MINDGAMES

PHIL JACKSON'S LONG STRANGE JOURNEY

ROLAND LAZENBY

CONTEMPORARY BOOKS

Library of Congress Cataloging-in-Publication Data

Lazenby, Roland.
    Mindgames : Phil Jackson's long, strange journey / Roland Lazenby.
       p.   cm.
    ISBN 0-8092-9707-8
    1. Jackson, Phil.   2. Basketball coaches—United States—Biography.
3. Chicago Bulls (Basketball team).   I. Title: Mindgames.   II. Title.
GV884.J32 L39   2001
796.323'092—dc21

00-64480
CIP

For Karen, Jenna, Henry and Morgan
And in memory of sweet Virginia

Interior design by Nick Panos

Published by Contemporary Books
A division of NTC/Contemporary Publishing Group, Inc.
4255 West Touhy Avenue, Lincolnwood (Chicago), Illinois 60712-1975 U.S.A.
Copyright © 2001 by Roland Lazenby
Printed in the United States of America
International Standard Book Number: 0-8092-9707-8

01 02 03 04 05 06 LB 19 18 17 16 15 14 13 12 11 10 9 8 7 6 5 4 3 2 1

CONTENTS

ACKNOWLEDGMENTS

Phil Jackson is one of the most complex figures in the history of American professional sports. Widely adored and held in the highest of esteem by fans in Chicago, New York, Los Angeles, and the world over, Jackson has built a career on finding success through a variety of unconventional approaches.

Interpreting his actions and discerning his motives could easily prove a daunting task for any biographer. If anything redeems this effort, it is the insight offered by Tex Winter, who has granted me numerous candid interviews over the past half dozen seasons. Long known for his frankness about the high-priced stars he coaches, Winter has taken the same approach with his own boss. He admires Jackson yet never hesitates to criticize him.

Jackson, for his part, seems to accept this criticism as part of his relationship with his mentor. In fact, the coach clearly relies on Winter's frankness, in spite of the fact that it frequently annoys him.

"Phil would like to control me," Winter offered during an interview in February 2000. "But he knows he can't."

Jackson has complained privately that I somehow duped Winter into providing inside detail for my 1998 book about the Bulls, *Blood on the Horns*.

Yet it was Jackson himself who volunteered most of the truly sensitive information during our interviews. It was Jackson who told me of the bathroom battles between Michael Jordan and Bulls VP Jerry Krause. And it was Jackson who revealed Scottie Pippen's drunken verbal assault on Krause on a team bus in Seattle that year.

I've interviewed Jackson several times over the years and have always found him to be forthcoming about events, even when the information he provides casts himself in a negative light.

By no means is this an authorized biography. As much as Jackson would prefer that I not write it, he has taken no steps to restrict my access to his team or to people who might provide information about him. As a result, Winter has offered some refreshing insight into a complicated figure.

I have also drawn heavily on Jackson's own published works, especially his first autobiography, *Maverick: More Than a Game*, a rawer, more daring account of his early life than his 1995 title *Sacred Hoops* provided.

Beyond Winter and Jackson's own works, my effort was aided immensely by a host of interviews and published material.

My accounts of Jackson's early years were greatly aided by interviews with Leon and Audrey Olson, Jim Simle, Bob Sathe, Peter Porinsh, Bill Shemorry, Dean Winkjer, Tom Kvamme, and Chuck Johnson. Also of great value were the archives of the *Williston Daily Herald* and the *Grand Forks Herald*, as well as Douglas S. Looney's work in *The National Observer*, and David Halberstam's fine biography of Michael Jordan, *Playing for Keeps*. Also helpful in discovering the history of Jackson's home region were *Montana* by Norma Tirrell and *The Smithsonian Guide to Historic America: The Plains States* by Suzanne Winckler.

Reporters Tim Layden, Mark Singelais, Tim Wilkins, and other staff reports from the *Albany Times-Union* provided excellent accounts of Jackson's days in the Continental Basketball Association, as did the reporting of Chris Young, who covered the CBA for the *Toronto Star*. Jackson's *Sacred Hoops* was also useful.

Phil Berger's book *Miracle on 33rd Street* provided a fascinating look at the New York Knicks during Jackson's playing days. Also helpful was Berger's illustrated history of the Knicks. In addition, Berger was kind enough to answer my follow-up questions, and Walt Frazier provided detail of his and Jackson's early years in the league in an interview.

Much additional help came from the host of periodicals and newspapers covering the Knicks during that period, including *The New York Times*, *Sports Illustrated*, *Sport*, the *Los Angeles Times*, the *Los Angeles Daily News*, and *The Sporting News*.

As for Jackson's success in Chicago, I have witnessed much of it first hand and conducted many interviews over the years.

Additional recent interviews for this project include Johnny Bach, Bill Wennington, Luc Longley, Michael Jordan, Jim Cleamons, and Winter.

Jackson's Chicago period received perhaps the most intense press coverage in the history of professional basketball, which was no small factor in my research. I was aided immensely by the work of a range of writers and reporters, including Paul Ladewski of the *Southtown Economist*; Sam Smith, Terry Armour, Melissa Isaacson, Karen Klages, and other staff writers at the *Chicago Tribune*; Lacy Banks, John Jackson, Rick Telander, Jay Mariotti, Mark Vancil, J. A. Adande, and other staff writers from the *Chicago Sun-Times*; Kent McDill and other writers from the *Daily Herald*; Greg Boeck, Roscoe Nance, and David DuPree of *USA Today*; Roy S. Johnson, Dirk Johnson, Thomas Rogers, George Vecsey, Ira Berkow, Sam Goldaper, and other staff writers from *The New York Times*; Richard Hoffer, Jack McCallum, L. Jon Wertheim, Frank DeFord, Jackie MacMullen, Ian Thomsen, Marty Burns, and other writers from *Sports Illustrated*; Dave D'Allesandro, Paul Dottino, Bill Pennington, and other writers from the *Bergen Record*; Peter Richmond and Mark Vancil from *The National*; Dave Kindred from *The Sporting News*; Terry Pluto from the *Akron Beacon Journal*; Jeff Coplon from *The New York Times Magazine*; Gary Binford from *Newsday*; Tom Callahan from *U.S. News & World Report*; Rachel Alexander and Michael Wilbon from *The Washington Post*.

For Jackson's tenure in Los Angeles, I am indebted to many who granted me interviews, including Kobe Bryant, Derek Fisher, Rick Fox, Jim Cleamons, Winter, Robert Horry, Shaquille O'Neal, Brian Shaw, Scot Pollard, Tim Kawakami, Howard Beck, Jerry West, Walt Frazier, Eddie Jones, Kevin Loughery, Tyron Lue, John Celestand, John Salley, Glen Rice, Ron Harper, Devean George, A. C. Green, and Travis Knight.

I was aided greatly by the fine coverage provided by Tim Kawakami, Randy Harvey, J. A. Adande, Bill Platschke, Lonnie White, and Mark Heisler of the *Los Angeles Times*; Howard Beck, Karen Crouse, and Tom Modesti of the *L.A. Daily News*; Kevin Ding, Janis Carr, Mark Whicker, Randy Youngman, and Steve Bisheff of the *Orange County Register*; Steve Brandon, Jim Beseda, Geoffrey Arnold, and Kerry Eggers of *The Oregonian*; Conrad Brunner, Mark Monteith, Bill Benner, and Phil Richards of the *Indianapolis Star-News*.

I was also aided by the work of dozens of writers who have covered the NBA, including Mitch Albom, Terry Armour, Jesse Barkin, Terry Boers, Clifton Brown, Kelly Carter, Mitch Chortkoff, Robert Falkoff, Bill Gleason, Bill Halls, Scott Howard-Cooper, Mike Imrem, Bernie Lincicome, Bob Logan, Jay Mariotti, Corky Meinecke, Mike Mulligan, Skip Myslenski, Glenn Rogers, Steve Rosenbloom, Eddie Sefko, Gene Seymour, Ray Sons, Paul Sullivan, Mike Tulumello, Bob Verdi, and many, many others. Their work has been invaluable.

Extensive use was made of a variety of publications, including the *Baltimore Sun, Basketball Times, Boston Globe, Chicago Defender, Chicago Tri-*

bune, Chicago Sun-Times, Daily Southtown, The Detroit News, The Detroit Free Press, Daily Herald, Hoop Magazine, Houston Post, Houston Chronicle, Inside Sports, Los Angeles Times, The National, New York Daily News, The New York Times, New York Post, The Charlotte Observer, USA Today, The Oregonian, Philadelphia Inquirer, San Antonio Express-News, Sport, Sports Illustrated, The Sporting News, Street & Smith's Pro Basketball Yearbook, and *The Washington Post.*

Also vital were many books, including *From Muscular Christianity to the Market Place* by Albert Gammon Applin II; *Holzman on Hoops* by Red Holzman and Harvey Frommer; *Sacred Hoops* by Phil Jackson and Hugh Delehanty; *Still Crazy About the Cats* by Jamie H. Vaught; *The Glory and the Dream* by William Manchester; *The Jordan Rules* by Sam Smith; *Transition Game* by Melissa Isaacson; *Why We Win* by Billy Packer with Roland Lazenby; *Trial by Basketball* by Mark Bender; *Cousy on the Celtic Mystique* by Bob Cousy and Bob Ryan

Beyond these contributions, I owe much to all the folks at Contemporary Books, publisher John Nolan, sales director Neil McNish, editors Rob Taylor, Marisa L'Heureux, and Julia Anderson, artists Nick Panos and Pam Juarez, and publicist Brigid Brown. Also a special thanks to Jorge Riberio for his support and outstanding editorial advice, and to Ken Samelson, plus the friendship and insight of Mitch Chortkoff, Larry Burnett, Mike Ashley, Mike Hudson, Greg Boeck, and Bill Adee.

INTRODUCTION

It was the same routine after every Bulls game: The publicity assistant would bring the two cigarettes and the beer. The coach would draw deep on the first cigarette, then take a drink of beer. Then a deep breath. A sigh would follow, the sort of sigh that seemed to contain all of Phil Jackson's pent-up energy from the game. Then he would gaze at the stat sheet, replaying the events in his mind as he read and smoked and drank. Nearby, Tex Winter, his longtime assistant, would be fussing over travesties . . . poorly thrown passes, errant shots, defensive breakdowns. Never mind that they had won by a dozen, that the team had long sustained a virtual orgy of winning—Winter still bubbled with indignation, which Jackson somehow managed to ignore and comprehend all at the same time.

His predecessor in Chicago, Doug Collins, was a nice guy who became a screamer, a raw, raving, frenetic man on the sidelines, thrusting his entire psyche out there for public view. Johnny Bach, Collins's old friend and assistant coach, laughed just recalling the difference between the two. "This guy would be worn out. Sweat was pouring off of him, veins were bulging. Doug had given every ounce of his energy. Phil, on the other hand, had this ability to sit there through the evening. He could walk off afterward and nod to people. He might have reached that same fever pitch as Collins had during the game. Phil had reached that pitch internally, but he never showed it externally."

Bach had his conflicts with Jackson, yet the older assistant had great respect for the younger coach's approach—especially during games, in the heat of battle. "Phil was at his best in that cauldron," Bach said. "Like the psychologist that he is, he's going to find a very different approach to solving problems. He will not get in your face and say, 'Let's get this settled now.'"

During games both Bach and Winter would beseech him to call timeouts. "Phil would just look at me," Bach recalled, "and he'd say, 'Johnny, I heard you, I'm just not gonna do it.'"

Bach said that he and Winter would request a timeout twice, and if he didn't respond they would give up. "He has this strength, this resolve," Bach said, "to endure whatever the results are."

It was Jackson's calm on the sidelines that immediately appealed to Michael Jordan. Dean Smith, Jordan's coach at the University of North Carolina, had displayed a similar presence of mind, and Jordan found it as comforting as he found Collins's frothing disconcerting.

Later, when Jackson joined the Los Angeles Lakers, Rick Fox, another former North Carolina player, was struck by how much Jackson's calm reminded him of Dean Smith. There was, however, one substantial difference.

"Phil swears," Fox explained with a chuckle.

Whereas Smith did not like foul language, Jackson decorated all of his expressions with it. "You could fuck up a one-car funeral," he told Toni Kukoc one night. (Jackson was later contrite about the comment.)

Both of Jackson's parents were fundamentalist preachers who tightly controlled his childhood, so it stood to reason that drinking, smoking, and cussing would bring him a liberating sense of satisfaction. Thus, he had to have the quick smoke, the quick beer, after each game before he could even address the team. Jackson called the smoke and the drink "getting his space." In his early years of coaching, that space came in the cramped bowels of Chicago Stadium, the old sandstone sarcophagus. In later years he would have the comforts of fancy offices in the United Center and Staples Center. Wherever it was, his ritual was mostly the same: the smoke, the drink, the replaying of events, the sigh, the quiet releasing of all that pent-up emotion from the game.

"He needed that few minutes of space before he could even talk to the team," recalled an associate. "After he talked to the team he would need another few minutes of space before he could talk to the media."

Jackson was always firm and direct in talking to his players after games, rarely raising his voice. And after tough losses he could be especially consoling, commending their great effort, telling them it just wasn't meant to be.

Later he would spend hours reviewing the videotapes and picking apart the performance play by play, isolating exactly what had gone wrong and why. But his verdicts were hardly ever delivered with anything that resembled insistence or stridence.

"He is a hands-on manager, but with a different approach in every way," Bach said. "It's deeply psychological. It's from the heart, except that he's able to separate it from his emotions. He's sort of a mystery to the players because he is not predictable. He doesn't overreact, or sometimes even react at all. Yet he has a firm hand. The great strength of Phil is that he is always very aware of what is happening. He could see things on the bench, or in the locker room, but he never moved too quickly to fix things. He would only do that after he had thought about it. Then he would do just what was needed to calm the situation and the problem.

"The most important thing is that he has never sought their love. There are many coaches who want to be loved, who have to be loved, and go down in flames as a result of it. Pro athletes just aren't going to do that. They aren't going to give you that love if you seek it."

Because he seemingly never sought it, Phil Jackson got what other coaches craved. He saw that on game nights, sitting there watching his players—first the Bulls, then the Lakers—execute his marvelously disciplined vision of the game. He would toast the results in private—the cigarette, the beer, the sigh, his communion in that mystic realm that only he understood.

1

EPIPHANIES

He ate the LSD for breakfast. It was one of those seamless Malibu mornings in mid-May 1973, just days after the New York Knickerbockers had defeated the Los Angeles Lakers, four games to one, for the National Basketball Association championship.

Phil Jackson was twenty-seven years old, and although the '73 Knicks were the first pro championship team he had played for, he was hardly in the mood to celebrate. First, he had a philosophical problem. He viewed the journey itself as the real celebration. Just getting to the championship round and winning it was the joyous thing—not all that whooping and hollering and hugging with people you hardly knew or didn't know at all. He wanted no part of that, thank you.

Then there were the injuries. He had performed well over the season, the best so far in his six years as a pro. He averaged 17 minutes of playing time per game, as well as 8.1 points, with better than 4 rebounds and an assist each outing, a superior contribution for a frontcourt reserve. He increased his scoring average to 8.7 points per game during the Knicks' title run, the second straight year he had done so. During New York's drive to the 1972 NBA Finals Jackson had averaged 9.8 points and better than 5 rebounds, though they ultimately lost that '72 series to the Lakers. The Knicks returned to the championship series in 1973 with the goal of completing unfinished business. But Jackson suffered a leg injury during Game 3, and his mood darkened. He craved being an essential part of the team, and in his mind the injury served to remove him from that essence.

His pro career had brought a series of physical challenges, and this was yet another. In 1969, he had undergone spinal fusion surgery after a serious disk injury. The recovery had been long and painful and had caused him to miss the Knicks' 1969–70 championship season. Instead of contributing to the most fascinating, magical moment in the franchise's history, he was left hanging at the edge of the group, dressed in street clothes, watching games from the stands or snapping photographs for a purported book. All in all, it was quite a miserable experience that left him feeling as if he had done nothing to contribute. It was no wonder that he felt an odd detachment from the euphoria that engulfed the team and its fans during that 1970 championship.

Beyond that separation from the group, the injury had increased his already substantial discomfort with his unusual body, one that as an adolescent had left him tagged with the unwanted nickname "Bones." The coathanger shoulders sat atop a 6'8" frame, and his 40-inch sleeves included an absolutely deadly set of elbows. Even Jackson himself didn't know when and where those elbows would strike next. This seemingly uncontrollable factor kept his Knicks teammates full of fear at practices.

"He seemed to be off-balance constantly. He seemed to be caroming off unseen opponents," teammate Bill Bradley wrote in his book *Life on the Run*, adding that it was as if Jackson's arms "served as separate sides of a scale which never achieved equilibrium. . . ."

As one might imagine, this imbalance would lead to frequent foul whistles and complaints from opponents that he was a dirty player. Jackson would contend that he was not, but those sorts of helpless arguments only contributed to the stereotype.

Despite this liability, Jackson had worked physically and mentally to get into the flow of this very good Knicks team. Somehow he had managed to help the team without ever really finding a comfort zone with his body. He had learned to fit himself into the changing pro game, a task that wasn't easy for a white player from a small college. But he had done that, and he was immensely proud of it. He could defend, he possessed a nice shot, and he knew how to move the ball and how to move himself without it. As a result, Knicks coach Red Holzman liked to introduce Jackson to the proceedings whenever New York needed to change the game's pace, to step up the pressure in hopes of producing turnovers. Jackson played well in the open court and usually helped produce the desired results.

His ballhandling, however, was more than suspect. Holzman jokingly told his players that everyone on the team but Jackson was allowed to dribble.

Regardless, he had willed himself to be a valuable part of the team. It wasn't easy for Jackson to be a defensive forward in the NBA, but that was his job. He wasn't strong enough to defend the power players, and he was too much of a roamer to stay glued to the shooters. But he had survived, then thrived, by learning to rely on his assets—his long arms, his mind, and his intensely competitive spirit. The long arms he used to deny his man the ball and to flick into the passing lanes for quick steals or even blocked shots. The mind he used to figure a means of adapting. The competitive nature provided gumption. Little by little his teammates began to trust him, then respect him, defensively. And little by little Jackson had worked himself into the Knicks' offensive equation, finding the places where he could fit in and use his jumper effectively.

The whole package had begun working nicely for him in 1972 and '73—until, once again on the eve of a championship, injury had separated him from the group. More than anything, the fiercely independent, individualistic Jackson seemed to crave being a part of the group, just one of many ironies in his curious makeup.

On the other hand, Jackson's need for the group was logical. Like other young inhabitants of that tumultuous time, he was in a search for identity. What would set him apart was the deeply complex nature of his search and the circuitous route he would take, finding and losing himself again and again over the years to come.

In that May of 1973, his personal life was a mess. He was in the process of coming to terms with the idea that he had a closeness problem with women. He suspected that it had something to do with his fundamentalist upbringing on the plains of Montana and North Dakota. His father, Charles, was a kind, Bible-believing Pentecostal preacher and church superintendent, a man large enough to live his life for the meager $100 weekly wages earned at the foot of the cross. Beyond his church life, Charles Jackson relished the earthy pursuits of an outdoorsman, the hunting and fishing, the things that defined his manhood.

At key moments, the elder Jackson could be stirred from his warmth to correct his children with a fiery discipline, but the real spark came from Phil's mother. Elisabeth "Betty" Funk Jackson was herself a Pentecostal preacher whose life was governed by the sure belief that the second coming of Christ was impending, that she, her family, and everyone she met should be prepared for that second coming. Of German heritage, with striking blonde hair and deep blue eyes, she was a proud, determined woman, a missionary brimming with integrity and toughness and commitment, as comfortable chopping wood as she was citing Scripture or speaking in tongues. She was also competitive—a characteristic inherited by Phil, the youngest of her three sons. Betty had captained her high school basketball squad and loved to win, whether the competition was a theological argument or a game of Scrabble.

Betty Jackson had a strong, manipulative nature that she used for a variety of purposes, mainly to ensure that her children observed the strict tenets of her religion. In time, that same talent for manipulation would become her youngest son's strongest and most unusual talent. In 1973, however, Jackson was more concerned with his problems than his promise. He had become increasingly aware of his fear of closeness. He certainly enjoyed the variety of women available to pro basketball players, particularly members of the New York Knicks in the early '70s, but he considered those brief encounters mostly expressions of physical prowess and male ego. His problem manifested itself in his relationship with his young wife, Maxine. He found himself alternately pushing her away from him, then pulling her back. Over the six years of their marriage, this process had proved emotionally exhausting for the couple and their young daughter, Elizabeth.

Jackson would later acknowledge that the couple's problems were clouded by his own insecurities and by his identity crisis, which he had sought to resolve with extramarital relationships, including an affair with a flight attendant and what he described as a desire for "a variety of sexual partners."

It seems little wonder then that during the 1972 offseason the young couple had decided to end their marriage, and by the spring of 1973 Phil Jackson found himself in divorce proceedings with Maxine. At the same time, he was pursuing a relationship with the woman who would become his second wife. He had met June at a pinochle game in 1972. She was enchanting, earthy in her own way, with a strong personality and a penchant for astrology. She had just graduated from the University of Connecticut and was working a difficult job at New York's Bellevue Hospital. They traveled and camped together for a time and she later moved into his loft in Chelsea on the lower west side of Manhattan. This, too, added to his anxiety because he was legally separated from Maxine but technically still married to her.

All of this only brought more turbulence to his private spiritual journey.

In his first days in high school, he had begun the long process of rejecting his fundamentalist upbringing, an exercise fraught with guilt, anxiety, and confusion. With his thirtieth birthday on the horizon, with his relationships in tangles, Phil Jackson recognized that he was more than a little lost that spring of 1973. He was far from alone in those feelings. It was a time of posers, populated by millions of young people moving from one pretension to another in their search for new identities.

The strains of '60s counterculture had somehow moved mainstream by the early '70s, except that the idealism had burned away, leaving mostly confusion. Kids in high schools and colleges across the country smoked pot, dropped acid, ate mushrooms, and snorted coke without really being sure why, except that it was something new and different. For many, the move toward recreational drugs was an answer to despair. The Vietnam War seemed to have the country caught in an inexhaustible pit of ugliness. Rocked by the National Guard's killing of four students at Kent State University in 1970, the antiwar protest movement had already lost much of its steam as the baby boom generation turned its focus to partying and redefining the essence of hip. At the University of California, Berkeley, a young editorialist complained that students were moving away from the activist mode in favor of a junkie lifestyle. The detachment of being strung out on drugs offered a strange allure, a freedom from the hassles of caring. "God isn't dead—he just doesn't want to get involved" read a pin popular among college students at the time.

Wearing a medallion and sporting long curly hair and a beard, Jackson fit right in with the times, at least in the eyes of Knicks fans. He was portrayed as the team hippie, and in that context he was clearly more radical than his teammates. But June Jackson actually found him to be on the conservative side, as opposed to the real freaks and radicals she had encountered in her undergraduate life. Jackson was "not nearly as radical as the people I knew in S.D.S. [Students for a Democratic Society] at the University of Connecticut," she recalled later. "He never dropped out, he always had money."

"I think the myopic way I grew up—and that's the best word to describe it—led to my experimentation," he would say later, trying to explain his drug usage. "Everything that happened to me in the 1960s was in tune with my background. The whole psychedelic experience or an LSD trip was, as Timothy Leary said, 'a religious experience.'"

For many, many others, the drug was a brain burner, a synapse-popping dance with psychosis. Jackson might well have been one of these victims had he not been so earnest about defining his relationship with God. Although he had rejected the fundamentalism of his parents, he retained their leanings toward mysticism. Part of his liberation in college had come with the reading of William James's *The Varieties of Religious Experience*. That comfort with mysticism left him free to sift through the many new religious and spiritual offerings that bubbled up in the rapidly evolving popular culture of the period. Jackson embraced a host of alternative thinkers, including the writings of Carlos Castaneda, and Joseph Chilton Pearce's *The Crack in the Cosmic Egg*.

His pursuit left his teammates with the notion that he loved the knowledge more than he loved the game. "He could have been a better player if he had applied himself to it more, as much as he applied himself to his books," Walt Frazier would later observe. "He'd read those weird books. They were weird to us anyway. No one else ever read them."

Jackson, however, was consumed by these new ideas, and they in turn fed his awareness of his own unfolding intuitive nature. In time, his substantial intuition would become a key factor in his success as a basketball coach. But in his twenties, Jackson was discovering his intuition as a child discovers walking. Shortly after coming to the Knickerbockers out of college in 1968, he had learned that one sure way to explore this intuition and his mystical nature was smoking marijuana. In time, friends and associates would caution him against smoking too much pot. And he would agree with them that the drug could be damaging. But he loved its effect on his mind, how it would allow him to see events and relationships in new and different ways . . . how the buzz lifted and pushed his intuition to places he had never imagined.

He greedily explored his mind, unrepentantly slipping into its recesses, which helps explain his foray into the popular recreational head drugs of that period. At the time, drug experimentation still offered a relative innocence, based on the '60s idealism that marijuana, mushrooms, peyote, mescaline, and stronger shades of hallucinogens could help people experience alternate realities and discover their kinder, gentler nature. Within five short years, those notions would quickly dissolve, leaving in their place a hard-edged drug culture adorned with guns and street gangs and a burgeoning human toll.

Jackson, though, in 1973 approached the drug culture with the innocence and idealism of a hippie, like millions of other baby boomers. He was on the road to find out, eager to be cool, to get high, to confront whatever God tossed in his path.

On that May morning in 1973, it was LSD.

Jackson later described it as the window-pane variety. He also noted that it was "good acid," which at least suggests more than a casual familiarity with the subject. If so, he was hardly alone in fancying himself a connoisseur of the hallucinogen. Young hipsters of the period faced an array of LSD consumer options. Purple haze. Sunshine. Orange barrel. Purple microdots.

Many preferred the purity of "blotter" acid, dabbed on creatively decorated snips of paper. One definition of poor quality was the amount of strychnine, or rat poison, used in the LSD home brew. High amounts of strychnine could leave the user with nasty stomach cramps and particularly vivid hallucinations. Considering that even the mildest acid trips consumed the best part of a day, a bad trip could leave one lost in a seeming eternity of confusion and pain, with all sorts of demons jumping in and out of one's consciousness.

Jackson, though, had "good acid," and he took it in beautiful surroundings with a beautiful stranger, which helps explain why he would later call it one of the peak experiences of his life. In fact, that one single day of tripping joyously on the beach would go far in determining the person he would become. Spiritual Being. Father. Teacher. Coach. Warrior. Illusionist. Minister. Manipulator. Master of Mind Games. Riddler. Recuser. Filmmaker. Artist. Counselor. Psychologist. Salesman. Shaman. Leader. Champion.

Even to those close to him, who watched him do it, it seemed strange, even mysterious, that he could combine all these facets of his very remarkable personality into the package of a basketball coach. Not just a coach but a truly great one, a coach who would reshape and redefine the nature of the job, broadening the position's parameters to the extent that he in some ways liberated the game.

He would prove himself as a psychologist, a master at group dynamics, an enhancer of athletic performance. One of the many things that separated him from other coaches is that he preferred to heap pressure on opponents as opposed to his own players. For them, he sought a million different ways to lessen the anxiety of performance, from meditation to mindfulness to yoga.

In retrospect, it should have seemed no surprise that other coaches would find him threatening. His approach proved to be a paradox, a mystery that few others could hope to match. He coached pro players with the control and discipline of a high school mentor and made no assumptions about their fundamental competence. Yet he provided those same men with frightening levels of freedom, building their individual sense of responsibility, all the while shaping them into a group, tightening the bonds, pulling even the players on the fringes tighter together than ever before.

It is safe to say that, after Phil Jackson, coaching would never be the same again. Strangest of all, perhaps, was the fact that the seed of his success was a clarity of vision that he began to achieve on an LSD trip. It wasn't the kind of thing that one could address frankly, especially not an athlete or would-be coach. Regardless, Phil Jackson, in a show of character, would attempt to do just that, and it would cause him and his family great pain.

The stranger who came into his life that May had actually phoned his hotel room the night the Knicks won the championship. She wanted to come up for a visit, but Jackson told her he was busy with friends. Early the next morning she phoned again. Jackson was packing up to check out and head back to New York with the team. But she persuaded him to give her a chance. He was met in the lobby by a stunning woman, a former child actress, a New Yorker. She made it clear just how badly she wanted to be with him. He explained that he had to return to New York, but the idea took hold that he should see her again.

Struck by the possibilities, he returned to New York and abruptly ended his relationship with June, dropping her off at a bus station to send her back home to Connecticut. At the time he explained that his action was the product of a Christian upbringing that left him uncomfortable with the idea of living with one woman while still being married to another.

Considering that June would eventually become his second wife and the mother of four of his children, it seems now like a particularly cold move, his detailing of the situation in his 1975 book *Maverick: More Than a Game*. But at the time, his frankness in the book was merely an attempt to be honest, to hold himself accountable for his actions. The volume, published by Playboy Press, would cause a stir around the NBA for Jackson's brutal candor about his drug use and details of his personal life.

In many ways it was a brilliant book about basketball, about a personal spiritual search; and it provided fascinating inside detail about NBA players and their insular world. But Jackson would come to regret the book, because reporters seemed to focus on his drug use to the exclusion of the rest of the book's details. June Jackson would hate it for other reasons, particularly for the revelation of painful details of their relationship. For years, it would serve as a reminder to Jackson that his openness could be disastrous and painful.

Even more challenging, this book would also leave him with the lingering image of a marginally compromised hippie. Years later, not long after he had become coach of the Bulls, he surprised his players one day by lighting a stick of sage in his office. Intrigued by the smell, his players would jokingly accuse him of toking a little reefer. By the fall of 1995, when Dennis Rodman joined the team and was immediately infatuated with Jackson's laid-back approach, the eccentric forward would tell reporters, "You know Phil. He likes to kick back and smoke a joint, drink a beer, chill out."

Even as a pro coach, he was known to frequent head shops on his trips to New York, browsing for incense and other knickknacks. That and his past led to rumors and speculation that he continued to enjoy smoking pot long after he came to the Bulls. But the team's employees who worked closest with him said that if Jackson pursued such a lifestyle he must have done so in the tightest of vaults locked away from the world, because in their daily association with him there was never a whiff of evidence.

"I had always heard the rumors, too," said one longtime Bulls employee who worked with Jackson. "But if he did it, he kept it well away from us."

To counter that image from his reckless youth, Jackson and wife June in later years would point out that many young people in their generation had innocently dabbled in the newness of recreational drugs, then moved on to evolve in their adult lives.

"The only thing in that book that's an embarrassment for me today," Jackson said in 1995, "is that people have picked out one or two phrases and said, 'This is who Phil Jackson is.' Sportswriters in the past have seized on one experience with psychedelic drugs or some comments I've made about the type of lifestyle I had as a kid growing up in the '60s and '70s. I've tried to make sure people don't just grab a sentence or phrase to build a context for someone's personality."

Yet, having said all that, Jackson himself acknowledged that his LSD trip that May of 1973 helped clear the way for who he was to become. Just hours after dropping June off at the bus station that May, Jackson was back on a plane to L.A. headed for a psychedelic tryst with the beautiful stranger. She had apparently disarmed Jackson with her intuitive sense about some of his deepest feelings, so much so that the unnamed woman served as his guide for the LSD trip on the beach at Malibu.

According to Jackson, it proved to be a day of epiphanies. Like many psychedelic experiences, this one began with Jackson and the woman waiting with anticipation to "get off," to begin feeling the drug's first effects. They sat in the morning sun at Malibu, washed by the sound of the sea and the ocean air. They talked. They listened to music. As the drug took effect, he found himself running up and down a two-mile stretch of the beach like "a lion." Known for producing deeply emotional and sometimes confusing revelations, the LSD brought Jackson face-to-face with issues about his body. He had learned over the years to trust his mind, but his relationship with his body was entirely different. The back pain and difficulties had pushed him to the conclusion that his body had somehow let him down.

However, under the influence of the drug, Jackson began to see the fallacy of his contempt. He felt a oneness between mind and body and with it a surge of power and strength like he hadn't felt in years.

Besides this physical rejuvenation, the day brought a host of other revelations—that he had to learn to love himself before he could love others; that he had to confront and subjugate his substantial ego, which in turn would lead to greater understanding about team basketball and his role in it. He saw that he had to rid himself of indecisiveness, that he had to begin taking responsibility for his actions.

Most important in the day was a "spiritual flash," the awe he gained at recognizing the Creator's power, a development that would send him on an intense search over the ensuing months for the best means of honoring and worshiping God. Jackson also saw that day the equality of people in God's eyes, the vast importance of every single person. And more important, he saw the bonds that connect people.

Out of this LSD trip came an enhanced love for the game of basketball and a new appreciation of team play, an appreciation that would be evident that next fall when he rejoined the Knicks. "I had to rediscover my ego in order to lose it. . . . I was able to become a totally team-oriented player for the first time," he would later write.

Not surprisingly, the 1973–74 campaign would become his most productive professional season. He would average a career-high 11.1 points per game and almost 6 rebounds per outing. Better yet, he experienced a new understanding of his teammates. When he looked at them, he felt that he saw all the forces and pressures pulling at them and affecting them. It was as if his team intuition had flowered into a sixth sense about the connectedness of basketball, a sixth sense that he would trust again and again over the years.

The experience in Malibu also opened his eyes to his personal life. He returned to New York, phoned June at her parents' home in Connecticut, and informed her that he was finally capable of love, a decision that would lead to their reunion and subsequent marriage and the birth of their four children.

In the months following the event, he would conduct a spirited investigation of his relationship with God, a move that would lead to his shunning of drugs and a change in friends and associates. During this period, he began reviewing Buddhist writings that he had discovered in college and struck up a friendship with a neighbor who was a practicing Muslim. That, in turn, would lead to his throwing coins and doing the I Ching. He even opened his mind to June's beloved astrology. As much as he took to these influences, he would finally decide that summer of 1973 that essentially he was a Christian, although he rejected the apostle Paul's denial of the flesh. Later, Phil and his brother Charlie, who had also experienced divorce, would meet with their parents to assure them that they still believed in God, that their spiritual search would remain active.

Jackson gained great pleasure from rereading William James's *The Varieties of Religious Experience,* a book that had been so meaningful to him in college. In his work, James recounted in first person the mystic experiences of a range of Christian sects, including Quakers and other intensely religious people. The mystic experience, James reported, wasn't an intellectual one, but a state of knowledge, in the sense that it brings sudden revelation and insight into fundamental truths.

James also discussed at length those mystical experiences induced by an intoxicant or drug, including alcohol, nitrous oxide, chloroform, ether, and anesthetics. That James gave these induced experiences "some metaphysical significance" was of comfort to Jackson, and the book itself left him eager to have another mystical experience, although this time in a natural state. Having felt the power of God, Phil Jackson wanted to feel it again.

That, in turn, inspired his move into meditation, an exercise that would become an increasingly important part of his personal growth. The practice would help him to complete parts of six more seasons as an NBA player, a remarkable run for a long shot out of North Dakota.

Later, meditation would become an important element in his coaching. He knew that it was his nature to be tight, precise, dogmatic, dictatorial. He also came to understand that such rigidity didn't work because "a dictatorial coach can frighten his team." His daily meditation became his means of freeing himself from those dictatorial tendencies.

Before he could move into coaching, though, he would have to outlive the reaction to his publishing of *Maverick* in 1975, and that would take some time. At the end of his playing career he moved to the New Jersey Nets and assisted coach Kevin Loughery with some duties as a player-coach. But from there, his only coaching opportunities would come in the Continental Basketball Association (CBA)—where he won a league championship and was named Coach of the Year with the Albany Patroons—and in summer work in Puerto Rico.

Despite those successes and experiences, Jackson came to realize that the NBA distrusted him, largely because of his openness and honesty in *Maverick* about his drug experiences. At one point the New York Knicks mentioned him as a candidate for an assistant coaching position, but that proved to be merely a courtesy.

"I thought I was ready to be an NBA coach at age thirty-five," Jackson recalled in 1995. "I had served two years as an NBA assistant in New Jersey. But I really didn't have a clue then, and I know that now. So I went to the CBA and had some success, but still nothing came in my direction. I had no mentor in the NBA. My coach when I played with the Knicks, Red Holzman, had retired and was out of the game. Although Dave DeBusschere, my former Knicks teammate, was a general manager, he had no control over my destiny as a coach."

That control, as it turned out, would come in the form of one Jerry Krause, a longtime scout who had admired Jackson's talents for many years. Krause had knocked around professional baseball and basketball for decades, and had himself been knocked around as well. A deeply secretive man, Krause held great enthusiasm for identifying talented people. Something in Jackson had led Krause to believe that he would make an outstanding coach. A guarded man, Krause confided to one of his few friends that if he ever became an NBA general manager he would eventually like to have Jackson as his head coach. That, in itself, was remarkable, that an outsider like Krause would want an outsider like Jackson as his coach.

Just when Jackson became frustrated with his inability to get a coaching job in the NBA, when he was thinking about giving up the profession and going to law school, it was Krause who stepped in as what Jackson would later call a "mentor."

"Jerry Krause was like the only person that really stayed in touch with me from the NBA world," Jackson recalled in 1995. "That was my connection. Jerry had seen me play in college, and we had a relationship that spanned twenty years."

Though he was meticulous in his conventions, Krause discounted the tales of Jackson's wild youth. What mattered were Jackson's intelligence and his talent, Krause figured.

"I've never read the book," Krause would later say when asked about *Maverick*. "I didn't need to. I knew about Phil's character."

And so he did. It would be Krause who would introduce this strange, intuitive duck of a coach to the NBA, setting in motion all that would follow— the high times and heartaches, the special passages and vagaries of Phil Jackson's very different curriculum vitae.

2

THE DIFFERENT
DRUMMER

The coach beat the tom-tom on game days. The instrument had routine purpose in the lives of the Native Americans, and he was determined it would have the same for his Los Angeles Lakers.

"I guess the drum is basically for gathering in terms of Indian customs," guard Derek Fisher explained. "They would hit the drum so that people would come together. Whether it was time to eat or time to meet or whatever. He just does that on game days when it's time for us to go in and watch film. It's different. But that's part of who he is, his life experiences. He chooses to share that with his teams."

On occasion Phil Jackson also burned sticks of sage. He had done the same during his time in Chicago, where he would walk around the Bulls' locker room with the burning sticks, waving them about when his team was struggling or facing a tough playoff foe. He would pause in front of each player's locker, moving the smoking stick up and down. One time he stopped and waved the sage twice at Toni Kukoc's locker. "He needs a little extra," Jackson said.

He did the same with the Lakers.

"That's done to drive away the evil spirits," Fisher said of the sage. "I think everybody kind of knew that he enjoyed doing different things. And he kind of touched on the things that he would like to do when he first talked to us."

At first, when they heard the drum and saw Phil Jackson chanting, many Lakers fought to suppress their snickers. Kobe Bryant had even read Jackson's book *Sacred Hoops* in preparation for the season. So he knew that the coach liked to blend basketball with spiritual exploration. But even that didn't prepare the young Lakers guard for the tom-tom.

"It kind of caught me off-guard," Bryant admitted. "I didn't know about that. I smiled. I laughed, as a matter of fact. It's funny. He said, 'You guys gotta get your hearts going. Just like warriors preparing for battle.'

"I said, 'OK, Phil. All right.'

"Phil said, 'Is your heart beating a little faster?'

"I was like, 'No, Phil. No.'"

In Chicago, Jackson had not beaten the drum as insistently. It wasn't necessary there. Over his years with the Bulls he had come to share a great intuitive feel for the game with Scottie Pippen and Michael Jordan. From that shared intuition, Jackson developed a deep and abiding love for his Chicago teams. Even the Bulls' employees who did not like him—and there were a few—could sense this love for his team, and they admired him for it.

Among his frustrations in Los Angeles was that his young stars showed little intuitive depth when it came to basketball. As a result, the coach found himself trying hard to love this Lakers team. He wanted his players to feel the game the way he and Jordan and Pippen had. He wanted to bring the Lakers together, to push them along to a single heartbeat. He wanted them to be a tribe, to feel bonds.

In Chicago, Michael Jordan had found great benefit in Jackson's Zen approach and mindfulness sessions. He advised the young Lakers to heed Jackson's ministrations, no matter how unusual they seemed, even though he himself had sometimes kept his own playful distance from them.

"Michael would always have some pithy or irreverent statement to make when Phil tried these things," former Bulls assistant Johnny Bach recalled. "It was nothing disrespectful. Phil is very able to handle relationships like that. I kind of enjoyed Michael's irreverence. It wasn't harmful, wasn't nasty. Michael's humor added that little spark in the coach–player relationship. It was exciting. We would all ask, 'What did Michael say?'"

Jackson searched for that same spark in his Lakers. Some of them did not understand him. Others were intimidated by him. But they all extended a measure of respect to him based largely on the fact that his Bulls teams had dominated professional basketball. They quickly came to see that the coach and his assistants brought an immaculately detailed approach to their work.

As Fisher explained, it was the detail, all the little things, that made them a great coaching staff. So it was easy for the players to accept the tom-tom, as strange as the drumming seemed to them, as part of the package of that detail.

"Even until a couple of months ago it still was funny," Fisher said late in the spring of 2000. "To see him and hear him walking through here chanting and beating on his drum. Sometimes he's smiling, sometimes he's chanting. Sometimes he's just hitting it."

"I wondered what he was doing," Robert Horry said. "Everybody says he always does crazy things, so I was like, 'This must be Phil being Phil.'"

Being Phil

For those misled by appearances, it's easy to underestimate Phil Jackson. As a coach, he enjoys displaying that studied nonchalance on the sidelines, even to the extreme of pausing to clip his fingernails while his Bulls lost an overtime game in Dallas in 1998. His eccentricities and offbeat approach are very much a part of who Jackson is, but they also mask a coaching style completely grounded in discipline and fundamentals.

"I do unusual things, yes, but I'm very, very sane," Jackson said in 1990, in the midst of his first season as an NBA head coach. "I'm a very centered person. I feel very much in control. I'll know more after I've done it for a while I guess. Then I'll know more about whether you can be successful without having to jump into a mold that's been prepared for you. There's no question it molds you. You can't escape it."

Contrary to those early fears, Jackson has somehow managed to avoid any mold whatsoever in the years since he offered that observation. In so doing, he has also set an unmatched standard for coaching success. His Bulls, featuring the incomparable Jordan, claimed their first title in 1991, then won five more over the next seven seasons. Jackson capped that run with a one-year sabbatical in 1999, then returned to the league to unite a once-fractured Lakers team and lead it to the 2000 NBA championship.

John Kundla won six championships with the Minneapolis Lakers (including one in the old National League before the Lakers joined the NBA), and Red Auerbach won nine while coaching Bill Russell's Boston Celtics in the 1950s and '60s. Then there was Alex Hannum, who won a title as a player-coach with the St. Louis Hawks in 1958 and later coached the Philadelphia

76ers to the championship in 1967, the only other coach to win titles with different NBA teams. And Bill Sharman directed the Utah Stars to the American Basketball Association title in 1971, then switched gears the very next season, guiding the Los Angeles Lakers to the 1972 NBA title. Longtime Jackson rival Pat Riley won four titles while coaching the Lakers in the 1980s and lost three other times in the championship series. From there, Riley moved to New York and coached the Knicks to the 1994 Finals, where he lost a fourth championship.

Jackson's results have eclipsed them all in one fashion or another, but that hasn't enabled him to elude his detractors, who readily point out that both his Bulls and Lakers teams featured the game's dominant player in Jordan and Shaquille O'Neal. Yet Jackson's many admirers quickly counter that between them, Jordan and O'Neal played thirteen NBA seasons without leading their teams to a championship. They only became champions when Jackson became their coach.

It's not a new debate in the NBA, long known as a league dominated by the talent of players, not coaches. John Kundla coached his Minneapolis teams to those six championships, then had to wait more than forty years for election to the Basketball Hall of Fame. The knock against him? He coached great players such as George Mikan, Jim Pollard, Slater Martin, and Vern Mikkelsen, which led to the assumption that Kundla's success didn't require much effort.

"Sure he had great players, but he did great things with them," Boston's Red Auerbach said in fussing about the Hall of Fame's long-running snub of Kundla. Indeed, Kundla spent his coaching career gulping milk to combat the ulcers irritated by the gnarly task of maintaining peace between feuding stars Mikan and Pollard. Pollard acknowledged the friction between them was "something that could have torn the team apart, but Kundla kept a very even keel."

"Kundla gets no recognition," Mikan agreed. "He did a great job of molding the team, taking care of the players' idiosyncrasies."

Although he was voted into the Hall with ease, Auerbach himself spent his career laughing off the critics who complained that he won only because of Bill Russell's dominating center play. In fact, Auerbach coached the Celtics to eight league championships before garnering enough votes to be named Coach of the Year. Auerbach's pat answer to his many critics was to simply light another victory cigar and puff away, further infuriating an NBA coaching fraternity seething with envy over his success and arrogance. "At first I didn't like Red Auerbach," a rival NBA coach once said. "But in time I grew to hate him."

"Red was hated around the league," longtime NBA player and coach Paul Seymour said in 1990. "He wasn't a very well liked guy. He always had the talent. He was always shooting his mouth off."

Having a great player like Russell made Auerbach a coach, said former Syracuse Nationals coach Al Cervi. "He's the biggest phony who ever walked the streets of America."

"Red was a very astute judge of talent," said Lakers coach Fred Schaus, whose teams battled the Celtics for several championships and lost. "When you have a lot of stars, you have to keep them happy and playing as a team. Red did that. I didn't like some of the things he did and said when I competed against him. Some of the things he said would bother me. But the guy who wore number 6 out there bothered us more. You had to change your complete game because of Russell." Schaus said he would have loved to shove the victory cigar down Auerbach's throat. "We came awfully close to putting that damn thing out."

Auerbach readily acknowledged that his teams won those championships because of Russell, but it was Auerbach who drafted Russell and made his talent work for the team. Russell himself took over as player-coach after Auerbach claimed his ninth title in 1966, and coaxed two more championships out of the Celtics. At a function honoring Auerbach's retirement from coaching, Russell told his mentor, "Personally, I think you're the greatest basketball coach that ever lived. You know, over the years . . . I heard a lot of coaches and writers say the only thing that made you a great coach was Bill Russell. It helped. But that's not what did it.

"Now this is kind of embarrassing, but I'll go so far, Red, as to say this: I like you. And I'll admit there aren't very many men that I like. But you I do. For a number of reasons. First of all, I've always been able to respect you. I don't think you're a genius, just an extraordinarily intelligent man. We'll be friends until one of us dies. And I don't want too many friends, Red."

The building of such relationships was essential for Auerbach. The Boston coaching legend even had a name for the bonds that developed between the players on his title teams: Celtic pride. From the first time he uttered it, the phrase rang with phoniness in the ears of his critics and opponents. Like all professional sports, the NBA from its earliest days has been a deeply cynical enterprise. In many regards, Auerbach was as hard-bitten as anyone who played or coached in the league. But his covenant with his players grew from the idea that their contracts would never be based on their statistics, only on their contribution to winning. That was particularly important for Russell, a shotblocking, rebounding machine who showed only a passing interest in offense. That covenant served well enough for the players' commitment to each other. They trusted Russell to block the shots or snare the rebounds to ignite their famous fast break, and they trusted Bob Cousy, Bill Sharman, Sam Jones, K. C. Jones, John Havlicek, Tom Heinsohn, and a host of others to finish those breaks with a bucket. When each season ended in victory, they trusted Auerbach not to shortchange them at contract time.

Like many Celtics of that era, Hall of Famer Frank Ramsey, who was sixth man on seven of Auerbach's championship teams, never had an agent. Ramsey recalled that he would sign a blank contract each season and leave it on the secretary's desk in team owner Walter Brown's office. Several weeks later, Ramsey would receive the contract in the mail with the amount he was to earn for the upcoming season filled in. Ramsey, who went on to a successful career in banking after his playing days, never made more than $20,000 in a single season, a level of pay he didn't reach until his final two years in the league. "We had great teams," Ramsey said in 1995. "I am not envious of the salaries they are making now. I don't wish I was playing today. What we did back then was a part of history."

All in all, that trust between Auerbach and his players added up to eleven titles in thirteen seasons. The degree of difficulty on that substantial accomplishment was that Auerbach achieved it on a relative shoestring, with no assistant coach and no scouts, in a league that usually featured eight or nine teams. As opposed to modern NBA teams, which employ dozens of front-office staffers, the Celtics of Auerbach's day had fewer than a half-dozen. He did everything, from booking the team's travel arrangements to scouting college talent, a workload that left him gray and exhausted long before his time. He began NBA coaching at age twenty-nine and retired at forty-nine, too worn out to continue.

Despite the burden he had faced, despite the fact that he had remained active for decades in managing the Celtics, Auerbach expressed no desire to work the bench in an age where coaches are flanked by a half-dozen assistants and a phalanx of scouts and personnel specialists. Asked in 1998 if he could duplicate his coaching success in the modern NBA, Auerbach expressed doubt. "It's different," he said. "The money has changed everybody. It's changed them from the time they're fifteen years old. They show some talent. The family gets in it. They talk to coaches, AAU coaches, whatever. They talk to agents. They change the whole thing as it used to be. It used to be fun. Years ago, the ballplayers would come to practice with a gym bag; today, they come to practice with attaché cases, followed by their agents, followed by the Madison Avenue boys or whatever. It's entirely different."

Auerbach said the perversion of big money makes it extremely difficult for a team or a coach to sustain success, to preserve the loyalty necessary to keep a championship team together. "How do you approach it because of the salary cap and other factors that have been involved in the game?" he asked. "I really don't know. When a player today who is getting $6 million a year says to the coach or the owner, 'Look, I want to be aware of any deal that's made. I want you to go over it with me.' And he tells that to the coach, too, and the coach says, 'What the hell is going on here?' The player tells the coach, 'Look, I don't have to take any crap from you. I got a no-cut, guaranteed, five-year contract, and if I don't like you, I'll get rid of you.' And there have been a lot of cases where players have gotten rid of coaches. And those are, to me, your big problems today. The players are getting more and more power, and they've taken it over."

This, perhaps, is what is most unusual about Phil Jackson's success. In an age when players have the power of astronomical salaries and guaranteed, long-term contracts, he has managed to snare their hearts and minds with an unusual blend of charms. Perhaps no player in the game wields more power than Lakers center Shaquille O'Neal. A gifted giant with a mammoth contract that averages better than $20 million per season, O'Neal has been known to demand a coaching change or even the trade of a teammate. Yet as soon as Jackson took over as coach of the Lakers in 1999, the center gave his unconditional cooperation.

Why?

Because after eight seasons of having coaches accede to his every wish, O'Neal said he had finally found someone to stand up to him and insist on discipline. "Not to take anything away from the other coaches that Shaq's played for, but this is the first time that I think he's really bought into what a coach is selling and what it takes to win," said Lakers guard Brian Shaw, a former teammate of O'Neal's for three seasons with the Orlando Magic. "Some of the coaches, because Shaq is who he is, didn't get on his case when Shaq wasn't doing what he was supposed to. And Phil does. If Shaq's not doing the job, Phil is the first one to point it out. He says, 'Hey, you're not doing this, you're not doing that. Get your ass up the court and do it.' I think Shaq respects that.

"I played with Shaq three years in Orlando," Shaw explained in November 1999 as the Lakers opened their first season under Jackson. "Shaq is really the one making the adjustment. Phil doesn't have to make any adjustments. He's coached the greatest players to ever play in Michael Jordan, Scottie Pippen, and Dennis Rodman. They've won championships. They bought into his system and what he preaches. Shaq has that respect for him just based on that. Michael Jordan listened and executed. If he did it, then there's something to it."

"He has his ways. Phil has his ways," says Ron Harper, who has played on four of Jackson's championship teams, three in Chicago and one in Los Angeles. "Guys take hold of the things that he says."

Somehow Jackson has managed the very difficult feat of blending fun and discipline and spiritual exploration for his teams, sort of like combining a trip to the dentist with a carnival ride. John Salley, who has played for Jackson in Chicago and Los Angeles, likens his style to the tough love of a friendly priest in a Catholic boys home, a father who uses the promise of sports to lure the boys to do good deeds. "That's Phil's attitude," Salley explained. "We're having fun. When we're not having fun he lets you know. He says, 'I don't want to be here and not have fun. We have to have fun, and we have to win, and we have to be together.'"

As a member of the Detroit Pistons "Bad Boys" championship teams in 1989 and '90, Salley had been an avowed foe, even a tormentor, of Jackson's Bulls. But in 1996 Salley arrived in Chicago as a Bulls substitute. Like most outside observers, Salley had assumed that Jordan really ran the team. Then Salley had the opportunity to see Jackson at work. "Phil understands the game better than most people," Salley observed at the time. "And he expects certain things that he knows his guys can give him. He gets the utmost respect from his players. A lot of people say Michael really runs the Bulls. But Phil runs this team. He runs the squad. He runs practice. He runs the film sessions. He splices the film. He organizes practice. He dissects the other team we're playing against. He knows his stuff.

"He understands the players' bodies. He understands when not to overuse them. He understands when he can rest you. He knows when to watch enough film. He knows when to push his players, when not to push 'em. He knows who to yell at, who not to yell at. He knows who can take it. And he treats you like a man, as opposed to downplaying you, or talking to you like you're less than him because of his position. He's a great coach. He laughs and smiles at life."

"From the outside looking in, I always thought he was intimidating," Brian Shaw said of Jackson. "Real serious all the time. But playing for him, I've found he jokes around and is real lighthearted. He wants you to come in and put in your work. He allows you to have input. I like that about him. Some coaches, it's like, 'I'm the coach. I'm the man with the power.'"

Many coaches, Shaw said, seem to tell their players, "I'll do the thinking; you don't have to think." Jackson, though, wants his players thinking and questioning.

This insistence on fun and freshness has been Jackson's means of battling the mind-numbing grind of the NBA lifestyle, circumstances that he had first come to detest as a player. "There's a danger because you get on the treadmill of pro basketball," he explained during his Chicago days. "You just keep running on the treadmill and you can't get off."

Asked how can a coach give himself to the game and not be consumed by it, Jackson replied, "You need diversions."

Which helps explain the tom-tom, the burning sage, the meditation, and all the other trappings of his approach. Rather than put his 1960s counter-culture experiences behind him like many of his baby boom contemporaries, Jackson has gloried in them as a coach, gaining notoriety for mixing Zen and Native American philosophy with proverbs from his Christian upbringing, and clinging to the Grateful Dead, Timothy Leary, and other icons of the period. It's well known that he loves preaching to his players about the great white buffalo, or giving them obscure books to read, or having them pause amid the looniness of the NBA for a meditation session. "He's our guru," Michael Jordan quipped as the Bulls were on their way to an all-time best 72–10 regular-season record in 1996. "He's got that yen, that Zen stuff, working in our favor."

Though they may joke, Jackson's players have come to see that his eccentricities aren't merely something he does for effect. They lay at the heart of the beliefs he holds dearly. Just as important, they are his means of self-preservation, of protecting himself from the rigors and stresses of his job.

Jackson has long realized that the faith his players show in him is no small thing. "I believe that there is a tenuous trial sometimes between coaches and players," he said in 1996. "I've found that I have the confidence of my group, so that they feel comfortable. And it's not anything where if I try experimental things that they feel threatened or can't deal with it. It's sort of something where I've had an open working forum to try a variety of styles and approaches, all of which seem to be enjoyable to them. The only thing they don't like is monotony and constancy. But we still make one thing constant, and that's fundamentals. The one thing that we always strive for is to make fundamentals and execution a part of our game."

All of those facets of his approach have added up to a magical mystery tour for a coach determined to be different. And circumstances suggest that the good times could run on for a while. Jackson celebrated his seventh league title over the summer of 2000 with the knowledge that he had a long-term contract paying him approximately $6 million per season and a team with two dominant players, twenty-eight-year-old O'Neal and twenty-one-year-old guard Kobe Bryant, under contract for years to come. Auerbach retired from coaching after the 1966 season with nine titles to his credit and 938 career regular-season victories. While it was assumed that someone would eventually surpass his total for regular-season wins (which Lenny Wilkens did in 1996), it had been almost unthinkable that someone could reach Auerbach's championships total. However, Jackson's success in Los Angeles in just his first year as coach there has suddenly made his catching Auerbach a distinct possibility.

How could a strange duck like Jackson pull off such a feat in an age when all the factors go against such success?

It's a question envious competitors continue to ask. If anyone knows the answer, it's probably Tex Winter, Jackson's longtime assistant and verbal sparring partner. He's studied Jackson up close for the past fifteen years and has been an integral part of the proceedings. One of the keys is Jackson's insistence that, while basketball is the heart of the endeavor, the whole thing has to be about much more than the game itself.

"Phil recognizes that there are a whole lot of things more important than basketball," Winter says. "He doesn't take himself too seriously. We all take basketball pretty seriously at times. Even then, he's inclined to relax. I'm amazed at times in the course of the game how he sits back and lets things happen. He likes people to be able to solve their own problems, and so he gives his players the reins. On the other hand, when he sees they're out of control, then he starts to pull them in a little bit. I think this is his strength, the way he handles the players and his motivation, his personal relationship with the players. That's borne out by the fact that they'll accept his coaching, they'll accept the criticism, even though sometimes it's pretty severe with certain players. They accept that because it's who he is, because he's Phil."

One of the fascinating elements of the Jackson story is how Winter has factored into it. The two first got to know each other in 1987 when Jackson joined the Bulls as an assistant coach. Over his decades on the bench, Winter had been the head coach at five colleges—Marquette, Kansas State, Washington, Northwestern, and Long Beach State—and had served as head coach of the San Diego/Houston Rockets in the 1970s. His specialty was the triangle offense, a system of team basketball that required stars to share the ball with lesser players. His Kansas State teams of the late 1950s and '60s hovered atop the national polls, and Winter enjoyed success against the rival Kansas Jayhawks. In fact, it was Winter's Kansas State team that defeated Wilt Chamberlain's team in the Big Eight conference in 1958, leaving the gifted giant so frustrated that he decided to leave Kansas early to play with the Harlem Globetrotters. For Winter, it was the ultimate victory of team basketball over the brilliance of an individual player.

Winter was mostly retired in 1985 when Bulls GM Jerry Krause, a longtime friend and admirer, lured him to Chicago with a handsome salary to be "the coach's coach." The only problem was, the Bulls' head coaches at the time didn't want to listen to Winter's advice. First, Stan Albeck declined to buy into Winter's view of the game. Then came Doug Collins, who saw Winter's triangle offense as unworkable in the modern NBA.

Jackson, though, came to the staff as an assistant and quickly adopted Winter as his mentor. Winter helped guide Jackson when he made the transition to head coach in 1989 and was delighted that Jackson chose to use the triangle for the team's offense. As the seasons of success unfolded, the older coach soon came to serve as something of a Merlin to Jackson's King Arthur.

When Jackson moved to Los Angeles, one of his first requests was that Winter move with him. It didn't take long for the Lakers' players to understand why. "He's seen so much basketball and all the players through the years, and he's seen all the coaches coach," Brian Shaw explained.

Indeed, Winter had once played junior college ball against Jackie Robinson and later wound up at Southern Cal, where he was a teammate of Bill Sharman and Alex Hannum playing basketball for the legendary Sam Barry. He also challenged for a spot on the U.S. Olympic team as a pole vaulter in the days just after World War II, when the standard weapon was a bamboo pole, but an injury ended his Olympic hopes. He served in the navy during World War II, and in the aftermath became one of America's premier college coaches, getting his first head coaching job at age twenty-eight.

"Whatever situation you see on the floor, he can talk to you about it, because he's seen them all," explained Bill Cartwright, who had worked with Winter first as a player, then later as a fellow Bulls assistant coach. "You ecall that everyone used to wear those Chuck Taylors, those canvas Converse shoes, and you talk to Tex, and he'll tell you, 'Oh yeah, I knew Chuck Taylor.'"

Having entered a new millennium with Jackson's Lakers, Winter takes the NBA one season at a time. If you're pushing eighty, as Winter is, that seems like a prudent approach. That's not to say that anything about him suggests frailty. Winter is a tough old cuss with a boyish charm. Somehow his fifty-three years in coaching haven't managed to turn his shock of hair completely gray. And it certainly hasn't dampened his fire. Former Bulls center Luc Longley has harrowing tales of Winter being physically restrained from coming after him during timeouts. Winter gets deeply offended if the game isn't played the way it's supposed to be played, and Longley has been known on occasion to commit this transgression.

Upon becoming a Lakers assistant coach in 1999, Winter grew fond of describing 7′1″, 330-pound Shaquille O'Neal as "the most impressive physical specimen in the history of the game." Actually, that distinction may belong to the seemingly ageless Winter himself. Lakers players got an indication of this after watching Winter spin through a jump-rope routine in his first days with the team. Most of them only knew him as the old guy who always sat next to Jackson during all those championship runs in Chicago, but the Lakers soon discovered a surprisingly nimble sort who was ready to challenge them or Jackson at every turn.

Brian Shaw recalled this scene from an early road trip during the 1999–2000 season. "We were practicing in Denver, and Phil had one of those heavy medicine balls. Tex was sitting on a table on the side. Phil took the ball and threw a bullet pass to Tex. The ball was coming right at him, and he jumped out of the way real quick. Then he got up and picked the ball up and fired right back at him. He was like, 'Oh, you wanna fire the ball at me?' Derek Fisher and I were sitting there, and we just started cracking up. We couldn't believe that he could move that fast. I hope that if I'm fortunate enough to make it to seventy-eight that I can have as much spirit as he does."

That spirit has often evidenced itself in Winter's determination to criticize modern NBA athletes about their play. Winter considers himself a guardian of the game, an assistant coach so ancient and untouchable that he can say whatever he wants to a high-salaried young player. It didn't take long for the

Lakers under Jackson to get a taste of Winter's fire. One night Brian Shaw took a shot when Winter thought he should have passed. During the ensuing timeout, the assistant coach pounced. Suddenly Shaw found himself in a heated exchange with a fire-breathing dragon who just moments earlier had seemed like an elderly gentleman. "He's old school, and he comes at you sometimes in a way that you aren't ready for," Shaw said, recalling the incident with a chuckle.

Winter hadn't been in Los Angeles long before his frankness chafed the supersensitive O'Neal, who would get angry at the criticism Winter offered about his play. Quietly fuming, the center would refuse to speak to the coach for several days. "He just kind of grunts his answers," Winter said. "He's got a heart of gold, but he gets mad at me and won't talk. He's very sensitive."

Winter acknowledges that this confronting of players is just one of the pressures he has taken off Jackson over the years. "I make his job easier," Winter says. "Phil knows that."

"They complement each other," said Bill Wennington, who played on three of Jackson's championship teams in Chicago. "Tex is the one that's gonna yell at you all the time. He's the one getting on you about the offense, so Phil doesn't have to do that."

Jackson himself was quite capable of leveling his own criticisms at players, but the more strident evaluations often fell to Winter, who grew so bold during the final years of his Bulls tenure as to fuss because Jordan's chest passes needed to be more fundamentally correct.

Winter also took it upon himself to regularly challenge Jackson himself, although it didn't take him long to bump up against Jackson's legendary stubbornness. If the head coach seemed too willing to sit passively on the bench without calling a timeout or making an adjustment, it was Winter who would jump in his ear, saying, "You better get off your ass and do some coaching."

Their debates were legendary around the Bulls' front offices, as was their friendship.

"Tex is Phil's buddy," Longley explained. "He helps him do everything."

"Like father and son," Wennington agreed. "They've got an understanding relationship. They do have their disagreements. But they understand each other well."

On many days in practice Jackson would speak to the team, Wennington recalled. "Then Phil would ask the assistants if they had anything to say, and Tex would go off on a tantrum and Phil would say, 'That's enough, Tex. Shut up.' He'd be getting heated up, so of course he would look hurt. But he'd stop and just let it go. Tex is a perfectionist, and sometimes he'd go off on a tirade and Phil would just be looking at him with a grin."

Methodical Madness

Winter has often marveled at his friend's intensely psychological approach to building a championship team. He says the key to Jackson's success lies in his ability to orchestrate relationships with his players, his assistant coaches, his fellow employees, the media, his opponents—in fact, just about all the parties inhabiting the rare environment of the NBA.

"Phil is a master manipulator," explained a longtime Bulls employee who worked daily with him. "You're talking about the media, the players, the staff, everybody."

Most important, Jackson possesses an uncanny ability to measure the impact of what he says and does on those around him, Winter said. "There's method in his madness. Always. If you see him do something, you can figure it's calculated. He might be impulsive every once in a while. After all, he is human."

For the most part, though, if Jackson says or does something, it is a move intended to elicit a specific reaction from his players, from the opponent, from the media. Just the amount of effort and intelligence such an approach requires is almost mind-boggling in itself, said guard Derek Fisher after watching Jackson renovate the Lakers.

To go with that manipulative nature, Jackson possesses a wide array of mental powers and a remarkably persuasive touch with his players. Former Bulls assistant Johnny Bach said one of Jackson's special gifts is the ability to establish a clear team structure. "We have in the league a lot of people who think they're a lot better than they are," Bach said. "And that's what coaches have to deal with. Can you get five people to play a team game when all the rewards seem to be for individual achievement? You're talking about fragile egos. Big egos. People who had status and can lose it in this game so quickly. Phil is great at defining roles and having people face up to what the hierarchy is. . . . And he does it in a very intelligent way. He doesn't do it to put you down. But he clearly addresses the problem."

"Phil is a very fine counselor," Winter explained. Jackson began establishing this approach almost from the very first moment he was named an

NBA head coach in 1989. Using his counseling techniques, he spent hours upon hours persuading a frustrated Michael Jordan that it was important to trust his less-talented teammates. In one private discussion after another with Jordan, Jackson encouraged the superstar to alter his views of the role players on the Bulls roster.

Such an approach may have seemed easy to outsiders, but it wasn't. Winter, who takes immense pride in the fact that he coached Jordan longer than anyone, recalled the fall of 1985, when he first joined the Bulls and began observing Jordan up close. "Like everybody else, I was in awe," Winter said of seeing Jordan in practice for the first time. "His reflections, his reactions, his quickness, just his overall ability to play the game."

The first thing he felt was intimidation, Winter said. Never mind that he was sixty-three at the time and owner of one of the best coaching reputations in America. Never mind that Jordan was a mere twenty-two-year-old heading into his second professional season. "I was in such awe of Michael that I was hesitant about even talking with him," Winter recalled. "I watched him a great deal and learned a great deal about watching him and his mannerisms. But it took a couple of years before I felt comfortable even visiting with Michael a whole lot."

Likewise, Jackson recalled the anxiety he felt upon taking over as head coach in 1989 and the strong urge he felt to please Jordan with his preparation and approach. It wasn't the kind of anxiety that kept him awake at nights, Jackson said. But it was intimidating.

Jordan was very bright and coachable, yet at the same time he could be quite difficult and demanding. In a half-century of coaching pro and college basketball, Winter said he had never been around a personality as complicated as Jordan's. "Personality-wise, he's a study. He really is," Winter said in 1998. "I'm really sorry that I . . . I guess I don't have the intelligence to grasp a lot of things that makes Michael tick, that make him what he is. I think I analyze him pretty good, but he is a mystery man in an awful lot of ways, and I think he always will be, maybe even to himself."

Without question, Jordan possessed tremendous personal charm, wit, and intelligence to accompany his legendary athletic skills. But it was the competitive drive that set him apart. One of Jordan's traits was a biting sense of humor that he used to chide teammates and staff members who didn't seem diligent enough in rising to his stringent competitive standards. And when the sense of humor didn't seem to work, Jordan never hesitated to singe them with his anger.

Winter portrayed a Jordan who seemed to enjoy belittling his teammates "even to the point sometimes that he can get pretty vicious, even to the point that he's insulting and ridicules them. But they seem to accept that because he does it in sort of a humorous manner. . . . He gets a big charge for some reason out of belittling people and putting them down. I think he does it because he feels it challenges him to be better."

"I can be hard when I want to be," Jordan acknowledged when asked about the matter, adding that his sense of humor was one of his main tools in coping with the rigors of stardom.

"That attitude," Jackson said of Jordan, "that tremendous competitiveness, sometimes makes it tough to be a teammate, because you see that tremendous competitiveness is gonna eat you up everywhere. It's gonna eat you up playing golf with him next week, playing cards with him next month. That attitude of arrogance is gonna be there. It's not always the best for personal connections and friendship. But it certainly makes for greatness."

Former Bulls guard John Paxson agreed. "Michael is easily the most demanding athlete I've been around," Paxson said, reflecting on his days on the team. "I don't want any of that to sound like there's something wrong with that, because there's not. . . . If you showed weakness around him, he'd run you off. He was always challenging you in little ways. The thing you had to do with Michael Jordan is you had to gain his confidence as a player. You had to do something that gave him some trust in you as a player. He was hard on teammates as far as demanding you play hard, you execute. So there had to come some point where you did something on the floor to earn his trust. That was the hardest thing for new guys coming in, and some guys couldn't deal with it."

In those early seasons of his career, Jordan displayed a growing frustration with his team's inability to win and with the critics who said it was his fault because he didn't display a desire to make his teammates better. They contrasted him with the Lakers' Magic Johnson, who was in the process of leading his team to five championships.

As much as Jordan disliked those comments, there was some truth to them, Winter said. "He was a high-wire act at that particular time. I often said back then it was more a degree of difficulty, a gymnastic feat, with Michael in those days than it was a matter of basketball."

It became Jackson's task, then, to help this very strong, very frustrated personality relate to his teammates. In a series of wide-ranging discussions with Jordan that lasted over their many seasons together, Jackson sought to soften the rougher edges of this raging competitiveness. At the same time, the coach worked at deepening and strengthening his own relationship with the superstar. Over the years, Winter marveled at the growing bond between the two, which was stronger than any that Winter had ever seen between a coach and star player. Later, some in the Bulls' organization would see this effort by Jackson as a power move to ally himself with Jordan against the team's front office. Jackson would disagree, saying he was only trying to do his job of building a winning team.

On that basis alone, Jackson's effort was remarkably successful. The coach began drawing out Jordan's understanding of himself and the team dynamics. But the talks went far beyond basketball. "I think Phil really has given me a chance to be patient and taught me how to understand the supporting cast of teammates and give them a chance to improve," Jordan explained in 1995, once he had an opportunity to reflect on the process.

In an interview given after he left the game, Jordan said he kept special memories of his one-on-one sessions with Jackson. "We talked about so many different things," he said. "We used to get into philosophies more than anything."

It was obvious that both he and Jackson enjoyed the talks immensely. "We used to challenge each other," Jordan said. "I think I would learn from him, and he used to learn a little bit from a player's perspective at that time. He had played years back, but I was giving him a thought process for a new era. It was a lot of give-and-take. Much more listening from me. Not disagreements but more or less concepts, with him saying, 'Think about this and think about that.'"

Always, the implied message was greater trust. Jordan said that his trust in Jackson grew as time went by, with the team's increasing success proving that what Jackson encouraged him to do had merit. As he won Jordan over and the Bulls began claiming championships, Jackson then employed his psychological approach in finding new ways to motivate the superstar and to keep offensive balance between Jordan and his teammates. From there, Jackson pulled together an array of influences to shape Jordan's mental approach to performing under the intense pressure that comes with high-stakes situations.

"Phil is the master of mind games," Jordan said at the time.

Faced every game night with the task of urging Jordan not to dominate the basketball in the fourth quarter, to include his teammates, Jackson spoke to Jordan through film clips inserted in the team's scouting tapes. In 1998, as Jackson guided the Bulls to their sixth championship, he chose to insert clips of the feature film *Devil's Advocate* into the Bulls' scouting tapes. In that film, the protagonist's wife slices her own throat with a shard of glass. Feeling the need to speak forcefully, Jackson showed his team a film clip of a possession where Jordan held the ball too long, then he cut to a clip of the woman cutting her own throat. Gruesomely effective, Jackson's editing spoke to Jordan in a way that no verbal communication could.

The passage of time has only increased the sharpness of Jackson's mental approach, Jordan said in March 2000 after observing his former coach's success with the Lakers. "He's still the master of mind games, only better," Jordan said. "He challenges you mentally. That's his strong point. You look at the Lakers. The Lakers haven't changed personnel-wise. Their mental approach has changed, and that's where Phil's best qualities are."

These mind games come in such variety that many times the people around Jackson proceed through the game without even being aware that they are participating, that he has engaged them in it.

"There's meaning in everything, and why things are done not everyone always knows," Bill Wennington explained. "Phil is a really deep thinker, and everything he says seems to have a lot of thought put into it. Most of the things he says have at least two meanings, and at times you have to figure out which one he means. But that's part of Phil. He wants you to think; he wants you to figure out what's going on. He doesn't want you to do things just by rote, and he uses that term a lot. He wants you to think and know what's going on and why you're doing things."

In the process of thinking about what Jackson has said to them, players sometimes discover that there was even a third or fourth intended meaning, Wennington said. "At times you think back and you find a third or fourth meaning that you maybe didn't see right away. He knows how to push buttons and get guys going and get them to achieve goals that maybe other people can't get."

The same can be said of Jackson's dealings with opponents, a practice that has drawn heated criticism over the years. His mind games with the other team usually involve sly comments made to the media, such as using the nickname "Van Gumby" for New York Knicks coach Jeff Van Gundy during the 1996 playoffs, or calling Sacramento Kings fans "rednecks" during the 2000 playoffs. Less obvious to the public is the way Jackson creeps into the minds of opposing players. Sacramento backup center Scott Pollard watched some of his Kings teammates fixate on Jackson's comments during their first-round playoff battle with the Lakers in 2000.

"He's great at working the media, I will say that," Pollard said. "If nobody who was playing in the games, or coaching the games, or reffing in the games, paid attention to the media, then there would be no head games, then he wouldn't be doing that. Some of us don't watch this or read that crap. Some of us don't pay attention to all that. Head games don't work on some people."

But others do pay attention, Pollard said. "People read that. If he says the other team doesn't do this well, then the other team reads that and they start thinking, 'We gotta prepare for this, because Phil says we don't do this well. So we gotta do this.' He's an intelligent man. If nobody read that stuff he wouldn't be saying anything. But he knows that everybody's reading it, the other players are reading it, the other coaches are reading it, so you know he's gonna throw out those little things here and there.

"He gets some people who read that and pay attention to it, and it hurts their feelings."

On more than one occasion over the years, Jackson has sat back during the playoffs and watched an opponent chase its tail over things he's said.

"I chuckle quite a bit at it," Tex Winter says. "He's an amazing coach. He's unorthodox. He likes to play those mind games, the way he comments about the things that happen during a playoff series. He likes to get a point across, likes to jab it into the opponent. The things he presents in his media sessions, he's calculating."

He uses all the devices of propaganda, including strong suggestion with his own players in the playoff scouting tapes they review over the course of each series. Years ago, Jackson adopted from assistant coach Johnny Bach the technique of splicing snippets of other information into those scouting tapes, including bits of Three Stooges skits and other images, all used to suggest and emphasize points to the players. Jackson then expanded this process by showing entire feature films, spliced in pieces around scouting tapes, during the playoffs each year. "He'll splice in little scenes from movies to try to send a little message," explained former Bull Steve Kerr.

For the first round of the 2000 playoffs, he used *American History X*, starring Edward Norton, a film about the lives of neo-Nazi youths filled with racial hatred. The film concluded with a moving passage about the futility of hatred and included an appeal for people to listen to the better angels of their nature. This message reemphasized Jackson's season-long efforts for Shaquille O'Neal to take a kinder view of Kobe Bryant.

But Jackson also played games with the film's starker images, juxtaposing shots of the skinhead Norton with his swastika tattoo and shots of Kings point guard Jason Williams, a white player with a shaved head. There were even allegations, based on a report in the *Washington Post*, that Jackson used shots of Sacramento coach Rick Adelman with his mustache to suggest Adolf Hitler. Exactly how this was supposedly done is not entirely clear, because Jackson fiercely guards his scouting film sessions and the Tribe Room, the Lakers' inner sanctum where he plays the tom-tom, chants, and pursues other group activities.

His mind games with opponents have made Jackson, like Red Auerbach before him, extremely unpopular with opposing coaches and teams around the league. "It's unfortunate," Winter said. "With the success he's had there's bound to be some natural jealousy. It behooves him to be humble and complimentary of other people.

"I think there's a lot of resentment in the league because of the success he had in Chicago," Winter added. "People seem to feel that Phil was lucky to coach Michael Jordan. I don't think they give Phil the credit he should receive, but at the same time Phil should have been a little more humble. There was the impression that Phil rubbed it in."

Clearing the Competitive Mind

Jackson also fiercely guards private "mindfulness sessions" given by psychologist and Zen enthusiast George Mumford. These efforts are in large part responsible for Jackson's image as a "Zenmaster," a tag he disdains because it elevates his status to that of those who have spent a lifetime engrossed in spiritual endeavors. Jackson's certainly serious about his beliefs, but he's no priest.

Mumford's sessions make sense for professional athletes because they are aimed at reducing the stress of competition by using a mix of meditation, Zen, tai chi, yoga, and common sense. When Jordan spoke of playing "in the moment" as he performed spectacularly in carrying the Bulls to their later championships, he was voicing the theme of these sessions.

Jackson said he considers the Mumford sessions a competitive secret and usually declines to discuss them in detail. Many of his players rave about them, except for some veterans, such as Lakers forward A. C. Green, who gave sessions a lukewarm response for religious reasons.

"George is pretty much there to relax your mind and body. To try and help you resolve the stress that's involved with everything," Bill Wennington said of Mumford's sessions. "He tries to get your basketball life, your whole life, in a peaceful, relaxed state so that you can compete. He doesn't want you to be stressed out about anything. George comes in and tries to teach the players a way to relax and regain your focus in a couple of breaths. To go out there and say, 'OK, I'm here, I've done this a million times before, we've gone over it in practice, and I'm just gonna go and do it.' If you take it seriously, you find it really works.

"It definitely made a difference with Michael," Wennington said. "You have to be in the moment. You can't worry about what just happened, the basket you missed, the foul you made two minutes ago, because it's over. You can't worry about what's gonna happen the next time down the floor. You have to be right there in the moment. It's most important especially in the playoffs because that's the time of year where you have to live for the moment. It doesn't matter what's gonna happen in Game 3 when you have to play Game 1. You have to be here right now to play basketball when it's happening. George tries to get it where you're only thinking about what's happening right now. And you're playing for that moment, and whatever is there is all that's affecting you. The second after it happens it doesn't affect you anymore because you're now living here. If you can get that down and just do that, it takes a lot of the pressure off because you're not worried about everything else."

Jackson believes in getting his athletes to train their minds, to clear the stress out of the way so that they can be successful. Phil Jackson's mind games add up to a very comprehensive approach, fun and victories for the believers and followers, and anguish and self-doubt for the opponents. In short, the Jackson formula is to take the mental pressure off your players and put as much as possible on the other team.

Viewed in terms of that formula alone, it's easy to understand the loyalty Jackson engenders. That's not to take away anything from other coaches, says Luc Longley, a former Bull who was traded to the Phoenix Suns, "but once you've played for Phil it's really hard to play for somebody else."

Mind Benders

Not everyone, of course, enjoys the Jackson approach. In particular, many Bulls staff members who had to endure his personality quirks were left harboring a long-burning resentment. Jackson's battles with team vice president Jerry Krause spilled over into an ugly display in 1998, but he also had many less-public clashes with the team's community services, marketing, and media relations departments. To many of these people, his mind games seemed unnecessary and sometimes cruel.

On more than one occasion, Jackson reduced staff assistants to tears with a good public upbraiding. Fans have often heard about the time he canceled practice and instead took the Bulls on a ferry ride in New York during the 1994 playoffs. What isn't known is that Jackson stopped the team bus that day as it was about to depart for the trip and ordered a longtime team publicity assistant, the only female on the bus, to get off. According to team sources, the woman was devastated by the move and has never forgiven Jackson for an unexplained and seemingly unnecessary humiliation.

Other staff members simply learned to adjust to Jackson's ways. They came to understand that for Jackson there were two groups: the players and immediate members of the team, and the rest of the world. Staff members belonged in the rest of the world, and Jackson didn't like them getting too close to the players and team. This, of course, is an attitude found among other NBA coaches. "Phil was a good guy," recalled one Bulls staff member who worked with Jackson a lot. "Phil was Phil. He would bust your balls a lot, a lot of times for no other reason than to exert that attitude that 'I'm the boss.' He just liked flexing his muscles. He was unpredictable. A lot of it was to keep you off-balance. If he saw you starting to feel comfortable at practice, in the locker room or on the team bus, he'd definitely put you in your place and let you know he was running the show. You always had to act subservient around him. He did that with the security guards, too. He had a way of saying things that would cut you to the bone.

"He wouldn't let you get too comfortable. He liked to keep everybody on edge. It was his way of control. If you asked him about it, he would tell you that it was his way of fucking with you or playing mind games with you.

"He always used to say, 'It's like I tell my kids, always ask. Don't assume things. Always ask.'"

This longtime Bulls employee said that as soon as he got comfortable around the team and forgot to ask if it was OK to make each move, then Jackson would cut him down to size. "Then, all of a sudden, you felt like a dick. He didn't just do this to me, but to everybody. It was never personal. It was just his way."

Another veteran Bulls employee said that Jackson had become increasingly difficult over the years in Chicago as the Bulls gained more and more notoriety and the demands on the coach increased. "You change a lot," explained one staff member who worked closely with Jackson. "That's because the landscape changes. We became the most popular sports team in the world. They all changed. The players. Phil. Everybody. Despite people thinking that he could be very, very arrogant, at times he could still be very funny. He could still take it all in stride and know that everything involving him was not the end of the world. But I can see where people would hate him. Those mind games after a while aren't funny. Those games are easy to play when you got Michael Jordan on your side. When you got Michael, all your games are gonna work. All the dice come up sevens.

"Another thing you've got to remember," the Bulls' employee added, "is that Phil's a former player. Just about all of those ex-players have this it's-all-about-me syndrome. They're taught to think that way and they never get over it. One other thing, Phil was the coach of the best basketball team in the world led by the greatest player in the history of the game. You have to have arrogance to coach a group like that. It's gonna be tough day in and day out if you don't. You do that job you better have some shit with you."

Some Bulls employees saw Jackson's approach as an outgrowth of his growing control battle with Jerry Krause. Anyone who held a private conversation with Krause over the course of the 1998 season heard his complaints that the Bulls' success had gone to Jackson's head, that he was an egomaniac hungry for power, that he had been disloyal to Krause, the one person who had allowed him back into the NBA, that the private Jackson was far different from the one admired by the public.

Winter was a friend and counselor to both Jackson and Krause. He had witnessed their success, then watched as the relationship began falling apart in 1996, leaving Winter playing the middle over the next two years trying to keep the two men working together for the team's sake. Winter acknowledged that there were things that Jackson could have done to make the situation more harmonious. But Winter privately pointed out that Krause had a difficult personality and that Jackson had spent years bending over backward to accommodate that personality until finally wearying of that effort.

Krause, though, portrayed Jackson as a two-faced character who really had very little regard for his assistant coaches, a perception that certain Krause associates in the Bulls' organization had sought to spread about Jackson. At the height of the hard feelings in the spring of 1998, one of Krause's scouts went to press row in Chicago's United Center to explain to a reporter the insidious nature of Jackson's ego.

Perhaps no NBA general manager had a more investigative nature than Krause, nicknamed "the Sleuth" for his secretive approach to scouting and compiling information about players and coaches. A Chicago native, Krause had worked in and around the NBA for four decades, which meant that he had a voluminous knowledge of the league's secrets. "I know where all the bodies are buried," he had once bragged when asked about his own franchise.

It was Phil Jackson's great misfortune that at the height of their discord Krause gained irrefutable evidence about one of Jackson's own misdeeds involving the 1994 firing of assistant coach Johnny Bach.

Like Winter, Bach had been an elderly influence on Jackson when he joined the team. A spirited sort who was popular with Bulls players, Bach apparently fell into Jackson's disfavor because he sometimes encouraged Jordan to follow his own inclinations and ignore the triangle offense. But Bach also was a strong supporter of Jackson's, which leaves his dismissal as something of a mystery. There was something about Bach that annoyed Jackson. "We were very different people," Bach acknowledged.

At the time and in later accounts, Jackson portrayed Bach's firing as a result of Krause's anger over the 1991 book *The Jordan Rules* by Sam Smith, a *Chicago Tribune* columnist. The text contained fascinating inside detail on the team's drive to its first championship, detail that portrayed Krause as something of a buffoon and Jordan as somewhat ruthless and selfish. Both Jordan and Krause hated the book, and Jackson later joked that *The Jordan Rules* was one of the few things the team executive and star player could agree about.

Krause alleged later that Jackson deceived him into believing that Bach was the anonymous source for most of the inside detail. Krause learned in 1998 that it was Jackson himself, not Bach, who was the source for much of Smith's book. How did Krause discover this? He learned it from Bulls chairman Jerry Reinsdorf, who was told of the situation in confidence by none other than Smith himself. Reinsdorf was not supposed to give that information to Krause, but he did.

Smith independently confirmed those events and Jackson's role in his book. "Phil and the players had much more of a role than Johnny Bach," Smith said in acknowledging that he had told Reinsdorf of Jackson's part in *The Jordan Rules*.

Jackson, though, had continued to explain Bach's firing as a result of the elderly assistant coach's involvement, clearly a prevarication on Jackson's part.

"It was Jerry Krause's relationship with Johnny Bach that created a very uncomfortable situation," Jackson said of the firing in a 1995 interview. "It made this have to happen eventually. It had gone all wrong. It was bad for the staff to have this kind of thing because we had to work together.

"Jerry basically blamed Johnny Bach for a lot of the things in *The Jordan Rules*. And there's no doubt that Johnny did provide that information. Jerry felt that Johnny talked too much. And Johnny, in retrospect, felt that animosity that Jerry gave back to him, the lack of respect, so Johnny refused to pay allegiance to Jerry just because he was the boss.

"It had gone on for too long a period of time," Jackson said. "I could have kept them apart, at bay from one another, I suppose for a while longer. But I didn't like the fact that it wasn't good teamwork. That was my staff and my area. I agreed to do it. I felt it was a good opportunity because Johnny had an opportunity to get another job in the league quickly. It worked out fine for Johnny, although I would just as soon have not put him through the disappointment, or have to go through the situation myself."

"Phil lied to me," Krause said in a 1998 interview. "Phil actually got Johnny fired."

"It was Phil's idea to fire Bach," Reinsdorf said in 1998. "Phil told me that the bad relationship between Krause and Bach had made things impossible. It was Phil's idea. Nobody told him to do it."

Contrary to Jackson's later assertions that things worked out fine for Bach, Bach himself said the firing came at a terrible time in his life, after the 1994 playoffs, just weeks shy of his seventieth birthday. The irony, Bach said, was that the coaching staff had probably never worked better together.

"At the end of that year I had every reason to think my contract would be renewed," Bach recalled in a 1999 interview. "The first person that told me was Phil. He said, 'We're not gonna renew the contract.' I was stunned. Before I could say much in defense, he said, 'It's really best for you that you do leave. The organization has made up its mind.' I was disappointed. Shocked is a better way of saying it. I didn't quarrel. I just couldn't believe it. I went to see Krause and he said the same thing. I just got up and left. I had a lot of crisis in my life at that time. I was in the divorce courts ending a long-term marriage. I had to move. I thought everything was collapsing around me that summer. Then I had a heart attack. It was all a shock, and it took some time to believe and trust people again."

An excellent coach, Bach was later hired by the Charlotte Hornets. He subsequently learned that he was supposedly fired for the inside information he provided to Smith. Bach said he went back and read the book three or four times looking for damaging information he might have provided. His quotes, though, were on the record and relatively basic.

"I didn't see a single quote in that book that was out of order," he said. "Sam is obviously a good investigative reporter. There was a portrait in there that Michael did not like, based on whoever gave it to Sam."

The book "was quite an accurate portrayal," Bach said. "I don't think Sam painted someone as he wasn't."

Krause was supposedly distraught more than three years later to learn that he had been deceived into firing an innocent Bach. By then, Bach was working in Detroit as an assistant coach. One night when the Pistons were in Chicago to play the Bulls, Pistons executive Rick Sund told Bach that Krause would like a word with him. "I had mixed feelings," Bach recalled. "You sort of protect yourself."

He agreed to the meeting, however, and was more than a bit surprised. "When Jerry spoke to me he was emotional, and so was I. I always thought the organization had made that move, not Phil. I thought it was a huge concession on Jerry's part to come up to me. I thought he meant it," Bach said of Krause's apology. "And I accepted that."

Bach said he had continued to greet Jackson whenever he ran into him and even addressed the issue with Jackson when they had a chance to sit down man to man over a drink. What he told Jackson that night will remain between the two of them, Bach said. "I'd rather leave it be. Certainly he knew how I felt. I always thought we had a relationship that was strong enough. We had sat there on the bench together for five years. As an assistant coach you don't always know about these things that are going on. It was always foolish, kind of an indictment that I could never defend myself. Now the whole thing is not important. Once it was."

The incident, however, begged several questions. Jackson had coveted the opportunity to coach the Bulls, just as he had worked diligently to build a relationship with Michael Jordan. Why would he risk his job or that key relationship in his professional life by providing a reporter with unflattering information about his boss and his star player?

One longtime Bulls employee who worked with Jackson on a daily basis figured the coach provided the information to Smith because it helped him gain more control over his team. The end result of the book was that it served to further alienate Krause from the players, thus securing Jackson's role as "the leader of the pack," the team employee said.

As far as the negative portrayal of Jordan, it was the ultimate mind game, a matter of " 'Let's get down on Michael. Let's whip this guy and keep him in line for my purposes.' It was his way of getting on Michael's side by alienating him from the media," the Bulls' employee suggested. "That was why Phil always used the us-against-the-media approach, the us-against-the-organization approach, because if he did that, then he could be the leader of the pack. That's why I've got a lot of qualms with the Zenmaster. You're not even smart enough to get along with your own bosses and your own fellow employees during the greatest run in basketball history. So how smart are you?"

These voices provide two distinctly different perspectives on Phil Jackson, of those who work for him and those who work with him. What emerges in both is his determination to control the competitive environment he inhabits. Some he cajoles and charms into line. For others he reserves harsher methods. Regardless, his purpose beats as insistently as his drum, moving them about for designs that only he sees. Yet even those who don't like him marvel at his mastery, at how he can do what no one else can.

Part of the employees' resentment stemmed from Jackson's insistence on shutting out everyone except the immediate group of players and coaches and trainers, thus dividing the organization into those within the team and those without. Jackson did this to increase camaraderie and group identification, but it led him to treat most approaching staff members as intruders. Regardless, the few staff members allowed a view of the team's inner workings marveled at what they saw.

"He really did love his team, really deeply" explained a Bulls staff member who worked around the team daily. "And the team trusted him totally. He included every player, top to bottom. You really knew he cared about them, about the whole group, on the deepest level."

3

SON OF THE
NORTHERN PLAINS

They came from everywhere. The first
were the Kootenai, probably ancestors of Montana's prehistoric inhabitants
from the west. Next were the Pend d'Oreille, followed by the Flatheads.
They all settled in western Montana, west of the Great Divide, in the lower
reaches of the Rockies. Later, in the 1600s, others came from the east, mostly
seeking haven from the spread of Europeans, from whom they had acquired
firearms. These newer inhabitants made their home on the region's vast
plains, east of the Great Divide.

The Crow got there early in the seventeenth century, having decided to
leave the Great Lakes region well ahead of encroaching whites. Next were
the Blackfeet, fine horsemen and warriors and the Crow's natural enemy.
They too abandoned the forests of the Great Lakes, migrating across the
Canadian Plains and bringing with them their Algonquian dialect.

The Gros Ventre, a northern arm of the Arapaho, arrived in the 1700s, as
did the Assiniboin, a Siouan-speaking people who took up residence on Montana's northeastern plains. The rest of the Sioux—the Dakota, Lakota, and
Nakota—pushed into the picture late, around 1800, having been driven into
the Dakotas out of Canada by white settlers. Known for their steam baths
and their purification rituals after battle, the Sioux would hold a particularly
strong fascination for Phil Jackson.

About 1830, the Northern Cheyenne finally abandoned their agrarian existence in Minnesota and moved to Montana's southeastern plains to find a new life as nomadic hunters, as did the Chippewa and Cree, who also left Michigan and Manitoba and joined the divergent mix of Native American cultures, the different languages and customs, that collected in the vast region.

And so the Montana territory, with its abundance of buffalo, became their land of exile and their battleground. "We were hunting the same herds in the same place," explained one Sioux legend, "and naturally we fought."

Later, many of them would put aside their differences and join forces to defeat Custer and the U.S. Seventh Cavalry at the Battle of Little Bighorn in Montana in 1876. Their prominent general was Sitting Bull (whose Sioux name was Tatanka Iyotake), from the Hunkpapa Lakota group, born at Grand River, South Dakota, in 1831. Said to have possessed an abundance of courage, wisdom, and generosity, he rose to lead the "Cante Tinza," an elite warrior society. The concept of such a society struck a note with Phil Jackson more than a century later, and it became his means of defining a code for his players.

Like the native tribes before them, Jackson's parents had traveled a rather circuitous path, both to Montana and to their beliefs.

The Jacksons were English Tories who settled in New Hampshire before the Revolutionary War. Once hostilities broke out between colonists and the English, the Jacksons moved to Canada, where they and other loyalists were rewarded with a grant of land from King George III.

Charles Jackson spent much of his early life back east in Ontario, working as a dairy farmer and lumberjack. His first marriage produced a daughter, Joan, but Jackson's wife and a second child died from birth complications. Despite the fact that he had left school in the eighth grade, he enrolled at Central Bible College in Winnipeg as his grief drove him to the ministry.

It was there that he met Elisabeth Funk. Her people were German Mennonites who had found their way to Saskatchewan, among a wave of European immigrants that swept across Canada in the late nineteenth and early twentieth centuries. There, Betty Funk's father ran a livery stable and gained notoriety for his strength and for his ability to break broncos and wild horses. Phil Jackson's grandfather was known for dealing with especially spirited horses by pulling them over on their backs while still protecting his own legs.

The outbreak of World War I, however, brought ethnic difficulties for the Funk family. The resentment of German actions in Europe meant that the

Funks' six children were forced to line up at school each day and sing songs and endure insults about the Huns. The circumstances also brought a chill to his livery business, which finally forced Grandfather Funk, as Jackson would later call him, to gather up his family and move south to Wolf Point, Montana, a hamlet on the banks of the Missouri River at the cusp of the Fort Peck Indian Reservation. According to legend, this northern plains town got its name in fur-trading days when trappers had poisoned and trapped hundreds of wolves. The traders were unable to skin the wolves before the onset of winter, so the frozen carcasses were stacked by a river landing to await the spring thaw. When the trappers returned at the first hint of warming weather, they found Indians had occupied the landing. The ensuing standoff resulted in the rotting of hundreds of wolf carcasses, a putrefaction that for some time would greet steamboat crews moving up and down the river. Thus the name, Wolf Point.

Jackson's Grandfather Funk found a new life in Montana running a boardinghouse and farming, but it was a meager existence verging on poverty. For good measure, he also rented out huts to Indians on a daily and weekly basis. It was as a child visiting his grandfather that Phil Jackson first came into contact with Native Americans. He recalls even then being fascinated by them, although he was strictly forbidden to go near the huts or attempt a conversation with them.

It was also at Wolf Point as a teenager that Betty Funk first heard the apocalyptic message of a minister during a revival. The Pentecostal movement had come to life around the turn of the century—first in a Topeka, Kansas, Bible college in 1901 when a young woman requested during a service that "hands be laid on her that she might receive the Holy Spirit." From that event grew several apparitions of Pentecostal expression, the most notable being the Azusa Street Revival between 1906 and 1909 in Los Angeles, a porchfront ministry that drew crowds to a city neighborhood. Word of the unusual worship, and accompanying complaints, spread until the *Los Angeles Times* sent a reporter to investigate. He reported the Pentecostals, or "gift people," as they called themselves, "breathing strange utterances and mouthing a creed which it would seem no sane mortal could understand. Devotees of this weird doctrine practice the most fanatical rites, preach the wildest theories, and work themselves into a state of mad excitement. . . . Night is made hideous in the neighborhood by the howlings of the worshipers who spend hours swaying back and forth in a nerve-wracking attitude of prayer and supplication."

Despite such negative reactions from the secular world, a number of revivals sprang up across the country, from Kansas to New York to Texas to Seattle, over the next few years, growing so rapidly that the Assemblies of God church organized in 1914 with the mission of spreading Pentecostalism around the world. In one short span, a hundred thousand followers were added in Wales alone, but that paled in comparison to the numbers reached in the American Midwest. By the 1920s, the movement had reached across the plains into hundreds of towns and farming communities.

It found Betty Funk in Wolf Point. She was a farm girl at the time but intensely driven, burning with frustration that the fall harvest had caused her to miss the first six weeks of school and prevented her from being class valedictorian by a mere two-tenths of a point. Her five siblings would all earn that valedictory distinction, and she seemed to live her whole life making up for the difference, caught in a belief that one should drive with unbending effort to realize God's gifts. Upon graduating high school, she earned a teaching certificate and took charge of a one-room schoolhouse at age eighteen, a position so poorly funded that she had to burn cow chips in winter to keep her classroom heated. Her real love, however, was the King James Bible, which she devoured on a daily basis, making note of her favorite passages in her voluminous memory.

"Christ is the only answer," she declared at an early age, a phrase that she intoned over and over again while raising her family.

Pentecostalism was a faith in which she could invest her intensity. She was immediately drawn to its mystical nature and the opportunity it provided to bond with the Holy Spirit. And there were other reasons to admire its practitioners. The denomination's focus on prophecy proved captivating in those uncertain days. Just as important, Pentecostalism didn't harbor the same sexism and racism of other denominations. From its very first days women and blacks had assumed leadership positions in the church. Specifically, the new movement pointed to Scripture to establish the leadership role for women: "Your sons and daughters will prophesy" (Joel 2:28, New International Version).

Betty Funk's passion for her faith grew to the point that as her thirties approached she felt a calling. She gave up her teaching and went off to the Assemblies of God divinity school, Central Bible College in Winnipeg. There she found Charles Jackson, with dark eyes, curly hair, and an inherent kindness immediately apparent to all who met him. Just as important, he possessed a faith to match her own.

Phil Jackson's recounting of family events varies in his two books, *Maverick* and *Sacred Hoops*, with one recalling that his parents actually met at the Bible college before Charles Jackson lost his first wife and the other suggesting that his first wife's death prompted Jackson to go to divinity school.

Regardless, about two years after Charles Jackson and Betty Funk met in school, they were married on March 20, 1938. Soon after, they moved back to Montana to pursue their evangelistic calling with the Assemblies of God church. As evangelists, they had sworn an oath of poverty and concerned themselves with things other than worldly possessions.

In addition to Jackson's daughter Joan, the couple brought three sons into the world, with Charles (Chuck) and Joe preceding Phil. The union of the Reverend and Mrs. Jackson in itself would set in motion a grand basketball karma: the game that was invented by a Canadian divinity student would come to feature a great coach, the offspring himself of two Canadian divinity students. In turn, this coach would become enthralled by what he described as the sacred, spiritual nature of Dr. Naismith's sport.

Keeping the Faith

Because his father was an itinerant preacher, Phil Jackson moved about Montana as a child, living in proximity to the range of native cultures that he grew to love at an early age. He was born in Deer Lodge, in the southwestern mountains in the heart of what was once Flathead country, on September 17, 1945, barely a month after the United States dropped atomic bombs on Hiroshima and Nagasaki. Jackson's parents actually lived in the shadows of towering smelter stacks in the nearby mining town of Anaconda, but a diphtheria outbreak there had forced Charles and Betty Jackson to go to Deer Lodge for the birth of their third son, Phillip Douglas.

The use of atomic weapons had brought an abrupt end to World War II, and in the days before the baby's arrival, the federal government had begun announcing an end to the wartime rationing of shoes, meat, butter, and other items. The War Manpower Commission had lifted controls on manpower, and President Truman had moved to restore the civilian economy, bringing the resumption of consumer production.

The war's end was a welcome development in the Jackson household, although it did little to ease either parent's conviction that the second coming of Christ was at hand, a belief only reinforced by the atomic devastation in Japan. Over the two decades since Betty Jackson had first been influenced by the fire and brimstone of that revival preacher, her faith had grown in intensity and depth, spurred on by her maternal instincts and her desire to prepare her children for the hereafter.

"Every Sunday since I was born, the apocalypse has been coming next year," Jackson once told Knicks teammate Bill Bradley in trying to explain his parents' view of life. Jackson's young world would be shaped by a growing awareness of his mother's intense devotion and her focus on the moment of Christ's return, what she called "the rapture of the saints," and he would spend his childhood years anticipating that rapture.

If anything, the cataclysmic events of the world war had only hastened the Jacksons' urgency to spread the word before the end of days. The arrival of this third son interrupted their busy work of revivals and thrice-weekly meetings. He was a large, active baby, thrashing about wide-eyed in his crib late into the night, which apparently presented such a disturbing sight that one fellow churchman of Charles Jackson came to believe that the infant was possessed and in need of an exorcism. The father declined that offer, but the baby's active nature soon brought its own sort of intervention. He steered his stroller down a flight of stairs and sustained a concussion.

Life was not easy in those early years for the Jacksons. They worked together, with the Reverend Jackson providing the Sunday morning ministry and weekday visitations while his wife taught Bible classes, played the church organ, and offered up the evening sermon with a fiery fervor. They lived in the basement of their church for the first four years of Phil's life while patiently waiting for the congregation to collect the funding to build a parsonage. With his parents involved in meetings and church business throughout the week, the toddler was often left to the care of others. In particular, he recalled staying with one older neighbor, a woman in her fifties, whose household was so foreign to him that he spent days afraid to go to the bathroom.

By the time Jackson reached age four, the family had packed up again and moved across the state, down into the lowlands to Miles City, near where the Yellowstone and Tongue rivers meet in the range country, a collection of vast ranches on what had once been lands inhabited by the Cheyenne. The time was 1949, when polio epidemics raged throughout the country. Though Jackson supposedly contracted the deadly, crippling disease, his family eschewed doctors and any sort of established medicine. Instead, they considered his recovery a sure sign of faith healing. At least one Assemblies of God minister was arrested and prosecuted for practicing medicine without a license during this period, as authorities in various communities tried to contain the more radical practitioners of faith healing. Faith, however, remained the abiding presence in the Jackson household, where daily life was shaped by a literal interpretation of the King James Bible. Like his brothers before him, Jackson was pushed from his first toddling moments to achieve all that he could in the honor of God. He was barely out of diapers when his mother informed him that at his age his brother already knew a thousand words.

From her third son's earliest moments, Betty Jackson filled his world with passages from the Good Book and definitions from the dictionary, all to be memorized. She would write down one verse after another in large letters on sheets of paper and place them about his room. Nights were reserved for family games, but there were also fire-and-brimstone discussions, often drawn from the book of Revelation, in which the children were instructed to prepare for the rapture.

In virtually every way, the Jacksons' spiritual beliefs shaped their children's lives. Phil's parents had no money to buy him a bicycle, but one fell off a passing car in front of the family house. Charles Jackson retrieved it, fixed it up, taught Phil to ride, then ran an advertisement in the local paper for the people who lost it to come pick it up. They did, and it would be more than a decade before Phil owned his own bike.

As he grew, Jackson would take his turn inhabiting the suits worn by his older brothers, suits that had already made many rounds in the Jacksons' schedule of church meetings Sundays, Wednesdays, and Fridays, a schedule that kept the Jackson children squirming in pews as many as twenty hours a week.

When Phil was seven, the Jacksons moved yet again, this time to Great Falls in central Montana, because Charles Jackson assumed the post of superintendent for all the Assemblies of God churches in the state, a position that required his constant travel to supervise more than seventy churches. The family's already hectic schedule would come to include regular trips to the train station to drop the father off for yet another excursion.

It was in Great Falls that Phil would be struck by the increasing awareness that he was different from the other children at school, that his family kept its distance from the secular world. In time, young Phil came to sense that he was an outsider, one of those Holy Rollers who practiced religion with the strange zeal of speaking in tongues, what seemed like bizarre babble to other denominations. To Jackson's mother, *glossolalia*, or speaking in tongues, was the grandest expression of her faith, a mystical experience in which she became filled with the Holy Spirit and began speaking in voices inspired by God. It was a true exhilaration she felt in these brushes with the Almighty, an experience that Phil wouldn't come to fully understand until he later read William James's *The Varieties of Religious Experience*. Other gifts of the Pentecostal faith included the laying on of hands, prophecy, and faith healing, all of which seemed quite foreign to secular neighbors, which in turn seemed to contribute to Jackson's growing feelings of estrangement in grade school.

His older brothers were all too familiar with such isolation, the inability to understand their peers' discussions of television shows and movies and other elements of the rapidly expanding popular culture. They had no earthly idea how to relate. "You could not go along with your peers in any easy way," Chuck Jackson would later explain. "The separation had already been done for you early on, and you had no control over it—so you're oddly objective and distanced from a lot of things most kids automatically accept and go along with."

These isolating circumstances led Phil to believe he wasn't popular, that he was different. At the same time, he and his brothers felt repelled by the religious practices that were supposed to be so much a part of their lives. The people they knew, seemingly normal people, would become wildly emotional during church services, falling onto the floor in convulsive states or babbling incoherently, all of which left Phil with a growing uneasiness.

Those feelings help explain his fascination with the Indian children who would show up at grade school. Their lives likewise seemed foreign; they didn't attend regularly; and they, too, were outsiders, inhabitants of another culture trying to find comfort in the mainstream public schools. Because of the cultural divide, there was little opportunity to hold anything more than cursory relationships with these Indian children, Jackson once recalled. But he was aware of them and filled with curiosity about them.

He began fantasizing that he was a Native American living in the 1850s before their world was overwhelmed by European encroachment, or even that he was an adopted Indian child. He went to the library and checked out every book he could find on Indians and Indian culture, bringing home an armload of them—as many as he could carry—to read and read again, picking through the details of the Native Americans' sad demise and their spiritual approach to life.

In many ways, this appreciation for Native American culture was one of Jackson's strongest connections with his mother. Having been raised in proximity to the Fort Peck Reservation, Betty Jackson had a familiarity with

Native Americans, and in later life her church work would extend to the reservation. In college and as a young NBA player, Jackson would conduct clinics and other outreach efforts to the Native American community. Those who saw the efforts and knew the Jackson family considered Jackson's efforts an extension of his mother's influence.

Years later, when he would reveal the nature of his beliefs about Native American spirituality, some observers, including opposing coaches, would assume that it was just so much blarney, that he had come to his views much later in life, as a function of the hippie lifestyle he had followed as a New York Knick. As a result, Jackson's adult fascination with Native American lifestyle was often greeted with derision, as if it were superficial, some New Age idea that he had gleaned from popular culture. To the contrary, it stemmed from the depths of his childhood, as mysterious in its origins as the other elements of his rather complex psyche.

After Jackson wrote extensively about his beliefs in his 1995 autobiography, *Sacred Hoops*, New York Knicks coach Jeff Van Gundy, who had shared a contentious relationship with Jackson, derisively dubbed him "Big Chief Triangle," a name that other NBA coaches and even some Bulls staff members began using to refer to Jackson behind his back during the final months of his tenure with the team. In interviews with reporters, Van Gundy began poking fun at Jackson's strange approach, mostly in response to the derision Jackson had aimed at Van Gundy. "Our biggest concern in the offseason," the Knicks' coach quipped in 1996, "was to find as many Indian artifacts as we could."

Although he never hesitated to needle an opposing coach, Jackson loathed the thought that his opponents would "demean" his beliefs in Native American spirituality, perhaps the main reason that Jackson sought to keep secret his tom-tom beating and other unusual coaching practices. In one form or another, these practices stemmed from those childhood feelings of being very different, of being an outsider.

"It was a fundamentalist type of belief," Jackson would explain to the New York media years later. "There was no smoking, drinking, dancing, or movies. TV was allowed, but we didn't have one. The only records were religious and classical and Christmas music. The only sectarian magazine in the home was *Reader's Digest*.

"I can remember waking up one night when I was eleven and discovering no one was at home. I panicked. Thought this was it. The second coming. And I'd missed out. I ran from room to room turning on lights, but nobody was there. I thought they'd all left, all gone to heaven."

In his autobiographical writings, Jackson actually recalled the panic as an afternoon event in which he came home from school and couldn't find anyone. Figuring the rapture had started without him, he grew fearful and rushed all over Great Falls looking for his parents until finally he found them down at the radio station taping an evangelistic show.

Regardless of the exact details, it was clear that Jackson's young life was dominated by a triangle of another sort: faith, family, and school. As a grade schooler, he discovered his increasing desire for recognition and acceptance and popularity, which immediately set him apart from his family in that his mother had taught him that it was nearly impossible to be popular and a good Christian at the same time.

If there was anything that made popularity possible, he soon discovered, it was sports, where his size and rawboned nature provided a decided advantage. Some of these characteristics Jackson inherited from his father, who was no pantywaist but rather a classic example of "muscular Christianity," a movement in the faith to demonstrate that followers could be spiritual and manly at the same time. It was the same concept that drove Naismith himself to invent basketball at the School for Christian Workers in Springfield, Massachusetts, in 1891.

Like Naismith himself, Charles Jackson had worked as a lumberjack at a young age, and he would remain an avid outdoorsman his entire life. One of Phil's vivid childhood memories was his favorite dog Smokey playing with severed deer heads in the family's back yard. With a limited income, Charles Jackson used his hunting and fishing skills to feed his brood from Montana's abundant supply of deer, moose, and elk. And he taught his sons to love the outdoors, to hunt and fish, leaving Phil with a lifelong taste for freshly killed game meat, although his relish for hunting was diminished as a child by watching his brother Joe struggle in the grisly task of finishing off a wounded deer by cutting its throat.

Other activities soon occupied Phil's time, mostly baseball, swimming, skating, and playground games. Somehow Charles Jackson found the time to build the family a home with his own hands and even included a basketball goal and concrete court in the backyard, which seemed to be the start of big things. Red Auerbach once explained that basketball fascinated people with its unique physics. "Because the floor is smooth, and the ball is round," the Celtics' coach said. That magical appeal quickly took hold with Jackson. By the fifth grade, he was serious about his hoops. A physical education supervisor at school taught him some things about the game, how to shoot and use his size. Jackson took a quick fancy to the hook shot, which he practiced over and over again with his dominant left hand. That year, his fifth-grade team won the local championship, an event that sparked Jackson's competitive fires.

He had always been a poor loser, whether it was family board games or athletic battles with his older brothers, but his intense dislike of losing grew even worse. He would storm away in tears after losses to Chuck or Joe. Outbursts of anger were not allowed in the Jackson household, and Phil would show a lifelong aversion to it. But he could barely contain his emotion over losses, and in turn that would become a recurring theme in his adult life. Phil Jackson would become known for many fine elements of his coaching, but graciousness often failed him as a loser, yet another factor that didn't endear him to opposing NBA coaches.

"To be successful you have to like to lose a little less than everybody else," Jackson would later explain.

The Jackson family soon faced bigger problems than the boys fighting over games, however. Phil's two older brothers had reached adolescence, and Joe in particular, who had always seemed to challenge the family's strict dictates, stepped up the intensity of his insurrection. By nature a kind, contemplative sort, the Reverend Jackson met these uprisings with his usual swift justice, a strapping with his belt in the basement. Phil himself recalled receiving only one such whipping, after which his father supposedly wept. Joe, on the other hand, became quite a challenge to his parents, a problem compounded by his father's intense travel schedule that often had him on the road days at a time.

The Jacksons finally decided that the only way they could cope with the situation was for Charles Jackson to give up his superintendent's job and return to a church as pastor, a move that would keep him home to more closely supervise the boys as they advanced through the difficult teen years.

In such circumstances, it is a Pentecostal minister's obligation to find a church that needs him, a calling, a flock on which to focus his spiritual gifts. Charles Jackson looked about the region and identified two locations: one in the scenic Idaho mountains, the other on the harsh plains of western North Dakota. His family wanted the mountains. Instead, he chose the plains, telling his family, "It's where the Lord wants me to go."

North Dakota

And so the Jacksons packed up their belongings and headed up U.S. Route 2 through the heart of Montana's big open country all the way to Williston, North Dakota, eighteen miles from the Montana state line and sixty miles south of Canada. The town sat just east of the confluence of the Missouri and Yellowstone rivers, at the geographic center of North America, where the arid prairie met a touch of the Badlands. The area's gently rolling hills were buffeted by winds that swept out of the Arctic, a deep chill in the winter. In summer, the winds would often shift, morphing into a hot blast from the south accompanied by stupendous nighttime thunderstorms.

"Across its empty miles pours the pushing and shouldering wind, a thing you tighten into as a trout tightens into fast water," Wallace Stegner wrote of the prairie. "It is a grassy, clean, exciting wind, with the smell of the distance in it. . . ."

Bill Fitch had his own take on it. "You can fly a kite there forever," the coach said of Williston.

"The wind blows like hell, all year long," agreed Bob Sathe, a North Dakota schoolmate of Jackson's.

Williston did have the smell of distance, with the horizon stretching out in every direction. Young Phil Jackson was there only a matter of weeks when he realized that on the prairie the sun and wind were seemingly always in your face, coming at you low, right off the vanishing point. The best thing about the wind was what it did for the sky, keeping it swept and clear and deep blue during the day, a grand spectacle that even people who lived there many decades could never quite get over. The days would begin with explosive sunrises and close with dramatic, blood-red splashes. At night, the spread of the stars could be overpowering, especially during the equinox, when the northern lights, the aurora borealis, presented a display of subtler, more intimate nature. Years later, when Phil Jackson was a famous coach and the local residents had finally coaxed him into coming back, he would insist on sleeping outdoors, forget the chill, because he wanted to see those lights, to get up close with that sky.

The price for all of this grandeur was the winters, which in a tough year could stretch from November to May, with the daylight fading not long after 3:00 P.M. It was then, at nightfall, that the wind had real teeth. It was then that you decided whether you really liked being a North Dakotan.

Williston had been founded in 1886, when the westward expansion of the railroad pushed all the way to the Missouri Breaks, in the heart of what had been fur-trading country. North Dakota, too, was a land once thick with Native American culture; much of the state had been occupied by the Mandans, those agrarian cousins of the Crow who lived in earthen houses and were pliable enough to scout for Custer's cavalry.

The town of Williston had begun life as nothing more than a cluster of tents and shanties, known as "Little Muddy."

"Just a scattering of old log houses and one damn thing and another," said Bill Shemorry, a local historian. "The railroad was gonna make a good town out of it, and they tried. I suppose they did a pretty fair job of it."

Needing to name the community, railroad officials decided to honor one of their investors, Willis James, by naming it after him, the only problem being there were already far too many Jamestowns, including one a few hours away. So the railroad concocted something different, figuring there would be only one Williston, a little jewel on the Missouri Plateau, the upper reaches of the northern plains that ran two thousand to three thousand feet above sea level.

By the time the Jacksons arrived seven decades later, Williston was a thriving hamlet of eleven thousand or so, riding on the wings of an oil drilling boom as wildcatters went for the region's riches. In 1952, geologists had discovered the Williston Basin, a vast underground oil reserve stretching into parts of Montana and South Dakota, which meant immediate growth for the town and assured that its economy would be attached to oil's wild ride, rising, then falling, booming, then busting, with the price of crude. Long a business center for the nearby farms and ranches, Williston quickly added drilling supplies to its economic mix, and its schools soon swelled with the children of oil workers.

The Jacksons were among a host of new faces arriving during the boom of the 1950s. Traditionally, the town's inhabitants were predominantly Lutherans of Norwegian ancestry, immigrants drawn to the area in earlier decades as homesteaders, wheat farmers, and laborers. The community also included a goodly number of Catholics, Methodists, and Congregationalists. But the Norwegians made up the overwhelming majority. "When someone wasn't Norwegian Lutheran, they were different," Bob Sathe explained.

That certainly included the Pentecostals, with their emotional style of worship. The Assemblies of God services were housed in a small building that would later be converted into apartments. "The Assembly at that time, it was just this tiny little church," recalled Audrey Olson, wife of the superintendent of schools.

In another setting, under other circumstances, it could have been quite difficult for a family like the Jacksons to move into a small, insular community. But the Norwegians were a friendly, open people, and Charles Jackson was a man who made a strong first impression with his quiet warmth. He represented a faith that was aggressive in its proselytizing, and he obviously worked at finding and helping lost souls. But the people of Williston could never recall him exercising anything but restraint in his approach with his new neighbors. "He was the type of person that wore very well," recalled Leon Olson, the principal at Williston High who later became the superintendent of schools. "Some of them wear their religion on their sleeves, but he didn't do that. He was very quiet, not someone who would be out in the crowd beating a drum."

One of the first things local residents noted about Reverend Jackson was that he didn't hesitate to climb onto the roof of his church to make repairs. "He really impressed me," Olson said. "I don't know too many pastors who could or would go out on that roof and do the physical work that he did."

Another who took notice was Fred Eckert, a wealthy wheat farmer. "He saw Pastor Jackson up on the roof of that church early one morning fixing shingles, and Eckert said, 'That's the kind of preacher I want,'" recalled Dean Winkjer, a Williston lawyer. Eckert, who had been orphaned as a child, was eager to use his wealth to start a home for children. To do that, he needed to set up a foundation to provide for the funding. In those days, such a foundation needed a church affiliation. Eckert got to know Jackson, liked him instantly, and made the unusual decision to use the Assemblies of God as the church affiliation for the Eckert Foundation. Then Jackson was named to the board of the foundation as part of a team that would oversee the building of two children's homes in Williston, one for boys and another for girls.

Although Eckert never converted to the Pentecostal faith, he admired Jackson and attended services at his church. "He wanted someone who was deeply committed to his faith, not someone going around looking for newer, nicer things," said Olson, who also sat on the foundation board.

That relationship between the foundation and Jackson was so strong that it continues to this day, with each Pentecostal pastor who has succeeded Jackson inheriting his seat on the Eckert Foundation board.

It would be easy to understand that a couple such as the Jacksons, who had gained immediate acceptance in the community with the appointment to the board, might seek other high-profile relationships, including memberships in Williston's various clubs and social organizations. The Jacksons, however, mostly kept to themselves and to their church duties. "They were the straight and narrow, but good, good people," Audrey Olson said.

"They were satisfied with living out of the limelight," Leon Olson agreed. "They didn't seem comfortable pushing themselves to the forefront." Mrs.

Jackson, in particular, kept a low profile, with her focus on her family and her faith.

The small Assembly church and its simple parsonage sat just across the street from Williston High School and its field house. Little could Charles and Betty Jackson have fathomed that the field house would one day be named for their youngest son. The Jacksons moved into the parsonage when Phil was in the seventh grade, and it didn't take long for conflict to arise. Jackson's dog Smokey, a German shepherd, got into a fight with another shepherd belonging to another boy, Bubby Brister. Jackson remembered being amazed at Brister's bravery in breaking up the snarling dogs, and the altercation proved to be the beginning of a lifelong friendship with Brister, who would go on to become a teammate, then a doctor in Wisconsin. He was the kind of friend that years hence Jackson could wake up with late-night phone calls to discuss whatever had bubbled up in his unusual life.

That dog fight was so horrendous that Brister's uncle, Dean Winkjer, a lawyer who looked after his sister's child in the wake of her husband's death, thought he should visit with Charles Jackson. What Winkjer discovered was a distinguished gentleman whose manner communicated character. That, too, marked the beginning of a long-term relationship, as Winkjer and Jackson worked together for years on the Eckert Foundation board.

"My nephew and Phil became very close friends," Winkjer recalled. It was a friendship driven by their mutual love of football, basketball, and baseball, and the two boys, both exceptional athletes, would form the heart of the town's most successful teams.

The twelve-year-old Phil made a quick impression on other schoolmates as well. "He was the new kid in town," recalled Bob Sathe, who would remain a lifelong friend of Jackson's. "And he loved any kind of sport. Baseball, football, basketball, he was always bouncing any kind of ball."

Or yo-yoing, another of Jackson's pastimes.

If he wasn't playing sports, he was reading. "His nickname was 'the Book,'" Sathe remembered. "He read an awful lot of books that none of us would have spent any time with. He was always curious. About everything. Very active mind. Loved to get around all kinds of information. Always curious. And knew lots of stuff about lots of stuff."

Perhaps no one ever made better use of a library card than Jackson. He particularly loved fiction, any story that could carry him away, but it helped if the story included tales about the West. Later, on Williston High's sports teams, Jackson faced hours of bus rides across the prairie to play games. Leon Olson recalled being amazed at the amount of time Jackson spent reading on those trips. "A lot of kids wouldn't be caught dead with a book on a trip," the principal said with a chuckle.

Jackson packed bundles of them. He relished the likes of Dostoyevsky and Pasternak and attempted to stretch his mind over their depth of thought, even if he didn't always understand.

The outgrowth of this reading, of his upbringing, was that he possessed a surprisingly mature intelligence for his age. "I have always found him challenging to be around. I still do. He was always restless in his thoughts. His mind was always moving to places that you didn't expect," said Sathe, who played guard on Jackson's high school basketball team and shortstop on the town's American Legion baseball team.

A large facet of this intelligence was Jackson's sense of humor, which at times could befuddle those around him. "It could be confusing," remembered Peter Porinsh, a former teammate. "When he had that smile on his face, that little smirk of his, you just didn't know what he was gonna do."

Jim Simle, Jackson's baseball coach, recalled hauling him somewhere in a car, when they pulled into a lane beside someone Jackson knew. He used his long arms to reach out and unscrew the gas cap from the other car. Then as Simle drove away, Jackson grinned and deposited the cap on the front hood of the other car. "He didn't even have to stretch to unscrew it," Simle recalled with a laugh. That same sense of humor would serve Jackson well over the years, particularly when it came to the mind games he played with his NBA opponents and the amusements he foisted on his own players. In one fashion or another, from his humor to his demeanor on the bench, much of Jackson's approach as a coach can be traced to the events of his young life in North Dakota, what many of Jackson's associates describe again and again as an ideal place to grow up.

As Providence would have it, Williston sported a healthy community ego, particularly when it came to its high school sports teams. "The winters are long," Sathe explained, "and athletics becomes an important part of everything that goes on. The kids are what the whole community revolves around. Our athletic facilities were second to none. The people dedicated their lives to the kids. The gym sat around 3,200, and it was filled every game."

Radio station KEYZ followed the Williston Coyotes around the state, broadcasting every contest live—football, basketball, and Legion baseball. Although the shortest road game was a 250-mile round-trip and just about always required overnight travel, the school's teams always took a strong contingent of fans wherever they went. A trip to the state tournament in Bismarck would easily draw four or five hundred Williston fans, each of them willing to spend three or four days out of town following the team, Winkjer explained.

"When you speak of the Williston Coyotes, we're known across the state as the gung-ho type," Leon Olson said proudly.

Such a community focus meant that the Jackson boys soon found a way to fit in, despite the family's outsider status. Joe was brown-haired and 6'3", but he was nearsighted, which prevented him from doing much in football or basketball, so he developed into a two-time state champion in wrestling. Six-one and blonde, Chuck was a track man, focusing on sprinting and high jumping. And Phil possessed those arms that would sprout to a 43-inch sleeve, which were connected to a most unusual frame. "He had this set of shoulders that never ended," said Chuck Johnson, a Williston native who went on to become a sportswriter and author. "They looked like a folding table with extra leaves in it." From the seventh grade on, Jackson discovered that his size and strange physique worked in football, basketball, and baseball. "It didn't take long for him to make a name for himself," recalled Bill Shemorry, who photographed just about all of Jackson's high school basketball games for the *Williston Plains Reporter*, a weekly. "He was bigger than most of those kids. He was just damn good."

In seventh and eighth grade, he was quarterback of the football team, center in basketball, and a developing pitcher and first baseman in baseball. Williston had a minor league baseball team, which contributed to Jackson's early fascination with that sport. In time, he would step into the Williston spotlight, which at the time was the biggest show on earth to those involved, fans and players alike. "Phil became quite the celebrity at a very young age," Sathe explained.

That newfound status didn't come without its share of frustration and even heartache, most of it attributable to Jackson's rapid growth. He was 6'1", 150 pounds by the time he began his sophomore year at Williston, and on his way to adding another four to five inches over the next twelve months—thus the nickname Bones. "Bones is cheating in biology," the kids at school would quip. "He's counting his ribs."

His size was enough to get him promoted to the varsity in both football and basketball as a sophomore. The two squads presented a stark contrast in the styles of their head coaches that would go a long way toward helping Jackson define his own approach to working with athletes. Harold Pederson, a former marine who had landed at Iwo Jima, was the taskmaster who ran Williston's football team with tough love and a searing temper. Jackson quickly came to dislike him and later described Pederson in *Maverick* as "a bullet head who scared the hell out of me." Pederson's football teams were among the best in the state, and most in the community held him in much higher esteem than Jackson did. Sathe, for example, pointed out that many of Pederson's players found the discipline and mental toughness that the coach instilled in them to be important in their lives.

"H.L. was a wonderful man. He was really hardcore, though," explained Peter Porinsh, a teammate of Jackson's who starred in football in Williston and went on to play football for the University of North Dakota. Pederson ran his physical education classes in strict military fashion, right down to the execution of calisthenics. "He was a real disciplinarian," Porinsh said. "But he was really important for all of us."

"I did not see him the way Phil saw him," recalled Olson, the school's principal at the time. "Harold Pederson had a tremendous amount of heart."

Jackson was moved from quarterback to center his sophomore year, and his good friend Bubby Carlson moved in as the signal caller. The Coyote football teams would enjoy strong success over the next few seasons, and Carlson would go on to earn a football scholarship to the University of Minnesota. Jackson would also play tight end and linebacker over his years of high school football, but it was not his primary sport and Pederson never grew on him, although Jackson's own teams would come to be known for exceptional discipline and mental toughness.

Jackson much preferred the coaching style of Bob Peterson, his deeply religious, mild-mannered basketball coach who after his days at Williston would go on to distinction in North Dakota Republican politics. As a coach, Peterson hesitated in making his decisions, almost to the point of appearing indecisive. Peter Porinsh laughingly remembered his early years on the basketball team when he wasn't playing much; all the subs would scramble to sit next to the coach because when Peterson did make a decision he seemed to go for the player right next to him, no matter what the situation.

Peterson also wanted his players to make decisions and share some responsibility for what transpired in the game. "He left a lot of stuff for us to do," Porinsh recalled. "He was a really gentle man. He never would get really angry."

Some of Jackson's high school teammates would note with interest years later that Jackson himself displayed an unusual patience as a coach, plus a knack for never rushing to make changes. Then there was Jackson's ability to put the game in the hands of his players, to allow them the freedom to make decisions. Many of those traits seemed to stem from his days playing for Bob Peterson in Williston.

Peterson offered constant encouragement to his players, never seemed to get riled at a loss, and proved instrumental in helping Jackson fight through the early crises in his young life—most of them related to the problems that attend rapid adolescent growth, awkwardness, ill-fitting clothes, and self-consciousness.

"At fourteen or fifteen, he really started to grow, and nothing seemed to work right with his body," Sathe recalled.

This adolescent clumsiness was easy enough to disguise on the offensive line in football. But varsity basketball, on its very public stage in front of the entire community, was quite another matter. Jackson seemed all shoulders and arms and wore thick-rimmed black glasses that contributed to an unusual countenance, which, combined with his tripping and thrashing about and his strange-looking left-handed hook shot, presented something of a spectacle to Williston's intense fans. Jackson was shy and especially sensitive; he quickly picked up on vibes from the crowd and felt he was being ridiculed and made fun of.

"We had a group of older guys that had that western North Dakota cowboy mentality," Porinsh recalled of the students in the crowd who made fun of Jackson. "He was so gangly and sort of all over the place. He was a misfit with a different religion. I think he was seen as a little bit of an oddball in a lot of ways. He was also an intellectual."

The students who ridiculed Jackson did so out of envy, Porinsh said. "They wanted to put a guy in his place."

Leon Olson recalled that it was obvious that Jackson was talented and intense and that he was going to develop into a fine young player. But in the interim the principal was so concerned about the situation that he sought a meeting with Peterson and the other coaches to make sure that they didn't put too much pressure on Jackson before he was ready. Even Jackson's friends weren't entirely aware of the embarrassment he felt at the time. Later it would become very clear that Jackson resented what he saw as a public humiliation. Bob Peterson saw the difficulties and went out of his way to encourage Jackson.

"Phil needed someone to say it was OK if he messed up," Sathe said.

Where the football coach demanded performance, the basketball coach took a more soothing approach. He never trumpeted his disappointment. In fact, Jackson was never made to feel that he disappointed Peterson. "I thought the world of him," Jackson would later recall.

"I think Peterson in some ways was a surrogate father for Phil, at least in high school," Sathe said.

How deep did Jackson's appreciation of his high school coach run? Years later, the residents of Williston found themselves having a hard time getting Jackson to return to his hometown. But when Peterson became involved in a political race, Jackson readily appeared at a fund-raiser for him, never mind that it was for the Republican party and Jackson had become a liberal Democrat.

As for those he suspected of ridiculing him for his clumsiness, Jackson's resentment of them grew the next season when he became a very good ball player. Those critics all seemed eager to jump on his bandwagon then. "By the time that he hit his junior year people really started to appreciate him," Peter Porinsh recalled. "Then they knew he was somebody special."

But that resentment would remain something of an unresolved issue in Jackson's adolescent life. As might be expected, it wasn't his only issue or perhaps even the largest one.

With his body rapidly changing and his perspective maturing as well, Jackson was moving into the first stages of defining himself. Like his brothers before him, what he found was something distinctly different from what his parents had sought for him. It was perhaps Betty Jackson's greatest disappointment that all three of her sons rejected the vision of faith that so engrossed her. Chuck recoiled so strongly as to leave Christianity almost entirely as an adult, and Joe became a psychologist who turned his interest to Eastern religions. Of the three, only Phil defined his soul as essentially Christian, with that well-publicized flavoring of Zen Buddhism and Native American spirituality.

The boys would bury their father in 1979, digging his grave themselves as he would have expected them to do. But Betty Jackson would live on, her mind clear, her faith strong, well into her nineties. She would spend her later years in a Bigfork, Montana, adult home, watching from afar as her youngest son gained unimagined fame and fortune. Even as he coached the Chicago Bulls, she held out the hope that he might give it up to return to the faith, to answer the call to serve a church as a pastor. "My mother still tells me, 'Fifteen hundred people witnessed you being given to God, given to the service of the Lord,'" Jackson said in 1995. "She really sees that as the fulfillment of my life, not basketball. I guess in some small way she considers me a success, certainly by financial standards. But spiritually? She has her doubts."

Those doubts began with early adolescence, when each of her boys was required to establish his own spiritual identity. Jackson recalled that the summers for his family were marked by tent revivals, large regional gatherings of the Pentecostal faithful that provided Betty Jackson an enthusiastic audience for her evangelism. It was only in this setting that she would accept the spotlight, but when she did she could be quite persuasive.

These gatherings were greeted by Phil in his early years as an opportunity to play with a host of other children, to get lost in their world of fun beyond adult concerns. Then one summer the proceedings took on new relevance. The time had come for Chuck to profess his faith and to be baptized in front of hundreds of witnesses. The oldest Jackson brother wept during the public ritual, something he rarely did, and Phil recalled being impressed by the emotion and meaning of the experience. But it also marked the nearing of his own coming out as a person of faith.

It was supposed to be the beginning of Jackson's adult relationship with God, where through prayer and meditation he would open himself to the Holy Spirit and be infused with "the gifts," the main manifestation of which was the ability to speak in tongues. Joe confided to Phil that when his turn came he had faked it. Phil, however, offered his best effort, praying and meditating as directed. But he told God he wouldn't give up athletics, no matter what. He underwent a public baptism, and his night for receiving the Holy Spirit finally came. He spent hours, until after midnight, waiting to be filled by the Spirit and to give voice to the tongues, but the evening was uneventful, other than his whimpering and brief bouts of tears. Finally, he was allowed to go home to bed.

His mother remained hopeful, spending many nights at home praying with her youngest son. Phil's feelings of failure persisted for several years thereafter, as did his mother's growing concern. Many other children in the faith were already leading church services. Jackson struck a fine figure at church, a gawking adolescent sprouting overnight out of his hand-me-down suits, a good son, given to standing with his father outside the church greeting worshipers. In the choir, he carried a strong tune, first as a tenor and then as a bass as his voice matured and deepened. Residents of Williston could see strong traces of that adolescent at church in Jackson long after he became a famous coach. "My father had a certain carriage and a certain character about him that made him distinguishable," Jackson recalled in 1995. "They say the apple doesn't fall far from the tree. I'll run into relatives, and they'll say, 'Gee, you look just like your dad. The way you carry yourself, the way you speak to your team.' I'll get a kick out of that because there's a lot more anger and ire that goes into coaching than goes into the ministry. But there is something to it. All my life, I had to carry myself as a minister's son. I pulled a certain status. It makes a responsible position easy, things like wearing a suit and moving in crowds."

Beyond appearances, however, other elements of his family's background proved more complex for him as an adolescent. As he perceived it, the Holy Spirit, or at least "the gifts," eluded him until he, too, began to pull away from his parents' sphere of influence, finding any means possible, mostly athletics and other school events, to avoid worship services and any in-depth involvement with Pentecostal faith.

"Even at fifteen or sixteen years old, he was always bumping up against his religion, trying to sort that through," Sathe recalled.

Jackson knew this situation troubled his mother, and he would later recall that she brought a great tenderness to her efforts to deal with him. He wished that there was some way around the situation. But communication and understanding travel a two-way path, and at no time did Betty Jackson ever venture across the street to watch her son play basketball. In fact, some of the people involved in Williston High athletics could never recall meeting Jackson's mother despite the fact that her son had become the town's brightest star.

Each game night, as the crowds gathered at the field house across the street to watch her son compete, Betty Jackson remained at home. The Reverend Jackson hardly missed any of the boys' athletic contests, but she seemed to be emphasizing a point, that no athletic contest should be elevated above the act of worship. In all likelihood, she sat home praying for her youngest son on those nights that she didn't attend his games.

Bob Sathe, however, cautioned against reading too much into Mrs. Jackson's absence. "Phil is an awful lot like his mother," he said. "He is very competitive, and he gets that from her. She is a wonderful lady. She may not have been at his games, but she was always very supportive of Phil, very proud of his accomplishments."

A few years later, once he had joined the New York Knicks, Jackson returned home and brought with him teammate Bill Bradley, who was struck by the similarities between Jackson's religious family and Bradley's own parents in small-town Missouri. The one difference that perplexed Bradley was the apparent distance between the people in the Jackson household and the seeming loneliness it produced.

Indeed, Phil Jackson recalled that in his junior year in high school, when his sister had married and gone away and his two brothers had gone off to college, he was left alone in the house with his parents and discovered he didn't really know them all that well. He loved them very much, but their world was not his.

Rising

The summer of 1961 belonged to Roger Maris, who belonged to North Dakota, then the state's most famous athlete. Schoolboys across the Dakotas followed the New York Yankees outfielder through that special but turbulent season as he hit 61 home runs to break Babe Ruth's single-season record.

Jackson and his American Legion teammates in Williston kept one eye on Maris and one eye on their own fortunes. Over the next two seasons, Jackson would develop into a prospect, rangy at first base when he played there and absolutely terrorizing on the mound when he pitched.

"He had a wonderful fastball and a breaking ball that was incredible," said Bob Sathe. Jim Simle, the baseball coach who also served as an assistant in basketball and football, thought so much of Jackson's abilities that he sat the young pitcher down to explain that probably his best chance of playing professional sports was in baseball. "I don't think that he ever had a run scored on him in tournament play," Simle recalled. "And with his size he was a fine first baseman."

Simle said Jackson was so enthused about baseball that he also coached younger kids in the Babe Ruth League and umpired Little League games as well. In those days, with the umpire in Little League standing behind the pitcher, the lanky Jackson presented a comical sight towering over the infield.

Bill Fitch, the University of North Dakota basketball coach, had also dabbled in baseball scouting, and he had first heard of Jackson through the baseball scouting grapevine. Fitch, though, heavily recruited Jackson for basketball and downplayed his baseball abilities, encouraging him to decide on a future in hoops.

"It was the right choice," said Fitch, who went on to coach in the NBA with Cleveland, Boston, Houston, New Jersey, and the Los Angeles Clippers. "He couldn't find home plate with a Geiger counter."

"He did have a little trouble with control," Sathe admitted when discussing Jackson on the mound. "I never saw anybody stay in the box on that sidearmed curveball of his."

Coach Simle, however, disagreed with Fitch. "Phil had excellent control," he said, adding that he also had a great release. "As tall and long as he was, it seemed like the ball was at home plate before he even released it."

Sathe always wondered what kind of pitcher Jackson could have been if he had trained in a warmer climate. The warm months were so few in Williston, it hardly allowed time for a big-league prospect to develop. Jackson himself would wonder the same thing over the years, privately harboring a fantasy of playing big-league baseball, a dream first stoked during the summer of 1961 when Maris hit 61 homers yet obviously struggled with being in the limelight and dealing with reporters' probing questions.

"I was able to take from what happened to him, the shyness he had," Jackson would say later of his experience following Maris's exploits. "I was an extrovert, I did have a voice, and I was able to be myself, without having to hide [as Maris did from the pressure that year]."

Indeed, Jackson obviously possessed a burgeoning sense of self, of identity, despite the adolescent problems he experienced. For that, much credit was due his parents—especially his mother, with her determination to push her children to do their best. Jackson took piano lessons, played trombone in the school band, and acted in high school productions. The Jackson clan still focused its Saturday nights on the dining room table for family games, especially Carooms, what Jackson would later jokingly refer to as "Christian pool," a rectangular board on which participants would flick wooden disks. When it came to cards, the family usually opted for hands of Rook—perhaps because the cards were faceless, free of graven images and the corruption they might bring. Jackson was allowed to go to school dances, but he wasn't permitted to participate—not that it mattered much, because he didn't know how to dance anyway. In that regard, he really wasn't that different from the other boys in Williston. "None of us knew how to dance either," Bob Sathe recalled with a laugh.

Still, it was hard not to want to try the Twist, the new dance by Chubby Checker, just one craze in a vast pop culture explosion ushered in during Jackson's high school days. The new music by Chuck Berry, Elvis, Jerry Lee Lewis, and a host of other nascent stars was bold, provocative, openly sexual. It brought a new energy and a new way of thinking. Young people loved it, and parents feared it.

As might be expected, Jackson craved the many new elements of popular culture, although he wasn't rebellious in going against his parents' strict rules. Yet these circumstances conspired to make him particularly beholden to athletic competition. The closest opponent for Williston High required a 250-mile round-trip. Others were much farther, meaning that the Coyotes' away games just about always featured an overnight trip, which required Jackson to miss Friday nights at church. His involvement in sports provided just the opportunity he sought to pull back from his family's religious intensity. It also allowed him a peek at the world outside. Even those who had televisions in Williston in those days had access to only two channels, but to Jackson those two channels offered an overwhelming sensory bombardment. To save on expenses, the school would pack six or seven athletes per room on those road trips. Jackson's teammates chuckled to find him up early on Saturday mornings, long before the TV channels had even come on the air, waiting with the tube turned on in anticipation of what it had to offer.

"The first thing that Phil wanted to do was get up on Saturday morning," Sathe recalled. "He had that test pattern on the screen and was waiting for the cartoons to come on."

If the test pattern fascinated Jackson, it isn't hard to imagine what delight he derived from the array of televised offerings. He was smitten by the rush of images and longed to sit in a movie theater as his friends did to take in a feature presentation on the big screen. He wouldn't realize that fantasy until Labor Day weekend of 1962, at the start of his senior year at Williston, when he snuck out of the house and stole away to the drive-in movies with brother Joe. They saw *Seven Brides for Seven Brothers*, beginning Jackson's long and amusing relationship with cinema, a relationship that he would exploit again and again as a basketball coach.

By his junior season in Williston, Jackson had sprouted to a certified beanpole, 6'5" and 160 pounds. He presented quite a bony spectacle, with his thick black glasses. "He was all shoulders and arms, and he wore those glasses," Jim Simle recalled. The arms were particularly important in gathering his teammates' misses and cleaning up on the offensive boards. He averaged 23.3 points per game that season.

In his memoirs, however, he recalled being possessed of a babyish attitude about competition, what he saw as a whining approach that left him looking for excuses and blaming others. Beyond that, Jackson felt that he lacked natural leadership qualities. He said it wasn't until he was into his junior season that he began to change, and his turnaround was prompted by one of his basketball teammates, who also played football, jumping in his face during the fifth game and telling him to grow up, that he was gutless, and that he just might get smacked.

Jackson admitted to being frightened by the incident, and he noted that the team went on a winning streak afterward, highlighted by his improved play. Porinsh, who was the senior captain of the basketball team that year, said he didn't recall whether he was the intimidator Jackson referred to. Porinsh and a couple of other players were late joining the basketball team because of their football commitments. Jackson did not play football his junior year, so he had been practicing before the others arrived on the scene. "We had all come off the football team," Porinsh said. "We all came in with a sort of tough attitude. I think he got tougher with us around."

Porinsh downplayed the incident, pointing out that Jackson was driven to improve in basketball without any goading. "It was obvious he really wanted to be good," Porinsh said, adding that Jackson was quite capable of dishing out punishment. "Nobody wanted to get underneath the boards with him," the former team captain pointed out. "If one of those elbows hit you in the head, it was just like a knife."

As for Jackson's perception that he lacked leadership skills, his former teammates failed to see that. In fact, they saw just the opposite, that he possessed extraordinary leadership for a high schooler, a condition that developed in the atmosphere developed by Peterson.

"Phil led in a different way," recalled Porinsh, a year older than Jackson. "He was not a rah-rah type. He just had this intensity on his face that told you he really meant what he was gonna do."

Sathe, a year younger than Jackson, saw him as something of a player-coach, even at that age, who did much to direct the team on the floor. "His senior year, he became a very dominant force physically, but he was even more dominant as a leader."

Both Sathe and Porinsh said they believed Jackson's ability to be honest and direct with people was the factor that drove his success then, as well as later as an NBA coach. As he matured in Williston, he showed an ability to approach a teammate about an issue without creating an incident or damaging team chemistry, Sathe said. "That was one of the things about Phil. He was respectful of who you were, but he had the ability to challenge you."

Jackson and his Coyotes improved dramatically that junior season. They became so good, in fact, that they made it all the way to the state championship game, where they lost to a team from the little town of Rugby, which was led by another player of distinction, Paul Presthus, who was about Jackson's height but who possessed a smoother set of offensive skills. The Coyotes tried to play man to man, but Jackson recalled that he couldn't contend with Presthus and the team had to switch defenses, to a box and one. Presthus, meanwhile, enjoyed a 44-point afternoon, and Rugby won by 10.

Jackson considered Presthus his main rival, and the loss was a decided setback. But he returned the next season at 6′6″, 175 pounds, with more muscle. Simle explained that there was no weight training for Williston's athletes in those days, but if there had been, Jackson's already rapid development might have reached phenomenal heights.

Jackson was also the team's only returning starter, meaning he took on an even larger role in Peterson's patterned scheme. "We had an offense that could be described in five words—'Get the ball to Phil,'" Bob Sathe recalled with a laugh. The regular-season highlight of this approach was Jackson's 40-point game against Minot in mid-February.

Jackson averaged about 23 points a game, but the Coyotes struggled early in the season as new starters found their way. Although the schedule included some disappointing losses, including a 66–39 demolition at the hands of Presthus's rugby team, Williston managed to finish 14–6, good enough to qualify for the state tournament, which the Coyotes approached with some apprehension.

On the drive all the way across North Dakota to the tournament in Grand Forks, Jackson's team stopped at a gas station. There Jackson tripped on a service station cord and plunged headfirst through a glass door, shattering it. In a later newspaper interview, Peterson remembered his instant panic that Jackson had been disemboweled. Instead, the team's star center got up and brushed himself off, embarrassed but unhurt. "I knew we were in good shape then," Peterson said.

Indeed, Jackson overcame that bout of clumsiness to turn in an impressive showing in leading his team to the state title. There, as in many of his other high school contests, he displayed a presence of mind that would become his trademark as a coach. "I have never seen anybody play an athletic event as intellectually as Phil did," Bob Sathe said. "I never saw him choke under pressure, and we had a lot of those situations. He was always so steady."

In the first round against Grafton, he scored 27 in a handy win and left the game at the end of the third quarter. Williston beat Minot Ryan in the second round to advance to the championship against Grand Fork Red River, where Jackson sparkled, scoring 35 while leading his team to the championship and earning Most Valuable Player honors.

The highlight of the contest was Jackson's stealing the ball from Grand Fork's guard Ron Bergh and going in for a dunk. Most Willistonians remember it as a stupendous dunk, but actually any kind of slam qualified as "stupendous" in those days. "It was a critical point in the game," Bob Sathe recalled, "and he went down and dunked it. It was quite a play, especially for a bunch of white kids from North Dakota."

"I had never seen a dunk in a ball game," assistant coach Jim Simle recalled. "Dunking was not legal in our state at the time. They disallowed the basket." Regardless, the play pumped up the Williston faithful and took its rightful place in North Dakota's athletic lore.

Years later, when he made a public appearance in North Dakota honoring his athletic achievements, Jackson spotted Ron Bergh, who had gone on to become a high school coach, in the crowd and made a joking reference to the play. "That, I guess, kind of made me a folk hero in the state of North Dakota," Jackson said of the dunk.

In the locker room after his team's championship victory, Jackson encountered University of North Dakota coach Bill Fitch for the first time. Ruddy-cheeked and reeling off one quip after another, Fitch made a strong appeal to sign Jackson for his team. Actually, Jackson had collected a number of cards and letters from various college coaches across the country, the first being a note from Lefty Driesell at Davidson College in North Carolina. The big competition for Fitch, though, came from the University of Minnesota, which offered the prestige of a Big Ten athletic scholarship. The Gophers were then coached by John Kundla, who had won six pro basketball titles coaching the Minneapolis Lakers. Jackson made a recruiting visit to Minnesota, where he met briefly with the older, gentlemanly coach. Much later, he and Kundla would come to share that rare, three-member coaching fraternity of men who had coached pro basketball teams to six championships or more. But at the time, Kundla's easygoing manner was no match for Fitch's nonstop banter and energy. The North Dakota coach braved a cross-state trip in a wicked snowstorm to speak at Jackson's high school basketball banquet. Fitch sealed the deal by joking and guffawing throughout the presentation. He, too, was a tough former marine, but he had a sense of humor to match Jackson's own.

Fitch had also lured a young assistant coach to help him, Jimmy Rodgers out of the University of Iowa, and he soon would become Jackson's good friend. Years later, Fitch, Rodgers, and Jackson would all find success as NBA head coaches, with Rodgers later serving as Jackson's assistant during the Bulls' glory days. "That shows you how good a recruiter Bill Fitch was," Jackson observed later. "He sold Jimmy Rodgers on the school and myself. It really is a distinct pleasure to have that fraternity."

Meanwhile, as the Coyotes were tidying up the remnants of their season, Leon Olson began putting away the team's uniforms. Broadcaster Bob Miller asked Olson what he planned to do with Jackson's number 22 jersey. "You ought to save Phil's number just in case," Miller said, "because I think he's going someplace."

Olson wasn't sure exactly why, but he took the number 22 home, where it found its way to one of his closets. It would not reappear until years later, when it looked strangely undersized to have fit somebody of such stature.

4

MONKEY TIME

Phil Jackson and his contemporaries entered college in the 1960s fully expecting to undergo a world of personal changes. What they didn't expect, perhaps, was to emerge four years later from the haven of university life to discover that civilization itself had slipped its moorings and was adrift. Soon they, too, would find themselves adrift, their lives tossed about in the upheaval. It was as if the infrastructure of the world had come unbolted. "Slipping is crash's law," Emily Dickinson once observed. It was certainly the law of the '60s and the early '70s. Things slipped, then crashed, and what once had been was no more.

Years later the participants would look back at photographs of themselves during the period and wonder if they weren't all wearing disguises.

Just about all of them found themselves making abrupt, unanticipated changes in direction. Peter Porinsh, Jackson's friend and teammate from Williston, was a good example. He had graduated high school in 1962, a year ahead of Jackson, and accepted that football scholarship at the University of North Dakota. He prospered there, playing in the defensive backfield and graduating in 1966. He planned to be a coach, and in fact served as a defensive backfield assistant at North Dakota for the next season after he earned his degree. But then came a tour of duty in Vietnam in the infantry, and thoughts of coaching vanished. In the wake of his war experience, he found himself studying counseling and therapy, mostly trying to deal with the unfathomable events of his young life.

Porinsh recalled that during part of that difficult period Jackson had brought a small piece of stability to the chaos. "Phil did a really nice thing," Porinsh remembered. "He started a circular letter about all the guys [from Williston and the University of North Dakota] and it went to those of us that were in the military. It went on for a while, a monthly thing that he would send out to keep us all in touch."

The fact that Jackson had emerged from the sports-intense climate at Williston to become a professional athlete, a New York Knick no less, only enhanced his friends' appreciation of the newsletter. All the guys from Williston watched intently each time the Knicks played, waiting in anticipation for Jackson to get in the game. "It was like a piece of us was there with him each time he played," Porinsh explained.

About 1973, Porinsh traveled to New York and spent a night with Jackson in his loft in Chelsea, a night of partying made vivid in Porinsh's memory by the ringing of the air hammer early the next morning in the machine shop directly under Jackson's loft. Porinsh remembered his disappointment at Jackson's brazen pot smoking that night. The young veteran couldn't understand how an athlete could do that, especially an athlete who had all the opportunity in the world. Porinsh's anger would be easy to understand. He had been required to serve his country, had seen his own opportunity dissipate into the crazy days and nights at An Khe, then had to return home to a world that expected him to resume his life as if there had been no detour into hell.

"I was a little bit strange at the time," Porinsh admitted. "I had done my own share of pot."

His disappointment cast the evening with an air of disagreement, but even that resolved itself in something Porinsh could accept. "Phil was just as open as you could be about that stuff," he recalled.

Open, indeed, agreed Phil Berger, a New York freelance journalist and author who interviewed Jackson for a profile in the *Village Voice* about the same time. Berger said he arrived at the loft for an interview to find Jackson rolling a joint, firing it up, and promptly offering him a toke. Berger, who knew Jackson socially, declined the offer and began pondering whether to mention it in his story. He decided against it, figuring the revelation would cause undue harm to his friend's reputation. But Jackson himself took care of the matter several months later with the publication of his book *Maverick*, in which he freely discussed his drug use.

"Phil was just very open," Berger recalled.

Porinsh remembered walking down the busy New York streets with Jackson during that weekend. Rather than distance himself from the fans by traveling to and from games in a chauffeured auto, Jackson walked or rode his bicycle or the subway seemingly everywhere he went in New York, which meant that his instantly recognizable bushy countenance attracted fans everywhere he went.

"Every kid would walk up to him," Porinsh recalled.

And Jackson seemed to have all the time in the world for them, joking around, talking, being real. "Often he walked to games in New York, and everybody talked to him—bums, kids, cops, businessmen. It didn't make a difference. Everybody just somehow trusted Phil," said longtime friend and *Maverick* coauthor Charley Rosen.

"His honesty is what made things work for him," Porinsh said. "It always has."

Years later this would factor mightily into his popularity with fans, who seized on the fact that Phil Jackson was no quibbler. He had inhaled, and it was something he had acknowledged from the very start. He was unafraid to be himself, and, more important, he would show over the coming years an amazing ability to help others be themselves as well. That honesty was the very first thing his players would perceive about him. "It is unique in some ways," he would say of that basis for his relationship with his players, "and not because they think I just smoked dope, went to parties and wore blue jeans and work shirts. There's been a lot of exchange of ideas there. We don't let things pass without talking about the whole of life. . . ."

For Jackson and many of those in his generation, grasping "the whole of life" had become something of a zeitgeist. His own transformation from sheltered child in Williston to streetwise flower child in New York was repeated millions of times over by baby boomers as cataclysmic events and sweeping changes struck one after another in a span of sixty turbulent months.

Jackson began the period at the University of North Dakota early that fall of 1963 as a tentative, youthful Republican bent on supporting archconservative Arizona senator Barry Goldwater for the presidency in 1964. Jackson hadn't been in school long when, on September 25, he and twenty thousand others hastened to the university's Hyslop Sports Center to hear President John F. Kennedy speak. It was one in a series of appearances Kennedy made that fall in the western states, the heart of Goldwater's stronghold. With the 1964 elections nearing, Kennedy's popularity was surging in the polls, boosted in part by his spending of billions to beat the Russians in a race to the moon. At each stop, the president departed from his prepared talk to mention his recent success with the nuclear test ban treaty, which had come in the wake of 1962's Cuban missile crisis, those seven days in May when the world seemingly sat perched on the brink of nuclear war. Kennedy's mention of the treaty efforts drew hearty applause from thousands of young Republicans like Jackson at stops in Denver, Montana, and North Dakota. He told them that, yes, these were "anxious days for mankind," but that the clouds had parted and better days were ahead.

Years later Jackson would reminisce about Kennedy's hope-inspiring appearance. But it would prove to be only a setup for the first of several cultural shocks awaiting the freshman and his contemporaries. Kennedy would be dead in a matter of weeks, assassinated before the semester was over, and afterward the trouble followed in strange, ugly bunches.

That same year, Dr. Timothy Leary would be booted off the Harvard faculty for his unbridled experimentation with LSD, a drug that the general public had never even heard of. The relevance of that event gained hardly any notice at the time because there was so much more happening. Each of the next three summers would bring an outbreak of deadly race riots in America's inner cities. In 1966 alone, forty-three different cities were left smoldering and scarred as the frustrations of decade upon decade of racial injustice and segregation exploded into fury.

Volatile as it was, race was just one of the items on the agenda. By 1965, President Lyndon Johnson had committed American ground troops to the war in Vietnam, meaning that hundreds of thousands of young people like Jackson's friend Porinsh would be drafted and shipped to the other side of the globe to fight a nasty jungle war for which there was no clear purpose or objective. This in turn would bring a civil insurrection, a blur of antiwar protests on college campuses across the country, culminating in the riot at the 1968 Democratic convention in Chicago. By then, Jackson himself had long left his Goldwater thoughts behind. He went to Chicago as a protester.

In the words of historian William Manchester, 1968 was "the year everything went wrong," beginning with the devastating Tet offensive; followed by the assassination of Dr. Martin Luther King Jr. in April in Memphis and another outbreak of race riots; followed by the assassination of Democratic presidential front-runner Robert Kennedy in June in Los Angeles, then the stormy Democratic convention just weeks later; followed by the election of Richard Nixon that November, and the revelation of the My Lai massacre of civilians in Vietnam.

These events forced an inevitable warping of the people and the culture. Folk music had reached something of an apex in 1963, with Bob Dylan gaining a following among the growing number of bohemians on college campuses, and Peter, Paul, and Mary offering up "Blowin' in the Wind" as one of their hits that year. They also issued "If I Had a Hammer" and "Puff, the Magic Dragon," a children's song purported to be about smoking marijuana, although the vast majority of the country's 190 million inhabitants had little idea exactly what marijuana was. The next year, 1964, the Beatles made their first visit to the United States, and music began the first quick steps in the rush to hard, acid rock. By 1966, Timothy Leary's admirers had begun following his admonition to "tune in, turn on, and drop out" in response to the strange, problematic events unfolding in each day's headlines. A year later, a newspaper reporter would describe Leary's flower child followers as "hippies." The idea was to escape the world's angry events by joining a community of peace and love and sex and drugs, a life as free from conflict as humanly possible. "Come on people now, smile on your brother, everybody get together, try to love one another right now," sang Jesse Colin Young.

The adult population stared in bewilderment and anger at this youthful rebellion, particularly the hippies. Yet mainstream America needed its own avenues of escapism. Many turned on their TV sets and tuned in to the new array of sports offerings, which, according to William Manchester, turned millions of viewers "into beer-drinking, flatulent spectators watching young athletes romp joyously in gilded playpens." The opening of the Astrodome in Houston that year helped usher in this age of hyperfascination with competition, as did the broadcast of the first Super Bowl. Critics pointed out that the Astrodome, with its forty-seven thousand upholstered seats, cost a mind-boggling $32 million to build—but that would prove to be a trifling sum compared to the billions that would be committed to arena construction over the ensuing decades.

The women's movement brought no riots but would shake society with quakes of a different kind. By Jackson's freshman year in 1963, a series of studies showed dramatic increases in the number of undergraduate coeds engaging in premarital sex, a trend documented that year by Gael Greene's book *Sex and the College Girl*. That same year the University of California, Berkeley, reported an alarming increase in sexually transmitted diseases among its female undergraduates, perhaps another factor in that school's students making one of the first-known requests for the public dispensing of contraceptives.

These, and a million other events, presented a profoundly bewildering atmosphere for youth in the 1960s. It could be argued that Betty Jackson's strict approach to child rearing had left her youngest son better prepared than most his age to deal with the times. But with so many innocents slaughtered by the turn of events, random fortune seemed to be the element that factored most heavily into all equations.

With his underwear and socks freshly labeled by his mother, Jackson took up residence at the University of North Dakota. It was all the way across the state in Grand Forks, hard against the Minnesota border, a full six hours' drive from his parents in Williston. Suddenly, for the first time in his life, he could breathe on his own, though his liberation after seventeen years as a Pentecostal ascetic didn't bring any wanton displays of hedonism. He still attended church every Sunday, still dutifully phoned his parents every two weeks.

He did, however, learn to dance, at the urging of a couple of his black teammates. A female acquaintance helped him find the rhythm to do the Monkey, one of a string of dances spun out of the soul music of that era. It was just one of many fad dances—the Watusi, the Jerk, the Swim, the Bossa Nova, the Frug, the Pony, the Twist, the Mashed Potatoes—that bubbled to the surface of popular culture in those early days, when the mood was still happy and dancing felt right. They would prove to be the first awkward steps of Phil Jackson's new identity, the one he would establish away from his family's watchful eye.

His identity as an athlete would also shift, though not as dramatically. Although freshmen were not allowed to compete on the varsity under NCAA guidelines of the era, Jackson was among a group of talented players Bill Fitch had brought to campus in his first year as coach. Jackson's UND freshman team would go undefeated and even split a pair of scrimmages against the varsity.

He was in the process of maturing, shooting to 6'8" as his frame filled out. From the start, he gained notoriety for his willingness to tumble across the floor going after loose balls. Soon his teammates nicknamed him "the Mop," which he figured was much better than "Bones." His long arms and active nature fit well in Fitch's fullcourt pressing style, in which all five players were expected to help trap the opposing ballhandlers. Jackson quickly showed in practice that he was hardly the typical center, that he relished the opportunity to cover guards and smaller players, even pressuring the point guard fullcourt. He was an overwhelming hydra, all legs and arms and elbows, ready to engulf any ballhandler who panicked and lost poise. This helped him acquire a second nickname at North Dakota—"Action Jackson"—which would follow him to New York and help define him as a Knick.

Although Jackson saw little of Fitch that first year, it was obvious they were a match. They both loved defense and took a cerebral approach to the game. A former marine, Fitch was a tough guy, a disciplinarian who would catch Jackson in some transgression and make him drop for push-ups, no matter where they were, on campus or in the gym. But Fitch leavened his approach with relentless banter and one-liners, the same sense of humor that would serve the coach so well when he moved on to direct the Cleveland Cavaliers during their first painful seasons in the NBA. "Last year wasn't all bad," he would tell reporters when they asked about his dreaded Cavaliers. "We led the league in flu shots."

No matter how many push-ups he dished out or how long he made players run wind sprints, it was impossible not to smile around Fitch. If his players screwed up on defense, he'd tell them they couldn't guard an elephant in a phone booth. In fact, the coach had first snared Jackson with a goofy routine at his high school basketball banquet. The guest speaker, Fitch called up Jackson and teammate Bobby McKenzie to get a present. He told them to hold out their arms and close their eyes, then he clamped a set of handcuffs on their wrists and announced, "When I go home I'm taking both of you with me."

If there was one thing that Jackson loved, it was a good laugh. "Fitch's humor rubbed off on Phil," Peter Porinsh recalled. "And Phil had his own sense of humor."

The whole North Dakota program showed a flair for fun. In his first seasons on the job, Fitch was reaching everywhere to bring in players. He talked a few football players into coming out for basketball just so they could set bulky, bruising picks for Jackson and his teammates. Soon Fitch's Fighting Sioux began drawing crowds, not only because they were good, but because they were fun, too.

Their pregame warm-ups began to resemble a Globetrotters circle. "We used to go to the arena early just to see what they were gonna do," Porinsh recalled. Their comedy routines would include rapid weaves that left the team's shortest man springing off the back of a kneeling teammate for a dunk. "It was hilarious, and people loved it," Porinsh said.

It was in this atmosphere, under Fitch's guidance, that Jackson would develop from a goofy, grinning freshman into a two-time All-American, the school's all-time leading scorer and holder of an array of records. Fitch was the kind of coach intent on developing his players, and not always on the court. Knowing that Jackson was from lily-white Williston, the coach assigned him a black roommate for road trips, to broaden his horizons and strengthen team chemistry. Jackson responded to it all, to Fitch's humor and discipline, with a work ethic that craved success.

"You wouldn't say Phil was blessed with a lot of natural talent," Fitch would explain later. "But he was a guy who always worked hard and always got better every year."

"He used to destroy us in practice with his elbows," former teammate David "Butch" Lince told an interviewer. "John Burckhard [another teammate] and I had more knobs on our heads from him. He was a gangly sophomore and uncoordinated. He had a 43-inch sleeve. How many guys do you know with a 43-inch sleeve?"

As he had in Williston, Jackson continued to amaze friends and teammates with his long-armed tricks in cars. Peter Porinsh remembered Jackson sitting in the middle of the front seat of a sedan and reaching through the rear windows to play with the door handle. "He could reach around when my alarm went off and tap me on the shoulder, and I had to get out of bed to do the same thing to him," Jackson's former roommate, Paul Pederson, recalled. "I think his arms were as long as our 7-footer's were."

In the classroom that first year, Jackson quickly found his maturity challenged. Foreign languages had always managed to expose a motivational weakness. He had flunked Latin in high school. In college, it was Spanish. Faced with an 8 A.M. class that required his rising before the sun, he cut it seventeen times. When he did show, he faced a showdown.

"I would climb up on a desk and whack him with a newspaper. That was the only way I could reach him," recalled Graciela Wilborn, his teacher, in a 1990 interview.

He was stalled at the time, unhappy as a political science major and unsure why. A turning point occurred late in his freshman year during a long drive with his older brother, Joe, who was a graduate student at the University of Texas. Always a skeptic about the family's religion, Joe was several steps ahead of his younger brother in the wrenching process of rejecting it. It had been tough digesting the principles of Darwinism taught in science class because they conflicted with the biblical story of creation, and the differences were too big to ignore for someone like Jackson, who seemed to enjoy pondering everything.

Jackson returned home that summer after his freshman year and promptly resumed his charade as a fundamentalist, all to keep his parents happy. But he returned to school that fall ready for the next stage in his life, which included a more intimate approach with girls. They, in turn, seemed quite eager to get to know him. He had done a bit of smooching in parked cars during his high school days but had spent most of his freshman year at North Dakota in social bewilderment. Many Saturday nights he had stayed in his dorm, playing gin rummy with his black teammates, who had few other options in the cultural isolation they faced in a predominantly white community.

From the immaturity of a typical freshman, he found something different his second year. First, he roomed with Paul Pederson, the team captain who was four years older and a role model for responsibility. Jackson grew increasingly political and was a vocal supporter of Goldwater that fall of 1964 in his campaign against Lyndon Johnson. When Johnson coasted in a landslide, Jackson was sure it meant the end of the Republican Party. He was also hawkish about the conflict in Vietnam and figured that the United States could clean up the whole mess if it simply bombed Hanoi.

By the second semester of his sophomore year, Jackson had decided to choose courses from across the academic spectrum, a step that would eventually lead him to a composite major in psychology, religion, and philosophy. The workload was well suited to his love of reading and his penchant for esoteric late-night debates. Once he got on track academically, college became his adventure, as he would later describe it, "to see what doors I could open."

On the basketball court, he mopped and hustled his way into the starting lineup, averaged 11.8 points per game, and helped his team to a 12–0 record in the North Central Conference—good enough to gain the first of his three straight nods for the all-conference team. As the season progressed, he and guard Jimmy Hester showed a knack for working together offensively, resulting in Jackson racking up a pair of 30-point games that January of 1965. The Sioux advanced through the regional NCAA playoffs all the way to the national semifinals against Southern Illinois, a team that featured his future Knicks teammate Walt Frazier. Jackson, in fact, was assigned to guard Frazier for much of the game. Frazier scored 18 points, and the Sioux lost in a rout.

Jackson found consolation on the pitcher's mound that spring and even threw a one-hitter against Arkansas State, which perpetuated his belief that any chance he had to play professional sports would come in baseball. His notion was confirmed when a scout from the Dodgers approached him after a game just to let Jackson know that he was watching.

His basketball play, though, zoomed off the next season as Fitch turned increasingly to Jackson as an offensive option. He answered with a pair of 31-point games in early December, followed by a 40-point performance in February. With Jackson averaging 21.8 points and shooting better than 54 percent from the floor (along with 12.9 rebounds per game), the Sioux were 11–1 in conference play that season and again made a strong run in the NCAA tournament, boosted by Jackson's 44 points in a win over Valparaiso. For the second year in a row, North Dakota advanced to the national semifinals to meet Southern Illinois. This time Walt Frazier was academically ineligible, but the Salukis still won, 69–61.

Jackson was surprised after the season when he was named an NCAA Division II All-American over Paul Pederson, his senior roommate, teammate, and friend. But Jackson's combination of scoring and rebounding had gotten him noticed. The distinction only served to increase the pressure on him that next fall when he was the only starter returning. The Fighting Sioux opened Jackson's senior season in Chicago for a pair of high-profile games. He scored 26 in the opener against Bradley but choked in the second against DePaul, with pro scouts in the stands, and totaled only 7 points. Disappointed, he went out with a female friend and got lost in the city, which caused him to miss curfew and catch Fitch's wrath. Fitch removed him as team captain and told him, "You can't make the pros without my help."

"Either be the leader or else you're not going to be anything," the coach said.

Jackson's answer to the call for leadership was a scoring outburst. Twice in December he scored 35 points in a game, then scored 40 in a road win over South Dakota State. He scored 36 and 37 in a pair of road wins in January, including one game where he was required to attempt a Shaq-like 27 free throws but responded in un-Shaq-like manner by hitting 23 of them.

"He was just an outstanding player," recalled former North Dakota sports information director Lee Bohnet in a 1992 interview. "He could dominate, and did dominate, games because of his wingspan, shooting ability, and intensity.

"He was very popular. The gals all liked him, and I think his teammates liked him. When he played for Bill Fitch, even though he was the star of the team, he got no special privileges. If he screwed up in practices—and I've seen this happen—he would do extra laps."

That February 24th he scored 50 in a home win over Northern Illinois, which helped North Dakota close out another conference title with an 11–1 record. Jackson was again the conference's outstanding player and was named to his third straight all-conference team. His averages of 27.4 points and 14.4 rebounds per game earned him yet another All-America distinction.

But with New York Knicks scout Red Holzman watching in the stands, Jackson got into foul trouble and had to sit out 17 minutes (he still scored 21), and the Sioux lost in the regional semifinals to Louisiana Tech. In a consolation game the next night, with no pro scouts on hand, Jackson scored 51 points in a win over Parsons, and his college career was over. Jackson owned eighteen different basketball records at UND and graduated as the school's all-time leading scorer with 1,708 points.

Among the pro scouts who had found their way to North Dakota was a chubby young Baltimore Bullets representative, Jerry Krause, who was the latest in a long line of people entertained by Jackson's car tricks. "I had quite a wingspan," Jackson recalled with a chuckle.

"Phil could do something no one else in the country could do," Krause would recall years later. "I was scouting Phil for the Baltimore Bullets, and I saw him get in an old four-door Plymouth, sit in the middle of the back seat, and then open both front doors at the same time."

For UND sports information director Lee Bohnet, it was Jackson's ability to tune the radio from the back seat that did the trick. "We were going somewhere in town," Bohnet recalled. "He reached over the front seat and dialed the radio without bending. He didn't like the radio program that was on."

Jackson hit it off instantly with Krause, a rotund little man with a hundred stories about the characters who peopled the world of baseball and basketball scouting. "Even as a scout back there thirty years ago, he was a very unusual type of fellow to be out there scouting a basketball player," Jackson recalled in 1995.

Despite the kick he got from surprising people with his reach, getting drafted by a pro basketball team wasn't Jackson's primary concern that spring of 1967. He had bigger things on his mind, notably the personal changes that had begun to escalate with the start of his junior year. He had pledged the Sigma Nu fraternity in early fall 1965 and at the end of pledge week had gotten drunk for the first time in his life, a mortifying experience in which he wound up on stage during a student gathering leading the audience in school cheers. That loss of control had left him so shaken that when marijuana began showing up on campus the next year he declined to try it for fear that he might lose it again.

Besides, he didn't need it. He was already having too much fun in his personal life. He met his first wife, Maxine, at the start of his junior year. She was a beauty who caught his eye in a campus academic building. He asked her out, took her to see the movie *Carousel*, and although he was already dating a girl from the University of Montana, decided to add a second romance to his agenda, a complication that grew a bit tangled the next year when his Montana girl transferred to UND.

More than Maxine's looks, it was her passion for liberal politics that caught his interest. She became an immediate influence. She cared a whole lot about public policy and almost nothing about sports. Jackson's conservative ideals melted in her presence. There was plenty for them to debate between the fall of 1965 and the spring of 1967 as their romance blossomed. Race riots and war protests gripped the country. Like a lot of people who had once favored the war in Vietnam, Jackson reversed his thinking.

Beyond his sports and his dating, Jackson immersed himself in his studies on his way to a composite degree in philosophy, psychology, and religion. A sociology class hit him hard his junior year with a lecture that depicted fundamentalists as people of a lower class. That summer, sitting in church services back home, he became increasingly irritated by how the ministers butchered the language, by their poor diction and grammar. That irritation and the desire to find something more sophisticated drove the intensity of his philosophy studies his last year in school. He took a special interest in the works of existentialists such as Sartre and Camus and the writings of Nietzsche (which years later he would suggest to Shaquille O'Neal). Ultimately, though, none of it filled Jackson's emptiness. He was in the process of vacating his former life and deciding what his new life would be. He particularly enjoyed that spring of 1967 with Maxine, but by late summer they learned she was pregnant. They married on September 7, 1967, just ten days shy of his twenty-second birthday. It wasn't long before Jackson realized that he didn't know Maxine all that well. What was worse, he didn't know himself either.

5

THE PROFESSIONAL

It wasn't until the day of the draft that Jerry Krause realized he'd been hoodwinked. By none other than Red Holzman. Krause had thought his team, the Baltimore Bullets, was going to steal Phil Jackson in the third round. He was wrong. Holzman's team, the New York Knicks, took him early in the second round, with the seventeenth overall pick. But there was this little problem of the Minnesota Pipers to overcome. The Pipers, an American Basketball Association team, offered Jackson $25,000 for two seasons. The Knicks offered $13,500 for one season plus a $5,000 signing bonus. Jackson did the math and signed with New York.

"I had wanted to draft Phil for Baltimore in the second round in 1967," Krause recalled years later, the disappointment still obvious in his voice. "We took a gamble on another player, and New York got Phil."

Holzman got Phil. *Holzman!!!*

It was the steal that mattered most to Krause.

Two years earlier, in 1965, he had purloined another Division II prospect, Jerry Sloan out of Evansville. "A tough kid," Krause liked to tell people. "He's got huge hands." Only the Bullets hadn't played him much as a rookie. Then they'd let him go in the 1966 expansion draft to the Chicago Bulls. The Bulls saw right away that Sloan was great. Two weeks into the season, the Bullets had phoned Chicago and asked if they could have Sloan back. "No," Bulls owner Dick Klein had told the Bullets. "A thousand times, no."

So Krause returned to looking for another steal, and was sure he had found one in Jackson. Way up in North Dakota. Nobody went up there. Not to see a big white kid. But he had these arms. And he was smart. Man, was he smart. And Krause had seen him. He'd been out there and had even flown this kid Jackson into Baltimore for a tryout. Holzman had seen him, sure, but had acted like he wasn't even interested.

But then fuckin' Holzman had gotten him. Just the thought of that made Krause ill.

It wasn't that he didn't like Holzman. He loved the guy. But that's what made it worse. He could even remember that red-eye in Kansas City. It was Krause's first year in scouting, in the early 1960s. Everywhere he turned he was running into Holzman. He had gone to Oklahoma to scout Flynn Robinson, who was playing for Wyoming at the time. The next night, Krause planned to see a game in Wichita, so he was on a late flight that stopped over in Kansas City. There, waiting to get on the same connecting flight, was Holzman. It must have been 4:00 in the morning! They gave each other looks that only scouts could.

"Where you been?" Holzman asked.

Already other scouts in the business were making fun of Krause, a chubby little guy who was secretive and wore a trench coat and a hat, like Inspector Clouseau or somebody. They called him "the Sleuth" and snickered behind his back. Krause's instincts told him to be coy in answering Holzman's question about where he had been.

"Down the road," Krause replied.

Years later, Krause would recall what happened next: "He looks at me and he says, 'Son, I want to tell you something. I know where you've been, and if you've got any brains in your head you know where I've been, so let's cut the bullshit and let's be friends.'"

Little did Krause realize it at the time, but he had just established the most valuable relationship in his professional life. Some umpteen years later Krause would find his way back into baseball scouting, working for Jerry Reinsdorf and the Chicago White Sox. Reinsdorf had grown up a kid on the streets of Brooklyn, a Knicks fan, and he would later come to idolize Red Holzman. Learning this, Krause would regale him with Holzman stories, and in 1985, when Reinsdorf put together a deal to buy the Chicago Bulls, he would reward Krause for those stories by naming him the general manager of the team. Reinsdorf then told the media that he wanted a team based on the Holzman vision of basketball, and Krause was going to give it to him.

The Red Holzman fan club, of course, was much bigger than Krause and Reinsdorf, although in the early days some people in pro basketball wondered if Holzman burned only a 60-watt bulb.

"Red is as dumb as he wants you to think he is," allowed former Knicks coach Carl Braun. "He's dumb like a fox."

"His own life was dedicated to creature comforts, to bottled scotch and good cigars and sirloin," Phil Berger once observed, "and he brought to the dinner table a homespun soul. . . ."

It was the soul that would nurture both Krause and Jackson—the former in scouting, the latter as a coach.

It was Holzman who picked Jackson up at the airport on his first trip to New York, a day made memorable when, on the ride to his hotel, some wanton youths standing on an overpass threw a rock through Holzman's windshield, providing Jackson with an instant and unforgettable lesson on the city's wretchedness and Holzman's unflappability.

He stood just 5'9", but had been a player himself in the bare-knuckled days of the game, a member of the Rochester Royals. They were owned and coached by a firebrand named Les Harrison and featured Hall of Fame ball-handler Bob Davies. In 1951, the Royals were on their way to the league championship when they hit a downturn, which Harrison corrected by taking his players to a roadhouse, watching them get uproariously drunk, then picking up the tab. Their vision corrected, the Royals went on to claim their title that spring, then retired to years of frustration as the Cincinnati Royals, Kansas City/Omaha Kings, and finally the Sacramento Kings.

Holzman, meanwhile, moved on to become coach of the Hawks when they perched in Milwaukee, where his teams lost 120 games and won just 83. He kept showing his players pictures of his young daughter, reminding them that her daddy didn't need to be out of a job, but it didn't work. He was fired, which contributed to the impression that he wasn't smart. But he somehow managed to move into the scouting hierarchy of the Knicks, the richest team in the league, where he became known for espousing wisdom that could only have come from his rough-and-tumble days with the Royals.

"Never talk about money with your wife at night," he would advise.

"Never get your hair cut by a bald barber. He has no respect for your hair."

"Never take medical advice from a waiter."

By the middle of Jackson's rookie year, Holzman replaced Dick McGuire as coach. McGuire probably knew a lot about basketball, Jackson had figured, but he was such a mushmouth that the players couldn't understand what he was saying. Jackson had taken to nodding in agreement whenever McGuire addressed him, but he rarely had an idea what the coach was saying.

Holzman, on the other hand, made his points with a spare precision, and only after he had thought things through. Later, his impact on Jackson could be found everywhere. In coaching, Holzman focused almost completely on defense. "On offense, you guys can do what you want," he would jokingly tell his players. "But on defense you do what I want." Holzman was tough and stressed discipline, but he was willing to listen. He allowed forward Dave DeBusschere to install several key offensive plays that freed forward Bill Bradley to shoot, a development that would be critical to the team's success.

The thing that defined Holzman's teams was the pressure. His Knicks became the first pro team to rely heavily on the press. In practice, he would stand courtside, dressed in shorts and a windbreaker, urging his players to "see the ball." On the press, he wanted them anticipating where the offense was going to throw it in attempting to escape the trap. Holzman wanted his players feeding off those passes. That would become their trademark, creating turnovers and converting them into points in easy bunches. "Any game we're down even 10 points going into the fourth quarter we can still win," Willis Reed explained at the time.

It was the press that would provide Jackson a reason for his NBA existence, the reason that Holzman wanted to sneak in ahead of Krause and draft him in the first place. In short time, Jackson would find a role coming off the bench with Holzman's pressing unit in the second period, where his arms and mobility were not just an advantage but a weapon. If the game slowed down into the halfcourt during Jackson's first years in the league, the crowds in Madison Square Garden would groan and hiss about his ineptitude. But when the pace was high, he was a difference maker.

It was his defensive mind-set that allowed Jackson to get along with Holzman despite his rapid transformation from preacher's kid to hippie. Jackson seemed to continuously complain about dress codes and other team rules. Like the pairing of Rodman and Tex Winter in later years, some observers took delight in Holzman, attired in his Brooks Brothers finery, having discussions with the bushy-haired, mustachioed Jackson. It was a cerebral connection of which neither fully understood the implications.

"Red was a big influence on my basketball philosophy," Jackson would explain a quarter-century later. "Everyone on those teams had their own sphere, but Red knew how to let everyone find their own niche."

Eventually, Holzman somehow managed to entrust this hippie to scout opposing teams while he was on the injured list. And it was Holzman who first saw Jackson's potential as a coach, something that none of his teammates did. "I thought he'd be growing his own food somewhere," Walt Frazier later admitted.

Jackson admired Holzman's "tender touch," the ability to compromise, to reconcile differences. "He never overloaded you with advice. He doled it out in small packets and in a variety of ways," Jackson explained. "He had a featherweight punch that hit you like a knockout blow."

And Jackson's knack for instigating a change of pace as a coach, giving his players books, or taking a side trip through the countryside instead of pushing his team through another practice—those things stemmed from the appreciation for the finer things in life that Holzman showed his players. Years later, as they watched Jackson at work, the former Knicks would note how much he was like Holzman.

Glory

Willis Reed earned the nickname "Wolf" when he played college basketball at Grambling University because he would hang around the boards gobbling up rebounds like a starved canine going after red meat.

At 6'9" and 235 pounds, he was a big man but not quite big enough to dominate the NBA with his size. Instead, he used his hunger, that red-meat factor. He was so serious and driven that he walked into New York Knicks training camp as a rookie in 1964 and immediately requested a copy of the NBA rule book.

"I just wanted to understand the game," he said.

He was a leader, not an overwhelming individual talent, although he could be overwhelming enough at times. Like Bill Russell before him, Reed was quick and intelligent. Unlike Russell, Reed had a smooth shot with plenty of range. Beyond all that, Reed had a presence that began with his overwhelming physical power. He wasn't a great leaper, but he was strong and determined that no one would outhustle him.

"As a player and a man, he was always on fire," Walt Frazier said of Reed.

As the story goes, Reed took on the entire Los Angeles Lakers team in a brawl during the first game of the 1966–67 season and whipped 'em all.

By himself.

"He just took over," recalled Sam Goldaper, the veteran writer for the *New York Times*. "The most unbelievable fight I ever saw in basketball."

It was a rough game, Reed recalled. "Rudy LaRusso threw a punch at me going up the floor, and the fight was on. I ended up hitting some people but I never did get a shot at Rudy. It was a wild fight."

After Jackson was drafted, the Knicks sent him a game film to view in North Dakota. Jackson, who had seen almost nothing of the NBA, sat down with some friends at school and watched in amazement. The film Holzman had sent him was of Reed's battle with the Lakers.

It was both good news and bad news for the rookie. It meant that he would play alongside Reed, who was a protector for virtually every Knick. Jackson also figured he would face something of a toughness challenge, which he did upon the opening of training camp. Mostly, though, it was a matter of ribbing. His Knicks teammates took one look at the new rookie's strange physique and dubbed him "Head and Shoulders," yet another in what was proving to be perhaps the longest string of nicknames in all of sport.

Jackson managed to survive, and even scored in, the Knicks' first game that season. Soon he and Walt Frazier, the team's first-round pick, found themselves in a whirlwind of fun on the Knicks' road trips around the country. Frazier recalled that in each city he and Jackson would check into their room only long enough to drop their bags before heading out for a night of fun on the towns. Chicago, Detroit, Boston, Los Angeles, Philadelphia, Cincinnati, Baltimore, St. Louis, San Francisco, Seattle, and San Diego—each offered its naughty delights, and Frazier recalled that he and Jackson seemed intent on sampling all of them in their first full view of the country's major cities. Meanwhile, back in New York, Jackson's young wife was pregnant and trying to find some meaningful way of relating to her new surroundings. Their daughter, sweet little Elizabeth, would arrive in March, as the Jacksons were coming to the understanding that they needed to find a way to get to know each other better in and around the NBA's 82-game schedule.

Beyond the hiring of Holzman, the season would be remembered for two other developments. The first was the Knicks' moving from the old Madison Square Garden to the brand new one on 33rd Street. This held some significance for Jackson. The old Garden was thickly populated with gamblers, which Jackson discovered after the fans kept booing him during garbage time at the end of games. He learned that his miscues and even his successes had great impact on the point spread.

The new Garden would still have its share of that crowd, but it was more uptown and quickly attracted a following of celebrities, especially as Holzman found ways to make his team better. By the time the glory years rolled around in 1970, Holzman's teams had transformed the Garden crowd into a loud, silly horde. The upper deck screamed "de-fense," and the city-hardened fans seemed to lose a little of their gaming edge and actually softened into something resembling cheerleaders. Like the Lakers in Hollywood, the Knicks soon acquired their courtside attractions. Woody Allen, Dustin Hoffman, Dianne Keaton, Elliot Gould, and Peter Falk were regulars. So was Soupy Sales. And author William Goldman. Suddenly it seemed that all of Manhattan wanted a seat in Holzman's Garden. Over the next several seasons, they would even find it in the kindness of their hearts to drop the murmur of despair when Jackson produced a miscue on the floor. Finally, they would go so far as to give up some love for Jackson and his mad-scramble ways. They would even take to calling him by his college nickname, "Action Jackson."

"I'm a person who gravitates to action. It's in my blood," he would tell an interviewer.

But all of that came long after his rookie season, a time reserved for inhabiting the shadows when he wasn't on a road trip having fun. Actually, Jackson preferred the road those first years in New York because he detested the city, its angry residents, and the complications it brought to everyday life. Truth be known, he didn't so much love the crowds he met on the streets during his walks and bicycle rides as much as he hated trying to find a parking space near the Garden on game nights.

The second memorable, major event of his rookie year was the arrival of Bill Bradley midway through the season. A national idol and the subject of a biography by *New Yorker* writer John McPhee before he even finished at Princeton in 1965, Bradley had accepted a Rhodes scholarship and put the NBA on hold while he studied at Oxford. Now, with his game having suffered from two years of atrophy, Bradley had returned with a fat contract and a massive media entourage in tow, reporters and writers eager to hang on his every word, every action. Though it would pale in comparison to the crowd following Michael Jordan in 1995, Jackson and his teammates were stunned by the sudden swarm that descended upon the locker room, leaving them all feeling like spectators of some bizarre drama.

Nobody greeted Bradley's arrival more eagerly than Jackson's parents back in North Dakota. They had read about his Christian upbringing in Missouri and, fearing the influences that young Phil might come under in Sodom and Gomorrah, were quite hopeful that Jackson could make friends with Bradley. Jackson himself considered Bradley a hero and had his own hopes for a friendship. Instead, he soon discovered a Bradley who was standoffish, embarrassed about the attention he was receiving, and quite aware that his game was nowhere near ready to match the buildup he was receiving.

The rejection stung Jackson, and it would take quite some time to get over it. In 1970, he enraged Knicks fans by confiding to writer Phil Berger that Bradley was strange, afraid to let himself go, that Jackson was weary of his "Platonic kind of shit."

"My parents love him because he's supposed to be a Christian, see," Jackson said. "They throw him up in my face a lot."

Faced with criticism for his comments, Jackson would complain about the dangers of commenting to freelance writers working on books. Berger would publish the critically acclaimed *Miracle On 33rd Street* after the Knicks' 1970 championship season. But Jackson himself would revisit his complaints about Bradley in *Maverick* in 1975. Eventually, over Jackson's ten seasons with the Knicks, he and Bradley would develop a deep and lasting friendship—so deep, in fact, that Bradley would offer Jackson the job of running his campaign for the Democratic presidential nomination in 1999, an offer prudently declined.

Jackson himself would acknowledge that Bradley had much bigger problems in 1967 than trying to find a middle ground for a rookie's deep discussions. With the world watching, his game was an obvious disaster. He was too slow to play guard, too weak at forward.

In the wake of his rookie failure, Bradley spent that fated summer of 1968 working days as a community volunteer in Harlem, then taking a train down to Philadelphia in the evening to work with Philly basketball legend Sonny Hill and play in the Baker League games, a summer proving ground for pro players.

"We played in the basement of a church. I was still trying to play guard, and Sonny was very positive," Bradley once recalled. "He told me I could do it. That was an important summer for me in terms of restoring my confidence, getting back some of the skills I had lost, getting the chance to go against great players like Earl Monroe and Wali Jones, and, above all, making a good friend [in Hill]."

Overnight that next season, there developed a glitch in the harmony that Holzman had begun establishing with his team. It came with the jockeying between Bradley and Cazzie Russell at small forward. The two had competed against each other in college, but Russell had gone right to the pros after the University of Michigan, while Bradley had left for Oxford. Russell had a fat contract, too, and an offensive game to match it. He was a finely tuned athlete, brimming with confidence as a young pro.

Bradley, though, was most comfortable at his natural position, forward—which, of course, was Russell's spot, too. The situation could have had explosive consequences for a New York team . . . a white guy and a black guy, both high-profile types, competing for the starting job. It was a story made for the New York press, and the writers had a go at it. The rest of the Knicks, though, left it alone.

"We stayed out of that," Frazier said of the controversy in a 1990 interview. "It was always remedied by some freak, uncanny circumstances."

Russell was given the starting nod for 1968–69 but broke his leg, and Bradley took over. Bradley kept the job when Russell returned the next season. The team would play well with Russell filling a big role off the bench. An incredible offensive talent, he obviously wasn't happy about the circumstances, but he wasn't loud about it either. Then, in the spring of 1970, Bradley was injured, and Russell moved back into the starting lineup—only the team didn't fare as well. They suffered some losses, and it became obvious they were better with Bradley as the starter.

"Cazzie had his chance," Frazier said. "But he was better coming off the bench when we needed something. He could come in and get us points when we needed them."

Russell had great moves and could create opportunities to get himself open for the shot. There wasn't much need for him to pass the ball. Bradley, on the other hand, didn't move nearly as well and couldn't always get his shot. The team had to set picks to get him free. If the play didn't work, he passed the ball and seldom forced a shot. That helped, Frazier said, because it created movement in the offense and kept everybody involved.

While immensely important for the Knicks, these events held little initial interest for Jackson. He recalled adopting his young wife's view of the people they had met in pro basketball. Most of them seemed to have only their interest in the game with little thought for the grave developments in society at large. That changed briefly in April of 1968 when Martin Luther King Jr. was assassinated. All of the Knicks felt a shock, and Jackson recalled his black teammates expressing anger and frustration. But Phil and Maxine Jackson saw the NBA as an unreal, even unfulfilling, realm. They made their way back to North Dakota quickly that first offseason, and Jackson gave much thought to his future, to perhaps a graduate degree in psychology. He even took some courses at UND, but found that experience strangely unsatisfactory.

Despite his misgivings, Jackson fell right in step with the Knicks in camp that fall, Holzman's first opportunity to really shape his team. However, the team's shortcomings quickly became obvious as the schedule unfolded, and much of the debate focused on center Walt Bellamy's inconsistencies. Finally, in December, twenty-nine games into the 1968–69 season, New York traded Bellamy and guard Howard Komives to Detroit for forward Dave DeBusschere, who would become the final element in their championship chemistry. Although he wasn't much of a leaper, he was a fine athlete. The first four years of his pro basketball career, he also worked as a pitcher in the Chicago White Sox organization. But in 1964, just months after DeBusschere's twenty-fourth birthday, the Pistons named him their player-coach, the youngest ever in the NBA. He threw baseballs one more season, then devoted his career solely to basketball.

Four seasons later he arrived in New York as a complete forward. Few people were better than the 6'6" DeBusschere at the subtleties of rebounding, of getting position and boxing out. He passed the ball as well as any frontcourt player in the game. And he had a smooth shot with great range.

The most important thing about the DeBusschere deal was the shifting of team roles that it brought. Komives had started with Dick Barnett in the Knicks backcourt, but his departure meant that Frazier moved in as a starter. Perhaps the best defensive guard in the league, the left-handed Frazier unmasked his offense once he got more playing time. His development as a scoring threat pushed the Knicks to the next level. But most of all, the DeBusschere trade benefited Reed, who had been playing out of position at power forward. With Bellamy gone, Reed moved to center, which set the team's identity.

"A lot of the pieces fell together at the right time," Reed said.

Unfortunately, they didn't include Jackson. Days after the trade, the Knicks were playing in Phoenix when the Suns' Neil Johnson shoved Jackson in the back as he was finishing a layup on a fast break. The resulting twinge required Jackson to leave the game. Although he felt well enough to play the next game in San Francisco, he got shoved again, this time by Clyde Lee. Days later he was diagnosed with a herniated disk, which resulted in hospitalization and persistent discomfort. At least one doctor suggested that he undergo spinal fusion surgery right away. But Cazzie Russell had just broken his leg, and Jackson got the impression from the team that he should hold off, just in case they needed him to play in an emergency. So he delayed the surgery until the offseason, which resulted in his missing the entire 1969–70 campaign.

With his muscles atrophying by the second, it seemed seriously doubtful that he could play even if asked. So he returned to North Dakota that spring of '69 and took a course in group therapy that involved a marathon session of intensely personal discussions within the group. The session was supposed to go on for hours, but the setting included a large aquarium, and Jackson, distracted by a strange fish in the tank, tapped so hard on the glass that he broke it. Hopes of anything constructive washed away with the ensuing mess, and Jackson would later use the memory to sum up his early efforts at graduate school.

Once the season ended for the Knicks, he underwent surgery and began the long, painful recovery and therapy that would prove to be the challenge of his young life, with atrophy reducing his muscles to mush, his game to gimpiness. Even worse, doctors ordered him not to have sex for six months after the procedure, which left Maxine and him with the creative fun of figuring a way around the directive.

Mostly, though, the situation meant that Jackson's journey of discovery took a detour into the dark recesses. He took to drinking, found that maybe he could enjoy smoking dope after all, and wondered if he would ever play again. He even ventured into a courtroom to watch an acquaintance go on trial for a drug charge. The district attorney recognized Jackson and told his investigators to check him out. Fortunately, someone tipped Jackson off with a phone call, and he cleaned up his act a bit and assumed a lower profile. Somehow he fought through this negative energy to do the hard work of rehabilitation, but it took a long time.

The recovery kept Jackson from playing a single game during the Knicks' glorious championship season. Still, he showed up at training camp, mostly out of curiosity about what offensive changes Holzman would make. Just days before camp opened he had gotten his back brace off, but the team made it clear he would spend the year on injured reserve. In those first days of camp Jackson endured teasing from his teammates about procuring a chastity belt for Maxine while he recovered. The second day of training camp, Jackson showed up late, prompting Holzman to take him aside and tell him, "If you're going to be part of this, be here on time."

Jackson's initial reaction was to withdraw, coming around only to work as a $75-a-game photographer for the *New York Post* when the team played at Madison Square Garden. But Holzman drew him in as an unofficial assistant, letting him perform limited scouting chores. Mostly he watched the Knicks from the sidelines and learned more than he ever imagined he could. Watching outstanding players such as Reed, Frazier, DeBusschere, Russell, and Bradley conduct themselves with unselfishness would have a profound impact on his ideas about team play. "I learned how to look at the game from the perspective of what the whole team was doing and to conceptualize ways to disrupt an opponent's game plan," he wrote in his 1995 book *Sacred Hoops*.

Just as important, he began to think about coaching as something that he could do. And he began to see the game as a coach.

Much of what Jackson saw involved Willis Reed's brilliance. First, he was named the MVP of the All-Star Game, then later that spring he was voted the league MVP. He capped that by picking up the MVP award in the Finals, the first player to capture all three in a single season. As captain of the Knicks, he was a natural and imposing leader. He was the link that seemed to keep everyone—rookies, veterans, coaches, even management—together and headed in the right direction.

They had finished the 1969 season with a 54–28 record but lost to Boston in the Eastern Conference finals. "DeBusschere said in the locker room after the Boston series that next year was going to be our year," Reed recalled in 1990. "We really believed it. Everybody went home eager for next year. We couldn't wait for the season to start. Everybody came back in good shape and ready to go."

After a great training camp, they opened the season by winning five, losing one, then taking the next eighteen, which at the time was the league record for consecutive wins. The Knicks rarely looked back from there, loping off to a league-best 60–22 finish.

For decades, New Yorkers had waited for a basketball team to love, and finally Holzman gave them one in 1970. With Dick Barnett and Frazier, the Knicks had the most stylish backcourt in the league. Frazier was "Clyde" from the movie *Bonnie and Clyde* because of his passion for gangsterish hats and fancy suits. Barnett had the Carnaby Street look, complete with a cane, cape, and spats. He spent many of his off-court hours engrossed in postcard chess, trading moves with other players around the country, often engaging in several games at once. In his book *One Magic Season and a Basketball Life*, Frazier called Barnett the funniest man in basketball. He was the team's graybeard, and he had a million tales to tell. He delivered them deadpan, with his considerable storytelling abilities (he would later earn a Ph.D. in education at Fordham).

Jackson hadn't traveled with this cast, but in the spring Holzman invited him along—and what he found would go a long way toward solidifying his fascination with pro basketball. The drama and excitement of the Knicks' playoff run would put to rest his doubts about the game, but they did little to abate his doubts about himself.

The Knicks clashed with Baltimore in the first round in a seven-game series. The Bullets had Earl "the Pearl" Monroe at guard, Gus Johnson at forward, and Wes Unseld at center. It was a brutal series, with Unseld and Reed laboring mightily in the post. The Knicks finally closed them out in the seventh game in the Garden, 127–114.

In the Eastern Conference finals, they defeated Milwaukee with rookie Lew Alcindor, 4–1, and New York stepped up to face the Lakers in the league championship series.

It had been an up-and-down year in Los Angeles. Butch Van Breda Kolff had been replaced by Joe Mullaney, the veteran coach from Providence College. Wilt Chamberlain, now thirty-three, had suffered a knee injury nine games into the season and appeared to be lost for the year. But as the playoffs neared, he announced his intention to return, a move that surprised even his doctors. He played the final three games of the regular season and was force enough to help the Lakers thrive in the Western Conference playoffs. They had finished second in the regular season behind the Atlanta Hawks and Sweet Lou Hudson, but with Chamberlain the Lakers swept Atlanta in the division finals.

Despite that win and the Lakers' overwhelming edge in playoff experience, the Knicks were favored by the oddsmakers. Game 1 showed why. Although Reed had been worn down by battling first Unseld, then Alcindor, he quickly ran circles around Chamberlain. Barnett also was eager to match up with Jerry West, who had gotten the ball and the publicity when the two played together in Los Angeles. New York opened a quick lead, pumped it up to

50–30, lost it, then blew by Los Angeles rather easily over the last eight minutes to win, 124–112. Reed finished with 37 points, 16 rebounds, and 5 assists. With that momentum, the Knicks went on to take a 3–2 lead in the series.

Game 5 in the Garden rang in as one of those golden moments in pro basketball history. Wilt came out strong and determined to cover Reed all over the floor. With a little more than eight minutes gone in the first quarter, Los Angeles had raced to a 25–15 lead. Then Reed caught a pass at the foul line, and Chamberlain was there to meet him. Reed went to his left around Wilt but tripped over his foot and fell forward, tearing a main muscle running from his hip to his thigh. The New York center lay writhing in pain as the action raced the other way and Holzman screamed for the refs to stop the game.

"I drove past Wilt and I just fell," Reed recalled later. "I was having problems with my knee, and I tore a muscle in my right thigh. I was on a roll, too."

Reed was out, and the Lakers had a hot hand. The Garden crowd grew quiet. Holzman tried to prop up his players' spirits during the timeout. He inserted Nate Bowman to play Chamberlain, and that worked for a time. Then Holzman went with reserve forward Bill Hosket, all of 6'7", who hadn't seen a minute of playing time in the entire playoffs. Hosket hounded Chamberlain effectively enough, but it really wasn't getting the Knicks anywhere. By the half, they were down 13.

In the locker room, Bradley suggested they go to a 3-2 zone offense, which would either force Chamberlain to come out from the basket or would give them open shots.

It began working in the third. The Knicks got bunches of steals and turnovers. The fourth period opened with the Lakers holding an 82–75 lead and a troubled hand. "Let's go Knicks. Let's go Knicks," all 19,500 spectators chanted over and over. At just under eight minutes, Bradley hit a jumper to tie it at 87. Then at 5:19, Bradley dropped in another jumper to give the Knicks the lead, 93–91. Then Stallworth scored. Then Russell with one of his acrobatic off-balance shots. Then Russell again on a follow, and it was 99–93. Bradley did the final damage with about a minute to go, pushing it to 103–98.

After a brief flurry, the Knicks took the 3–2 edge, 107–100. Los Angeles had been forced into 30 turnovers for the game. In the second half, West didn't have a field goal, and Chamberlain scored only 4 points.

"The fifth game," DeBusschere said proudly twenty years later, "was one of the greatest basketball games ever played."

The Lakers returned home and corrected their mistakes in Game 6. With Reed out, Wilt scored 45 with 27 rebounds. The Lakers rolled, 135–113, to tie the series.

The stage was set in New York for the Game 7 drama. Would Reed play? The Knicks left the locker room for warm-ups not knowing. Before he had left, Bradley and DeBusschere had asked Reed to give the team just one half. About twenty minutes would do it, they figured. In the training room, Reed was set to receive injections of carbocaine and cortisone through a large needle. There were problems, though, because the skin on his thighs was so thick. The doctor had trouble getting the needle in.

"It was a big needle, a big needle," Reed recalled. "I saw that needle and I said, 'Holy shit.' And I just held on. I think I suffered more from the needle than the injury."

The doctors had to place the injections at various places and various depths across his thigh in an effort to numb the tear. As they did, Reed howled in pain, and Jackson, who had been hovering in the locker room with his camera, captured what he described as some excellent shots of the moment. However, he never published them because Holzman asked him not to.

"I wanted to play," Reed recalled. "That was the championship, the one great moment we had all played for since 1969. I didn't want to have to look at myself in the mirror twenty years later and say that I wished I had tried to play."

Reed appeared on the Garden floor just before game time that Friday, May 8, bringing an overwhelming roar from the crowd. "The scene is indelibly etched in my mind," Frazier said, "because if that did not happen, I know we would not have won the game." The Knicks watched him hobble out, and each of them soaked in the emotion from the noise.

The Lakers watched, too, and made no attempt at furtive glances. Reed took a few awkward warm-up shots. Then he stepped into the circle against Chamberlain for the tipoff but made no effort to go for the ball. Once play began, Reed scored New York's first points—a semi-jumper from the key— and played incredibly active defense. Seventeen times the Lakers jammed the ball in to Chamberlain in the post. Reed harassed him into shooting 2 for 9. And Reed hit another shot (he would finish 2 for 5 with 4 fouls and 3 rebounds). But it was enough. The emotional charge sent the rest of the

Knicks zipping through their paces, while West answered for the Lakers with a flurry of turnovers, many of them forced by Frazier. New York rushed to a 9–2 lead, then 15–6, then 30–17. When Reed left the game, having delivered the half that Bradley had asked for, New York had assumed complete command, 61–37. From there, they rolled on to Holzman's first title, 113–99. Frazier hit 12 of 17 from the field and 12 of 12 from the line to finish with 36 points and 19 assists. Barnett had scored 21, and DeBusschere had 17 rebounds. But their efforts were second to Reed's appearance.

"There isn't a day in my life that people don't remind me of that game," Reed would say decades later.

"It was," DeBusschere said, "a warm, wonderful time."

Doubt

The outcome of the 1970 season had left Jackson with a mix of public elation and private doubt. The players met three days after the final game and voted him a full share of playoff money, $12,000, on the reasoning that the Knicks had made the decisions that kept him out of action. As glad as he was to have it, the money only increased his feelings of not having done his share to earn it. He recalled these feelings of low worth spilling over into his personal life. On one hand, he was torn by the desire to be free of his commitments so that he could enjoy an active social life. On the other, he felt more guilt.

Not surprisingly, his relationship with his parents had reached a cool distance. Jackson took his family to Grand Forks that summer but never made it over to Williston. To pull their children together, the Jacksons organized a family reunion in a group of cabins in Montana later that summer, affording Phil the chance to see Chuck, who was married and working in Dallas in retail sales; Joan, a mother of four; and Joe, a psychologist in New York. Jackson recalled Joe being alarmed at his state of mind and pressing him to come clean on all his issues, including an ambivalence that was obviously wrecking his marriage. Jackson, though, chose to avoid producing any sort of answers. He enjoyed the time with his family, then headed back to New York for training camp. He did so with serious doubts that he would find much success. In fact, he thought his playing career was probably over.

He had eventually found his way back to activity that previous spring, mixing with his workouts some pickup basketball and even volleyball on L.A.

beaches while the Knicks were battling the Lakers. But those things were entirely different from resuming the banging and physical play in an NBA frontcourt. He quickly found upon his return that every little opportunity for contact left him fearful of a reinjury. The league is uncompromisingly unforgiving of any such reluctance.

Because he was on injured reserve the previous season, he hadn't been included in the expansion draft that summer. Instead, Dave Stallworth and Bill Hosket were lost to new NBA teams, which meant dramatically weakened depth in the Knicks frontcourt. Jackson could see that he was expected to step in and play a major role. The circumstances were further complicated by Willis Reed's poor health. His heroics during the championship series would mean that he struggled with injuries the balance of his career. That struggle began with the 1970–71 season. He was out, and Jackson had to play. It wasn't a pretty sight on many nights, but with Frazier, DeBusschere, and Bradley around him, the Knicks remained in the thick of the playoff race.

"I remember him coming in and lighting a spark," DeBusschere would say of Jackson during the period. "I also remember Red yelling at him, 'Don't dribble it!' And Phil would dribble it off his knee, and the ball would go two rows deep into the stands."

Reed even returned late in the season in time to be a factor in the playoffs, and Jackson and his teammates figured they were headed back to the NBA Finals to battle for another championship. However, they found themselves embroiled in a seven-game series with the Baltimore Bullets, which the Knicks expected to win—right up to the final moments of that seventh game, when Baltimore managed to blunt Bradley's final field goal attempt.

The offseason brought a major infusion of talent to New York. Earl Monroe, who had just played a major role in defeating the Knicks, arrived in a trade from Baltimore, and 6'8" center Jerry Lucas came from the Warriors. Reed, however, would lose another season to injuries, and Jackson would again have to offer up major support.

His physical circumstances were steadily improving, but his relationship with Maxine was fraught with confusion and insecurity, a torture that seemed capable of wrecking his career along with his home life. He had spent quite some time trying to pull away from her, but as the relationship neared its obvious end he attempted to revive their union. Maxine, however, had had enough of his pushing and pulling. She wanted out. And the 1971–72 season became the setting for the end of the relationship. They cried and hugged after the separation papers were signed. She went off to explore the opportunities that a new age of women's liberation seemed to offer. And Phil Jackson went back to his basketball life, just in time to turn in a splendid effort in the playoffs. It was in an early series against Baltimore that Jackson first allowed himself the delight of intentionally goading an opponent into a mistake. He coaxed Jack Marin into a sixth foul, and out of guilt pledged that he would never do such a thing again, but it would prove to be the first perhaps in his long history of mind game fun.

New York advanced to the championship series, and he played well against the Lakers in the 1972 Finals. The Knicks figured they had an opportunity to upset West, Chamberlain, and company, who had just turned in an all-time best 69–13 record in the regular season, including a 33-game win streak. New York even gained a split of the first two games in Los Angeles, despite the fact that Reed was unable to play. Monroe and Lucas had come in and played brilliantly for Holzman, but Dave DeBusschere injured his hip early in the championship series and was lost. With him went any hope the Knicks had of winning, and the Lakers handily swept the next three games.

Jackson, though, had salvaged much with the season, not the least of which was his teammates' confidence and respect. "Whenever Phil got out there, you knew he was going to get physical and make something happen," DeBusschere remembered. "People talk about what a free spirit he was, but he always worked hard and always played within the structure of the team."

"Jackson's style as a player developed in accordance with his build, which reminds me of a clothes hanger turned upside down," Bradley later explained. "He surprised big men by his defensive skill and made them feel they were being guarded by a man with three sets of arms."

Beyond the revival of his career and the expiration of his marriage, the spring also brought him June, a 5'4" redhead, courtesy of a Tuesday night pinochle game that Jackson shared with her sister's boyfriend. She had just moved to Manhattan after graduating from the University of Connecticut, Storrs, in her home state. "I enjoyed basketball, but I wasn't a crazy fan," she later recalled.

By 1975 they would be married and on their way to adding four grandchildren to Charles and Betty Jackson's expanding clan.

What attracted Phil and June to each other in those first days was their mutual inclination to earthiness, which at the time also involved heavy overtones of freakiness. "He struck a common chord in me," she once explained to an interviewer. "I think we had a similar sort of social consciousness and maybe even intellectual consciousness. We were both a product of the times."

They both liked the idea of political activism. They were hippies, but not "crazy wild," Jackson said.

Somehow, the good people of North Dakota didn't seem to agree.

Dating back to his college years, Jackson had served Boys State, the American Legion's summer program for youth in North Dakota. Some years, he served as chaplain, but after the 1970 playoffs he headed back to Fargo to fill the dual role of chaplain and assistant dean of boys. Having grown his hair long and taken up pot smoking, he arrived with a different look than the one he had brought to his earlier duties with the program.

Not long after assuming his duties, Jackson and a group of his friends attempted to give Boys State a similar kind of makeover. He instigated group discussions on protest and avoiding the draft and made plans for a seminar on ecology, all to the great alarm of conservative-minded Legion officials. Afterward, they directed pointed public criticism at Jackson and his friends.

"It was a real heavy thing," recalled Peter Porinsh, himself a recent Vietnam vet who joined Jackson for the program. "We got into a whole political thing. With his political activism, Phil brought a different awareness back to that little piece of North Dakota, which was very, very conservative."

"It was a troubled time when I grew up, like when I was involved in Boys State," Jackson recalled years later. "I was interested in giving those boys a chance to be draft dodgers if they didn't want to go into the service. So there were a lot of things I stirred up as a kid, and I think it ran against some of the established people in the state.

"It was with great embarrassment that a lot of North Dakotans looked at me then, and in my early days in the NBA, with my alternative lifestyle—and they also looked away."

The incident and two later misunderstandings served to alienate Jackson from his hometown and his state. He returned with June for his tenth high school reunion in Williston in 1973, and although he enjoyed catching up with old friends, Jackson picked up some negative vibes. Those vibes were confirmed when a local newspaper blasted him afterward for his personal lifestyle.

"He took a little heat when he came back for that first class reunion," Dean Winkjer, a Jackson friend and Williston lawyer, acknowledged. "He had that hippie lifestyle and was a little bit out of sync with the mores of the community at that time. There was a female gossip writer in the weekly newspaper here who was quite critical of him. He never really felt comfortable here after that."

"My star rose and fell rather quickly in this state," Jackson would offer years later, after he had time to think about it.

He vented his anger with the publication of *Maverick*, which further irritated the good people of North Dakota, even some of Jackson's friends. "I was very unhappy with some of the things that were written about him when he was with the New York Knicks. And I read his book. . . . Some of the things in there I didn't agree with," former UND sports information director Lee Bohnet told a reporter in 1992.

Jackson's comments about his high school football coach and a shot he took at North Dakota hit a sour note. But what really angered folks back home was his story about his family's disappointment over moving to North Dakota. "North Dakotans had the reputation of being ignorant farmers," he wrote.

After that, the relationship would never be quite the same, although both sides came around considerably after a number of years had passed. Jackson was honored with North Dakota's Cliff Cushman Award, an award of excellence from the governor; but even more important, he received the state's highest honor, the Theodore Roosevelt Rough Rider Award, given to North Dakotans of distinction and accomplishment.

In the early 1990s, Williston renamed its field house for him, and Tom Kvamme, editor of the *Williston Herald*, came up with the idea of naming the high school's most valuable athlete award after Jackson. "His sentiments hadn't been great about Williston," Kvamme explained. "I started the award with the idea of keeping him connected here."

The editor pointed out that Jackson had always been particularly gracious in writing a personal letter to each year's recipient, and he had always managed to pony up some prized item whenever Williston had a fund-raising raffle for its athletic programs. One year he sent Michael Jordan's autographed warm-up, no small feat in that Jackson disliked prevailing upon his players for autographs and favors of that nature.

The state awards and local honors all came after he had vaulted to success as head coach of the Bulls, and Jackson couldn't help wryly noting that no one from the state had seemed eager to honor him when he coached in the Continental Basketball Association.

Indeed, it was Jackson's conversion of his reluctance into persistence in and around the pro game that kept him alive and well in North Dakota hearts.

"Phil's one of those guys who would have been successful at whatever he did," Bill Fitch would offer after looking back at his career, "because he's intelligent, thorough, and competitive."

He wound up playing ten seasons for the Knicks over eleven years, all of it a rush of loose angles and hook shots, stray elbows and crafty play. The run ended when they traded him to the New Jersey Nets before the opening of the 1978–79 season. In training camp, Nets coach Kevin Loughery asked Jackson to go for a ride, leaving him certain that he was about to be cut. Instead, Loughery asked him to accept a reduced role, to stick around as a player-coach, to dress for practice and work against the younger players on the roster and to play in games as needed. Jackson was happy to stick around and was immensely grateful to Loughery for the opportunity.

The thing most people didn't realize, Loughery would explain later, was that despite his hippie image Jackson was incredibly tough, a feature hardened by his long years trading elbows in the Knicks frontcourt. He was competitive, too. On occasion, Loughery would get tossed from games and Jackson would get to take over. At one point, Loughery even threatened to quit and offered up Jackson as his replacement. The team's owners, though, didn't think he was ready. Jackson claimed that he was, but later would admit that he was dead wrong.

Still, the coaching bug had taken a bite.

"I don't see anything else out there as far as a business, career, or anything that compares with motivating eleven basketball players into a winning team," Jackson told the *Williston Herald* in 1980. "The thrill, drama, pressure, and intensity of playing the game can't be duplicated. There's not the same feeling of being part of the action as a coach, but there are greater pressures. And the wins and losses are felt more intensely than as a player."

Eventually the Nets' run would come to an end as well, and for the first time in many years, Jackson saw no involvement with basketball in his immediate future. With his playoff money from 1973, he had bought land on Flathead Lake in Montana and built a home there. So he packed up his family, which had expanded by three children, and headed there, spending an ill-fated year trying to run a health club and dabbling in junior college basketball. That didn't work, and it occurred to him that pro basketball was just about all he had ever known. Yes, he had toyed with the idea of education and graduate school, but over the years hoops had thoroughly infested his blood. It was then that he truly came to regret writing *Maverick*.

"If I had a chance to do it over again I would not," he told an interviewer later.

Armory Days

Jackson cast about the basketball world looking for an opportunity, hearing between the lines with each phone call that he was a pariah. Then came a contact with the Albany Patroons, an expansion CBA team coached by Dean Meminger, one of his former Knicks teammates. It was Meminger's sad fortune to be fired, and Jackson's to be hired.

So he packed up his family and moved to Woodstock, New York, in 1982 to take over an 8–17 Patroons team. "It was important for us, it was important for me," Jackson would say of the experience. "I was just in the process where I was concerned whether coaching was going to be something I was going to do or not do. Or if I was going to be any good at it."

The Patroons were owned by the local government and run by Jim Coyne, their founder as well as Albany County's executive. Later, Coyne would end up serving a four-year jail term in a federal prison camp in Fort Dix, New Jersey, but at the time he was the one man in pro basketball to give Jackson a break.

Actually, Coyne had wanted to hire former UCLA star Henry Bibby, but that didn't work out. So Coyne dialed up Jackson. "I told Phil how things were going, and I told him I just wanted him to finish out the year and see if he liked it or not," Coyne recalled several years later. "He told me to call back in an hour, and when I called back, he said, 'I'll be there.' Fate is a funny thing. It's just being in the right place at the right time. If I didn't make the phone call, maybe fate would have turned out a different way for Phil and he might not have gotten back in basketball the way he did."

The job paid $17,500 that first year and left Jackson with a one-way commute of exactly forty-seven miles from his Woodstock home to the Washington Armory in Albany. Jackson pulled in his zany friend and occasional tripping partner from their wilder days, Charley Rosen, as a volunteer assistant. Rosen nicknamed the CBA the "Cockroach Basketball League."

"The only thing I don't miss is the hour and ten minute drive from the Armory to Woodstock," Rosen would say later of the commute he and Jackson made each way.

Jackson's coauthor of *Maverick*, Rosen was 6'8" inches and had played ball at Hunter College. He had met Jackson in the early 1970s when Rosen was running around with Stan Love, the brother of Beach Boy Mike Love. Rosen, a freelance writer, had been an English professor at Hofstra University in the late 1960s. He would quickly become known as an emotional boiling pot on the Patroons bench. He loved the league, and his antics would soon make him a viable entertainment attraction in his own right.

"Charley is a showman," Rockford guard Kenny Natt, a former Patroon, once explained, "but that kind of thing can work against a team. Everywhere we go, the focus is always on Charley. He talks to the fans, he gets on the refs. He might like that, but the players don't. I don't. When you're a player, you don't need the extra distractions."

Jackson, though, loved the friendship and the amusement. Together, they would make an immediate impact in Albany.

"Phil turned the franchise around," Rosen later recalled. "When he took over for Meminger, it was a very dangerous situation for the franchise."

The Patroons would eventually fold, as most CBA teams have at one time or another, but not until Jackson had pushed them off on a rather distinguished journey. After his tenure there, he would be followed by future NBA coaches George Karl and Bill Musselman, and the Patroons' all-time roster would feature a long list of NBA players, including Sidney Lowe, Vince Askew, Scott Brooks, Tony Campbell, Mario Elie, Kenny Natt, Albert King, and Micheal Ray Richardson.

Not many of those guys, however, populated the rosters during Jackson's five-year tenure with the team. Instead, he dealt with the likes of Frankie Bryan and Michael Graham.

Displaying his counterculture idealism, Jackson's initial strategy was to pay all of his ten players the same, with married guys getting a $25 weekly boost over the single guys. Jackson gave each of them ample playing time. "It was really kind of a taught thing," he said. "We talked these guys into that. We talked them into sharing time."

It was a Shangri-la that allowed him to claim the league championship in 1984. But pro basketball has always been a star system that pays the players with the flashiest games. Eventually Jackson had to give in to that, leading to three immensely frustrated seasons that caused his tenure there to end badly. In one of his last playoff games, he lost his cool and tossed not one but two folding chairs onto the floor, a Bobby Knight type of display far from the laid-back posture he would adopt in his later NBA seasons.

Despite such histrionics, Jackson left mostly fine memories for the people he worked with there. "Phil was just a great guy to play for," recalled Derrick Rowland, the franchise's all-time scoring leader, who played five seasons for Jackson. "He understands a lot of the dynamics of the game, the dynamics of people, and brings them together."

"He'd always come to practice in a tie-dyed shirt, and he was living in Woodstock, so we'd kid him that he was stuck living in the '60s," recalled Greg Grissom, who played for Jackson in 1986–87. "He was a kind of player's coach, but you also knew with him when it was time to be serious."

When Jackson was about to claim his seventh NBA title, the *Albany Times-Union* sent a reporter to Los Angeles to ask Jackson to reflect on the difference between his approach then and later. "It's still playing for the group, I think," he replied. "It's still playing for your team. It's still a desire to win and play hard every time you're on the floor. I think it's easier at this level because of the audience and television that comes with this game to motivate players, and the fact that their life is so much better."

Not to mention easier. The CBA is a league designed to test just how much those involved love the game. This was especially so for those playing in the drafty old Washington Avenue Armory, which seated all of twenty-one hundred. "I remember the first time I was in Albany and we drove by the Armory," George Karl recalled. "I said to the guy driving, 'You mean we've got to play there?'"

"The Armory certainly shines the brightest of my memories," Jackson told the *Times-Union*. "It had character. Practicing in the cold of the gym, dealing with the people in the reserve or the guard or whatever it was. There was always just a little bit of not being a basketball court feeling but it certainly warmed up in the middle of a winter night.

"I used to talk our commander of the Armory into keeping the balls in a warm spot in the ticket office so that the guys wouldn't have to use balls that were 50 degrees, because that was the temperature in the building," he recalled. "And we had to always go out and sweep the floor and mop the court because they used it for everything. We had to measure the temperature in the middle of the day when it was the warmest so guys could have a good practice. Usually, they'd come out in their parkas or stocking caps and mittens on."

The players had to shower in full view of an adjacent public restroom, which meant fans weren't above asking for autographs with the water running. So much has been written about the road trips that they've reached legendary status, with Jackson driving the team van for umpteen hours to Toronto or Bangor, steering while he worked *New York Times* crosswords.

"It was difficult," he said. "We'd play four games in four nights on some road trip out West. We fly out to some place, grab a van and then drive to wherever. You'd get four or five hours of sleep at night. It was almost impossible to win on the road. But the players all performed very well. I was impressed by their cohesiveness, their desire to win. They were motivated."

Ugliness invaded the circumstances in the 1985 playoffs when Jackson got into a shouting match on the bench with star Frankie Sanders, who hated coming out of games. Jackson promptly suspended his star, only to have Coyne, the public official who ran the team, reinstate Sanders over Jackson's protests.

"Frankie was a prolific three-point shooter, but he got into an argument with Phil and Phil suspended him during the playoffs," Coyne later explained. "But I said, 'Hey, without Frankie, we're not going to continue in the playoffs.' So I flew Frankie up to Toronto [against Jackson's wishes] and we won. That was a little bit of controversy, and Phil took it personally."

The Patroons won that series but lost the next to a Tampa Bay Thrillers team coached by Bill Musselman, the first of three straight playoff losses Jackson's teams would suffer at the hands of Musselman's clubs. The 1985 series involved a typical CBA brouhaha when Musselman placed an early morning call to Sanders to tell him to behave. It would be one of the few times that Jackson himself was the victim of an opposing coach's mind games. The Patroons and their fans were so incensed by the call that they lost focus on the game. Musselman made a big deal of having bodyguards in the Armory in Albany for the third game of the series.

"He will be remembered as the guy who brought stability to the franchise—and the guy who couldn't beat Musselman," the *Times-Union* would later say of Jackson's tenure there.

The incident in his third season left Jackson depressed and looking around for an exit. During the summers he coached in Puerto Rico, another test of wild players and unruly, sometimes dangerous, fans. Before he left for Puerto Rico that spring of 1985, Jackson got a call from Jerry Krause, who had just been named general manager of the Chicago Bulls. "I kept up with Phil as a player through the years," Krause recalled. "We'd talk from time to time, and I followed his coaching career in the CBA. When I got the job in Chicago in 1985, I talked to him again. I told him I needed scouting reports on the CBA. Within a week, I had typewritten reports on the whole league, details on every player. What I saw in Phil was an innate brightness. I thought that eventually he'd become the governor of North Dakota. I saw a lot of Tony LaRussa in him. A feel for people. A brightness. Question-asking. A probing mind. A coach."

Jackson turned in the reports to Krause and departed for Puerto Rico. Later, he was called to Chicago to interview with Stan Albeck, the man Krause had hired as head coach to replace the fired Kevin Loughery.

"I was coaching in Puerto Rico," Jackson recalled in 1995, "and I flew up directly from San Juan. It was a quick trip. I had to drive into San Juan and catch a morning flight. When you live in the subtropics, you get a lifestyle. I was wearing flip-flops most of the time. I wore chino slacks, because of their social standards down there, and a polo shirt. I had an Ecuadorian straw hat. Those hats are really expensive. They're not like a Panama, which costs twenty-five bucks. It's a hundred-dollar hat. You could crush-proof it. As a little flair item, I had a parrot feather that I'd picked up at a restaurant. I had messed around with a macaw in the restaurant and pulled a tail feather out and stuck it in my hat.

"There was a certain image I presented," Jackson admitted. "I had a beard, had had it for a number of years. I was a little bit of an individualist, as I still am. I have a certain carriage about myself that's going to be unique. I just came in for the interview. I don't know how it affected Stan Albeck. Stan was a good coach. He'd been around and had some success. Stan and I had a very short interview. It wasn't very personal, and I knew right away that Stan wasn't looking to hire me, although Jerry Krause had locked us in a room and said, 'I want you guys to sit down and talk Xs and Os.' Stan found a different topic to talk about."

"Stan came back to me after the interview," Krause recalled, "and said, 'I don't want that guy under any circumstances.' "

Rejected, Jackson returned to the CBA to endure two more frustrating seasons. With his coaching in Puerto Rico, he had no time to search for talent to upgrade his roster, and with the Frankie Sanders incident, his system of sharing time and money went by the wayside. It didn't help that his bench talent dropped off considerably.

"I think it was a system that, for the first two and half years, worked," Jackson told reporters at the time. "Everyone played and everyone got the chance to contribute to a team that was highly successful. A year ago we felt a little talent shortage and we didn't have enough to get by with ten players and we could only play seven or eight. That changed my philosophy a little."

Jackson had to do his last season in Albany without Rosen, his colorful sidekick, who had accepted his own CBA head coaching job in Savannah. "I think Phil found it tougher to coach alone," Albany point guard Lowes Moore said. "I think he found he really wanted to talk to someone."

The last season closed in particularly painful fashion. Jackson's team was an underdog to Musselman's Thrillers but still managed to take a 3–2 lead in the series, only to drop the last two games.

"I knew I couldn't go back anymore," Jackson would later tell local reporters. "I'd had enough of CBA coaching. I knew I couldn't become mired there, that it was time to leave. It happens that no matter how you plan things, they don't turn out that way."

He had made $30,000 in that final season, but he didn't end the relationship right away, preferring instead to keep Coyne on the line while he searched around for college or pro opportunities, anything that would take him away from the situation. He was also pushing the Patroons for more money and turned to reporters to emphasize what he wanted. "With all the accolades and the won-loss record, I'm still not one of the highest-paid coaches in the league," he said. "If nothing is coming up ahead of me then I will have to find something that is gainfully appealing to me as a breadwinner.

"I might as well get a job in some bureaucratic institution that has a health plan and other benefits and get on with my life."

His time in Albany, however, had given him more of a resume, a five-year record of 117–90, a CBA championship, and a Coach of the Year award. The previous year he had applied for jobs at the University of Minnesota and at Colorado. Even Yale had seemed interested in his resume.

"I felt I did a good job," Jackson, then forty, told reporters. "I felt comfortable with the team and I feel comfortable that I am getting better as a coach."

"Phil made the Patroon organization very classy," Moore told reporters. "He accomplished many things and he knew it was time to move on."

Jackson's hesitation mostly centered on how much June and the kids, twin sons Ben and Charley and daughters Brooke and Chelsea, loved Woodstock. June was director of a hospice there, and both she and Jackson had taken an active role in the affairs of Woodstock's eclectic community.

Coyne himself wasn't sure he wanted Jackson to come back for another season. In short time, it would become clear that Jackson had put himself in a bad position, twisting in the wind with no job. Then the Patroons hired his old nemesis, Musselman, and what seemed like Jackson's only real door of opportunity had slammed. "He beat us three years in a row," Jackson told the *Times-Union* when informed of Musselman's hiring. "I would say he is the most logical choice."

Jackson's friends in Woodstock began to worry about him. He spent long hours watching basketball on television that spring and continued to prepare scouting reports on teams, even though he had no purpose for them. One friend asked why he watched so much basketball on TV. Because hoops was the only thing real on TV, he replied.

Jackson contacted the Phoenix Suns and the Knicks but failed immediately to get an interview with either team. "I guess you could say I have had get-to-know-you talks, or nice-to-meet-you sort of things," Jackson said. "I talked a little bit to [Phoenix general manager] Jerry Colangelo for an assistant job but I think that would be a long shot."

With the Knicks, it was another unproductive phone chat. "The Knicks are looking for the best possible people," Jackson said. "And I have a very dedicated niche in the organization as far as being a former player and one that is generally interested in that organization. But, as far as being one credited with NBA know-how [coaching], I have yet to prove my point."

Finally, he was called in for an interview with Madison Square Garden vice president Jack Diller. Jackson was desperate enough by then to tell them he would take anything. "I want to have a job in this organization, but not any specific job," Jackson told reporters after the interview. "Most good organizations have quality people who go across the board. That is the way I believe the Knicks want to go."

Jackson waited by the phone until time to leave again for Puerto Rico, where he also took up a position by the phone. That time, too, passed, and he returned and took his family back to Montana, again with no contact.

Even Coyne began pitying Jackson's situation and made a public call for him to be hired as CBA commissioner. Reporters phoned Jackson for his response. "It piques my interest, sure," he said. "I find it thought provoking and soul searching."

His forty-first birthday came and went, and still no call from an NBA team and no call from the CBA either. The phone didn't ring until October, after Jackson had already come to the realization that his career as a professional was over.

It was Jerry Krause on the line. This time, he told Jackson, get a haircut and shave.

"Things didn't work out like I planned," Jackson would say later, "but they worked out like I hoped."

6

THE ASSISTANT

Michael Jordan left the University of North Carolina after his junior season in 1984 and entered the NBA draft. The Houston Rockets selected center Hakeem Olajuwon first. With the second pick, the Portland Trail Blazers took Kentucky center Sam Bowie, leaving many observers dumbfounded. With the third pick, the Chicago Bulls grabbed Jordan.

Portland's mistake would go down as the greatest blunder in draft history, but the matter was barely a blip on the radar screen of Phil Jackson's busy life. He was working hard for the money—a little better than $20,000 per year in his second as a CBA coach. His Albany Patroons had just won the league title, and he had headed to Puerto Rico to spend a few weeks coaching hoops tropics style. Little did he understand that a great miracle had occurred: an angel had touched down in his presence, sitting there waiting, fluttering his wings in a holding pattern, biding time for the final magical elements to fall together in Jackson's semi-charmed kind of life.

Jordan, meanwhile, led the United States to the Olympic gold medal in Los Angeles that summer, then exploded into an instant phenomenon that fall when he joined the NBA.

Bill Blair, who was then an assistant to Bulls coach Kevin Loughery, recalled that the coaching staff decided to have a scrimmage on the second day of practice to see whether Jordan was going to be as good as the team thought. "Michael took the ball off the rim at one end," Blair said, "and went to other end. From the top of the key, he soared in and dunked it, and Kevin says, 'We don't have to scrimmage anymore.'"

"When we started doing one-on-one drills," Loughery recalled, "we immediately saw that we had a star. I can't say that we knew we had the best player ever in basketball. But we always felt that Michael could shoot the ball. A lot of people had questioned that. But Michael had played in a passing game system in college under Dean Smith and in the Olympics under Bobby Knight. So people never got the opportunity to see him handle the ball individually the way he could handle it.

"We saw his skills, but you've got to be around him every day to see the competitiveness of the guy. He was gonna try to take over every situation that was difficult. He was gonna put himself on the line. He enjoyed it. But as much as you talk about Michael's offensive ability, he's probably one of the best defensive players to play the game. His anticipation was so great, he could see the floor, his quickness, and then his strength. That's another thing that's overlooked, how strong Michael is. He really had the whole package."

In just his ninth pro game, Jordan scored 45 points against San Antonio. Six weeks later he burned Cleveland for another 45. Then came a 42-point performance against New York. Another 45 against Atlanta, and his first triple-double (35 points, 15 assists, 14 rebounds) against Denver. Then, just before the All-Star break, he zipped in 41 against defending champion Boston.

It wasn't just Jordan's point totals that thrilled the crowds. His appeal began with his energy level. He played all-out, every minute. On defense, he was a roaming thief. On offense, he was simply a cornucopia. Jumpers. Elegant dunks. Reverses. Finger rolls. Short bank shots. All executed with a style that bordered on miraculous. When he couldn't get to the hoop by land, he traveled by air. Literally, he could fly. (The definition of flying, according to the *Random House Dictionary of the English Language*, is "to be carried through the air by the wind or any other force or agency.")

For the first time in the Bulls' history, the "force" was with them, and it meant a profound transformation for both the team and its young superstar. Chicago had joined the NBA in 1966 as an expansion franchise and had suffered through two decades of frustration. The Bulls had fallen into deep misery in the half-dozen seasons before Jordan's arrival, and crowds in Chicago Stadium had dwindled to a few thousand many nights.

The fans returned in droves to see Jordan, although he still didn't generate regular sellouts that first season. The Bulls would have to become winners to draw regular crowds.

Seeing that the Bulls' young star was going places, Nike soon built a multimillion-dollar shoe and clothing deal around his image. Michael, the player, quickly became Air Jordan, the incomprehensibly successful corporate entity. Before long, he was making far more money off the court than on it. Rather than dull his unique drive, this off-court success seemed to shove it into a higher gear.

"He's as much an image as he is a symbol," agent David Falk said late that October 1984 after revealing that Jordan had already signed promotional deals with Nike, Wilson Sporting Goods, and the Chicagoland Chevrolet Dealerships Association. The Nike deal alone paid him $500,000 per year. "I know everybody's eyes are on me," Jordan said, "and some of the things I do even surprise myself. They aren't always planned. They just happen."

Two Jerrys

A second unseen miracle occurred in Jackson's life just a few months after the first. Jerry Reinsdorf had reached an agreement in October of 1984 to purchase the Chicago Bulls.

Perhaps the greatest part of this miracle was that one of Jackson's friends, Jerry Krause, would soon be named vice president of basketball operations for the Chicago franchise. It would be his second go-around with the job (and his third stint with the team). Almost a decade earlier, Krause had been named executive of the team but only managed to keep the job about six weeks. Krause had gotten into a rather public disagreement with DePaul coaching legend Ray Meyer, a candidate for the Bulls' coaching job. Arthur Wirtz, then the chairman of the team, was embarrassed that his roly-poly GM had bungled his first task, hiring a new coach, so he cut Krause loose.

Already something of a laughingstock around Chicago, Krause was humiliated. The people who made fun of him behind his back now had more ammunition. He healed his wounds by taking a scouting job with the Los Angeles Lakers and doing a fine job of finding players for them. The Lakers needed a guard, and he suggested they draft an unknown by the name of Norm Nixon, who would play a key role on the Lakers' championship team just two years later.

The son of a Russian Jewish immigrant, Krause had grown up in Chicago. In media interviews over the years, he recalled being a distinct minority in his own neighborhood, where he was called "kike" and "sheeny." After those interviews some people who knew Krause at the time came forward to question whether he hadn't perhaps overstated the circumstances. Regardless, one of the beacons on his landscape was Jim Smilgoff, the legendary baseball coach at Taft High School. Not only was Smilgoff a mean, tough competitor, he was Jewish. Needless to say, Jerry Krause worshiped him. When Krause's family moved to another neighborhood, Krause recalled that he decided to ride his bike eight miles each way each day so he could continue at Taft playing for Smilgoff, never mind that he would never be more than a warm-up catcher.

It so happened that Krause had a high school teammate who was a good enough pitcher to attract pro scouts—including the Yankees' Freddie Hasselman, who quizzed Krause about the prospect. It was then that Krause discovered being a warm-up catcher was a good way to get to know the big-league scouts, who would hang around the batting cage asking about the strength of the pitcher's arm and other issues.

The exchange led to a friendship between Krause and Hasselman, who was portly and had never played the game. Krause wondered how someone like that could be a scout, and Hasselman passed along this secret: "You don't have to be a chicken to smell a rotten egg."

It would prove to be the revelation of revelations for Jerry Krause. He later attended Bradley University and worked his way into a spot as the student assistant to Braves basketball coach Chuck Orsborn. His duties were to chart offensive and defensive plays, and that proved to be a major training ground for his scouting days. He also managed to hang on with Bradley's baseball team.

After college, he found his way into a series of scouting jobs for a variety of pro and semi-pro teams. It was a hard life, 280 nights on the road each year for roughly $100 a week, but Krause consumed it with relish. Later, he would joke about naming his unwritten autobiography *One Million National Anthems*. Wherever they played a game, he tried to be there, hanging out in the locker room, talking to coaches, watching and charting players. He wore a snap-brim hat and a raincoat and was obsessively secretive, so they began calling him "Sleuth."

"Jerry Krause is an enigma to the athletic world," Jackson pointed out in 1995. "But Jerry has done whatever it took to get to the top and hold his position. That's why he has such a great knowledge of the game, from A to Z. He did whatever it took, from going and getting the sandwiches and coffee, to whatever, just to keep hanging around the game and learning. And he's always been able to pick out talent. He was down there at Kansas State when Tex Winter coached there in the '60s, hanging out with Tex the way he would later hang out with Bighouse Gaines at Winston-Salem State. He's always had an eye for people who are dedicated to what they do."

Heavily influenced by Holzman, Krause smugly operated by his "two-cocktail rule": While other scouts were having two cocktails, he was down the road, seeing another game, searching for that great undiscovered talent to send up to the big leagues. One of his first big scores was a scouting gig with the old Baltimore Bullets. First came the drafting of Jerry Sloan, and later Krause pushed his bosses in Baltimore to select Earl "the Pearl" Monroe, out of little Winston-Salem State.

Those early successes, however, didn't buy Krause any seniority. The scouting circuit was a hard road in those days, and Krause soon left the Bullets to join the Bulls in the late 1960s, shortly after they had entered the league as an expansion team. But a poor relationship with Bulls coach Dick Motta meant that Krause had to move on after a couple of seasons in Chicago. The next stop was another expansion team, the Phoenix Suns.

People would marvel that, given his appearance, he could be so effective as a scout. Krause would answer them with Freddie Hasselman's wisdom: "You don't have to be a chicken to smell a rotten egg."

The Bulls' executive job in Chicago had seemed like his first really big break. The Bulls were looking for a coach, and DePaul's Ray Meyer told reporters that Krause had offered him the job. Krause insisted he had done nothing of the sort, but somehow the incident got blown up into a local media firestorm. Abruptly, Wirtz fired Krause, turning his triumphant homecoming into public humiliation. This forever shaped Krause's view of the media.

After his stint with the Lakers, Krause met White Sox owner Bill Veeck in 1978 and was so impressed that he returned to Chicago and baseball. Krause's toughness and acumen were already well established in 1981 when Reinsdorf put together an investment group to purchase the baseball team. The new team chairman soon grew to admire the plucky scout, and four years later, when Reinsdorf put together a group to buy the Bulls, Krause was his first choice to run the organization, despite the fact that the team's previous owners and management had loathed him.

"Jerry's been around forever," said one Bulls employee. "He knew all the coaches, the assistants, the scouts in the league. The previous Bulls administration despised Jerry. They had all these stories and tales and ripped him all the time. Lo and behold if he didn't come back here and get the job as general manager."

His resurfacing in basketball amazed many people, including Orlando Magic executive Pat Williams, who had known Krause for years and had worked with him in the early Bulls days. "Part of the saga of the Bulls is the incredible scent, the life of Jerry Krause," Williams said. "It's phenomenal. He starts out in Baltimore, then gets hired and fired in Chicago. So he's out and he ends up going to Phoenix. He bats around and ends up with the Lakers. He ends up working for me in Philly. He's hired back by the Bulls, and Arthur Wirtz ends up firing him after a few months on the job. He's gone, just gone, and he wheels out of that and he battles his way back and works for Reinsdorf. His life story and what happened to him is phenomenal. He's a hard worker who has really paid his dues. He may make a mistake but it won't be from a lack of effort."

"I would run into Jerry in the early '80s when he was still scouting baseball," said Bruce Levine, a radio reporter who has covered Chicago sports for many seasons. "Jerry was known in the scouting business as just a very tough cookie, very similar to what he is now. Very intense. A guy that would spend fifteen hours a day going to baseball games."

Many of the people competing against Krause as scouts in baseball were former players and coaches, people of standing in the game. Krause, on the other hand, came from nowhere, so he had to outwork them, had to fight through the circumstances with a fierce, unflinching determination.

This and Krause's deep store of Holzman tales immediately appealed to Reinsdorf when he and Eddie Einhorn took over the White Sox in 1981. At the time, no one would have dared think that somehow Jerry Krause would wind up running the Bulls again. But Phil Jackson had a charmed future that he didn't even know about, and another miracle was about to happen.

A Knicks Fan in Chicago

It was through his baseball connections that Jerry Reinsdorf learned he might have a chance to purchase the Bulls. He had grown up in Brooklyn, where his industrious father worked alternately as a mechanic and a cabbie and ice cream truck driver before settling into a business buying and reselling used sewing machines. In Brooklyn, "being a Dodgers fan was almost a religion," Reinsdorf explained, and he worshiped just as hard as every other kid on Flatbush Avenue. He was also a Knicks fan (Carl Braun was his favorite player), and later in life, even after he had finished law school and was well on his way to amassing a fortune in real estate investment in Chicago, he would hold in awe the Knicks' teams of the early 1970s coached by Red Holzman. As Reinsdorf built the market value of Balcor, his real estate investment company, he had dreamed of owning a sports team. Then in 1981, Reinsdorf and partner Eddie Einhorn purchased controlling interest in the White Sox from Bill Veeck. They soon began an aggressive revamping of the team, structured around Carlton Fisk, which led to a divisional championship in 1983. A year later, Reinsdorf was in New York having dinner with New York Yankees owner George Steinbrenner, who was also a minority owner of the Bulls. Reinsdorf told Steinbrenner he would love to own and operate the Bulls. Very quickly the Bulls' owners got back to him. They had been losing money for years and were eager to unload the white elephant of sports franchises.

"I worked out a deal in October of 1984, before Michael Jordan had played a game," Reinsdorf said.

In the settling of Arthur Wirtz's estate in 1984, the Bulls had been valued at $14.8 million. Pulling together a group of twenty-four investors, Reinsdorf bought out the majority shares of the team. "I will be visible, I will be seen," Reinsdorf said in announcing the acquisition. "I will be actively involved with this franchise. . . . I have a theory about how to run a basketball team, and I've always wanted an opportunity to run one."

Reinsdorf brought in Krause, and they began making plans to fire GM Rod Thorn and coach Kevin Loughery. "I just didn't like the whole culture of the organization," Reinsdorf explained, "and I didn't like the way it was being coached. I felt we had to break from the past."

On the day they made the changes, Reinsdorf and Krause drove over to Bulls offices, and Krause waited on the street in the car while Reinsdorf went up and delivered the bad news. He came back downstairs ashen-faced, admitting to Krause that he hadn't fired anyone in years, especially not a good guy like Thorn.

"I want a team that will play Red Holzman basketball," Reinsdorf said in announcing the changes. "An unselfish team, one that plays team defense, that knows its roles, that moves without the ball. Jerry Krause's job will be to find the DeBusschere of 1985 and the Bradley of 1985."

The news hit the sports desks at Chicago newspapers like a bomb that spring of 1985. Jerry Krause is running the Bulls? Krause is gonna be Michael's boss?

"I wouldn't have taken the Bulls' job had it not been for Jerry. Michael or no Michael," Krause would explain later. "My consideration there was not Michael Jordan. I had worked with Jerry with the White Sox for several years. I had turned down chances to come back in the NBA during that time. I'd had a couple of strikes against me, and I didn't want to come back unless I knew I could work for an owner I felt comfortable with and that I knew would back me and do the things that needed to be done. When Jerry bought the ball club in February, it totally shocked me. I was getting ready to leave for spring training. I said to him, 'Take a look at the thing for a year, and if you don't like what you see I'd be interested in going over there and running the thing for you. You're the one guy I'd go back in that league for. It's a potential gold mine now because you got it.'"

"Krause was atop the scouting hierarchy at the White Sox, and I had gotten to know him," Reinsdorf explained later. "There had to be a cultural change in the Bulls' organization, and Krause believed the same things I did. I hated to fire Rod. He was one of the two or three nicest gentlemen in the NBA. But the change worked great for us."

Putting Reinsdorf's grand vision of Holzman-style ball into place would take a bit of maneuvering. Krause's first step was to fire Loughery. Then he turned his attention to the roster, which was riddled with drug abusers. "I had a brutal start," Krause recalled. "I had nine players I didn't want and three I did. I wanted Dave Corzine, I wanted Rod Higgins, and I wanted Michael. The rest of them I couldn't have cared less about. And they were talented. All of them were very talented. But it wasn't a question of talent."

Once Krause took over, Phil Jackson began taking a keen interest in events in Chicago. "Jerry took away a lot of things that this franchise didn't need," Jackson would say later of those early moves. "It didn't need certain types of people on the club. He had a certain idea of what type of person he wanted. He brought in character, or what he liked to think of as character. Good solid people. People who wanted to work hard."

Krause and Reinsdorf soon became known around Chicago as "the two Jerrys," because they worked so closely together, almost like mental conjoined twins.

After two decades of upheaval and misfires in the team's front office, Bulls fans were openly leery of Krause's seemingly unorthodox approach. Early missteps were greeted by loud hisses from the media and fans. In retrospect, it seems obvious that a pattern of success was emerging. But at the time, the entire enterprise was a burgeoning gamble with careers on the line. Looking around in a hurry for a coach, Krause hired veteran Stan Albeck. "I knew it was a mistake almost as soon as I did it," Krause would say later.

At the time, though, Krause had bigger problems on his hands. He had been on the job a matter of months and had already alienated Michael Jordan with one of his first personnel moves: trading Rod Higgins, Jordan's best friend on the team, because Higgins had market value and could be swapped to upgrade the roster.

"We traded Rod Higgins," Krause admitted later. "Michael was upset about that."

But that paled in comparison to the conflict to come. The Bulls opened the 1985–86 season, Jordan's second year, with three straight wins—but in the third game, at Golden State, Jordan broke a bone in his left foot, an injury that had altered or ended the careers of several NBA players. He would miss the next 64 games while the team sank in misery.

But in March, with the Bulls' record at 22–43, Jordan informed the team that his injury had healed and that he wanted to resume playing. Immediately, Krause, Reinsdorf, and the team's doctors questioned that decision.

"I was scared to death," Krause said of the situation. "I didn't want to go down in history as the guy who put Michael Jordan back in too soon."

"It was like a soap opera," Reinsdorf recalled. "We were too honest with Michael. We let him hear the report from the three doctors we consulted with over when he could come back. All three said the break had not healed enough. They said if he did play there was about a 10 to 15 percent chance of ending his career. Michael was such a competitor. He just wanted to play. . . . But Michael insisted that he knew his own body better than I did."

"The thing that got Michael and me off on the wrong foot," Krause said, "was that he thought I said to him, 'You're our property, and you'll do what we want you to do.' I don't remember ever saying it that way. He just misinterpreted me. I was trying to keep him from playing because he had a bad foot and the doctors were saying, 'No, no, no.' And Reinsdorf was telling him about risk. He was a kid who wanted to play. And I couldn't blame him. But that's where it all started because we said 'We're gonna hold you back.'"

Jordan was infuriated by what he saw as a stall by Bulls management. "Here you are dealing with big businessmen who make millions, and my millions are like pennies to them," he told reporters. "All I wanted to do was play the game that I've played for a long, long time. But they didn't look at it that way. They looked at it as protecting their investment, to keep their millions and millions coming in. That's when I really felt used. That's the only time I really felt used as a professional athlete. I felt like a piece of property."

Jordan vented his anger by almost single-handedly driving the Bulls through an amazing turn of fortunes. They managed to claim the Eastern Conference's eighth and final playoff spot, earning themselves the right to play the Boston Celtics in the first round. Considered to be among the best teams of all time, the 1986 Celtics defeated Chicago in three straight—but not before Jordan turned in one of his early masterpieces, a 63-point performance in Boston Garden, the all-time single-game playoff record.

In the aftermath, Krause wasted little time in firing Albeck. Reinsdorf felt that Albeck had only made difficult their task of holding Jordan back from his foot injury. Plus, Albeck had shown little interest in the offensive advice of Tex Winter, who had been hired by Krause to coach the coaches.

The choice of replacement came down to two men, broadcaster Doug Collins and Phil Jackson. It was here that another favorable development ultimately aided Jackson's cause. Krause chose Collins, which would later afford Jackson the opportunity to learn the job as an assistant coach. He wasn't thrown into the fire without the chance to prepare and grow. (On the other hand, one could argue that perhaps Jordan's Bulls could have won more and sooner had Jackson gotten control earlier.)

The choice, though, was Collins, a CBS broadcaster with no coaching experience whatsoever. But he had been a player. A star at Illinois State, he was the top pick of the 1973 draft and had played a pivotal role on the ill-fated 1972 U.S. Olympic team that lost a controversial last-second decision to the Russians. Selected by the Philadelphia 76ers, Collins helped that club climb out of the wreckage of its disastrous 1973 season into championship contention by 1977. A 20-points-per-game scorer in his best seasons, Collins ultimately fell victim to the injuries that prematurely ended his career.

"It was very uncomfortable because Collins was a broadcaster and had traveled with the team before he was hired," recalled Chicago broadcaster Cheryl Raye. "Stan Albeck would look over his shoulder, and there was Doug Collins. He served as a consultant briefly, and there was speculation that Collins was taking Stan's job."

"When I hired Doug, everybody laughed at me," Krause said. "A lot of people said, 'What the fuck are you doing hiring a TV guy?'"

"At the time, I was thirty-five," Collins would later recall, "and there had been nine coaches in ten years in Chicago. I was the kind of guy to roll up my sleeves and make something happen."

Jordan wasn't so sure about that. "When I first met Doug, I didn't think he knew what he was talking about," the team's star recalled. "I wondered when he first got the job. I mean, he was so young. But once I got to know him, I liked him a lot. He was bright, he was in control, and most of all, he was positive."

Not only did he bring this strength, but he added assistant coaches Johnny Bach and Gene Littles to the equation. Bach, in particular, would become a force in his own right with the team. "I had coached him at the Olympics in 1972 and we had a good friendship and respect for each other. Doug called me and said, 'I'd like you to come here and join the staff,'" Bach recalled. "It was a pleasure to go with Paul Douglas Collins. He was emotional and exciting, fired-up. He really started this franchise, the Bulls, to winning again."

Having made the coaching change, Krause began dumping the veterans on the roster in trades exchanged for draft picks. He was obviously making moves for the future, but suddenly the cupboard looked bare, which led to a round of preseason predictions that the Bulls would struggle to win 30 games. Who was going to score? observers asked.

Jordan gave the first big clue to that in the opening contest against the Knicks in Madison Square Garden. The Knicks, with twin towers Patrick Ewing and Bill Cartwright, were in control with a five-point lead midway through the fourth quarter when Jordan looked at Collins and said, "Coach, I'm not gonna let you lose your first game."

He then scored the Bulls' last 18 points to finish with 50 and give Collins the win, 108–103. It was the most points ever scored by an opponent in the Garden, erasing the 44-point mark shared by Rick Barry and former Bull Quintin Dailey.

"I've never seen anything like Michael Jordan. Ever. Ever. Never," Collins said after hugging each of his players. Yet, as the coming months would reveal, the Air Show was just getting started.

Twenty-eight times that season, Michael scored better than 40 points. Six times, he ran up better than 50. Over late November and early December, he scored more than 40 in nine straight games, six of them coming on a West Coast road trip.

"I had to be the igniter, to get the fire going," Jordan said later of his explosion that season. "So a lot of my individual skills had to come out."

He won the Slam Dunk Contest at the All-Star Game. Then he resumed his assault on the league's rims and records. In late February, he scored 58 against the Nets, breaking Chet Walker's old Bulls regular-season, single-game scoring record of 57. A few days later, despite a painful corn on his left foot, he blasted the Pistons for 61 in an overtime win before 30,281 screaming fans at the Pontiac Silverdome. Down the stretch, Jordan and Isiah Thomas and Adrian Dantley of the Pistons swapped baskets furiously.

"I don't know how he did it," John Paxson said. "Every night someone else was standing in his face, and he never took a step back."

March brought another scoring outburst, including a streak of five 40-plus games. In April, he had an opportunity to become the first and only player since Wilt Chamberlain to score more than 3,000 points in a season. (Chamberlain had done it twice in the 1962–63 season.) Jordan scored 53 against Indiana, 50 against Milwaukee, and 61 against Atlanta in the Stadium to finish with 3,041 and a league-best 37.1 scoring average. He also set Bulls records in six different single-season categories, all enough to drive Doug Collins's first team to a 40–42 record and another first-round playoff meeting with the Celtics. Bird and Boston, however, swept the series in three and taught the Bulls a primary lesson—that team strength could easily outshine a one-man show.

"He's a guy whose highlight films you most want to watch," Boston guard Danny Ainge said of Jordan. "But I don't know how much fun he'd be to play with."

The Opportunity

Thank goodness June Jackson was both resourceful and resilient: her life as a pro basketball wife had demanded both qualities in spades. "I'm a pro at moving," she once boasted. "I can pack and unpack with my eyes closed."

Not that it was ever easy. Rather, the tasks, as big as they were, were never bigger than her determination.

"She had an independence about her that assured me she could withstand the NBA life," Phil Jackson would say later.

She thought she had seen the worst of it during the tail end of Jackson's playing days. "When the kids were little and he was a player, it was very stressful," she told Chicago writer Paul Ladewski. "While he was on the road I'd be at home alone with sick one-year-old twins. I hated it. The season he retired as a player was one of the worst."

She would soon discover that Jackson's transition from CBA to NBA coaching was worst of all. The waiting had dragged out from late summer into fall of 1987, and still no job. So the kids started in Woodstock's schools, and June took a job at a local hospice service. Hope dimmed for Phil Jackson. June questioned his decision to leave the safety of the CBA, but he told her the only way to make the leap to the big league was to leave the security blanket behind. But as the days passed and no job offer came, it looked as if Jackson just might eat those words.

Then, out of the blue, Jackson was on a plane to Chicago to interview with Doug Collins. This time his arrogance was in check. He wouldn't dare show up for the interview in flip-flops and a feathered hat. This time, per Krause's directive, he had a nice shave and a haircut.

Afterward, he would feel extremely grateful to Doug Collins. The head coach, who was five years younger than Jackson, certainly had reasons not to pick him. After all, Jackson had finished second behind Collins in the head coaching search just two years earlier. If there's one thing NBA coaches dread, it's having your successor sitting there on the bench beside you like a vulture waiting to pick your sorry carcass. But Collins knew that Krause badly wanted to bring in Jackson, and felt grateful himself for the opportunity to be a head coach. The interview had a much nicer feel to it than the previous session with Stan Albeck, Jackson recalled: "The next time I came in for an interview, with Doug Collins in 1987, it went a little better. Doug was a much more open person to deal with."

Better yet, he offered Jackson a job.

"A gamble," Jackson would say later of Collins's move. "He only knew me casually."

Johnny Bach, Collins's confidant, recalled that it was Jackson's background that got him the job. "He had obviously played in the league and been in the CBA," Bach said. "That was, and still is, a real battleground, a real testing ground. It's a league of difficult players, frustrated many times in their NBA failures, a league of long drives and changing rosters. Phil had to cope with a lot of unusual problems in his time in Albany. It was a place where the coach was also the trainer. And Phil came from being a luminary on the Knickerbockers' championship team, a guy with a little bit of notoriety. People knew about him. He had the full beard and the wild hair and went back to Montana in the summers."

Like that, Jackson was back on the plane to New York to make a decision with his wife. "I had just taken a job, the kids were in school," June Jackson said later. "We felt it would be too upsetting to move."

So Jackson's wife and children stayed in Woodstock, and he flew off to his future in Chicago, where he joined Collins's staff that consisted of two gruff old assistants, Johnny Bach and Tex Winter.

"My first two years as an assistant coach with the Bulls, it was very much like going to graduate school," Jackson recalled. "My first year I was hired after my children were already in school and my wife had a job. So my family stayed in Woodstock. I had a lot of free hours to spend learning basketball from Johnny Bach and Tex Winter. There was Tex's western input and Johnny's eastern input. So I got about thirty years of basketball history real quick."

He took up residence at the Sheraton in Deerfield near the Bulls' practice facilities and resigned himself to long hours—first, helping with training camp; then, as the season got under way, as the team's advance assistant, spending numbing hours watching videotape of the Bulls' opponents and diagramming their tendencies.

"He came in and wanted to do a job. He welcomed the opportunity that obviously had been denied to him for some time. He was appreciative of that chance to work in a role as an assistant coach," Bach recalled. "He was there to be a good scout, a guy to help with drills in practice, to work with the team's big men, but not someone to offer his full-time input into decisions."

Later, there would be whispers that Jackson was Collins's dreaded vulture, but Bach disputed that. "I didn't see any vaulting ambition. Phil was very professional and had a good relationship with the team and was obviously trying to fit in. I saw Phil come in very quietly and take my place on the road as the advance guy. He fit in well with us. You could see that we had a nice group for pithy work. I thought it was a good mix right away. The first year was a very good one."

Jackson himself was asked about the issue and told a reporter, "I'm not making any heavy-duty push to get a head coaching job. This is a real good place for me right now. I'm getting re-educated to the NBA, and this is a team for the future. My good friend, Jimmy Rodgers, has been an assistant coach for seventeen years; but he's only forty-five, still young. He knows the right jobs come to the ones who are patient."

Still, the forty-year-old Jackson confided that he didn't want to be scrounging around for a head coaching job at age fifty, either. He knew that this would get him into the slot, and he knew that Krause had almost hired him as a head coach two years earlier. Billy McKinney, who had moved up as Krause's personnel assistant, was ahead of him in the coaching slot, perhaps. Perhaps not. Everyone around could see that the insecure Krause made life difficult for his coaches. He didn't generally interfere with what they wanted to do, although he could be meddlesome at times. It was just that Krause was so unusual. Coaches had to adjust their approaches in a million different ways. For example, there was a comical story making the rounds within the team about Krause and Collins checking into a hotel. Their rooms were on the same floor, and as they got off the elevator to drop off their bags, Krause announced that he couldn't wait, that he had to go to the bathroom *right now*. So he went to the toilet in Collins's room and christened the coach's abode with an overwhelmingly foul odor. Then he finished, picked up his bags, and headed off to his own room.

Hearing the story, Bulls coaches and staff members chuckled. Every day was a new adventure with Krause.

Jackson would later explain that his one lifeline to the NBA had been Krause. The new assistant coach knew that his future in the league would depend on his ability to get along with this unusual little man.

At the very least, the Bulls were a team on the rise, and Jackson knew that if he did his job and took advantage of the learning opportunity, he would get noticed, maybe even by the Knicks.

With Jackson away from his family, the other coaches went out of their way to make him feel at home, to include him in activities whenever possible. But his main diversion was work.

"You spend a lot of time," Jackson said at the time, "a lot of time at this job. And that's very fortunate for me, because time is all I have. I live in a hotel at home and hotels on the road. I have no family, they're all back in Woodstock. I've been able to throw myself into basketball up to my elbows."

June Jackson figured that over the season she and the kids saw her husband maybe five times. "I don't mind being two weeks apart," she confided to an interviewer, "but nine months was difficult on our marriage. You begin to wonder if you're married."

And you begin to wonder about your husband. "I hadn't been jealous in years," she said, "but I started to think about a lot of things. I became insecure. It was too much."

Enter the Dobermans

Although he wasn't fully aware of the implications at the time, Phil Jackson had returned to Chicago for training camp that fall and discovered two more gifts that had been bestowed upon his coaching life. The previous spring the Bulls had drafted two fine young forwards.

One of them, Clemson's Horace Grant, was a player Doug Collins had requested. Jordan, the team's star, had wanted Krause to draft North Carolina senior Joe Wolf. Krause deliberated long and hard on draft day before deciding to select Grant.

The other fine young forward was Scottie Pippen, a gem in the rough if ever there was one. After playing all of his young life in relative basketball obscurity, Pippen had quite suddenly and dramatically sprung to the NBA's attention in the spring of 1987. An unknown from the hamlet of Hamburg, Arkansas (population 3,394), Scottie had grown up in poverty, the baby in Preston and Ethel Pippen's family of a dozen children. Later, visitors would be taken aback by the living conditions of the Pippen family, with so many children and a father disabled from millwork. Pippen, though, was hardly aware of anything but the good feelings among his siblings. "It was fun," he said of his family life. "With all those brothers and sisters I always had a friend around."

Later, his Bulls teammates would be amazed at how strong a factor Pippen was in pulling them together as a group. Steve Kerr, in particular, would be amazed by this, telling friends that Pippen was simply the best teammate he had ever had.

Pippen attended Hamburg High, where as a junior he barely got off the bench for the basketball team. As a 6'1", 150-pound senior, he became the school's starting point guard. That hardly brought him any notice from college recruiters, however. The fall of his junior year, he had agreed to become manager of the football team, and if his prospects for higher education seemed bright, it was as a manager.

Don Dyer, the basketball coach at Central Arkansas, agreed that he could attend school there on a federal grant while serving as manager of the basketball team. "I was responsible for taking care of the equipment, jerseys, stuff like that," Pippen once explained. "I always enjoyed doing that, just being a regular manager."

"He wasn't recruited by anyone," Don Dyer recalled. "He was a walk-on, a 6'1½", 150-pound walk-on. His high school coach, Donald Wayne, played for me in college, and I took Pippen as a favor to him. I was prepared to help him through college. I was going to make him manager of the team and help him make it financially through college. When Scottie showed up for college, he had grown to 6'3". I had had a couple of players leave school. I could see a little potential; he was like a young colt."

"I really wasn't that interested in playing," Pippen later confided. "I had gone through some hard times not playing in high school, but my coach had it in his mind that basketball was the way I would get an education."

"By the end of his first season, he had grown to 6′5″," Dyer recalled, "and he was one of our best players. . . . He had a point guard mentality, and we used him to bring the ball up the floor against the press. But I also played him at forward, center, all over the floor."

"I felt myself developing late," Pippen remembered. "I kept seeing myself getting better and better. It was a great feeling, something like I could be as good as I wanted to be. I developed confidence in my abilities."

For Central Arkansas, Pippen became a two-time NAIA All-American. As a senior he averaged 23.6 points, 10 rebounds, and 4.3 assists while shooting 59 percent from the floor and 58 percent from three-point range. NBA scouting guru Marty Blake had gotten a tip about Pippen, which he passed on to the Bulls and other teams. Pippen was invited to the NBA's tryout camps, and the rest of the story became the Bulls' sweet fortune—but only after Jerry Krause had maneuvered through a trade to get him. Seattle selected him fifth overall in the 1987 draft, with the idea that they would immediately trade him to Chicago for draftee Olden Polynice and a draft pick.

As a player from a small town and a small school who was suddenly thrust into the spotlight in Chicago, Pippen was understandably lost. But he quickly developed a friendship with Grant, the Bulls' other first-round pick. They did everything together. Shopped. Dated girls. Partied. They both drove $74,000 Mercedes 560 SELs. They moved within a mile of each other in suburban Northbrook. And eventually, they got married within a week of each other, serving as each other's best man.

In the Bulls' 1988 yearbook, Pippen's profile contained a question: If you were going to the moon who would you take along?

Pippen's answer was "Horace Grant."

"Scottie is like my twin brother," Grant told reporters.

"We talk about every two hours," Pippen agreed. "Just to see what's going on. Horace is my best friend, the closest anyone's ever been to me."

Although he would later drive them to excellence, Doug Collins took a light touch with his rookies, pushing them in practice but showing patience in their uneven performances in games. This perhaps sounded easy enough, but the Bulls were in dire need of talent. They had Jordan and they had tough young forward Charles Oakley, but little more. Still, Collins knew that if he rushed Pippen and Grant he might well ruin them.

"In the early years with Michael it was fun, but we weren't very good," former Bulls guard John Paxson recalled. "And that was hard. Because we didn't have a lot of talent. Other teams would disrespect us. The good teams would. Especially Boston. They did that a lot. Michael was so good and Charles Oakley was pretty decent. It wasn't really until Scottie and Horace came into the picture that the talent level rose and you had the feeling that you were going to get better as a team. Those first years it was hard to play confidently every night because when you looked at our talent and other teams around the area we didn't match up."

On other days, however, it was clear that the two young forwards needed time to mature. "Scottie called in one day and skipped practice because his cat died," recalled former Bulls trainer Mark Pfeil. "Horace called about fifteen minutes later and said he was with Scottie because of the grieving. Johnny Bach was absolutely furious. He got Horace on the phone and said, 'You get here. You oughta throw the cat in the garbage can.' Horace, when the team got together, wanted to have a moment of silence for Scottie's cat."

Given time, Pippen and Grant would develop into what Bach called "the Dobermans," the athletic attack players in the Bulls' pressure, trapping defense. In his first weeks on the job, Jackson befriended the young forwards and began working with them. Years later, Pippen would look back on his first experiences working with Jackson as some of the prized moments of his NBA career. "Phil just had his ways," Pippen recalled. "It wasn't just basketball." From there, the relationship would deepen over the years with coach and player developing an unusual trust in one another. Michael Jordan would become Jackson's weapon, but it was Pippen who, despite being a forward, would become Jackson's point guard, the executor of virtually everything the coach wanted to do. But it would not be a typical coach–player relationship, because Jackson would open the agenda to what Pippen wanted to do as well, creating a shared vision.

In 1987, they began the first steps together, and it was immediately fun. After five years in the CBA carrying the burden of being head coach, Jackson found that he enjoyed the duties of assistant coach, particularly the freedom it offered. "It's nice to be friends with the players, instead of dealing with their egos and playing time and all the things a head coach has to do," Jackson said at the time. "When you're an assistant coach, you can be an instructor, a teacher, and not have that sleepless tension that comes with winning and losing."

That tension, in fact, was already beginning to show on Doug Collins. In late October, the hypercompetitive Jordan angrily stalked out of practice after accusing Collins of doctoring the score of a scrimmage. The incident made headlines in Chicago and left in its wake a stony silence between the young coach and his star.

"He has his pride; I have mine," Jordan told reporters. "We're two adults. In due time, words will be said. I'm not going to rush the situation."

The team issued Jordan a light fine, but the task of reestablishing relations with the superstar was left to Collins. "Doug knew he had to kiss and make up," John Paxson recalled, "and that's what he did. He had to calm his superstar. That was a little test he had. Had another player done that, you don't know what would have happened because guys just don't walk out of practice. Just don't take off."

Some observers wondered if Collins hadn't lost some respect and undermined his authority by seeking to soothe Jordan's anger. "It's got to be very difficult as a head coach to have a relationship with Michael and try to have that same type of relationship with other players," Paxson observed. "You just can't do it. You have to give Michael leeway. On the floor you can't be as critical of him as you can with other players because of what he can do and what he means. As a head coach you're walking a fine line with Michael Jordan. Not that he would ever do anything like that, but we all knew about the situation with Magic Johnson and Paul Westhead at the Lakers, when Westhead got fired after disagreeing with Magic. That's the power Michael could have wielded if he chose to. So Doug was walking a fine line. Early in Doug's career he handled it the best way he knew how."

It was during one of those first uneasy days that, as the coaches were gathered after practice, Jackson remembered a bit of his old coach's wisdom. "Red Holzman had a saying, that the difference between superstars and great players is that a superstar makes everybody on his team a better player," Jackson would explain later. "I happened to mention that one time when I was an assistant coach, and Doug Collins heard me and said, 'You gotta go tell Michael that. That's kind of the penultimate position.' I said, 'C'mon. I don't want to go tell Michael Jordan something that's just a statement.' He said, 'No, no, you really gotta go tell him. I really want you to do it.'"

Collins insisted—why, Jackson wasn't sure, because the circumstances weren't suitable for offering such information. "I got up out of the coaches' room and went out to the players," Jackson said. "It was thirty to forty minutes after practice one day."

As Jackson spoke, Jordan gave him something of a bewildered look, although he betrayed nothing of what he thought of the message. "I told Michael about it, and Michael thanked me for it," Jackson said. "That was one of the most amazing things, that he took it. And that's one of the best things about Michael Jordan, he's a great coachable player."

Jordan's respect for coaching had prompted him to listen politely, although the subject was a hot-button issue with him at the time, because his critics had offered the opinion that he was not the kind of player to make his teammates better. But Jordan was impressed by Jackson's directness. It was one of Jackson's first conversations with the star, among hundreds they would have over the next dozen years.

In the three seasons since Jordan's arrival, the value of the Bulls' franchise had more than tripled and was growing with each tipoff. Jerry Reinsdorf was so pleased with these developments that he extended Doug Collins's year-old contract and began plans to give Michael Jordan a new, extended deal. With the increased popularity and cash flow came a new atmosphere of confidence around the team. "We've reached a respect factor in this city," Collins told reporters. "We're no longer considered the 'Bad News Bulls.'"

Yet there was little argument that the team still faced major challenges. To plug their perennial hole in the middle, the Bulls brought back thirty-eight-year-old Artis Gilmore to share center duties with Dave Corzine. Oakley was well established at power forward, but he continued to call for more opportunities to get the ball in Collins's play-oriented offense. The coach seemed to agree with him. "We have to get to the point where Michael Jordan is not the sole source of energy on this team," Collins said.

The situation dictated that Collins would shift his approach with both Pippen and Grant, incrementally increasing the demands on them. "Doug brought them to a level of competing hard every night," Bach explained. "He drove them. He emotionally got involved with them and got them to understand how important each game and practice was, and he drove them. Some people lead young players; he drove them."

"We knew even as rookies that Scottie and Horace were going to be very fine players," Tex Winter recalled. "They had exceptional quickness, exceptional physical abilities. It was a question of them learning the pro game, maturing a little bit, getting a little bit stronger, and becoming little bit more familiar with the way we wanted to play. I thought Doug Collins did a tremendous job of utilizing their talents as rookies. He kept them on the bench and didn't rush them. He did put a lot of pressure on them during practice sessions to see how they would respond. I think he did an outstanding job of handling rookies of that caliber. He set a good stage for them to step forward. When Oakley was gone and Grant and Pippen moved into the starting lineup, they were ready."

Steps to Success

The opening night lineup in 1987 had featured Brad Sellers, the Bulls' first-round pick in 1986, at small forward, with Gilmore at center and Oakley at power forward. Jordan and Paxson were the guards. Management had planned for Jordan to play fewer minutes and to share the responsibility with his teammates, but just the opposite happened. Collins continued to run a large number of isolation plays for Jordan and to rely on him heavily. The reasoning was simple: they needed him.

Chicago ran off to a 10–3 start, which earned Collins Coach of the Month honors for November. A five-game losing streak in late December dipped them back toward .500, and the hopes for Gilmore soon vanished. The team released him before Christmas. But the Bulls zoomed off again on their way to a 50–32 record, an accomplishment that came with a heavy price.

Each night Collins seemed to fire up his team by wrenching a piece of his heart from his chest. "Doug was a perfect coach for our team when he got the job because we needed some young, aggressive guy that you could feed off of," Paxson recalled. "He was energetic, and a lot of games we fed off of his energy. Michael was in the early stages of his career and athletically could do some amazing things, but Doug got us going. He was very active, very vocal up and down the sidelines, and at that time that was what we needed."

"Doug was such an intense guy," remembered longtime Bulls equipment man John Ligmanowski. "It was almost like he wanted to be in the game. He'd come downstairs soaked in sweat, totally drained after a game. It was fun because we were just really starting to get good. The team had come around."

"Doug was screaming and yelling and jumping and throwing," recalled Chicago radio reporter Cheryl Raye, who watched from press row. "He definitely was demonstrative in his actions, and the guys who were key to this team were extremely young. Horace and Scottie, they hated him.

"He was growing up with them. He was new to the job. Here's a guy who came from the television booth. He was learning the process, too."

It was a process that rapidly ground down Doug Collins, one that Bach would recognize repeating itself several years later when Collins took on the task of coaching a young Detroit Pistons team. "Doug is a driven coach with unbelievable energy. It exhausts Doug first," Bach explained. "When he finds himself exhausted emotionally and torn in shreds, then he isn't the same person."

The approach Collins took was different from the one Jackson would later use with the same team, Bach explained. "They are diametrically opposed people. If there's something on the floor that Doug sees, he's gonna go right to it, like a moth to a flame. He wants to solve the problem immediately and really get at it."

That would leave Collins making rapid changes from the bench, calling numerous timeouts, designing and redesigning plays as he went along. "He could change a play during a timeout that we'd worked on in practice," Bach recalled, "and he could make those changes with unusual success."

Collins had an excellent memory and a superior vision of what was unfolding on the floor, attributes that made him an excellent television analyst. But those attributes, and his desire to make changes immediately, came to work against him as a coach. "The team saw that as his calling every play," Bach said, "and the backcourt people found that the changes Doug made were rapid. Doug had his tempo and his machine driving the team. The players got the notion that the coach was orchestrating everything for them."

It didn't take long for them to begin resenting it. Collins was especially hard on point guards. He couldn't seem to find one who satisfied him, resulting in a constant sifting through players. Yet whatever turmoil this caused, Collins seemed to have enough personal energy to drive the team past it.

And he also had Jordan, who again led the league in scoring in 1987–88, this time with a 35.0 average, and for the first time he was named the NBA's MVP. "It's a thrill," he said. His 3.2 steals per game also led the league, and he was named Defensive Player of the Year and a member of the All-Defensive Team.

Krause, meanwhile, was named Executive of the Year, and Charles Oakley again pulled down more rebounds than any player in the league, with 1,066.

In preparation for the playoffs, Johnny Bach began adding extra messages in the scouting videotapes he prepared for the team. The son of a maritime officer, Bach himself served in the navy during World War II and had lost his twin brother, a torpedo squadron bomber, during the conflict. His coaching was filled with stark references to combat, which made him a favorite of the players. Bach added those same references to the scouting tapes he prepared.

"I put in all kinds of extras for the team," he recalled. "It was interesting for the players, and I kind of enjoyed it. I just always put it in as a whimsical thing." He would punctuate basketball footage with images of exploding bombs, profound sayings from war movies, "anything to keep people's attention." The idea was always to prepare the troops for combat, Bach said. "It just started as a whimsical thing."

The practice drew Phil Jackson's immediate interest. He didn't particularly care for the violent military messages at the time. But he was amazed at the effectiveness of the effort with the players. It was just one of several facets of coaching he picked up from Winter and Bach during his "graduate school." Jackson took particular interest in Tex Winter's triangle offense and made an effort to absorb the multifaceted basketball philosophy that Winter had put together.

"Phil began to understand the triple-post offense," Bach recalled. "He spent a lot of time going over that with Tex. Tex is a summer fanatic. He loves teaching the young players. Tex did the summer league every year. Phil began to work with him, and he found parts of the triangle offense that he liked better than others."

The 1988 playoffs afforded Jackson a view of the team's preparation, which culminated in the Bulls' first playoff series win since 1981, a 3–2 defeat of the Cleveland Cavaliers. In the decisive fifth game, Collins decided to give Pippen his first start. He replaced the ineffective Sellers and scored 24 points. Krause was overcome afterward. "This is a baby from Conway, Arkansas, upon whom we've put tremendous pressure," he told reporters.

"When I played against Scottie last summer, I could see he had the skills," Jordan said. "It was just a matter of, how do you get them out of him in a season? It took 82 games for him to do it, but he's done it. And I think it's going to help him for the rest of his career."

To celebrate, the Bulls donned T-shirts that said, "How do you like us now?"

"We're ready for the next round!" Jordan had announced after the victory. At first, it seemed they were. They claimed the second game at the Pontiac Silverdome in their series with the Detroit Pistons, and suddenly the Bulls had the home-court advantage. But from there the Pistons zeroed their double- and triple-teaming defense on Jordan and forced him to pass. They also resorted to their Bad Boy tactics. In Game 3, a 101–79 Pistons blowout in the Stadium, Jordan and Detroit center Bill Laimbeer scuffled. "I set a pick," Laimbeer said. "I guess he wasn't looking."

Detroit took the next game and was in control in Game 5 when Jordan hit Isiah Thomas in the face with an elbow and sent him to the locker room. The blow knocked Thomas unconscious, but he returned later in the game to make sure the Pistons advanced, winning the series 4–1.

In the aftermath of the loss, Krause prepared to make another personnel move that would infuriate Jordan. Just before the 1988 draft, the Bulls' GM traded forward Charles Oakley to New York for center Bill Cartwright. The trade created yet another stir among Bulls players and fans, because Oakley had established a reputation as a strong rebounder, and Cartwright, a 7'1" post-up center, had been plagued by foot injuries and was thought to be near the end of his career. Several days later, the Bulls drafted Vanderbilt center Will Perdue in the first round as a backup.

"Charles was strong and tough and mean," Bach recalled. "He was the hardest trade that we had to do because Jerry Krause not only loved him as a player, but I think he had a great affection for him as a person. And to give him up and get Cartwright was almost against the grain. But the coaches really believed we couldn't win without Bill Cartwright, so we made the trade."

"I think Oak was in Atlantic City with Michael at a fight, and I couldn't find him to tell him," Krause remembered. "Oak found out about it because somebody ran up to him at the fight and told him. He told Michael, and Michael went bananas. 'How in the hell could Krause do this? He's screwing the franchise.' Michael went nuts."

"I didn't find out about it until Oakley told me during the fight between Mike Tyson and Michael Spinks," Jordan recalled. "We were in Atlantic City watching the fight. I was pretty upset about the deal and also to have to find out about it that way."

"It was traumatic for the team," Bach admitted, "but I think it just took us the next step up. Our defense was anchored by a real professional. Bill was good in the locker room. He was good in practice, and he earned the respect of the team because he could play Patrick Ewing straight up. We didn't have to double Patrick Ewing. And that gave us a great deal of confidence. What made the trade so tough was that Michael looked at Oakley as a protector. Charles was ready to fly into any tangle. You hit Michael; you had to face Charles. But Bill, in his own way, toughened up the big guys we had, and, in his own quiet way, Bill became very much of a terminator. Things stopped at the basket."

"We knew we couldn't win without a dominant defensive center," Reinsdorf said. "I didn't care about offense. We needed a defender. We needed a guy who could clog the middle, and we weren't going to win without one. I also knew that Horace Grant was coming on and thought that he'd be a better player than Oakley anyway. With Grant at forward, our team was built around a quick defense. Johnny Bach called them the Dobermans. With Grant, we could keep on pressing and pressuring the ball, which we couldn't do with Oakley. But we were trading Michael's friend and protector, so he didn't like the deal at the time. But he has since acknowledged that without that deal we wouldn't win any championships."

Reinsdorf rewarded Jordan with a contract extension two months later, in September 1988, worth a reported $25 million over eight years. A short time later, Reinsdorf also extended Jerry Krause's contract.

This financial success did little, however, to alleviate Jordan's frustration over the team's seeming inability to compete for a championship. Writers and reporters continued to compare Jordan to Larry Bird and Magic Johnson by pointing out that Bird and Johnson were the type of players to make their teammates better while Jordan often seemed to be playing for himself. This criticism infuriated Jordan, and the trade for Cartwright only deepened his anger because he thought the team had been weakened.

"Michael didn't really know Bill Cartwright as a person," Krause recalled. "He made Bill prove himself to him. Michael did that with everybody; that was Michael's way of doing things and I didn't mind that. I knew what Bill was, Bill was going to be fine with Michael. And I told Bill it's coming. He's going to needle you, he's going to drive you crazy and you're going to hate it. Bill said, 'He's not going to bother me.' "

"At the beginning of the year it was frustrating and hard to accept," Jordan later admitted. "Things were not going well, and it was getting to me. I had very high expectations, just like everyone, but there was a transition period we had to go through."

The season opened with Cartwright at center, Sellers and Grant at forwards, and Jordan in the backcourt with Sam Vincent, who had come to Chicago from Seattle in a trade for Sedale Threatt. On opening night, the Bulls got shoved around in the Stadium by the Pistons, and the tension built from there. Jordan again scored at a league-leading clip, but by January the club still struggled to stay above .500.

Discord built on the coaching staff until Collins blocked Tex Winter from coming to practice. "Tex was basically out of the picture at that time," Jackson recalled. "He did some scouting for Jerry Krause and took some road trips. He didn't go on all of our game trips. When he was with us, he sat in a corner and kept notes on practice and didn't participate in the coaching. He was out of it."

"It was a mix of an emotional Doug Collins and a very obdurate Tex Winter," Bach recalled. "As an assistant coach, you can speak for what you want, but there comes a place where you have to stop."

Keeping Winter away was Collins's means of keeping the control that he wanted, Bach explained. "Doug was not going to give up his thinking and his timeouts."

"I was upset because Doug basically wasn't listening to Tex, and he wasn't listening to Phil Jackson," Krause recalled. "Doug did a great job for us for a couple of years. He took the heat off me from a public relations standpoint. Doug was great with the media. But he learned to coach on the fly, and he didn't listen to his assistants as much as he should have. Doug had a thing with Phil, too. As time went on, he was like Stan in that he got away from what we wanted to do."

"Doug didn't get along with Jerry Krause," trainer Mark Pfeil recalled, "and on a day-to-day basis, that began to grind on us."

As his relationship with Krause deteriorated, Collins became increasingly suspicious of Jackson, due in part to June Jackson's being caught by television cameras sitting at a game with Jerry Krause's wife Thelma. In public, however, the head coach would praise his assistant, leading reporters to joke that Collins seemed to be going out of his way to help Jackson find a head coaching job.

By the end of January, the team had begun a turnaround with a series of winning streaks. A big factor in the change was the improvement of Pippen and Grant. "Scottie and Horace made a big progression from the start of their second to the end of the second year going into the playoffs," Will Perdue recalled. "You knew that those were guys that you could rely on. You knew what you were going to get out of them. A guy like Scottie, he was just so explosive and so talented that you knew if he could play up to his potential, which he did, it was going to be a real boost for us. I think Michael saw what kind of player Scottie and Horace could be, and he was very difficult on them at that time. Yet at the same time he was supportive. I mean he wasn't negative to the point that it drove them out of the game, or drove them to become not as good as they are. He did it in a positive way, but at the same time he was challenging them to see if they would answer the challenge."

By March, Vincent had become the latest point guard to displease Collins. He was benched, and Jordan made an unprecedented move to the point while newly acquired Craig Hodges stepped in at shooting guard. "It'll be interesting to see how Michael likes it," Collins said. Jordan responded by turning in seven straight triple-doubles, and the Bulls went on a six-game winning streak. But that was followed by a six-game losing streak, and the team's management worried that Collins, who had placed more of a burden on Jordan, just might wear the superstar out.

"I felt we lacked a system," Krause later explained. "It got to be a play-of-the-day thing with Doug. There wasn't a fundamental way we were playing. Collins would see a play that Boston or somebody ran, and he'd add that to our playbook all the time. There were all kinds of rumors about him, but none of them were true. Doug had some incidents where I told him to tone down his personal life a few times, but those weren't the reason we let him go."

"Doug had a lot of plays," Jackson said. "There were forty or fifty plays we ran. We had a lot of options off of plays. We had five or six different offensive sets. You see that with a lot of teams. But that's not where I came from as a basketball coach, and that's not where Tex was philosophically. We believed in Tex's organized system. Doug's a very emotional guy. He throws his heart into it, and from that standpoint he was very good for this basketball club. He was good at getting them directed to play with intensity and emotion. Then there came a level where they had to learn poise and control."

They finished the schedule at 47–35 for fifth place in the conference.

Once again Cleveland was the first-round opponent, but this time the Cavaliers had the home-court advantage. The Bulls took a 2–1 series lead and had a chance to close it out in the Stadium in Game 4. But, despite scoring 50 points, Jordan missed a key late free throw and the Cavaliers evened the series in overtime.

Game 5 in Cleveland produced an incredibly tight fourth quarter. There were six lead changes in the final three minutes. Craig Ehlo scored for Cleveland and seemed to give them a 100–99 victory with just seconds left. But Jordan got one final shot. With Ehlo draped on him, Jordan put up a spinning, double-clutch jumper as time expired to break the Cavaliers' hearts, 101–100.

"I saw him go up," said Cleveland center Brad Daugherty, "and I turned to box out, to look for the flight of the ball. I didn't see it, because Michael pumped, then brought it down. Then he went back up and hit the bottom of the net. I still don't know how he fit all of that into three seconds."

The dominant image from the videotape was Jordan's fist-pumping celebration as he was mobbed by teammates.

The energy of that win carried over into the second round, where the Bulls dispatched the Knicks in six games as Jordan averaged 35 points despite playing with an aggravated groin injury. For the first time since their ill-fated

1975 loss, the Bulls returned to the conference finals. Once again they faced the Pistons, and once again the rivalry hit new lows. In an April game, Isiah Thomas had slugged Bill Cartwright and had been suspended for two games. The memory of that tussle was prevalent in the series, as was a 1988 fight in which Detroit's Rick Mahorn had thrown Collins over the scorer's table.

"The Bulls always seemed a little intimidated by the Pistons, except for Michael," trainer Mark Pfeil recalled. "And he was always trying to get it across to the guys that this is the team we have to bridge ourselves over to get to the next level. Sometimes it took some yelling to get his point across. But against the Pistons, I think that's when Michael started stepping up as a leader. In the backs of their minds, our guys were always thinking that something dirty would happen against the Pistons. Detroit would intimidate you bit by bit every time they came in your building. We had a big fight with them one time. There was a tussle in front of our bench, and Doug Collins tried to grab Ricky Mahorn. Hell, Ricky threw Doug down twice. Threw him down on the floor. Doug jumped back up, and Ricky threw him over the scorer's table. Those were the things that always stood out in our minds. The Pistons were constantly doing those kinds of things. They just constantly beat and battered you."

"You couldn't play Detroit in an emotional way," Paxson said. "You couldn't because that's the way they wanted you to play. They wanted you to retaliate against them. They wanted you to start throwing them around and get out of your game. We didn't have the big banging bodies to play that way, and when we got angry that played right into their hands. Unfortunately, that was Doug's emotional makeup. Our crowd would play into that whole thing, too. And it never worked to our advantage. The Pistons were so antagonistic that it was just hard to maintain that control. It turned out to be a terrific rivalry for us, once we learned how to beat them. But for a while it looked like we were never going to get past them."

With Jordan at point guard, the Bulls surprised the Pistons in Game 1 at the Palace at Auburn Hills. The loss ended Detroit's twenty-five-game home-court winning streak and nine-game playoff winning streak. It also marked the first time in nine games that the Bulls had beaten the Pistons.

The Pistons won Game 2 at home, but Chicago fought back for a 2–1 lead when the series returned to the Stadium. But the Pistons stepped up their intimidation in Game 4 and covered Jordan so closely that he took only eight shots. Detroit won in Chicago, then went on to finish the series 4–2. Piston center Bill Laimbeer infuriated the Stadium crowds with his rough treatment of Pippen, leading Bulls fans to chant over and over, "Laim-beer sucks!"

During the series Krause informed Reinsdorf that Collins had to go. "We were in the Eastern finals against Detroit when I said to Jerry, 'I want to let Doug go.' Most owners would have said, 'Wait a minute. You brought him in here. He's your creation. He's just won 50 games and got us to the Eastern finals.' Jerry didn't say that," the GM remembered. "He said, 'Why?' And I told him I didn't think we could win the world championship this way, and I thought this was a club that could win the world championship."

A New Path

During the Pistons' series, New York Knicks coach Rick Pitino announced that he was leaving the team to take over as head coach at the University of Kentucky. When Dallas Mavericks coach John MacLeod said he wasn't interested in the job, speculation turned to Jackson. "Sure, I want to be a head coach," Jackson told reporters. "The Knicks know I'm interested."

"I don't expect to hear anything until the playoffs are over for us," he added. "Anyone who has played as many games in the Garden as I did has to feel some attachment."

Asked why he was being considered, Jackson said he expected that the Bulls' dramatic playoff success, including their defeat of the Knicks, had something to do with it. "Anytime a team does well, it rubs off on the assistants," he said. "I think we did a good job defensively against the Knicks."

Instead of moving rapidly to fire Collins, Krause and Reinsdorf paused to evaluate their options and the ramifications. "Jerry and I waited and sat down over the Fourth of July weekend and talked for three days," Krause recalled. "When the decision was made to let him go, Jerry said, 'I'll back you totally. We'll co-fire him. I don't want all the heat on you.' And in the end, the owner has to go along with you. No manager, no matter how strong he is, can fire the head coach without the owner's approval. We brought Doug into the office, and I think Doug thought he was going to talk about a contract extension. He had his agent with him. I said, 'Doug, we're going to have to let you go.' The look on his face was shocking."

On July 6, 1989, Jerry Reinsdorf and Jerry Krause announced the dismissal of Doug Collins, citing the coach's "philosophical differences" with management. Collins was fired despite a 137–109 regular-season record during his three-year tenure and solid playoff success. His three years with the team had been the longest for any Bulls coach since Dick Motta led the team for eight years before leaving after the 1975–76 season.

The move surprised and outraged many of the team's fans. "Whoever fired him is an asinine fool," one fan told reporters. "I think it's the most ridiculous thing I've ever heard of."

It also led to a round of gossip and media speculation that Collins had been let go for a variety of reasons, including that he was unpopular with his players, that Collins had angered Reinsdorf by trying to get Krause fired, that Collins "had become involved romantically with a daughter of one of the team's owners," and that Collins had become exhausted by the job and was headed for a breakdown.

The hottest rumor was that the firing had come at Jordan's request. "I firmly want to put that to rest," Krause quickly told reporters. "Michael Jordan had nothing to do with the decision."

"The media said, 'How could he fire Doug Collins? It must have been for this or that reason.' It was just pure basketball," Krause recalled in 1995. "And people to this date don't understand that. There were rumors, all kinds of rumors, why we fired Doug, and none of them are true. We fired Doug because we didn't think he could win the championship."

In a prepared statement, Collins responded to his firing: "When hired three years ago, I willingly accepted the challenge of leading the Bulls back to the type of team this city richly deserves. I'm proud of the fact that each year the team has taken another step towards an NBA championship, and played with intense pride and determination. Words will not describe the void I feel not being a part of Chicago Stadium and this great team."

"Doug was extremely popular with the media," Krause later recalled. "Everybody loved him except me. I had an owner who backed me in whatever I thought was best for the team. Most guys would have said, 'Wait a minute.' But Jerry just said, 'Why?' I told him. He said, 'I'll back you totally. I'll take the big heat.' Everybody with a typewriter castrated me. 'That dumb little sonofabitch,' they said. 'He went and did it again.'"

"I remember when Doug left, a lot of people were hurt," said longtime Bulls equipment manager John Ligmanowski. "They were shocked. There were people in the office crying."

Radio reporter Cheryl Raye didn't see the same thing among the city's media contingency. "Most of the local media weren't too surprised that Doug was fired." she said. "There was a lot of anger by the fans. They didn't understand it. The Bulls had gone to Cleveland and won that series, and everybody thought, 'Gosh, Cleveland should have won.'

"The fans reacted bad, but there was so much tension, there was tension amongst the players; there was tension between Doug and management, it didn't seem like it was gonna be long-term."

With no successor named immediately, speculation centered on Jackson, with good reason. Krause recalled that when he first told Reinsdorf he wanted to fire Collins, "he said, 'Who do you want to coach the team?' I said, 'I don't want to make that decision until we decide that we're going to let Doug go. Let's decide Doug's merits first.' So we did that. After that, I said, 'I want to hire Phil Jackson.' I'd brought Phil on two years earlier as assistant coach. Jerry said, 'Fine.' We had our conversation with Doug, and I called Phil, who was fishing out in Montana. I told him, 'I just let Doug go.' He said, 'What!?!?' And I said, 'Doug's gone, and I want you to be the head coach. You need to get your ass in here on a flight today. Soon as you can. I got to talk to you.'

"I brought Phil in and we talked philosophy," Krause recalled. "The first thing he said was, 'I've always been a defensive-oriented guy, as a player with Red Holzman, and as a coach. That's what you want me for.' I said, 'Yeah.' He said, 'I'm going to turn the offense over to Tex, and I'm going to run the triple-post.' I think some people who know me thought that I had set that all up, that I'd brought Phil in because he'd run Tex's stuff. I wish I'd been that smart, but I wasn't. It was all his idea. But I said, 'Great. That's super.' Because I knew the damn stuff would work. But I couldn't impose that on Doug. You couldn't impose anything on Doug. I would never impose what a coach runs on them anyway. Phil made his own decision to run Tex's stuff, but I agreed with it."

In the interim, coaches around the league weighed in on Krause's surprise move. "With the success that Doug had," Dan Issel told reporters, "it was a pretty bold move to fire him. It certainly doesn't seem like a spur-of-the-moment thing."

"Whatever the reason, it just doesn't make me very proud of our profession," Don Nelson, then the coach and general manager of the Golden State Warriors, told reporters. "Here's a franchise that didn't know success until Collins arrived. Now the future looks bright, and to tell him he can't be a part of it is a real slap in the face."

"It hurt Doug a great deal," Bach recalled. "But he had this marvelous recovery rate." Although he would indicate to associates that he felt betrayed by Jackson, Collins never made such claims publicly. He quickly gathered himself in the days after getting the news and met with the media. "I don't think it's important to keep talking over things. . . . I know this is a situation that everybody wants to hear a lot of talking," he said. "But I'm not going to say a lot of things. I have nothing but the utmost respect for this organization."

On July 11, the Bulls announced they had hired Jackson as their next coach, a little more than two months shy of his forty-fourth birthday.

"To ignore the circumstances would be thoughtless," Jackson said. "Doug Collins was instrumental to my arrival."

Reporters then asked if Bulls management had created a climate where he needed to be worried about his job. Jackson told them, "No. I've got a good basketball team with me and the future's very bright."

The *Chicago Tribune* reported that Jackson would receive a four-year contract with the first two years guaranteed. The deal called for about $275,000 the first year and escalated to about $350,000, similar to what Collins had been paid. The former coach was hardly surprised by the naming of his successor.

"He knows the temperament of the team and he was really great with me last year. I wish him well," Collins said. "I came to this city with one goal in mind and that was to win an NBA championship. And even though I won't be a part of that, I want them to win it."

"I made the decision to fire Doug Collins in large part because I thought it was the best thing for Doug Collins," Jerry Reinsdorf said in 1995. "And I thought it was the right decision for the Chicago Bulls. I knew it was the right decision for Doug Collins. You know, I have a very strong attachment, personally, to Doug Collins. I really like him as a person, I think he's brilliant, but he's driven, maybe to the detriment of his own benefit, overly driven, and I wanted to remove him from a situation where I thought he was going to grind himself up. Unfortunately, coaches have different periods when they're useful. It's not a long-term job. There's no tenure associated with it."

"Everybody liked Doug," John Paxson recalled. "The thing about it was, we had just come off of getting to the conference finals, of taking Detroit to six games. Our future was out there. The coach who had spent three years helping us do that was gone. That's where you give Jerry Reinsdorf and Jerry Krause credit. They truly believed that Doug had been good for that team to a certain point, but that there had to be a different type coach to get us to the next level. That was a pretty good read on the situation."

Reporters began phoning around to interview people from Jackson's past. Who was this man who had been named to coach Michael Jordan? Why should he get the job?

"He reads the game as well as any coach and makes adjustments," Charley Rosen, Jackson's old CBA assistant and friend, told them. "He has the ability to see a team play, watch them on tape, and figure out how to beat them."

Quickly Jackson would begin demonstrating just how true that was, and how very different he was from Collins. "It seemed like especially in the last few minutes of a game, there was no calm amid the chaos with Doug. And that's where Phil is such a difference," radio reporter Cheryl Raye would observe later. "By sitting on the bench, Phil had an opportunity to learn the personalities of these players. So when he took over, it was much easier. He knew their hot buttons. He knew when to press them and when not to press them. When he got into those fiery situations, he had better control of himself than Doug did."

"When Krause and Doug brought Phil here as an assistant coach, I didn't make a big thing about it because it never dawned on me that someday he'd be head coach," Reinsdorf recalled. "I know that the year before, when Stan Albeck was the coach, Jerry tried to talk Stan into hiring Phil. But, as I understand it, Phil came to the interview with a beard. I don't know what the hair looked like, but I know he had a beard. I didn't see him. And then, when Jerry brought him in to interview with Doug, he told him to get a haircut, and to get rid of the beard. He said it made a better presentation. He was an assistant here, I believe, for two years. So I got to know him pretty well during that time, and there was no question in my mind that he was the guy to succeed Doug, that he would be a stabilizing influence."

"I've always been impressed by Phil," John Paxson said in 1994. "He's an intellectual guy, and I think that's the first thing that stood out to me. You don't run into too many intellectual guys in the NBA. The thing that impressed me is that he hasn't allowed this game to consume him. It can be so consuming for a coach. But Phil has other interests. His family has always been important to him. And he has never let the game take a toll on him mentally. When you're around him, you can see that he has a good mind, and whatever he chooses to apply it to, he's been good at it. He's a take-control type of person, and when he was an assistant coach, you got the impression with Phil that someday he was going to get a job and be in control."

7

MICHAEL'S COACH

Phil Jackson's hiring as head coach of the Chicago Bulls brought to an end a long and varied apprenticeship. After prepping in sports-crazy Williston, he had played pressure defense under Bill Fitch in college for three years while studying religion, philosophy, and psychology. From there he spent a decade in Red Holzman's much-needed academy of common sense, with more pressure defense. Summers were reserved for graduate courses in counseling and therapy. He also learned a meaningful lesson in the limits of a pro basketball player's body. Next came his three seasons in New Jersey, a synthesis of playing and coaching and media; followed by a period of induced humility with his failed business in Montana; and then his protracted internship in the Continental Basketball Association, aided by summer school in Puerto Rico. His doctoral work had been performed in Jerry Krause's Intense Finishing School, two seasons under the individual tutelage of two old masters, Johnny Bach and Tex Winter.

Now it appeared Phil Jackson was ready—except that he needed one final brush-up.

After accepting the job that July, Jackson rushed to coach the Bulls' team of draftees and young free agents in the NBA summer league. The summer team was always Tex Winter's domain, but Jackson took the time to examine the triangle one final time to decide which parts of it, if any, he could use that first season. There simply wasn't time to get the whole thing in. As badly as he wanted to see his offense in place, Winter knew that as well.

"It is complicated and it does take a lot of experience," Bach said. "Phil found parts of it that he liked better than others. Phil himself began to understand the triple-post. He spent a lot of time with Tex."

They both agreed that before the offense could be fully installed, a lot of prep work had to be done with the players, beginning with Jordan. That would be Jackson's job. And it wasn't just about the offense. It involved the entire culture that had grown around Jordan. Jackson as an assistant coach had been careful to cultivate a good relationship with the star. But now Jackson would have to elevate the nature of that relationship. He had to keep Jordan as an ally while effecting big changes. Winter would later marvel at the effort and quiet tenacity that Jackson brought to the task.

By the time Jackson took over as head coach of the Bulls in 1989, Michael Jordan was twenty-six years old and facing explosive fame and wealth. His annual off-court income was ballooning from $4 million to $30 million. Overnight he had become a cultural icon. As an assistant Jackson had watched Jordan struggle personally to cope with this newfound status. Now, his immediate fear as head coach was that both Jordan and the team might well be consumed by it.

"I was nervous when I took over the Bulls," Jackson admitted, "but it wasn't the kind of nervousness where you lose sleep at night. I wanted to do well. I was anxious about having a good relationship with Michael. I was anxious about selling him on the direction in which I was going.

"You knew what Michael was going to give you every single night as a player. He was gonna get those 30 points; he was gonna give you a chance to win. The challenge was, how to get the other guys feeling a part of it, like they had a role, a vital part. It was just his team, his way.

"He had such hero worship in the United States among basketball fans that living with him had become an impossibility," Jackson explained. "Traveling in airports, he needed an entourage to get through. He had brought people along on the road with him. His father would come. His friends would come on the road. He had just a life that sometimes alienated him from his teammates. It became a challenge to make him part of the team again and still not lose his special status because he didn't have the necessary privacy.

"I had roomed on the same floor of hotels as he did. Michael always had a suite because of who he was, and the coaches got suites, too, because we needed the space for team meetings and staff meetings. Michael basically had to have someone stay in his room with him. I'd hear murmuring in the hallway, and there'd be six or eight of the hotel staff, cleaning ladies, busboys, getting autographs and standing in the hallway with flowers. It was incredible, and he was constantly bothered."

Most coaches, particularly first-year coaches, wouldn't have dared to begin changing the rules for Jordan, especially if those new rules separated him from his entourage of family and friends. But Jackson began that process.

"I knew," he explained, "that we had to make exceptions to the basic rules that we had: 'OK, so your father and your brothers and your friends can't ride on the team bus. Let's keep that a team thing. Yeah, they can meet you on the road, but they can't fly on the team plane. There has to be some of the team stuff that is ours, that is the sacred part of what we try to do as a basketball club.'"

Jackson had decided that dealing with and controlling the ever-growing media contingency would be another major task. He figured Jordan and the team needed a shield as much as anything. And behind the shield he wanted to create a sanctuary, an inner place that was only for the team.

"I got a curtain for our practice facility, so that practice became our time together," he explained. "It was just the twelve of us and the coaches, not the reporters and the television cameras. It wasn't going to be a show for the public anymore. It became who are we as a group, as people. Michael had to break down some of his exterior. You know that when you become that famous person you have to develop a shell around you to hide behind. Michael had to become one of the guys in that regard. He had to involve his teammates, and he was able to do that. He was able to bring it out and let his hair down at the same time."

The effort would involve getting Jordan to rethink his own personal parameters—a major undertaking, because those parameters were growing and changing daily. "Over his years in pro basketball, Michael had learned to mark out his own territory," Jackson explained. "He had his own stall at every arena where he might find the most privacy, or he might find a territory in the trainer's room. He had two stalls in the old Chicago Stadium. That was his spot because there were twenty-five reporters around him every night.

"We continued the protocol of all that, but we also made efforts to create space for him within the team. If we hadn't done that, the way he was going to treat us was that the rest of the world was going to overrun us, if we hadn't done things the right way. So we said, 'Let's not all suffer because of his fame. Let's give ourselves space and exclude the crowd.' I guess I created a safe zone, a safe space for Michael. That's what I tried to do."

"Phil's handled Michael so well," John Paxson would say later. "If I could ever take a page out of the manual for handling a superstar, it would be the way Phil's handled Michael Jordan."

One of Jackson's delights as a Bulls assistant was to spend hours studying videotape of Jordan's performances—many of them absolutely phenomenal athletic feats, things no one had ever done in basketball. "Some nights he could take on a whole team," Jackson explained. "They'd say, 'That son of a gun, he beat us all to the basket.' As a coach, you can run that tape back all day. You say, 'Look at this guy go around that guy and that guy. He beat four guys going to the basket that time.' That's destructive. That's something that Michael's been known for, and I know it grates at the heart of the other team. It's an amazing feat this guy has been able to accomplish. But I think his power is very addictive. You know the fans were there looking for him. Everybody's waiting. They loved it. He had this tremendous vision of basketball. He was this tremendous entertainer."

Jordan's "greatness," however, was tempered by that same old issue: Was he the kind of player who could lead a team to a championship? Could he make his teammates better?

As an assistant, Jackson had come to appreciate the exceptionally keen nature of Jordan's mind. As a head coach, he relished the opportunity to fully engage that mind to pursue the goal that both of them wanted badly. He wanted to challenge his player, but only mentally. He wanted to use Jordan's mind to bring about the discipline that the Bulls so badly needed. Jackson suspected that Jordan would respond to a mental challenge, if it was issued on a daily basis—not issuing directives as Collins had, but suggesting paths and leaving Jordan and his teammates free to choose.

"When Phil came along, I thought he did much more than adopt the triple-post offense," Bach observed. "I think Phil threw the game back to the players. 'It's your game. You're out there on the floor. You make the decisions.' It sounds like wild freedom, but it was not wild freedom, just a change in philosophy."

Such an approach required immense advance work to prepare the players to make their own decisions, in practice and in the discussions that Jackson began with Jordan.

"He has more psychological sayings to make you think about things," Jordan observed in those early days. "He reminds me of Dean Smith a lot. Dean used to play a lot of mind games. Both of them make you think about your own mistakes. Instead of yelling at you, Phil makes you think about it and you eventually realize that you made a mistake. That type of psychological warfare sometimes can drive a person crazy, yet it can drive you to achieve, too. I like mind games, so Phil is great for me."

These subtle changes soon gained notice by the rest of the team.

"I think there came a point where he understood his greatness was going to be defined by winning," John Paxson said of Jordan. "That's why I saw a change in his real commitment to winning championships and, to that end, dealing with teammates and getting guys he felt comfortable with, that were able to play with him. It was really that understanding that championships mean a lot, when it comes down to who's the greatest. There are great NBA players who've never won championships, and it's always been a blot on their careers."

Jackson took quick measure of the messages he was sending to all those involved with the team. As with his players, he assigned substantial latitude to his assistant coaches. Each member of the staff had assigned duties and was given ample room to perform them, a development that the players quickly picked up on. Unlike many coaches who were control freaks, Jackson seemed eager for his coaches to have free input.

He hired Jim Cleamons, an old Knicks teammate, as the team's third assistant. Cleamons, in his early forties, actually didn't know Jackson all that well. They had both been reserves for the Knicks in Jackson's last season there. Cleamons remembered that they had played well together in practice, had approached the game the same way. But he hadn't seen Jackson in years until he came to Chicago in the spring of 1988 to visit Brad Sellers, who had played for Cleamons at Ohio State. At the time, Cleamons was the coach at Youngstown State. He came to the Bulls' practice and saw Jackson (an assistant at the time) and had a nice chat. Several months later, Cleamons got a phone call from the Bulls. He assumed they wanted to ask him about a college player. Instead, it was Jackson, asking whether he wanted to come for an interview. The next thing Cleamons knew, he was back in the NBA doing the advance scouting chores that Jackson himself had done.

Winter focused on offense, and Bach was the defensive specialist. Like Winter, Bach relished debating Jackson. "He was his own man; he loved to play devil's advocate," trainer Mark Pfeil said of Bach. "Sometimes people took him too seriously. I always called him Doctor Doom. I don't care what we were doing, he always thought the worst was going to happen."

Jackson was keenly aware of Bach's influence on players, an issue that would develop as an undercurrent over the coming seasons. "Phil had called

Johnny the locker room coach, which meant he was the liaison with the players, especially for Horace Grant," explained radio reporter Cheryl Raye. "Horace was extremely sensitive, took everything at face value. So Johnny was there to explain everything. While Phil would be screaming at him, Johnny would be there, 'OK, Horace.' He'd be stroking him and telling him everything was all right. So Johnny was very close to Horace. The players had so much respect for him, especially defensively."

With so many questions about their offense, Jackson and his assistants knew that their ability to play defense would buy them time to evolve at the other end of the floor. They knew they had the personnel to pressure the ball, which could produce turnovers and easy baskets, another factor in taking pressure off the offense.

"When Phil came in, our first training camp was as difficult a camp as I'd ever had," recalled guard John Paxson. "It was defensive-oriented. Everything we did was, start from the defensive end and work to the offensive end. Phil basically made us into a pressure-type team. Defensively, he knew that was how we would win."

"We were gonna play fullcourt pressure defense," Jackson said. "We were gonna throw our hearts into it."

In many ways, the players seemed to draw their defensive identity from Bach. "They seemed to take their pride from him," Cheryl Raye observed. "It just rubbed off, especially the defense. When he put the Aces up, the military term that signaled for the pressure, it got everybody going."

Coming out of camp, the players and coaches knew they were much better, and the energy was tangible as they finished the preseason 8–0. Yet everyone knew that a big adjustment lay ahead. The Bulls had to find a comfort level playing in the strange new offense. And then there was the matter of Cartwright. Michael Jordan openly resented the big center, who seemed to have trouble catching the ball in traffic. It wasn't just Cartwright, because Jordan cast a hard eye at any teammate who was not ready or willing to get better.

"I guess I expected more from a lot of them," Jordan said. "But some of them didn't want to take more responsibility. . . . We were inconsistent and I was frustrated."

"He was always challenging you in little ways," Paxson said of Jordan. "The thing you had to do with Michael Jordan is you had to gain his confidence as a player. You had to do something that gave him some trust in you as a player. He was hard on teammates as far as demanding you play hard, you execute. So there had to come some point where you did something on the floor to earn his trust. That was the hardest thing for new guys coming in, and some guys couldn't deal with it. Some guys could not play consistently enough or well enough, or they would not do the dirty work or little things. That's one of the reasons why Michael liked Charles Oakley, because Charles played hard. He did little things on the floor that Michael appreciated, but a lot of guys didn't understand that.

"Michael demanded nothing less than playing hard. If you missed shots when you were open, he didn't want to see that either. If Michael came off the screen and roll a couple of times and threw a quick pass to Bill Cartwright and he couldn't handle it, Michael wasn't going to go there again. That was kind of what happened early. If you do something and one of your teammates doesn't respond to it, you're going to think twice about going there. It's a natural thing. You always sensed with Michael that he was looking for perfection out of himself. There's a part of him that expected that of those around him, too."

"I feel I'm very observant about the game and how it's played," Jordan would later explain. "I try to be aware when my team needs my creativity and scoring or my passing or rebounding. If things were going well, I didn't have to score too much. I could stay in the background and get everyone else involved."

"Michael challenged guys," Paxson explained, "and for some, their game didn't live up to that challenge. Brad Sellers, for example. It was tough for him to handle what Michael expected of him. Michael had a tendency to look at certain guys and say, 'You're capable of doing this. Why aren't you? I look at your physical skills. Why can't you?' I'm sure he looked at me many times and said, 'You're not capable of doing that on the floor.' But I had an advantage with Michael in our basketball relationship. We spent a month overseas together when we were in college as part of an international team in 1981. I made a shot to win a game over in Yugoslavia, and I've got to believe that in the back of his mind, Michael remembered that about me as a player. He was able to trust me. It's all about earning his trust and his knowing that he could rely on you when there was pressure and the game was on the line. At the same time, I don't remember Michael early on putting any pressure on Scottie Pippen or Horace. He knew that a lot of guys have to grow into the league.

"Michael was always more than fair with me. He was always positive with me and never said anything negative about me in the papers. That meant a lot to me. You can get battered down when the great player of the team says something critical of you personally. He didn't do that. I thought early on he was too reserved toward players at times. I'm sure he felt he was walking a fine line. 'Should I be critical? Should I just lay back and let these guys do their own thing?' I felt the more vocal he became as a leader, the better we were. Once he really started challenging guys, it made us better. We had to learn how to play with Michael as well as Michael had to learn to play with us."

They went 8–6 over the month of November, and there were few smiling faces. December, however, brought a trend: they would find bursts of momentum and consume the schedule with winning streaks. First came a five-game run right before the holidays, then another five heading into the new year. Their offense continued to struggle, but the secret was their defense. Across the league, other coaches began talking about it—and fearing it.

Then, just as suddenly, their magic faltered, and during a West Coast road trip things reached a low point with four straight losses. Even worse, Cartwright was struggling with sore knees and missed several games. Jackson saw their play without Cartwright as critical to their development. He was looking for much more from Grant and Pippen.

"My first year here you could read their facial expressions like a book," Jim Cleamons would recall later. "They were easily frustrated when things did not go right. But over their first three years, they learned how to play, and they learned to keep their composure on the court. They matured and grew more confident."

"I think the physical demands on Scottie were what got to him the most," Cheryl Raye observed. "When he got here, he was very fragile mentally. I tie that to his being from a very small school, being from a different background, a different setting. Scottie never had any of the grooming that guys like Michael who went to big programs had. At the big schools, they groom those guys with the media. Usually they have some sort of maturity about them when they get to the NBA. Scottie did a couple of things on his own. He hired a speech coach from Chicago. She's a radio person and worked on how he handled questions, what to say."

"My first year or two, I admit that I messed around a lot," Pippen said later. "I partied, enjoyed my wealth, and didn't take basketball as seriously as I should have. I'm sure a lot of rookies did the same thing I did. You're not used to the limelight or being put in a great situation financially. . . . There were nights where I should have been more focused on basketball."

Pippen's career had been interrupted by back surgery in his second year in the league, but he was able to make a successful comeback. With playing time under Jackson, he made dramatic improvement, turning in stellar performances throughout 1989–90. That February of 1990, he was named an All-Star for the first time, joining Jordan on the Eastern Conference team.

"He's on the cusp of greatness," Bach said of Pippen. "He's starting to do the kinds of things only Michael does."

"It's just a matter of working hard," Pippen said. "I've worked to improve my defense and shooting off the dribble. I know I'm a better spot-up shooter, but I'm trying to pull up off the dribble when the lane is blocked."

Jordan led in scoring, but it was Pippen who gave opposing coaches nightmares. Few teams had a means of matching up with him, particularly when they also had to worry about Jordan.

"Starting out, you could see Scottie's possibilities," Jackson recalled. "He could rebound yet still dribble. He could post up, but he also had those slashing moves. You knew he could be very good, but you didn't know how good. He played a few times at guard in his first few seasons, bringing the ball up against teams with pressing guards, but mostly we used him at small forward. As more and more teams pressed, however, we decided we had to become more creative. More and more we had to go to Michael to bring the ball up. We didn't want to do that. We came up with the thought of Scottie as a third ball advancer, of an offense that attacked at multiple points. From that position Scottie started to take control, to make decisions. He became a bit of everything."

Fortunately, the All-Star break provided relief. Jackson's players regained whatever confidence they'd lost, and won nine straight. They lost a game to Utah in Chicago Stadium, then won six of eight and followed that with another nine-game win streak.

The win streaks propelled them to a 55–27 finish in 1990, good for second place in the Central Division behind the 60-win Pistons, the defending world champions. And Jordan harvested another batch of honors: All-NBA and All-Defensive teams, and his fourth consecutive scoring title. Plus he led the league in steals.

With the playoffs approaching, Jackson cast an eye toward the scouting footage that Bach was putting together. "Phil wanted to put in the theme," Bach recalled. Instead of the older assistant's military motifs, Jackson, an outspoken advocate of gun control, offered up his own take. "He introduced Pink Floyd and the story of the white buffalo."

Bach chuckled at the difference in their selections. "We are very different people," he recalled. "His mother and father were tent preachers. My father was a maritime officer."

The Bulls sailed into the playoffs with new confidence and Pippen playing like a veteran. First they dismissed the Milwaukee Bucks, then followed that by humbling Charles Barkley and the Philadelphia 76ers. But Pippen's seventy-year-old father died during the series, and the young forward rushed home to Arkansas for the funeral. He returned in time to help finish off Philly. Next up were the Pistons and the Eastern finals. In essence, it was the big exam for Jackson's new style of play. "Detroit was still an enigma," the coach later recalled.

The series was a gauntlet. The year before in the playoffs, Pistons center Bill Laimbeer, one of the primary advocates of their physical style, had knocked Pippen out of Game 6 with an elbow to the head. The Detroit center claimed the shot was inadvertent, but that wasn't the way the Bulls saw it. To win a championship, they knew they had to stand up to the Bad Boys.

Jackson said he had never had a cross word with Pistons coach Chuck Daly, yet Jackson had no doubts who issued the directives for excessively physical play.

"I thought they were thugs," Reinsdorf said of the Pistons, "and you know, you have to hold the ownership responsible for that. I mean, Billy Laimbeer was a thug. He would hit people from behind in the head during dead balls. He took cheap shots all the time. Mahorn and lunatic Rodman, I mean, they tried to hurt people.

"They called themselves the Bad Boys, and they marketed themselves under that name. I would never have allowed that. You know I blame the league and David Stern a little bit for that, too. It was terrible."

"There were times," Pippen said, "a few years before the flagrant foul rules, when guys would have a breakaway and [the Pistons] would cut their legs out from under them. Anything to win a game. That's not the way the game is supposed to be played. I remember once when Michael had a breakaway, and Laimbeer took him out. There was no way he could have blocked the shot. When you were out there playing them, that was always in the back of your mind, to kind of watch yourself."

The Bulls, however, thought they were ready to challenge Detroit in 1990. At first, their conference final series seemed to develop as a classic, with each team winning tight battles at home to tie it at 3–3 heading into Game 7 at the Palace at Auburn Hills. The Pistons had home-court advantage, but the Bulls had worked for years to get to this point. Things went dreadfully wrong, beginning with Paxson limping from a badly sprained ankle and Pippen developing a migraine headache just before tipoff.

"Scottie had had migraines before," trainer Mark Pfeil explained. "He actually came to me before the game and said he couldn't see. I said, 'Can you play?' He started to tell me no, and Michael jumped in and said, 'Hell, yes, he can play. Start him. Let him play blind.'

"Horace Grant kind of backed up a little bit that game, too," Pfeil added. "It was more a matter of maturity than wimpin' out. It took a certain period of time before they would stand up and say, 'Damn it, I've been pushed to the wall enough.' Scottie played with the headache, and as the game went on he got better."

Pippen played, but the entire roster seemed lost. They fell into a deep hole in the second quarter and never climbed out. With the Bad Boys' skull and crossbones banners flying and their "Bad to the Bone" theme music playing, the Pistons advanced easily, 93–74.

"My worst moment as a Bull was trying to finish out the seventh game that we lost to the Pistons in the Palace," Jackson recalled. "There was Scottie Pippen with a migraine on the bench, and John Paxson had sprained his ankle in the game before. I just had to sit there and grit my teeth and go through a half in which we were struggling to get in the ball game. We had just gone through a second period that was an embarrassment to the organization. It was my most difficult moment as a coach."

Furious with his teammates, Jordan cursed them at halftime, then sobbed in the back of the team bus afterward. "I was crying and steaming," he recalled. "I was saying, 'Hey, I'm out here busting my butt and nobody else is doing the same thing. These guys are kicking our butt, taking our heart, taking our pride.' I made up my mind right then and there it would never happen again. That was the summer that I first started lifting weights. If I was going to take some of this beating, I was also going to start dishing out some of it. I got tired of them dominating me physically."

With each Chicago loss in the playoffs, observers grew more convinced that the Bulls were flawed because Jordan made them virtually a one-man team. Some pointed out that it had taken Wilt Chamberlain, Jerry West, and Oscar Robertson many years to lead teams to the NBA title. Some critics said Jordan fit into the category with those players. Others wondered whether he wasn't headed for the same anguish as Elgin Baylor, Nate Thurmond, Pete Maravich, and Dave Bing, all great players who never played on a championship team.

Jordan was understandably angered by such speculation and by the criticism that he was a one-man team. He was also pained by the losses each year to Detroit. He and Pistons point guard Isiah Thomas weren't fond of each other, which made the losses all the more difficult.

"When Scottie and Horace came in, Michael sensed the thing could be turned around," trainer Mark Pfeil recalled. "But the thing that frustrated him was that they didn't have the same attitude. They were young enough to say, 'Hell, we get paid whether we win or lose.' And it was good enough for them just to get close. In their second year, we went to the Eastern finals and lost. Then with Phil we lost again. After that second loss, Michael said, 'Hey, now we've gotta go over the top, and I'm gonna take us there. If you don't want to be on the boat, get off.' I think those guys really matured. You had your petty jealousies, but Michael, to me, bent over backwards to help all kinds of people, from Oakley to Paxson to Scottie to Horace."

The burden of the loss fell on Pippen. Everyone, from the media to his own teammates, had interpreted the headache as a sign of faintheartedness. Lost in the perspective was the fact that the third-year forward had recently buried his father.

"I'm flying back from the migraine game," recalled Cheryl Raye, "and who should be sitting across from me but Juanita Jordan. And she says, 'What happened to Scottie?' I said, 'He had a headache.' She goes, 'He had a headache!?!?' And she just shook her head."

"It grabbed me and wouldn't let go," Pippen later said. "It's something the fans will never let die."

In the wake of that first season, Jackson reflected on what he had learned. He learned that practice time was precious and that the emphasis in pro basketball had to be on defense, because that had the greatest impact on winning.

He also had learned much about his psychological approach. "When I was a player," he said, "I went to graduate school in counseling psychology for three of the summers I was playing in the NBA. A lot of times at that point I thought that group psychology and group encounter sessions could be really important in basketball, getting guys to react and work together better. Of course, I learned that those things can be applied at times and can't be applied at other times, particularly in our type of game, where a lot of it's nonverbal—unlike the office situation or in motivational meetings in a corporation, where the verbal is more important and groups can come together and have discussions. There are a lot of things I thought at that time could possibly work and now that I've grown into adulthood, I've realized that some of the hopes I've had and aspirations for group behavior are not applicable to professional basketball. There's a lot of envy and jealousy on a basketball team, where somebody's making $200,000, somebody else is making $2 million, and those things can't really be ironed out in a group situation. So there are a lot of limits to what hopes and aspirations can accomplish."

One reporter discovered that Jackson was meditating and talking to his team about Indian lore. The coach tried to dissuade the reporter from disclosing those facts. "The NBA is a very closed world," Jackson told him. "But I think there's a lot of room to operate out on the fringe."

The First Championship

June Jackson found herself celebrating her sixteenth wedding anniversary at a Bulls team luncheon in the fall of 1990. The occasion was the beginning of a new basketball season. Her husband had climbed high in recent seasons, but that hadn't calmed her fears. From everything she could see, pro basketball coaching was a matter of quick rise, quick fall.

During that luncheon, Jerry Krause stood at the podium and told her husband, "I got the players for you. Now it's up to you to make it work."

The Jacksons had felt secure enough to begin a major addition to their home in Bannockburn in suburban north Chicago, but her husband had not had time for the details. Those would be left to her, as were all the other details of their lives. She asked Jackson about the house. He told her he only wanted to pick out the front door; the rest was up to her. "That sort of typifies our relationship," she said at the time. "If it's a major decision, then he'll be part of it. But generally speaking, the kids, the finances, the social engagements are left up to me."

Her husband, out of necessity, was consumed by basketball.

Despite the outcome, Jackson and his assistants had come away from the 1990 playoffs with tremendous optimism. They knew they would have to sell Jordan and his teammates on using the triple-post offense, and they would have to get tougher defensively.

Without question, Winter said later, it was the rise of Jackson to the position of head coach that made the use of his triangle offense possible. It was not, however, an easy transition.

Winter had spent years developing the triangle, or triple-post, offense. It was an old college system that involved all five players sharing the ball and moving. But it was totally foreign to the pro players of the 1990s, and many of them found it difficult to learn. Where for years the pro game had worked on isolation plays and one-on-one setups, the triple-post used very little in the way of set plays. Instead the players learned to react to situations and to allow their ball movement to create weaknesses in defenses.

Among the offense's strongest questioners was Jordan.

"I've always been very much impressed with Michael as well as everyone else has been," Winter once explained. "I've never been a hero worshiper. I saw his strong points, but I also saw some weaknesses. I felt like there was a lot of things that we could do as a coaching staff to blend Michael in with the team a little bit better. I thought he was a great player, but I did not feel that we wanted to go with him exclusively. We wanted to try and get him to involve his teammates more. Until he was convinced that that was what he wanted to do, I don't think we had the chance to have the program that we had later down the line."

"Tex's offense emulated the offense I had played in with New York," Jackson said. "The ball dropped into the post a lot. You ran cuts. You did things off the ball. People were cutting and passing and moving the basketball. And it took the focus away from Michael, who had the ball in his hands a lot, who had been a great scorer. That had made the defenses all turn and face him. Suddenly he was on the back side of the defenses, and Michael saw the value in having an offense like that. He'd been in an offense like that at North Carolina. It didn't happen all at once. He started to see that over a period of time, as the concepts built up."

"It was different for different types of players," recalled John Paxson. "For me it was great. A system offense is made for someone who doesn't have the athletic skills that a lot of guys in the league have. It played to my strengths. But it tightened the reins on guys like Michael and Scottie from the standpoint that we stopped coming down and isolating them on the side. There were subtleties involved, teamwork involved. But that was the job of Phil to sell us on the fact we could win playing that way."

"Everything was geared toward the middle, toward the post play," Jordan said, explaining his opposition. "We were totally changing our outlook . . . and I disagreed with that to a certain extent. I felt that was putting too much pressure on the people inside."

"What Michael had trouble with," Jackson said, "was when the ball went to one of the big guys like Bill Cartwright or Horace Grant or some of the other players who weren't tuned in to handling and passing the ball. They now had the ball. Could they be counted on to make the right passes, the right choices? I brought Michael in my office and told him basically, 'The ball is like a spotlight. And when it's in your hands, the spotlight is on you. And you've gotta share that spotlight with some of your teammates by having them do things with the basketball, too.' He said, 'I know that. It's just that when it comes down to getting the job done, a lot of times they don't want to take the initiative. Sometimes it's up to me to take it, and sometimes that's a tough balance.'

"All along the way it was a compromise of efforts," Jackson said. "Everybody made such a big issue of the triple-post offense. We just said, 'It's a format out of which to play. You can play any way you want out of the triangle.' Because if it's a sound offense, you should be able to do that. One of the concepts is to hit the open man."

Jordan's presence also stretched the flexibility of Winter's concepts and challenged the older coach's thinking. "There were times when Michael knew he was going to get 40 points," Jackson said. "He was just hot those nights. He was going to go on his own, and he would just take over a ball game. We had to understand that that was just part of his magnitude, that was something he could do that nobody else in this game could do. And it was going to be OK. Those weren't always the easiest nights for us to win as a team. But they were certainly spectacular nights for him as a showman and a scorer."

"It took some time," Paxson recalled. "Michael was out there playing with these guys, and unless he had a great deal of respect for them as players, I think he figured, 'Why should I pass them the ball when I have the ability to score myself or do the job myself? I'd rather rely on myself to succeed or fail than some of these other guys.' The thing I like about Michael is that he finally came to understand that if we were going to win championships he had to make some sacrifices individually. He had to go about the task of involving his teammates more."

"A lot of times," Jackson said, "my convincing story to Michael was, 'We want you to get your thirty-some points, and we want you to do whatever is necessary. It's great for us if you get 12 or 14 points by halftime, and you have 18 points at the end of the third quarter. Then get your 14 or 18 points in the fourth quarter. That's great. If it works out that way, that's exactly what it'll be.' Who could argue with that? We'd tell him, 'Just play your cards. Make them play everybody during the course of the game and then finish it out for us.' I think that's why sometimes Michael has downplayed the triangle. He says it's a good offense for three quarters, but it's not great for the fourth quarter. That's because he took over in the fourth quarter. He can perform."

"Phil was definitely set on what we were going to do and he wouldn't waver," Winter recalled. "Even though the triple-post offense evolved through my many, many years of coaching, Phil was sold on it even more than I was at times. There's times when I would say, 'We should get away from this. Let Michael have more one-on-one opportunities.' And Phil was persistent in not doing so. It's to his credit that we stayed to his basic philosophy of basketball."

Jackson's tenacity in keeping with the offense in the face of all that opposition is what defined him as a coach, at least in Winter's thinking.

The key to the Bulls' defensive toughness was Cartwright. His career had featured one frustrating battle after another with injuries, but what the Bulls saw in him was the defensive intimidator they needed. Either way, Michael Jordan was not pleased to have him on the roster. Jackson, however, had seen his value, not only as a defender but as a leader. The coach began calling Cartwright "Teacher," and the name stuck.

More than that, his teammates and opponents around the league knew Cartwright for his elbows. He held them high when he rebounded or boxed out, something that Jackson liked and could understand. Cartwright's elbows weren't as notorious as the Pistons' style of play, but they were close. "You had to be cognizant of those elbows because they could hit you any time," recalled Bulls backup center Will Perdue. "I got hit constantly in practice. That's just the way Bill played. He was taught to play with his arms up and his elbows out."

Jordan, however, was irritated that Cartwright sometimes had trouble catching the ball, and often set up in the lane, in the way of Jordan's drives to the hoop.

The relationship eased as Jordan realized that Cartwright could anchor the Bulls' defense. "I'll never forget the battles Willis Reed had to fight against Kareem to get to the championship in 1970," Jackson recalled, "the fight Willis had to wage against Wilt Chamberlain in both '70 and '73. We, the Knicks, had to have this guy who said, 'You're gonna have to come through my door, and you're gonna have to get over me to win a championship.' At some level, that sacrifice had to be made. That's what Bill Cartwright brought to the Bulls as a player. He was the one who said, 'You're gonna have to come through me.'

"Bill's an extremely stubborn person, and he believes you've got to work real hard to get what you want in life. He gave us that element, that 'I'm-gonna-work-real-hard-to-get-this-accomplished' attitude. He was dogged, dogged persistence. One of the things that got to us was that Detroit used to have a way of bringing up the level of animosity in a game. At some level, you were gonna have to contest them physically, if you were gonna stay in the game with them. If you didn't want to stay in the game with them, fine. They'd go ahead and beat you. But if you wanted to compete, you'd have to do something physically to play at their level. Bill stood up to the Pistons. Bill's statement was, 'This isn't the way we want to play. This isn't the way I want to play. But if it is the way we have to play to take care of these guys, I'm not afraid to do it. I'm gonna show these Detroit guys this is not acceptable. We won't accept you doing this to us.' You can't imagine how much that relieved guys like Scottie Pippen and Horace Grant, guys who were being besieged constantly and challenged constantly by more physical guys like Dennis Rodman and Rick Mahorn."

With Cartwright providing the necessary toughness, Jordan and his teammates matured into a determined unit over the 1990–91 season, although their progress was sometimes frustrating and difficult. Jordan again led the league in scoring at 31.5 points per game (to go with 6 rebounds and 5 assists per outing). Another key development came with the 6'7" Pippen. He had been stung by criticism, most of it stemming from his migraine headache in Game 7 of the 1990 Eastern Conference finals. A gifted swing player, Pippen performed with determination over the 1990–91 campaign, playing 3,014 minutes and averaging nearly 18 points, 7 rebounds, and 6 assists.

"I thought about it all summer," he said of the migraine. "I failed to produce last season."

Pippen made the transition from wing to point guard, Jackson said. "He became a guy who now had the ball as much as Michael. He became a dominant force."

Other key factors were power forward Horace Grant (12.8 points, 8.4 rebounds); point guard John Paxson (8.7 points while jump shooting .548 from the floor); and center Bill Cartwright (9.6 points and interior toughness on defense). Jackson also made great use of his bench with B. J. Armstrong, Craig Hodges, Will Perdue, Stacey King, Cliff Levingston, Scott Williams (a free-agent rookie out of North Carolina), and Dennis Hopson, who had come over in a trade with New Jersey, all contributing.

These efforts resulted in impressive displays of execution. In December, the Bulls' defense held the Cleveland Cavaliers to just five points in one quarter at Chicago Stadium. Crowds there presented an atmosphere that no opponent wanted to face. The Bulls lost to Boston there in the third game of the season. They wouldn't lose at home again until Houston stopped them March 25—a run of 30 straight home wins.

The Bulls won the Eastern Conference with a 61–21 record, and Jordan claimed his fifth straight scoring title with a 31.5 average. During the play-offs, he was named the league's MVP for the second time. The Bulls, how-ever, had seen all that window dressing before. The only awards they wanted came in the playoffs. They opened against the Knicks and won the first game by a record 41 points, then went on to sweep them 3–0. Next, Charles Barkley and the Sixers fell 4–1, setting up the only rematch the Bulls wanted: the Pistons in the Eastern Conference finals. To prepare for the playoffs, Jack-son had taken to splicing footage of the *Wizard of Oz* in and around sequences of his own players, which had them laughing until someone pointed out that Jackson was suggesting they had no courage, no heart. It was a challenge.

The Bulls answered by hammering the Pistons, who were reeling from injuries, in three straight games, and on the eve of Game 4 Jordan announced they were going to sweep. "That's not going to happen," responded an infu-riated Isiah Thomas. But it did.

At the end of Game 4 the next day in Detroit, Thomas and the Pistons stalked off the floor without congratulating the Bulls, a snub that angered Jordan and thousands of Chicago fans.

"I have nothing but contempt and disgust for the Pistons' organization," Reinsdorf said later. "Ultimately, David Stern felt the pressure and made rules changes to outlaw their style of play. It wasn't basketball. It was thug-gerism, hoodlumism. . . . That's one of the things that made us so popular. We were the white knights; we were the good guys. We beat the Bad Boys, 4–0, and they sulked off the court the way they did. I remember saying at the time that this was a triumph of good over evil. They were hated because they had used that style to vanquish first the Celtics and then the Lakers, who had been the NBA's most popular teams for years."

Actually, Brendan Malone, a former Pistons assistant, recalled that it was Jackson's mind games that angered the Pistons that day and induced them to walk off without shaking. Jackson's comments in the press had infuri-ated Detroit's players. They felt he had disrespected their two NBA titles, Malone explained. "They were angry at Phil and the disrespect he showed them."

Krause, meanwhile, was deliriously happy as he got on the team plane after the game. "He comes in the front of the plane and he's celebrating," Jackson recalled. "He's dancing, and the guys are going, 'Go, Jerry! Go,

Jerry!' He's dancing or whatever he's doing, and when he stops, they all collapse in hilarity, this laughter, and you couldn't tell whether it was with him or at him. It was one of those nebulous moments. It was wild."

The Portland Trail Blazers had ruled the regular season in the Western Conference with a 63–19 finish, but once again Magic Johnson and the Lakers survived in the playoffs, ousting Portland in the conference finals 4–2.

For most observers, the Finals seemed a dream matchup: Jordan and the Bulls against Magic and the Lakers.

Although the 1991 Finals wouldn't be a one-on-one matchup of the superstars, it still provided a great opportunity to see them battle. Many observers, including former Lakers coach Pat Riley, figured the Lakers' experience made them a sure bet. Los Angeles was making its ninth Finals appearance since 1980, and had five titles to show for it.

"The Lakers have experience on us," Pippen said as the series opened in Chicago Stadium, "but we have enough to win."

Just as important, the Lakers' James Worthy had a badly sprained ankle, which took away much of his mobility. Some insiders figured Worthy's injury would cost the Lakers the series. Others figured that without Abdul-Jabbar (who had retired after the 1989 season), Los Angeles just wasn't as potent as a playoff team. Game 1, however, seemed to confirm Riley's prediction. The Lakers won 93–91 on a three-pointer by center Sam Perkins with 14 seconds left in the game. The Bulls got the ball to Jordan, but his 18-foot jumper with four seconds left went in the basket and spun out. It seemed that Jordan was human after all and that the Lakers' experience just might deliver them.

Suddenly, the pressure was on the Bulls for Game 2, and they struggled with it. Then, a huge basketball accident occurred. Jordan got into early foul trouble, and, forced to make a decision, the Bulls' coaches switched the 6'7" Pippen to cover the 6'9" Magic Johnson. In retrospect, that would seem logical, but at the time there was an assumption that the twenty-five-year-old Pippen would struggle to handle the wily Johnson, the master point guard of his time.

Just the opposite happened. The long-armed Pippen was on Johnson like a hydra, and just like that, the momentum in the championship series shifted. Pippen harassed Magic into 4 of 13 shooting from the floor while Pippen himself scored 20 points with 10 assists and 5 rebounds as the Bulls won Game 2 in a swarm.

The tale of terror was written on Johnson's face. "I can't believe this is happening," he told reporters as the Bulls swept four straight games from Los Angeles.

"It's true," Jackson said in 1998 when asked if the switch of Pippen covering Johnson was entirely accidental.

"We started to see that we were wearing him down from a physical standpoint," Pippen happily recalled, "especially myself being able to go up and harass him and trying to get him out of their offense. He wasn't as effective as he had been in the past against some teams, being able to post up and take advantage of situations. I saw the frustration there."

The Bulls blew out the Lakers in Game 2, 107–86. The Chicago starters shot better than 73 percent from the floor, with Paxson going 8 for 8 to score 16 points. "Does Paxson ever miss?" the Lakers' Sam Perkins asked.

Paxson shrugged at reporters' questions and said his job was to hit open jumpers. "When I'm in my rhythm, I feel like I'm going to make them all."

Jordan himself had hit 15 of 18 to finish with 33.

Even with the loss, the Lakers were pleased. They had gotten a split in Chicago Stadium and were headed home for three straight games in the Forum. The pressure was on Chicago.

But the Bulls met the challenge in Game 3. Jordan hit a jumper with 3.4 seconds left to send the game into overtime. The Bulls then ran off eight straight points for a 104–96 win and a 2–1 lead in the series. Jordan was elated, but he refused to dwell on the victory. The Lakers had plenty of experience in coming back, he said.

Yet experience proved no match for the Bulls' young legs and determination. For Game 4, Chicago's weapon was defense. The Bulls harassed the Lakers into shooting 37 percent from the floor. Chicago won, 97–82. The Lakers' point total was their lowest since before the shot clock was adopted in 1954. They managed a total of 30 points over the second and third quarters. Perkins made just 1 of his 15 shots.

Suddenly, Jackson's Bulls were on the verge of the improbable.

"It's no surprise, the way they've been defending," Lakers coach Mike Dunleavy said of the Bulls. "They are very athletic and very smart."

And very hot.

On the eve of Game 5, Jordan publicly acknowledged the team's debt to Cartwright. "He has given us an edge in the middle," he said. "He has been solid for us. . . . This guy has turned out to be one of the most important factors for this ball club, and he has surprised many who are standing here and who play with him."

Told of Jordan's comments, Cartwright said, "That stuff really isn't important to me. I've always figured what goes around comes around. What's really important to me is winning a championship."

"We went up 3–1 and had a long wait, from Sunday to Wednesday, for Game 5," recalled Bulls equipment manager John Ligmanowski. "Those three days took forever. Before we had even won it, Michael would get on the bus and say, 'Hey, how does it feel to be world champs?' He knew. That was a pretty good feeling. We just couldn't wait to get it over with."

As Jordan predicted, the Bulls turned to their offense to claim the title in Game 5, 108–101. Pippen led the scoring parade with 32 points, and Paxson did the damage down the stretch, hitting five buckets in the final four minutes to score 20 points and seal the win. Time and again, Jordan penetrated, drawing the defense, then kicked the ball out to Paxson, who hit the open shots. In the bedlam on the Forum floor following the victory, Lakers super-fan Jack Nicholson hugged Jackson, and Magic Johnson tracked down Jordan to offer his congratulations. "I saw tears in his eyes," Johnson said. "I told him, 'You proved everyone wrong. You're a winner as well as a great individual basketball player.'"

By the time Jordan squeezed through the crowd to the locker room he was openly weeping. "I never lost hope," he said, his father James and wife Juanita nearby. "I'm so happy for my family and this team and this franchise. It's something I've worked seven years for, and I thank God for the talent and the opportunity that I've had."

It had been a long haul.

The tears flowed freely for Jordan. "I've never been this emotional publicly," he said.

"When I came here, we started from scratch," he said. "I vowed we'd make the playoffs every year, and each year we got closer. I always had faith I'd get this ring one day."

Jackson and Jordan agreed that the key to the game had been Paxson hitting the open shots. "That's why I've always wanted him on my team and why I wanted him to stay on my team," Jordan said.

"It was done and over, and it was dramatic, like a blitzkrieg," Jackson recalled. "Afterward, there was a lot of joy. There was Michael holding the trophy and weeping. For me, it was doubly special because the Forum was where I had won the championship as a player nearly twenty years earlier, in 1973. This was the same locker room where the Knicks had celebrated. With the Bulls, what made it extra special was the way we won it, to split our first two games at home and then to sweep three on the road. It was special."

Afterward, the Bulls' quarters at the Ritz Carlton became Party Central. "I remember going up to Michael's room," equipment manager John Ligmanowski said. "He told me to order like a dozen bottles of Dom Perignon and enough hors d'oeuvres for forty people. We're at the Ritz Carlton, and I call down to the concierge. I said, 'Yeah, send up a dozen bottles of Dom and hors d'oeuvres for forty people.' So they were like, 'Wait a second.' They didn't want to send it up because they knew it wasn't Michael on the phone. So I handed the phone to him. He grabbed the phone and said, 'Send it up!'"

As the parties wound down in the wee hours before sunrise, Jackson headed to the elevator to go up to his room. The doors popped open and there were Jerry and Thelma Krause, headed for the hot tub in their bathing suits.

"It was a perfect cap to the evening," Jackson recalled years later with a chuckle.

The Bulls returned to Chicago and celebrated their championship in Grant Park before a crowd estimated at between a half-million and a million. "We started from the bottom," Jordan told the screaming masses, "and it was hard working our way to the top. But we did it."

The Second Championship

Perhaps the most amazing thing about the Bulls' second championship was the amount of discord and controversy they had to overcome to win it. Long-festering resentment surfaced during the 1991 championship celebration when Michael Jordan decided not to join the team in the traditional Rose Garden ceremony with President George Bush. Much of the discord stemmed from the relationship between Horace Grant and Jordan.

"I think it was a situation," Jackson later observed, "where Horace felt demeaned, felt that he was made light of, and he wanted to be a person of importance. There were some things about Horace that bothered Michael. Basically, Horace says whatever comes into his mind in front of the press. One of the situations that was exacerbating to Michael came after our first championship when Horace and his wife and Michael and his wife went to New York. They went to dinner and to see a play. While they were out, Michael basically told Horace that he wasn't going to see President Bush. Michael said, 'It's not obligatory. It's on my time, and I have other things to do.'

"Horace at the time had no problem with it," Jackson added. "He knew about this in a private situation and said nothing. Yet when the press came into the picture later, after the story became public, and asked Horace if it bothered him, he made a big issue of it. Basically, the press had put the words in his mouth, and he felt it was a good time to make this kind of statement. It was immediately team divisive and made Michael look bad and basically got that whole thing started. That bothered Michael about Horace, that he would do something personal like that. Horace had problems in that area, where a lot of times he said things that the press had put in his mind, or in his consciousness. I would call him in and remind him that he could be fined for making comments that were detrimental to the team. I'd say, 'Horace, I have every reason to fine you, but I'm not going to because I know the press put words in your mouth.' He would say, 'I'm not ever gonna tell lies.' I told him, 'No one's saying you have to tell lies. You have to be conscious of what you're saying. You don't want to be divisive.' "

Another major source of controversy was the book *The Jordan Rules* by *Chicago Tribune* sportswriter Sam Smith. Marketed as the inside story of the Bulls' championship season, the book and its unflattering portraits of Jordan and Jerry Krause rocked the franchise just as the 1991–92 season opened.

"Those kinds of stories there's no reason for," Jackson would say later, without disclosing his role as an anonymous source. "And people believe it's the truth. I read about seventy pages of it, and I realized there's a lot of things represented that I didn't believe to be true, or that I knew didn't happen to the team. I felt, 'This is like anything else. It's one guy's perspective on life. Another guy knows it's not real.' When I sat down with Jerry Krause the week after that book came out, he had a list with 176 things on it. Of lies. One hundred and seventy-six lies."

"I went to the best libel lawyer in the country," Krause said. "He said I couldn't do a thing because I was a public figure. Sam Smith made some money on that book. I hope he chokes on every dollar."

At the time, Jackson did not acknowledge his major role as an anonymous source. Later, he tried to bring about a reconciliation between Krause and Sam Smith. "I tried to patch those two guys, Smith and Krause, up a couple of years ago. Sam said, 'You know, Jerry, I've never really hurt anybody.' Jerry knew right there he couldn't believe that," Jackson said later, adding with a smile that at least the Smith book was something Krause and Jordan could agree on.

"*The Jordan Rules* was very divisive to the team," Jackson said later. "But the one great thing about this group of guys. They never let the external stuff bother the team's play on the floor."

Indeed it didn't. Krause set the roster with a November trade, sending disgruntled Dennis Hopson to Sacramento for reserve guard Bobby Hansen.

The Bulls raced out to a 37–5 record—including a 14-game winning streak, the longest in history. They slipped over late January and February, going only 11–8. By the first of March, the Bulls were back on track and closed out the schedule with a blistering 19–2 run to finish 67–15, the franchise's best record. Jordan claimed his sixth straight scoring crown and won his third league MVP award. He and Pippen were named to the All-Defensive first team, and Pippen earned All-NBA second team honors.

"We really had an outrageous year," Jackson said. "We won 67 games, and basically I felt like I had to pull back on the reins, or they would have tried to win 70 or 75. The playoffs were an entirely different story from the regular season. We had injuries, and we had to face New York. And teams were coming at us with a lot of vim and vigor. We lost seven games in our championship run. It wasn't as easy this second time. There had been a challenge to our character as a team."

In the first round of the playoffs, the Bulls faced the Miami Heat, a 1989 expansion team making its first postseason appearance. Chicago quickly claimed the first two games in the best-of-five series, then headed to Miami for Game 3.

"In Miami's first playoff game ever, it was clacker night," recalled Bulls broadcaster Tom Dore. "What they said was, any time Michael gets the ball or shoots a free throw, go nuts with those clackers. Make all kinds of noise. Well, it worked in the first quarter. The Heat had a big lead. And in fact, we were wondering, can the Bulls come back from this? And Michael stopped by the broadcast table and looked at Johnny Kerr and me and said, 'Here we come.' That's all he said. Boy, did he ever. He went absolutely berserk, scored 56 points, and the Bulls won, swept the series."

Next up were the New York Knicks, now coached by Pat Riley and employing a physical style strikingly similar to the Pistons. The Knicks used their muscle to claim Game 1 in Chicago Stadium. B. J. Armstrong helped even the series at 1–1 by hitting big shots in the fourth quarter of Game 2. Then the Bulls regained the home-court advantage in Game 3 in New York when Jordan finally broke free of New York's cloying defense for his first dunks of the series.

The Knicks, powered by Xavier McDaniel, fought back to even it with a win in Game 4.

In the critical Game 5, Jordan took control by going to the basket. The Knicks kept fouling him, and he kept making the free throws—15 in all—to finish with 37 points as the Bulls won 96–88. "Michael is Michael," Riley said afterward. "His game is to take it to the basket and challenge the defense. When you play against a guy like him, he tells you how much he wants to win by how hard he takes the ball to the basket."

The Knicks managed to tie it again with a Game 6 win in New York, but the Bulls were primed for Game 7 in the Stadium and walked to the win, 110–81. "We got back to playing Bulls basketball," Chicago guard B. J. Armstrong explained.

They resumed their struggle in the conference finals against the Cavaliers, who managed to tie the series at 2–2, but the Bulls had just enough to escape Cleveland 4–2. "John Paxson turned to me in the locker room and said, 'What a long, strange trip it's been,'" Jackson confided to reporters. "And he wasn't just quoting the Grateful Dead. It has been a long, strange trip. Last year was the honeymoon. This year was an odyssey."

The NBA Finals against the Portland Trail Blazers brought more turbulence, which was intermittently calmed by Jordan's memorable performances. The Blazers—driven by Clyde Drexler, newly acquired Danny Ainge, Cliff Robinson, Terry Porter, and Buck Williams—answered with a few performances of their own. Ultimately, though, the glory was Jordan's. In Game 1, he scored 35 points in the first half—including a record six three-pointers—enough to bury the Blazers, 122–89.

"The only way you can stop Michael," said Portland's Cliff Robinson, "is to take him off the court."

"I was in a zone," said Jordan, who had focused on extra hours of practice shooting long range before Game 1. "My threes felt like free throws. I didn't know what I was doing, but they were going in."

In Game 2, the Blazers' hopes dimmed when Drexler fouled out with about four minutes left. But they rallied with a 15–5 run to tie the game, then somehow won 115–104 on the strength of Danny Ainge's nine points in overtime. "Momentum is a fickle thing," Ainge mused afterward.

"It was a gift in our hands and we just gave it away," Horace Grant said.

The Blazers had their split, with the series headed to Portland for three games. But the Bulls' defense and a solid team effort—Pippen and Grant scored 18 each to go with Jordan's 26—ended thoughts of an upset with a win in Game 3, 94–84. Later, Jackson would explain that the Blazers rushed to take a late flight home after Friday night's Game 2, which cost them important sleep, while the Bulls waited until Saturday to travel. "They controlled the tempo; we shot poorly and never got in the groove," Portland coach Rick Adelman admitted.

Having regained their rest, the Blazers struggled to stay close through most of Game 4, then moved in front with just over three minutes left and won it 93–88 on a final surge. The outcome evened the series at 2–2.

But Game 5 was another Jordan showcase. Going to the hole repeatedly, he drew fouls and made 16 of 19 free throws to finish with 46 points, enough to give the Bulls a 119–106 win and a 3–2 lead. Again, the Blazers had stayed close, but Jordan's scoring had kept them at bay over the final minutes. His raised fist and defiant grimace afterward served notice to Portland.

Game 6 back in the Stadium should have been a Chicago walk, but the Bulls fell into a deep hole, down 17 points late in the third quarter. Then Jackson pulled his regulars and played Bobby Hansen, B. J. Armstrong, Stacey King, and Scott Williams with Pippen. Hansen stole the ball and hit a shot, and the rally was on. Strangely, Jordan was on the bench leading the cheering.

With about eight minutes to go, Jackson sent Jordan back in, and the Bulls powered their way to their second title, 97–93, bringing the Stadium to an unprecedented eruption.

"The final against Portland was a dramatic night for us and all Chicago fans," Phil Jackson recalled. "We came from 17 down at the end of the third quarter to win the championship. What followed was an incredible celebration."

"The team had gone down to the dressing room to be presented with the Larry O'Brien Trophy by David Stern and Bob Costas," remembered Bulls vice president Steve Schanwald. "Jerry Reinsdorf and Jerry Krause and Phil Jackson and Michael and Scottie stood on a temporary stage and accepted the trophy. But we didn't have instant replay capability, so the fans were not able to share in that moment. Up in the Stadium, we were playing Gary Glitter on the loudspeaker, and the crowd was just reveling in the championship. It had been a great comeback in the fourth quarter, really initiated by our bench. So the victory was a total team effort. I went down and asked Jerry Reinsdorf if we could bring the team back up. He said, 'It's all right with me, but ask Phil.' I said, 'Phil, the fans are upstairs. They're not leaving; they're dancing. We've got to bring the team back up and let them enjoy this thing.' Phil thought for a moment, and Bobby Hansen was standing nearby. Phil asked Bobby what he thought, and Bobby said, 'Let's do it!' Phil has the ability to whistle very loud. He put two fingers in his mouth and whistled over all that noise and champagne and everything. He got everything quieted down. He said, 'Grab that trophy. We're going back up to celebrate with our fans!' With that, Michael grabbed the trophy, and we went back upstairs.

When we started emerging through the tunnel, we started to play the opening to our introduction music. It's very dramatic. It's 'Eye in the Sky' by the Alan Parsons Project. So the crowd knew when the music started playing something was happening. The team came up through the tunnel, and all of a sudden the crowd just exploded. It was a ten thousand–goose bump experience. All of a sudden some of the players, Scottie and Horace and Hansen, those guys got up on the table so that everybody could see them in the crowd. Then Michael came up and joined them with the trophy, and they started dancing. It was just an electrifying experience, and I think for anybody that was there it was a moment that they will never forget as long as they live."

"They told me the fans were still celebrating up top," Jackson said. "Everybody said, 'Let's go up.' I heard that and went upstairs with the players into this scene of bedlam. But I got tripped up by some television people, from the cables on their equipment. It occurred to me that this was a little bit wilder than I wanted it to be. I got hit and got tripped. I thought, 'I guess this really isn't something I have to be a part of. This is a time for the fans and the players.' I stood and watched them for a while celebrating on the tables. Then I went back downstairs and collected myself and my thoughts. My family stayed up there and was a part of the celebration. But I went back downstairs and enjoyed some private thoughts. How the first championship had been more of a glory ride, and the second one was more of a journey. It had been a special time of nine months together. Things had been up and down, but we had had this one goal together, and despite our differences, we had focused on that one goal. I told the guys, 'A back-to-back championship is the mark of a great team. We had passed the demarcation point. Winning that second title set us apart.'"

The team opted for another rally in Grant Park a few days later to rejoice with their fans. Again, hundreds of thousands gathered to scream and celebrate. "We will be back," Bill Cartwright promised.

"Let's go for a three-peat," Pippen suggested, and the crowd's roar in response made it clear that no one in Chicago doubted that it was possible.

The Third Championship

Jerry Krause had hoped that Scottie Pippen and Michael Jordan would decline their invitations to play for the United States on the Dream Team in the Olympic Games in Barcelona over the summer of 1992. Krause wasn't being unpatriotic; he just wanted the Bulls' superstars to rest. They both agreed to the honor, however; and despite the United States's easy breeze to the gold medal that August, both players came home thoroughly tired by the experience.

Horace Grant, who had said many times that no one understood his importance to the Bulls, seemed jilted by the attention showered on Jordan and Pippen. And when Jackson allowed the two stars to take a casual approach to training camp in early October, Grant complained to the media about "double standards" and "preferential treatment."

Later in the season, he would accuse Pippen of arrogance. Ultimately, this sniping would prove to be a minor rift between the two friends, but both agreed that they weren't as close as they had been.

Besides the "divisiveness" that Jackson loathed, the Bulls encountered a rash of physical ailments. Cartwright, thirty-five, and Paxson, thirty-two, had offseason surgery on their creaky knees, and Pippen was troubled by a bad ankle for most of the season. For Jordan, the pains were first his arch and then his wrist.

B. J. Armstrong, who had long struggled with the Bulls' triple-post offense, finally found enough of a comfort level to replace Paxson in the starting lineup. Finding his playing rhythm coming off the bench clearly stumped Paxson, and the media kept steady track of the difficulties brought on by the shift. But no rift developed between the two guards. The twenty-five-year-old Armstrong was simply better equipped to play in the Bulls' pressure defense, and that would make the difference in the playoffs. Plus, he would lead the league in three-point shooting, hitting better than 45 percent.

For the regular season, however, Jackson backed off from the pressure defense, thinking that he needed to conserve the players' energy and health. But the other problem for this veteran club was boredom, and the slowed pace worked against them. At one point during the season, Jordan called a conference on the court and told his teammates to resume the pressure. Later, Jordan debated Jackson's strategy with reporters. "Maybe we gamble and we lose our legs," Jordan said. "I still don't think we get conservative now. When we try to slow down, things get too deliberate."

All of these wrinkles ultimately proved no hindrance. Their only real opponent was the sameness. Jordan called it "monotony." For most teams, that might have meant 38 wins. For the Bulls, it meant another divisional championship, 57 wins (their fourth straight 50-win season) and a seventh straight scoring crown for Jordan, tying him with Wilt Chamberlain.

On January 8, Jordan scored his twenty-thousandth career point, having reached that total in just 620 games. The only man to do it faster was Wilt Chamberlain, who reached the milestone in 499 games. "It looks like I fell short of Wilt again, which is a privilege," Jordan said. "I won't evaluate this until I'm away from the game. I'm happy about it, but we still have a long season to go. I'm sure as I get older, I'll cherish it more."

In another game, an overtime loss to Orlando, Jordan scored 64 points, although Pippen complained afterward that Jordan had taken too many shots.

Jordan would be named All-NBA first team again, and both he and Pippen would make the All-Defensive first team. In the NBA Finals, Jordan would collect an unprecedented third straight MVP award.

For Jackson, December would bring his two hundredth win; he had reached the mark faster than any coach in league history. Even with the accomplishments, it was not a regular season to treasure.

"Guys were hurt," Jackson explained. "Pippen with his ankle, Jordan with his plantar fascia. All of those things prevented us from getting a rhythm. We weren't in great condition. So when practices were done hard and precise, we ended up suffering in our game effort."

"I have always liked practice," Jordan said, "and I hate to miss it. It's like taking a math class. When you miss that one day, you feel like you missed a lot. You take extra work to make up for that one day. I've always been a practice player. I believe in it."

"They were tired," recalled Bulls trainer Chip Schaefer, who had replaced Mark Pfeil in 1991 and would become a close Jackson friend. "No question. Michael and Scottie were tired in the fall of '92. That was just a tough, long year, and really a tough year for Michael. It seemed like one thing after another. The press was picking on him, things just happening all year long. As soon as one thing would let up, it seemed like another came into play. There was one book or one incident constantly. It got to be not about basketball but personal things that really shouldn't have been part of it at all. You could just see it starting to wear on him a little bit. In some private moments, he expressed that. It was really evident that he was getting tired. Tired physically, tired mentally of the whole thing."

Jackson's answer was another series of psychological ploys to motivate his players. "Phil played a lot of mind games," Jordan recalled. "He waged psychological warfare to make you realize the things you have to do to be a winner."

"It's a funny thing to look at the history of the NBA and the way teams kind of rise and fall," Schaefer noted. "For all intents and purposes, it looked like it was going to be New York's year. They paid their dues. The Knicks absolutely destroyed us, beat us by 37 points in late November that year. They played like it was Game 7 in the playoffs. We went in kind of yawning. No big deal. Michael sprained his foot early in the game, and they just crushed us. We still won 57 games that year, but we just kind of foundered."

For two years, the New York Knicks had seen their championship hopes end in seven-game playoff battles with the Bulls. With good reason, they figured they needed the home-court advantage to dethrone Jordan and his teammates. So coach Pat Riley turned the full force of his considerable intensity to driving New York to 60 wins and the home-court advantage in the Eastern Conference.

The Bulls, meanwhile, slipped quietly into second place and seemed almost distracted heading into the playoffs. But they quickly picked up the pace, sweeping three from Atlanta in the first round, then devastating the Cleveland Cavaliers again by winning four straight. Jordan capped the series with a last-second game winner in Cleveland that closed the chapter on his domination of the Cavs.

"Once the playoffs rolled around," Schaefer recalled, "Michael managed to turn it on again. But we faced New York again. We didn't have home court so there really wasn't much reason to be optimistic about it."

Jordan loathed the Knicks' brutish style. "They play like the Pistons," he said testily. Perhaps New York's frustration made them worse. Plus, Jackson and Riley made no great effort to hide their dislike for one another. In Game 1 in Madison Square Garden, the Knicks banged Jordan into a 10 for 27 shooting performance and won 98–90. "I told the team I let them down," Jordan said afterward.

The acknowledgment did little good, because the same thing happened in Game 2. Jordan missed 20 of 32 shots, and the Knicks won again, 96–91. Afterward, the smugness in New York was tangible. "Now the Bulls are down two games and have to beat the Knicks four games out of five games if they are going to have a chance at three titles in a row," crowed *New York Daily News* columnist Mike Lupica.

A media firestorm then erupted after a *New York Times* report that Jordan had been seen at an Atlantic City casino in the wee hours before Game 2, suggesting that perhaps he wasn't properly rested for competition. The headlines brought Jackson and Krause quickly to his defense. "There is no problem with Michael Jordan," Krause told reporters. "He cares about winning and is one of the great winners of all time."

"We don't need a curfew," Jackson added. "These are adults. . . . You have to have other things in your life or the pressure becomes too great."

With this issue hovering over the events, the series moved to Chicago.

"The Bulls came back for practice at the Berto Center," recalled Cheryl Raye. "I've never seen as much media gathered for an event. Michael stepped out of the training room, and I said, 'Michael would you just go over the chain of events for us? Would you tell us what happened and where this story is coming from?' He did, and then a television newsperson from a local Chicago station started grilling him as though he were an alderman being convicted of a crime. Chuck Gowdy from Channel 7 was saying things like, 'Do you do this before every game? Do you have a gambling problem?' He kept hammering and hammering away, and eventually Michael just shut up and walked away. He didn't talk until the first game against Phoenix."

Jordan ceased speaking with the media, and his teammates followed suit. With Pippen taking charge, the Bulls won big in Game 3 in the Stadium, 103–83.

"The moment I knew we were going to win that series was after Game 3," Schaefer recalled. "After we'd beat them pretty soundly and brought the series back to 2–1, Patrick Ewing made a comment that, 'We don't have to win here in Chicago.' As soon as I heard him say that, I knew we were going to win the series. If you have that attitude, you may lose a game and lose your edge. You can't assume you're going to win all of your home games. As soon as he said that, it told me he was counting on winning all their home games, which wasn't going to happen. It was Scottie who got us that series. He always seemed to have a knack when Michael might have been having a tough time, to step up and do what needed to be done."

Jordan scored 54 points to drive Chicago to a win in Game 4, 105–95; and Jordan's triple-double (29 points, 10 rebounds, 14 assists) dominated the statistics column in Game 5, when Chicago took the series lead 3–2. But it was Pippen's successive blocks of putback attempts by New York's Charles Smith late in Game 5 in New York that closed off the Knicks' hopes. Then, when the Bulls completed their comeback in Game 6 in Chicago, it was Pippen again doing the final damage, a corner jumper and a trey, in a 96–88 victory.

The Bulls had persevered to return to their third straight NBA Finals. This time, Charles Barkley, now with the Phoenix Suns, was the opponent. After several frustrating and troubled years in Philadelphia, Barkley had been traded to the Suns before the 1992–93 season—and just like that he was reborn, earning league MVP honors and leading the Suns to 62 wins and a trip to the Finals.

It was a memorable series—not so much for the basketball, but for the extracurricular activities, which included sightings of Barkley and Madonna at a Phoenix restaurant. In the championship matchup with Jordan, Barkley was a fitting opponent. Having come into the league together in the fall of 1984, the two superstars had formed a solid friendship over the years. While Barkley had shown no forethought, no hesitation in trashing his own public image during his early NBA seasons, the more circumspect Jordan had proceeded cautiously, always saying and doing the correct corporate things while persistently building Chicago into a winner. At times, when Barkley's occasional bar fights or misguided public statements boiled over into controversy, Jordan had even taken on the task of trying to explain his friend to writers and reporters, the primary message being that Charles may tend to run his mouth before thinking, but he's an honest, genuine person and a tough competitor.

For these defenses and for Jordan's friendship, Barkley was quite grateful—in fact, some said too grateful to be successful in the 1993 championship series. Later, Scottie Pippen, Jordan's teammate, would berate Barkley for "kissin' Michael's ass," an accusation that left Sir Charles bristling. Yet it would remain one of the great unanswered questions of his career. The Lakers' Magic Johnson and the Pistons' Isiah Thomas had formed a similar friendship in the 1980s, but that relationship fell apart when their teams met in the 1988 and 1989 Finals. There was no way, Johnson later admitted, that their intense competition could not get in the way of their friendship.

Faced with the same tough choice of building and nurturing an intense dislike for his championship competition, Barkley had chosen to remain a good guy and Jordan's friend. The Suns had won 62 games and had the home-court advantage for their brand new America West Arena. The Bulls, though, had plenty of confidence. They had always done well against Barkley's Philadelphia teams. Pippen's and Grant's defense would shackle him again, and B. J. Armstrong had the quickness to stay with Phoenix point guard Kevin Johnson.

Those plans eventually worked out, but in the short term there was more turbulence ahead. No sooner had Jordan's Atlantic City casino jaunt slipped out of the news than Richard Esquinas, a San Diego businessman, stepped forward with a book claiming that Jordan owed him $1.2 million from high-stakes losses from betting on golf games.

In a taped interview on NBA at halftime of Game 1 of the Finals, Jordan answered, admitting that he had lost substantial sums to Esquinas, but nowhere near the figure claimed. Questions about whether this distraction would hinder the Bulls were quickly put aside when Chicago claimed the first game, 100–92. Jordan hit for 31, Pippen for 27, while the Bulls' defense harassed Barkley into shooting 9 for 25.

"I don't think anybody was scared or had the jitters," said Phoenix guard Kevin Johnson, a statement that was met with no amens. Frankly, the Suns seemed quite nervous. And they sank deeper into trouble in Game 2. Barkley and Jordan both scored 42 points, but the Bulls' defense clamped down on Kevin Johnson and Phoenix guard Dan Majerle to take a 2–0 series lead, 111–108. Bulls assistant Johnny Bach had devised a defensive scheme, deployed by Armstrong, that had Johnson talking to himself and sitting much of the fourth quarter.

Suddenly, Phoenix faced three games in Chicago and the prospect of a sweep. The Suns answered by scratching out a 129–121, triple-overtime win in Game 3. This time Johnson had played an NBA Finals record 62 minutes and scored 25 points with 7 rebounds and 9 assists. Majerle had scored 28 and Barkley 24.

"I thought it was never going to end," Jackson said afterward.

Sensing a vulnerability in his team, Jordan came on strong in Game 4, scoring 55 points and driving the Bulls to a 108–98 win and a 3–1 series lead. The Suns had allowed Jordan time and again to glide inside for handsome little dunks and bank shots. Phoenix was only down two, but Armstrong's pressure and a key late steal propelled Jackson's team to a 111–105 victory. Jordan's point total tied Golden State's Rick Barry for second place on the all-time single-game list. The record was held by Elgin Baylor, who had scored 61 in a game against Boston in 1962.

The Bulls were up 3–1 with Game 5 on their home floor. However, they strangely teetered at the brink of their accomplishment. Jordan swore to his teammates that he wouldn't accompany them back to Phoenix if they failed to deliver the championship in the Stadium. Regardless, the Bulls stumbled, and the Suns busied themselves with defense. Jordan's easy baskets disappeared as Phoenix congregated in the lane. Suns rookie Richard Dumas scored 25 points. "It was just a matter of slipping into the open spots," he explained. "There were a lot of them."

With Johnson scoring 25 and Sir Charles 24, the Suns got the win they needed, 108–98, to return the series back to their home court. Afterward, Barkley forecast a Suns title. "It's just that I believe in destiny," he said.

There had been speculation that if the Bulls won Game 5 in Chicago, the city would be racked by the riotous celebration that had marred the team's previous championships. In fear of that, many merchants had boarded up their stores.

"We did the city a favor," Barkley said as he left town. "You can take all those boards down now. We're going to Phoenix."

So was Jordan, contrary to his vow, and the Bulls were fighting feelings that they had let their best opportunity slip away.

"Michael seems to sense what a team needs," recalled Bulls broadcaster Tom Dore. "They had just lost. But Michael walked on the plane going to Phoenix and said, 'Hello, world champs.' He's got a foot-long cigar, and he's celebrating already because he knows the series is over. He knew, going to Phoenix, that they were going to win. It wasn't a question with him, and I think that's what the team had. They just had this arrogance. They weren't mean about it. They just felt like they were going to win."

Barkley had claimed that "destiny" belonged to the Suns, but over the first three quarters of Game 6 it seemed the Phoenix players were feeling pressure more than anything else. Meanwhile, the Bulls' phalanx of guards—Jordan, Armstrong, Paxson, and seldom-used reserve Trent Tucker—fired in nine three-pointers over the first three periods to take Chicago to a 87–79 lead.

From there, however, it was the Bulls' turn to succumb to the pressure. They missed nine shots and had two turnovers the first eleven times they got the ball in the fourth quarter. The Suns closed within a point, then surged to take a 98–94 lead with 90 seconds left. Then Jordan pulled down a defensive rebound and wound his way through traffic to the other end for a short bank shot. It was 98–96 with 38 seconds to go. Majerle's shooting had helped Phoenix back into the series, but on their next-to-last possession he shot an air ball.

The Bulls had another chance with 14.1 seconds to go. After a timeout, Jordan inbounded the ball to Armstrong, then got it back and passed ahead to Pippen. The ball was supposed to go back to Chicago's Superman, but Pippen saw that Jordan was covered and motored into the lane, where he was greeted by Suns center Mark West.

Alone on the near baseline was Grant, who had scored a single point in the game, and who had almost thrown the ball over the backboard on a stickback opportunity moments earlier. Pippen whipped him the ball, and, scrambling out of his personal terror, Grant passed up the shot to send the ball out to John Paxson, all alone in three-point land to the right of the key. "I knew it was in as soon as Pax shot it," Jordan said.

Paxson's trey and a key Grant block of Johnson's last shot moments later delivered the Bulls' third championship.

"That's instinct," Paxson said of the shot afterward. "You catch and you shoot. I've done it hundreds of thousands of times in my life. Horace gave me a good pass."

Reporters converged upon Jordan afterward to ask if he planned to retire. "No," he assured them. "My love for this game is strong."

Time would reveal that it was more than a matter of love. Still, the effects of Paxson's big shot and three straight championships would linger sweetly in Chicago.

"It was like a dream come true," Paxson recalled in 1995. "You're a kid out in your driveway shooting shots to win championships. When you get down to it, it's still just a shot in a basketball game. But I think it allowed a lot of people to relate to that experience, because there are a lot of kids and adults who lived out their own fantasies in their backyards. It made the third of the three championships special. It's a real nice way of defining a three-peat, by making a three-point shot.

"I'm not sure what winning did for us outwardly, but inwardly it justified all the effort and hard work that we put into it. It confirmed our belief that we could win, and with that comes a confidence that carries over into your personal life as well as your professional life. I saw that in a lot of my teammates after we won the first one and we continued to win. It was like, outside of Michael and Scottie, who were already established stars, the other guys kind of blossomed. It was recognition. We all became a little more noticed as players. For so long, it was Michael Jordan. Can these other guys hold up their end and help him win? We proved to the basketball world that we could.

"That's the greatest part about winning, is how you feel as a group. You're happy for one another. You look at small plays that happen in a game, the people who come off the bench and provide something that the group needs. In our first championship run, Cliff Levingston provided some key minutes in the games out in Los Angeles. Craig Hodges did the same thing. You understand how important each individual is to your success. It's not just the best player. It's from one to twelve, the coaches included, and your appreciation for each is very high."

For Jackson, the exhilaration somehow outlasted his exhaustion. For four seasons, he had juggled between being a teacher, a coach, a friend, and a counselor.

"You have to be all of them," he said. "You have to be able to wear all of those hats. At times you have to be a person who is concerned, as you obviously are, about the welfare of the individuals who are under your care, people who are directly responsible to you for their production or performance level. Other times you have to be able to give advice as far as basketball goes or regarding personal life. And sometimes you have to be able to call people to perform at a greater level because they're not living up to their expectations—you have to get more from them."

He had gotten everything from this group of Bulls, but the circumstances were about to change dramatically. The negative energy had steadily collected about his team, and it was something that no burning sage could drive away.

Jackson (22) scrambled for rebounds in a 1963 high school playoff game against Grafton. He led Williston High School to the Class A North Dakota state championship and was honored as the tournament's outstanding player.
© *Bill Shemorry*

The 6′8″ Jackson was cocaptain of the University of North Dakota Fighting Sioux.
Photo courtesy of the University of North Dakota Media Relations Department

Not long after arriving in New York, Jackson became known as the team hippie.
© *Corbis*

Jackson, shown here with a beard and short hair, has frequently changed his look as an adult.
© *Bettmann/Corbis*

Jackson's long arms helped him in the transition from small-college player to pro substitute.

© *Bettmann/Corbis*

In 1976 action between the Knicks and Philadelphia, Jackson got a step on 76er Joe Bryant, father of future Lakers star Kobe Bryant. Bryant was whistled for a foul on the play.
© UPI/Corbis-Bettmann

Jackson used his long reach to pull in this 1974 rebound as Knicks teammates Jerry Lucas (32) and Walt Frazier (10) look on.
© UPI/Corbis-Bettmann

Jackson was known as a tough, crafty NBA reserve. He's shown here in the post against the Buffalo Braves.
© Sports Illustrated/Walter Iooss Jr.

Jackson celebrated quietly in his cramped office in the bowels of old Chicago Stadium after the Bulls won their second championship in June 1992.
© Sports Illustrated/*Bill Smith*

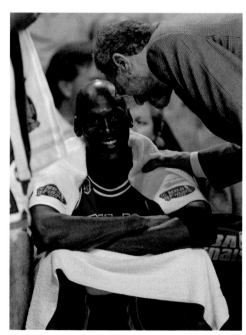

Jackson shared his thoughts with Michael Jordan during the fourth quarter of Game 4 in the 1996 NBA Finals, as the Bulls took a 3–1 lead in the series and neared completion of their masterful run to their fourth championship.
© *AP Photo/Beth Keiser*

Jackson watched as Michael Jordan led the Chicago Bulls in May 1996. The Bulls became the first team in NBA history to win 70 regular season games.

© Sports Illustrated/*Chuck Solomon*

Jackson found a strange measure of delight in some of his star forward's antics during Dennis Rodman's first season in Chicago.

© *AllSport/Jonathan Daniel*

8

STRANGE DAYS

At the conclusion of the 1993 playoffs, Michael Jordan sat atop the NBA mountain, too weary to look back and find much joy in his swift climb. One championship had somehow become three, and the immense energy needed to claim the third had emptied him. Years later, Jackson and his assistants would look back and realize that three championships in a row was about all that Jordan could stand in any one burst of success. They said this with some amazement, because they had just watched this very unique man bump up against his limits. For the longest time, Jackson and his lieutenants had wondered if Jordan had any limits at all.

For the casual fan, Jordan's magnificence became such an assumption that his winning almost seemed easy. To those with him, though, there was nothing easy about the grind of what he accomplished. Jordan had been successful because he had infused his teammates with huge doses of will, mental strength, and leadership.

From their earliest days together, Jackson had shown a strong intuitive sense of what Jordan would need to realize and sustain his talent. Jackson, then, became Jordan's companion and guide on this unusual quest. And Jordan did the same for Jackson, their ideas and separate visions invigorating one another. The tool Jackson employed most often was the mind game, the deceit, the motivational hide-and-seek, and then—when necessary—the rarest frank assessment, or even confrontation. As their time together went on, the nature of Jackson's effort became more political, more soothing and understanding. The respect he showed Jordan presented an obvious double standard.

"Phil would make references to things with Michael as 'We need to do this,'" Bill Wennington explained. "Whenever there was a problem with Michael in a meeting, it was like 'We need to do this.' If it was me, it was like, 'Bill, you have to go box out.' When it was a Michael thing, it was a 'we' thing. For us, it was, 'Steve, you need to take that shot.' Michael would maybe miss a boxout, and it was like, 'Well, WE need to box out now.' Just little things like that. But if you understand the reason for it, and the reason that the team was good, it's all part of it."

They all understood that the reason was Jordan, Wennington said.

In his earlier seasons in the league, most of his teammates hadn't achieved that understanding, and more than a few found Jordan to be an impossibility. He was walled off by his talent and celebrity and his demanding nature, which allowed the conflicts and resentment to fester.

Jackson's efforts to take down those walls when he first arrived as coach helped immensely in calming some of those conflicts.

But by and large, it was the triangle offense that answered the bigger question. It provided a format that allowed Jordan to relate to his less talented teammates. The structure of the triangle demands that the ball be passed to the open man. Once Jordan began complying with that, once he trusted enough to do that, the tension began to ease.

There quickly evolved a system in which Jordan would play within the triangle for three quarters, and then—depending on the pace and rhythm of the game—would break out of the offense in the fourth quarter to go on scoring binges.

Jordan's conspirator and early instigator in these departures was Bach himself, who whispered his opinion. "Johnny would say, 'Fuck the triangle. Just take the ball and score. Get everyone else to clear out,'" Jordan recalled.

Jackson would tolerate Bach's insubordination only so long, but it played a role in the evolution of the team's style of play.

These fourth quarters each night produced a sizable tension of their own, with Tex Winter on the bench anxious that Jordan was trying to do too much by himself. Many nights he would, and the team would stumble. But far more often, Jordan would do too much, and everyone in the arena would become mesmerized.

That had certainly been the case in 1993. To claim that third title, he had averaged 41 points per game during the NBA Finals, breaking the championship series record of 40.8 points per game set by San Francisco's Rick Barry in 1967.

Jordan had never seemed more masterful, yet Jackson and other close associates could see that he had grown weary of the grind, of the lack of privacy. In his public comments during the 1993 season, Jordan had made oblique references to his retirement. Then, in the euphoria of the locker room victory celebration in Phoenix, Jordan had relented, saying he would return for another campaign come fall.

Just two weeks later, in July, Jordan's popular father, James Jordan, was found murdered in South Carolina, ostensibly the victim of a random roadside killing. Yet the news of Mr. Jordan's death was followed quickly by wild speculation that somehow Jordan's golf wagering might be a factor. That, as much as anything, seemed to be the final insult.

"That's what killed us about Norm Van Lier, who works as a broadcaster here in Chicago," Jackson would explain later. "He was broadcasting theories about Michael's father's death and gambling and the NBA and all this stuff. Michael had to go talk to Van Lier and say, 'Norm. Cool this stuff about gambling and the NBA and the grand scheme and all this other stuff about my father's death. There's no conspiracy going on here.' That's the paranoia that builds in people's minds and sometimes drives you crazy."

As training camp neared that fall, Jordan informed Jerry Reinsdorf that he was prepared to retire. The owner recalled that he asked Jordan if he had spoken with Jackson, and Jordan replied that he was hesitant to do that.

"Knowing Phil, the psychology major, he was going to try to get in my head and see where I stood," Jordan recalled.

Jordan, though, knew what he wanted. While Jackson certainly knew how to push his buttons, the coach made no such effort. He pointed out that Jordan possessed a great gift from God and that leaving the game would deny millions of fans the benefit of that gift. Jordan was firm that it was his time to go. But before they concluded their half-hour discussion, Jordan had a question of his own for Jackson. He wanted to know how the coach would get him through another 82-game regular season, because he had absolutely no motivation to do it ever again, saw no challenge in it. Jackson tried, but had no good answer for it. Jordan simply didn't want to end his career on a down note, with declining skills and facing excessive criticism, the way Julius Erving had ended his career.

So Jackson changed course one final time and asked Jordan if he had thought about a sabbatical. Jordan wanted no lingering, no loose ends.

Jackson realized it then, and told Jordan he was on his side. Then he told him that he loved him and began weeping. Although he had braced himself for a difficult encounter, Jordan was caught off-guard by the depth of the emotion. He realized then that people could spend years working together and not know the depth of their feelings for each other until it came time to move on.

On October 6, 1993, Jordan announced his retirement from the Bulls. The move came so swiftly that he didn't even have time to notify his mother. "I was in Kenya with Michael's mom and a group of school kids," recalled Bulls vice president Steve Schanwald. "It had been so peaceful out there. We were on safari in a remote portion of Kenya, living in tents. No newspapers, no radio, no TV, no nothing. I told the people that the world could be coming to an end, and we wouldn't know. Two days later we flew back to Nairobi, back to civilization for the first time in about ten days. I got off the plane and got on the bus that was going to take us to have lunch. The bus driver was reading a newspaper, a tabloid called the *Daily Nation*, Kenya's national newspaper. On the back page, there was a picture of Michael, and the headline said, 'Michael Jordan Retires.' I thought it was somebody's idea of a bad joke. But two days earlier, Michael had announced his retirement. Apparently, Michael's mom didn't know. I went up to her and thanked her for lending us her son for nine great years. She said, 'What are you talking about?' I said, 'Mrs. Jordan, your son retired two days ago.' She said, 'He did! I don't believe it.' So I went and got the newspaper and showed her. That was how we found out about Michael retiring.

"That night at dinner I bought some champagne for everybody, and we toasted Michael on his great career. But by the time I got back to Chicago, the festive mood was gone. People were definitely depressed. It happened with such suddenness, it was so out of the blue, that it kind of took the wind out of people's sails."

Perhaps the greatest emptiness was felt in the NBA's administrative offices, where staff members began trying to figure out how to replace the greatest attraction in basketball history.

Jordan soon announced that he would try his hand at minor league baseball in the Chicago White Sox farm system with the hopes that he might someday make it to the big leagues.

"It was really his father's dream that he play baseball," Jackson pointed out. "His father wanted to play pro ball and did play semi-pro. When his father passed away, I think Michael was kind of living out his father's dream. That's one of the things I thought when I heard it. 'Geez, this guy wants to go play baseball in the major leagues!?' But then I realized basketball players are always fantasizing that they could play baseball."

The situation brought to mind Jackson's own playing days. He remembered DeBusschere, who had been a big-league pitcher, and Bradley getting into a debate that spilled over into a challenge one day. Bradley was contending that he could hit DeBusschere.

"OK, Bill, let's see if you can hit," DeBusschere said. "We'll go out to Shea Stadium."

"I jumped in," Jackson recalled with a smile, "saying 'I was a pitcher, too. I want to be part of this.' "

Bradley had cast a dubious glance at the wild-haired, bearded Jackson and said, "I won't stand in for any pitches that you throw."

"I used to tell Danny Whalen, who was the manager of the Pittsburgh Pirates, 'Danny, you think I could come back and play baseball?' I was twenty-five or twenty-six and I had this desire to go play baseball," Jackson recalled. "He said, 'Phil, you been a basketball player for how long now, four or five years? You haven't thrown a baseball hard in four years? Forget about it. Just stick to basketball. It's been pretty good to you.' I think there are a lot of players who would like to play [two] sports, like Deion Sanders has been able to do. Looking back on it, it was a beautiful thing Michael did. What a risk he took trying to play baseball. The whole idea that he's going to go out and give up everything to try that at his age. That's the wonderful thing about it. Michael is such a special person."

Jordan's abrupt retirement came just as training camp was set to open in 1993. Suddenly, Jerry Krause found himself hustling to patch together a replacement combination for the backcourt. As he once explained, it had been nearly impossible to keep a young off guard as an understudy for Jordan because his immense competitiveness consumed them in practices. Now, Krause had to pull together a group of free agents. Ultimately, the coaches decided to go with an old standby—Pete Myers, a hard-working, scrappy journeyman who made Tex Winter remember why he loved coaching. Myers moved into the starting lineup on opening night and played solidly and consistently all season.

There were several other new faces on the roster. After years of trying, Krause had finally lured 6'11" Croatian Toni Kukoc. Krause had pursued Kukoc since the Bulls drafted him in the second round in 1990. It had never been a move popular with Jordan, Pippen, Grant, and other Bulls, but Krause had persisted, even after Jordan and Pippen made a point of trying to humiliate Kukoc when the U.S. played Croatia in the 1992 Summer Olympics.

The general manager had also signed free agent Steve Kerr with the idea that he would eventually replace Paxson, who, like Cartwright, was struggling to return for one more season. For the frontcourt, Krause signed 7-foot journeyman Bill Wennington and later traded Stacey King to Minnesota for 7'2" Luc Longley.

There was immediate speculation that these newly reconstituted Bulls would fail miserably without Jordan. But just the opposite happened. Jackson and his assistants did what some observers saw as their best job in Jackson's tenure with the team. And Scottie Pippen, Horace Grant, and B. J. Armstrong showed that they had developed into outstanding players in their own right. All three were picked for the All-Star team, the first time that three Bulls had been selected.

Amazingly, these Jordanless Bulls won 55 games and made a strong-but-controversial run into the 1994 playoffs. Their first-round opponents, the Cavaliers, fell easily, leaving the Bulls to face Pat Riley's Knicks in the Eastern semifinals.

"We'd used more energy to get 55 wins than we'd ever had to use in the past," Jackson recalled. "Maybe my better job was holding them back a little bit in years past so that when we went into the playoffs we had energy and expertise that could be unleashed. This time, it was a matter of how much did we have left for the playoffs."

In Game 1 in New York, the Bulls had a 15-point lead but seemed to run out of energy and suffered a bitter, frustrating loss, the kind that Jackson feared could do harm to his team. So instead of practicing, he decided they needed a break, which turned out to be an impromptu ride on the Staten Island Ferry.

"One of the things I like to do in New York is observe its grandeur," Jackson explained. "Sometimes when you step away from it, you can see it for what it really is. New York can be overwhelming if you're on its streets, if you're in the canyons between the skyscrapers. Something about New York in Game 1 overwhelmed us. We had a 15-point lead and we got overwhelmed, with the intimidation of the crowd and the team together. That home court got to us. I just wanted to take that away. These guys knew how to play. They were in great shape. There wasn't any strategy change that we had to have. We had two days off between games. But yet we had to do something together as a group.

"One of the things I've always enjoyed was the Staten Island Ferry ride. In fact, sometimes I'd come back from Jersey and go through Staten Island just to take the ferry ride back to New York City. So I misdirected the bus.

I didn't let anybody know. I misdirected the bus because where we were practicing, the downtown YMCA was about six to eight blocks from the Staten Island Ferry. What I didn't know was that the press was following us in cabs. I thought they were already at the YMCA. Then I'd have the excuse, 'Well, while we were going down there, I got this idea. . . .' But the other thing I didn't anticipate was that the Staten Island Ferry runs every fifteen minutes or so. There's a clock on it. When I got there, there was still ten minutes on the clock. I thought we'd be lucky and hit the clock late. But I knew the guys on the Staten Island Ferry would treat us great; they're great guys; they're city employees. They hustled right up to the top of the ferry. We rode on the top of the ferry out and back. We could go in the pilot's house; we had complete freedom. There was some stuff there, where the press got ahold of us. I was disappointed that we couldn't just jump on the ferry and escape all that. But it was beautiful, because President Clinton was flying in. They had a helicopter hovering over the pad, where he was gonna land down by Wall Street. It was a beautiful day. We had a neat ride and a lot of fun."

Radio reporter Cheryl Raye was among the media contingency that day. "We were at practice, and all of a sudden we see the bus drive by," she recalled. "The bus takes them to the ferry, and Phil shows them the sights of New York. They get back on the bus, and go back to the hotel. We see the bus going back the other way, so we hop in a cab and get back to the Plaza."

Desperate for interviews, Raye got into the lobby in time to see an elevator about to close with some players on it. "I jumped on," she said, "and there's Bill Cartwright and John Bach and B. J. Armstrong, so I say, 'Can I talk to somebody about this?' So I get up to Bill Cartwright's room and he tells me, 'You know Phil. He's got these ideas in his head. But I know New York. I know what's going on. But Phil was trying to relax the guys, and he's telling them the history of Staten Island and the history of the Statue of Liberty. Most of these guys could care less.' Bill said, 'To be awakened to go to practice is one thing. But to be awakened to go on a tour?' That was one of Phil's ways of handling the stress and handling New York and the media."

"I think they were feeling the stress," Raye said. "Here they were, defending champions, playing the Knicks without Michael. It was one of those times where you said, 'That's Phil. What other coach could do that?'"

"It was OK," Horace Grant told reporters. "I was hesitant about getting on a big boat like that because I get a little seasick. But we had fun."

"Phil was pointing out all the different boroughs," Scott Williams said. "It was kind of cool. It was the first time I ever saw the Statue of Liberty, and it was a lot smaller in person."

"Phil is great," Wennington recalled. "He cancels practice and we go on the ferry ride to the Statue of Liberty. Things like that are just phenomenal. The team was really stressed and we were feeling down, and it was something to just break everything. Like, 'You know what? We're here, and we're good. We know what we have to do. Let's go and forget about it for two hours, have fun, get our minds straight, and tomorrow we'll go take care of business.'"

The trip on the ferry, played out in front of the New York media, brought a new level of focus to Jackson's unusual approach. "That's the thing that makes coaching really enjoyable and fun for me," he said later when asked about his beliefs. "You need diversification. If you have that, you can keep it interesting for these guys."

He pointed out that the NBA was populated by career coaches so focused on basketball that they hardly realized the world included anything else. "You get on the treadmill of pro basketball," he said. "You just keep running on the treadmill and you can't get off. It's something that can be generated from a season to one year to ten years to twenty years. You look at some of these guys, they've been around the game for thirty years. And they just stay in that same pattern. But you should try to make the pattern just a little bit better. Sometimes I think you have to jump off the treadmill, step back a little ways from it, relook it, and rethink it."

He had gained notoriety at first for giving his players books to read, as if he were a college coach who also happened to be teaching a section of English lit. "Horace Grant really likes to read," he said. "I started him out with some simple books. *Joshua.* I knew he was into religion. I'd read the book. Somebody gave it to me. He liked it, and he trusted me a little bit. Then I gave him *To Kill a Mockingbird.* He loved *To Kill a Mockingbird.* So Horace and I had this communication through reading. He liked a lot of the stuff I picked out for him. What I liked about Horace is that he is not stagnant. He always wanted to learn more. He believed in self-involvement and self-improvement. And he's got this optimistic attitude about life."

Deft as his coaching touches were, the ferry ride did not bring his Bulls a win in Game 2 of that 1994 playoff battle. The Knicks strong-armed a second victory, and the series moved to Chicago with the Bulls down 2–0. There, in Game 3, they seemed poised to fall off the edge. The score was tied at 102 with 1.8 seconds left. Chicago had the ball and called a timeout, where Jackson issued instructions for the ball to go to Kukoc for the final shot. Pippen was infuriated. He was the superstar of the team, burdened all season with the load of carrying the Bulls alone. He believed the shot should have been his to take. So he refused to go back in the game. Cartwright was at first stunned, then furious. Unflustered, Jackson substituted, and Kukoc hit the game-winning shot.

"Those times are the moments in games that you live for," Pippen later explained. "And I thought it was an injustice the way Phil treated me, and I had to say something, right or wrong. So it wasn't what people wanted to hear."

"Phil defuses confrontations so quickly and easily," Bill Wennington offered. "It's amazing how fast he can just get a situation under control. Once we got into the locker room Scottie realized that he had made a mistake and was really feeling bad for it. Bill Cartwright was talking and had words to say. Everyone was just really disappointed at the time, but Phil was there in control of the situation. He just said, 'Enough said. We don't need to talk about this anymore.' And that was really in my eyes the perfect way to handle it. He just let it go at that."

The moment illustrated a key factor in Jackson's approach: he was not a believer in confrontation. "He never did anything openly," Wennington explained. "I'm sure he had to talk to players about things, but he did that sort of thing behind closed doors where it was just sort of taken care of between him and the party involved. He never brought things out into the open for all eyes to see when it was a private matter. He didn't want to demean anybody, didn't want to take anything away from anyone's manhood. He wanted you to feel proud on the court, not to feel belittled or threatened by something he was gonna do. Because he was gonna be there every day coaching you and asking you to do things for him and trying to motivate you. He didn't want any feelings to get in the way of that."

Jackson did, however, leave the locker room that day and go to the postgame media session. Reporters were unaware of the situation until Jackson began discussing it. Certainly he couldn't have kept it quiet, but again, the series involved the Knicks, meaning that New York reporters were there to magnify the incident, to throw it on the global agenda.

Krause was furious with Pippen and immediately began planning to trade him, leading to the many heartaches and frustrations and disagreements that would follow. There had long been an undercurrent of discontent with the Bulls, of dislikes and difficulties. But this was the incident that loosed a putrefaction upon the organization, bringing a flare-up in long-simmering hostilities between Krause and Pippen, which in turn would finally prompt

Jackson to rebel against his mentor. If they hadn't been so successful as a group, it might have ended quickly. Instead, it would drag out over four seasons, three of which were overwhelmingly successful, so that all of their lives—especially Jackson's—would be a mix of the highest and the lowest, the best and the worst.

Somehow, the team shook off the Pippen incident and claimed a 12-point win in Game 4 to even the series. The Bulls then could have won the crucial Game 5 in New York, but they let it slip away by a point. In the closing seconds, the Bulls had the lead, and seemingly an assured win, when referee Hue Hollins whistled Pippen for a late foul on New York's Hubert Davis. The incredulous Bulls protested, and supervisor of officials Darrell Garretson later said the call was terrible. But it still cost Chicago the game and the series, and a chance to win a fourth straight championship.

Back in Chicago for Game 6, the Bulls played well and evened the series at 3. But the Knicks had home-court advantage, and a week of ferry rides wasn't going to break the spell that cast on Jackson's team.

In the wake of the loss, Jackson fired Johnny Bach.

"That's the twist in life that fate does to you," Bach said.

He had come to the team as Doug Collins's chosen man, and Jackson had come to view him perhaps as an unnecessary filter in his communication with his players. Krause had continued to despise Bach since *The Jordan Rules*, and he appeared to express his displeasure at every little turn, in staff meetings and casual discussions alike.

"It was Jerry Krause's relationship with Johnny Bach that created a very uncomfortable situation," Jackson explained a few months later. "It made this have to happen eventually. It had gone all wrong. It was bad for the staff to have this kind of thing because we had to work together."

Krause had also set out to trade Pippen, but it had been extremely difficult to find a deal that would bring a player of comparable value to the Bulls. Finally, he had put together a deal with Seattle that would have brought power forward Shawn Kemp plus a draft pick that would possibly have given the Bulls Eddie Jones out of Temple. But Seattle's owner backed out of the trade at the last minute, and a series of news stories followed that revealed Krause's plans. Pippen, who was already unhappy over his contract, was further enraged that the team planned to trade him.

The ensuing turmoil had left the fans and the media eager to pump up the volume on their rejection of Krause. He, in turn, responded by withdrawing even deeper into his suspicions and unhappiness.

"Poor Jerry's been kicked around from pillar to post by everybody, including me," observed longtime Chicago sportswriter Bob Logan. "But he got what he wanted in life. He's running the franchise. He's got three championship rings. Yet I don't think he's ever spent a day where he's completely satisfied. There's always something else he wants, or something that doesn't quite work out."

A classic example of that misery followed a few months later, in November 1994, when the team held "A Salute to Michael," a ceremony to retire Jordan's number 23 jersey in the United Center. It was the night the team unveiled a bronze statue of Jordan in action, called "The Spirit," just outside the building.

The event quickly became something of a nightmare for the Bulls' staff. The trouble, it seems, began when NBA Entertainment took control of the event away from the Bulls to make it into a nationally broadcast program for Turner Network Television. As first envisioned, the "retirement" was to be a night of intimacy and warmth involving Jordan, his coaches and teammates, and the fans. Instead, NBA Entertainment turned it into a dimly conceived TV special in which every line was scripted. Rather than a memorable evening with the Chicago crowd that followed Jordan's every jump stop on his rise to greatness, the session unfolded as a vapid showcase of television business connections.

Instead of a circle of friends, there was a "cast," including broadcaster Larry King and actors Craig T. Nelson, Kelsey Grammer, Sinbad, George Wendt, Woody Harrelson, and Robert Smigel, all of whom had little or no real connection with Jordan and the Bulls. The show moved from one hollow segment to another. The script writers had effectively removed any emotion from the format, except for odd moments when the crowd grew impatient with the awkward silliness of this staged event.

Sadly, the only impromptu moment of the evening was one of profound embarrassment, especially for Krause. When he and Reinsdorf were introduced, the crowd of twenty-one thousand booed lustily.

"C'mon, now," Jordan chastised the fans. "Both Jerrys are good guys."

It was an uncomfortable moment, but not unprecedented. At virtually every rally or celebration of the Bulls' three straight championship seasons from 1991 to 1993, Krause had been the target of merciless booing from Chicago crowds. Never mind that by just about all accounts his personnel moves factored heavily into their success; the fans took a special delight in deriding him.

This night, however, was perhaps the worst for Thelma, Krause's wife of many years. She began crying, and Krause himself grew furious. For years, he had ignored the booing and hardened himself to the fans. "I learned long ago that when we won, Michael would get the credit," Krause has explained, "and when we lost, I would get the blame. I knew that. It was something I accepted."

But this was different. The booing had finally gotten to his wife, and she was openly weeping.

"One of the really sad moments that I've seen before," said former Bulls trainer Chip Schaefer, "is at the retirement function for Michael at the United Center when Jerry was roundly booed, and Michael had to say, 'Don't be hard on him.' I could see from where I was sitting Thelma Krause just broken down in tears over it."

Later, Dean Smith came up to Thelma and sought to console her. Smith pointed out that it was nice of Jordan to speak up for Krause. The comment sparked the pent-up anger and emotion in Thelma Krause, and she told Smith in clear terms what she thought of Jordan's effort. It was too little, too late, she said angrily. "Too damn late."

Smith and Jordan had often been at odds with Krause over the years, particularly when it came to the Bulls' personnel decisions regarding University of North Carolina players. Both Jordan and Smith had lobbied long and hard to get Krause to draft Joe Wolf in the first round of the 1987 draft, and their efforts had created a tension-filled draft day dilemma for Krause. But then Reinsdorf told the general manager to "go with his gut" because his instincts on personnel had served the franchise well. So Krause selected Grant, who developed into a key player. Wolf, meanwhile, went on to become an underachieving career role player.

So Thelma Krause had no compunction about telling Dean Smith off that night. Krause himself didn't seem to mind it too much either.

Faced with a diminished roster and dissension within the organization, Jackson held a certain dread for the 1994–95 season. Later, after Jackson had found himself thoroughly mired in hellish circumstances, trainer Chip Schaefer, Jackson's good friend, said he was almost sure it would be the coach's last season. Things had simply become too difficult.

But then Jordan abruptly returned that March, Schaefer said, and the entire team's spirits were lifted, especially Jackson's.

It had been the kind of season to chase away even the best of coaches, and the trouble and swirl of changes had started long before the first tipoff.

Angered by Jackson's assessment that he would spend his NBA career as a bench player, Scott Williams became a free agent and accepted a lucrative offer to play in Philadelphia. "Have a nice life," Krause had told him.

Then the re-signing of Horace Grant got mired in nasty dispute, and he left the Bulls for the Orlando Magic after publicly exchanging insults with Reinsdorf. His departure, combined with the retirements of John Paxson and Bill Cartwright (who would abruptly unretire when the Seattle Sonics offered him a substantial two-year contract) left the roster noticeably weaker.

The bottom line to these changes meant a significant struggle over the first months of the season. The game-related battles were made worse by a public dispute between Pippen and management over his efforts to have his multiyear contract renegotiated. Pippen asked repeatedly to be traded. Tangled in the mess and offering much less firepower, Jackson's team struggled to stay above .500.

By January, Pippen and Krause were engaged in an open war of words in the press, a development that brought the first public cracks in what would become a rupture of Jackson's relationship with his boss.

"The thing that happened with Pippen was avoidable," Jackson would confide after the season. "The things that have happened in the past were avoidable. Somehow or other they got pushed to greater limits. But that's part of who Jerry is. He wants to directly confront when he feels that there has been a problem. He wants to challenge and overrun people and be brusque. He's very brusque and sets people on edge just by walking into the locker room sometimes. We've had to talk to him about his manner in the locker room. On the other hand, Jerry keeps his space very well. He doesn't overrun us, the coaches. He allows a coach to do what he wants to do as far as strategy and how he wants to handle the players. Jerry has a very good attitude about protocol.

"He's just a very unusual guy."

Informed that Jackson had labeled him brusque, an angry Krause called Jackson into his office. He saw the comment as one of the first signs of betrayal. Jackson countered that he had meant nothing of the sort, that he was only trying to maintain an air of cooperation with his team.

But how Bulls employees viewed the issue would go a long way in deciding where their loyalties fell. Some perceived Jackson as being the instigator of these troubles in that he coaxed and reinforced Jordan and Pippen's dislike of Krause. Jackson's supporters saw him as only trying to maintain his relationships with his star players.

One thing was certain: Krause needed no help in fomenting disagreements. His life had been a virtual whirl of conflicts in and around pro sports. With the media. With fellow NBA executives. With players. It was a pattern that had existed long before he met Jackson. But as Jackson grew weary of his trials with Krause, he seemed to focus more on his boss's shortcomings.

"Jerry's never been able to project a good personal image," Jackson offered in 1995 as the issues with Krause heated up, "and that's been the thing that's destroyed his public persona as far as the audience goes here in Chicago. They see him as someone like the mayor. The mayor always gets booed in public. Jerry represents that kind of guy. He has to do a lot of the dirty jobs. The fans remember the dirty jobs, and they remember his comments. What has happened with Jerry is that he has alienated a lot of sportswriters, and the sportswriters form the public opinion.

"Jerry Krause is an enigma to the athletic world. He's not what you would consider an athlete. So it's everybody's challenge to define him as a person. He's a Damon Runyon–type character who is undefinable. But Jerry's a watchdog. He keeps the press away, he keeps the public away, he keeps company policy always. He's ever vigilant at mind control and spin control to the point that it wears people out. He has a tendency to alienate people. I don't know if there's ever been a story done on him here in Chicago where he hasn't had a conflict with the writer.

"He's willing to call people up on the phone and challenge them. 'Why did you say this?' And, 'That's a lie!' And, 'You missed the point!' He'd done that to the point where he's sort of made himself an unlikable character."

Actually, trainer Chip Schaefer had seen the beginning of trouble three years earlier with the building of the team's fancy practice facility, the Berto Center, in suburban Deerfield. "There are events that happen in the course of life that are like pebbles in a pond, that sort of ripple off of it," Schaefer said. "As wonderful a facility as the Berto Center is, I think a lot of it started with the building of the Berto Center in 1992, when people were all forced to really be around each other a lot more. Prior to that, when we practiced at the multiplex, there were people who worked downtown, which meant there wasn't as much contact. I don't think Phil and Jerry saw each other as much. Once the Berto Center was built, we all had to be together every day, and I think that may well have been the start of it."

The new building meant that the coaching staff began sharing space with Krause's organizational staff, which engendered little misunderstandings between the two groups. Slowly, all those involved came to see two distinct and often opposed groups: the team, meaning Jackson and his assistants and the players; and the organization, consisting of Krause and his scouts and the rest of the front office. Over time, the two groups became polarized, Schaefer explained. "The Bulls became a house divided, and you were either Jerry's guy or Phil's guy, whether you wanted to be or not. I think it was a situation where Phil had his coaches, Jerry had his scouts. . . . Sometimes what I think happens, because they're being combative, they draw people close to them, whether you want to be or not. There were times on issues that Phil pulled me to him when in fact I may well have wanted to remain neutral on that issue. . . .

"I'm trying to remain neutral, like Switzerland, and I just can't. I'm getting pulled to one side or the other and it's really difficult. There was no one activating event. I think it was a series of events. If you have personalities that don't exactly mesh, then familiarity breeds contempt. If you don't care for somebody, but you're around them twice as much or three times as much as before, then you notice everything."

Over time, the "team" became the code word for Jackson's clan and the "organization" was Krause's domain.

"The 'team' was the group of people you'd see on the bench during a game," Schaefer said. "But I never wanted it to be that. It was kind of a shame. I think people are going to look back years from now and say, 'What a shame. What a shame that we all couldn't kind of rise above it.'"

The major complication would come with the 1995–96 season as Jackson entered the last year of his contract. Around the NBA, a number of untested coaches from college were receiving large sums to move to the pro game, which prompted the accomplished Jackson to expect a proportionate pay raise. It was an issue that would soon divide the coach and general manager. Krause had long insisted that the Bulls would not pay such sums for a coach, that the NBA was a players' game, that coaches had minimal impact if the "organization" did its job.

Jackson was willing to concede that Krause had been pivotal in his own opportunity to coach. "One of the things that he does well is that he hires the best people that he can find," he said. "That is really important. And when he does that he gives them the autonomy to move inside the field, even though he sometimes has a controlling tendency. He likes to keep things under the lid, he's very good at that."

Yet even Krause's intense focus on finding and developing talent annoyed Pippen and Jordan no end. Pippen, in particular, bristled at the idea that

Krause "discovered" him. "How the hell is he gonna find me in the draft if I'm the fifth player picked?" Pippen said. "If he 'found' me in the draft, I would have been picked in the second round, not the fifth player taken in the draft and not to the point that he had to work his way up to draft me from the eighth pick."

The resentment Pippen and other players expressed about Krause was that in his boasting about deals, he came across as if he were taking credit for their careers.

He's Back

By early March, the Bulls were struggling to stay above .500, and speculation abounded that once the season was over Pippen would be shipped to another team. Observers figured that, short of some miracle, the roster would have to be rebuilt, and the Bulls would have to start over.

Then came word that Jordan was about to abandon his baseball career and return to the Bulls. The next ten days brought the greatest tease in the history of sport. Was Michael Jordan returning to basketball or not? From Warsaw to Waukegan, the planet clamored to know.

Then on Saturday, March 18, 1995, he broke his silence with a two-word press release, issued through his Washington-based agent, David Falk:

"I'm back."

Sure enough, the next day, shortly after noon, he emerged with his Bulls teammates from the visitors' locker room at Market Square Arena in Indianapolis, where the Bulls were scheduled to meet the Pacers.

Standing before the crowd gathered in the hallway outside the locker room was Superman himself, chomping his gum fiercely. Jordan was ready to resume the career that had been prematurely interrupted by an eighteen-month "retirement."

Camera bulbs flashed, and people wiggled with excitement. "This is just like the president appearing," commented one Chicago TV reporter.

"Are you kidding?" somebody else said. "Michael's more important than that."

Only now, just as he was raring to take the floor and restart his career, something was wrong. Jordan's face tightened.

Somebody was missing.

The Bulls did a quick head count. Only eleven. "Who's not here?" Jordan asked as he searched the faces around him.

They all turned to see Pippen sheepishly slipping out of the locker room.

With his jaws working the gum and his glare policing the roster, Jordan gathered his teammates in their traditional huddle.

"What time is it?" somebody yelled.

"Game time!" they answered in unison.

With that, the Bulls broke and made their way out into the arena, opening the latest chapter in a strange, dramatic saga.

Air Jordan was back, and the news flashed around the world. "He is like a gift from God to the basketball game," Huang Gang, a twenty-one-year-old professional player in Beijing, told reporters. "We try to imitate his ground moves. But you can't copy him in the air. He is unique."

Waiting for the competition to begin that Sunday in Indianapolis, Pacers coach Larry Brown quipped that the atmosphere was so zany, it seemed like "Elvis and the Beatles are back."

The proceedings did have a dreamlike feel about them. But Jordan had always been defined by his ability to suspend reality. The circumstances were never more ethereal than that March, when the first rumors leaked out that he was contemplating another career move.

Without question, the Bulls were caught off-guard by Jordan's decision to abandon the professional baseball career he had launched upon leaving basketball. Many people in baseball had questioned his skill level after he immersed himself in the White Sox minor league farm system, but no one doubted his work ethic. In his determination to learn to hit big-league pitching, Jordan came early and stayed late each day at practice.

But the futility was obvious almost from the start. He was too tall, some said, and presented too big a strike zone. "He is attempting to compete with hitters who have seen 350,000 fastballs in their baseball lives and 204,000 breaking balls," Rangers pitching instructor Tom House appraised shortly after Jordan joined the AA Birmingham Barons for the 1994 season. "Baseball is a function of repetition. If Michael had pursued baseball out of high school, I don't doubt he would have wound up making as much money in baseball as in basketball. But he's not exactly tearing up Double A, and that's light years from the big leagues."

If he was light years away, Jordan, a thirty-two-year-old .200 hitter, certainly didn't have time to waste with the protracted baseball strike that loomed over the game for six months. Hoping it would soon be resolved, he reported to spring training in Florida only to realize that the fight between owners and players over money wasn't going to end anytime soon. So he packed up and went home.

Within days of his departure from Florida, a Chicago radio station reported that Jordan was secretly working out with the Bulls and contemplating a return to basketball.

On March 10, he announced his retirement from baseball, saying his minor league experience had been powerful because it allowed him to rediscover the work ethic that had made him a great basketball player. "I met thousands of new fans," he said, "and I learned that minor league players are really the foundation of baseball. They often play in obscurity and with little recognition, but they deserve the respect of the fans and everyone associated with the game."

Jordan hadn't failed baseball, Jackson would later note. "Baseball failed him."

Soon the Bulls confirmed that Jordan was working out with the team, and Jackson revealed that Jordan had actually been contemplating a return since October.

Like that, the situation exploded. Scores of media representatives from the major networks and national publications converged on the Berto Center in anticipation of Jordan's holding a press conference announcing his return.

Yet each day at practice, large screens covered the picture windows through which reporters observed Bulls practices. The media could hear the shouts, the squeaking of sneakers on the gym floor. They were told that Michael was practicing with the team but that he hadn't yet made up his mind about returning, that the details were being worked out.

On the Berto Center floor, Jordan displayed the intense competitiveness that for years had charged Bulls practice sessions. Wearing the yellow vest of the second team, he ran point guard against the regulars. "Just to be able to play with him is fun," said center Will Perdue. "Just to be able to watch him."

Yet Jordan wavered that week, pausing, as he would later explain, to contemplate whether he was returning to basketball out of disappointment over the baseball strike, or if he was in fact returning because he loved the game. While the media speculated and fans kept the lines buzzing on sports radio talk shows, Jordan remained silent. The closest he came to making a statement was the revving of his burgundy Corvette, warning the media to get out of the roadway as he left practice each day. His silence drove reporters and fans alike to distraction, with some callers on Chicago's sports radio talk shows claiming that Jordan was toying with the public.

Meanwhile, *USA Today* reported that the stock value of companies that employed Jordan as a spokesman had zoomed up $2 billion on the various stock exchanges in recent days, leading to further speculation that Jordan was engaged in some kind of financial manipulation.

Finally, on Thursday, March 16, Jackson told Jordan not to attend practice that day because the media crowd at the Berto Center had gotten too large. After practice, Jackson revealed to a swarm of reporters that Jordan and Jerry Reinsdorf were engaged in negotiations and that a decision was three or four days away.

That Friday night, the Bulls capped a three-game winning streak and raised their record three notches above .500 by defeating the Milwaukee Bucks in the United Center. Speculation had been high that Jordan might make a sudden appearance in uniform for that game, but only his security advisers showed up to evaluate the arena.

Early the next morning, the Chicago radio waves were abuzz that Jordan would make his announcement that day, and that he would play Sunday on the nationally televised game against Indiana. Down on LaSalle Street, the managers at Michael Jordan's Restaurant heard the news and decided that they had better restock the gift shop yet again. The restaurant's business had been slow in February, but the hint of Jordan's return had turned March into a boom, with crowds packing the place virtually every night. ESPN hosted an NCAA tournament special there, and the various TV crews in town appeared every night to interview fans and "capture the atmosphere."

As a result, the gift shop was doing a whopping business, selling miniature bats, trading cards, jerseys, posters, coffee mugs, and other trinkets. Other fans gathered at the Jordan statue outside the United Center. Revealed at his November "retirement" ceremony, the statue had quickly become a hot spot for fans and tourists in Chicago. On this Saturday, as the anticipation grew, small groups were drawn to the statue.

"This is like the Colts returning to Baltimore," said one fan, "with Johnny Unitas as quarterback!"

Over at the Berto Center, crowds of fans and reporters milled about, with many fans hanging from the balconies and walls of the Residence Inn next door. Nine different TV satellite trucks hovered over the building, waiting to blast the news around the world.

Suddenly practice was over, and just like that, Jordan's Corvette appeared on the roadway, with him gunning his engine and the fans cheering wildly as he sped off. Next came Pippen in a Range Rover, pausing long enough to flash a giant smile through the vehicle's darkly tinted windows.

Moments later, NBC's Peter Vecsey did a stand-up report outside with the fans rooting in the background. He told the broadcast audience that Jordan was returning; that the superstar had negotiated to keep Pippen, guard B. J. Armstrong, and Jackson with the team; and that Jordan would play against Indiana on Sunday and probably wear his old number 23, which had been retired in November.

Chicago, quipped one radio sportscaster, was in a state of "Jorgasm."

Jordan did not fly to Indianapolis with the team that Saturday night. A crowd of fans and media gathered at the Canterbury Hotel, awaiting the Bulls' arrival. When a limousine with a police escort pulled up, the crowd surged forward. But out stepped a bride and groom. "Who are these people?" the stunned bride asked her new husband.

The team showed up moments later and was roundly cheered. But Jordan flew down the next day on a private jet and showed up at the arena with an armada of limousines carrying his security force of twenty to help hold back the crowds.

Outside the arena, tickets were going for $150 to $200, and the Wheaties marketing staff was creating a stir by passing out five thousand T-shirts and about ten thousand posters that read "Jordan's Back, and He's Eating His Wheaties."

Shawn O'Grady, Wheaties marketing manager, said the company had hastily printed the posters and T-shirts the night before in Minnesota and airfreighted them to Indiana. The company, he added, was already working on a special edition cereal box to be distributed May 1 as the playoffs opened.

Jordan wore jersey number 45, his minor league and junior high number, instead of the number 23 that he had made so famous. Number 23 was the last number his father James saw him compete in, Jordan later explained, and he wanted to keep it that way.

Champion, the sportswear manufacturer that holds the NBA license for jerseys, immediately added an extra shift and began producing more than two hundred thousand number 45 jerseys for sale around the world.

Jordan played against Indiana like someone who had taken two years off. He made just 7 of 28 shots, but his defensive intensity helped the Bulls take the division-leading Pacers to overtime before losing. Afterward, Jordan broke his silence, saying he had been "embarrassed" by all the hoopla of the preceding ten days. "I'm human," he said. "I wasn't expecting this. It's a little embarrassing."

He said he had taken his time evaluating his love of the game and had come to the conclusion that it was real. That, he said, was the reason he returned, not financial considerations. He pointed out that the league had a moratorium on renegotiating contracts while it worked out a new labor agreement with the NBA Players Association, so he was required to play for the $3.9 million salary he left behind in 1993. He also added that he received no assurances about Pippen, although he asked.

His return, he said, was based solely on his love for basketball.

"I wanted to instill some positives back into this game," he said of his return, indicating his displeasure at some of the NBA's highly paid young players. "There's been a lot of negatives lately, young guys not taking care of their part of the responsibility, as far as the love of the game. I think you should love this game, not take advantage of it . . . be positive people and act like gentlemen, act like professionals."

For months, fans and media had speculated that Jordan's retirement had been a deal with NBA commissioner David Stern to serve as punishment for revelations in 1993 that Jordan had lost hundreds of thousands of dollars gambling on golf. "I had to let him know what some of my thoughts were," he said of Stern, "and to see if he wanted me back in the league."

But as to implications that he was suspended, Jordan said, "It was strictly my decision."

So it was.

Three nights later, he scored 27 points by shooting 9 of 17 from the floor in a win over the Celtics at Boston Garden. In two short games he had served notice that he was indeed back—which, in turn, led to a revival of the NBA's fortunes. Sagging television ratings abruptly jumped, and suddenly the whole country was watching Michael Jordan's return.

"Everybody was complaining about the season," Jackson said. "It was a lackluster year. It wasn't any fun. All of a sudden Michael comes back, and suddenly people start paying attention to the NBA. They see there's a lot of dynamic things going on here. A couple of television people told me, 'It brought back our audience.' And the NBA really enjoyed a very good post-season tournament because people got their minds set on pro basketball again because of this great attraction."

The circumstances engendered an overwhelming belief among Chicagoans that Jordan was about to perform his grandest miracle of all: he would return after a two-year absence, play just 17 games of the regular season, then lead an undermanned Bulls team into the playoffs to capture a fourth title.

It had all the appeal of a storybook ending, which is what it proved to be. Instead of magic, Jordan's return engendered mostly unrealistic expectations. The Bulls finished in fifth place in the Eastern Conference and had no home-court advantage in the playoffs. Still, they managed to oust the Charlotte Hornets in six games. But it became increasingly obvious that Jordan still lacked the stamina and timing to deliver a miracle.

In the second round, against the Orlando Magic with Shaquille O'Neal, Anfernee Hardaway, and Horace Grant, the Bulls and Jordan found themselves out of sync—particularly in Game 1 in Orlando, when Jordan committed two late turnovers that cost the Bulls the game. From there, Jordan missed shots, made miscues, and watched Grant and the Magic celebrate a 4–2 series victory.

What made the loss worse was that the Bulls' primary executioner was Horace Grant. In preparing to defend Orlando center Shaquille O'Neal, Jackson had decided to double-team the Magic post while leaving Grant unguarded. It was a logical move. The rest of Orlando's starters were deadly three-point shooters. Jackson figured that leaving Grant open would mean that if he made shots, they would only be two-pointers. Logical as it seemed, Jackson's move backfired. Grant, who always felt that he had been disrespected during his playing days in Chicago, took umbrage and answered Jackson's strategy by scoring early and often, a performance that further emphasized Chicago's weakness at power forward. The final insult came when the Magic closed out the series on the Bulls' home floor, and the young Orlando players hoisted Grant to their shoulders and carried him off in celebration.

Bad as it seemed, the loss hurt most because the Bulls' coaching staff studied the tape of the series in the aftermath and came away with the firm conclusion that Chicago could have, should have, won the series and possibly even swept it.

"We should have won all six games," Jim Cleamons said of the 4–2 outcome. "The reality of it was we didn't win, but we weren't that far from winning. . . . We lost games at the end of the clock, on last-second shots and turnovers, matters of execution. Good teams close the doors; they end the case. The teams that are trying to become good teams have those straggling situations, those dangling participles, if you will. They just don't quite get the job done."

Strange as it seemed, the Orlando loss left the Bulls realizing that they now resided in the latter category: a team trying to become good. It wasn't a status they wanted to inhabit very long, "The day after we were out of it we started planning for next year," team chairman Jerry Reinsdorf said.

The only acceptable goal would be winning the team's fourth NBA championship.

One critical aspect of that would be reestablishing a home-court advantage in Chicago. For years, that had been a foregone conclusion when they played in the creaky old Chicago Stadium, the "Madhouse on Madison," whose thundering crowds and intimidating acoustics had hammered many an opponent into submission. But the Stadium was now headed toward life as a parking lot, having been razed to make way for the United Center, the fancy new $175 million building just across Madison Street.

Brand new when the 1994–95 season opened, the United Center seemed awkward and foreign to Jordan, who had once vowed never to play there. He relented, but didn't like it and quipped that he'd like to "blow it up." The remark was something of a setback to the Bulls' administrative staff, who had hoped to establish the United Center as the "New Madhouse on Madison," a snazzier, high-tech version of the old barn. But then the Magic won two playoff games in Chicago, and those hopes dimmed.

Rebuilding

In the aftermath of the 1994–95 season, Chicago's sports radio talk show airwaves were filled with anguished calls for changes, particularly for ditching Winter's triple-post offense. The offense had played a large role in the team's three championship seasons, but now even Winter expressed doubt. In all their years of working together, Jordan had never told Winter what he thought of the offense. In the wake of the Orlando loss Winter wanted to know, so he pushed Jackson to discuss the issue with Jordan in the season-ending conference Jackson held privately with each player.

"With his impulsiveness, Tex said, 'Phil, I'd like you to ask him, does he think we need to change the offense,'" Jackson recalled. "'Is it something we should plan on using next year? I want you to ask him just for me.' So I did, and Michael said, 'The triple-post offense is the backbone of this team. It's our system, something that everybody can hang their hat on, so that they can know where to go and how to operate.'"

For others, the concern wasn't the offense or the United Center but rather Jordan himself. It seemed pretty clear that his time as the game's dominant player had passed, which meant that the Bulls' fortunes were declining as well. There was even speculation among some Bulls administrative staff members that Jordan might retire again rather than deal with the hassles of NBA life. Failing his team against Orlando had been a setback for Jordan, one that bruised his giant pride. For years he had thrived on taking the Bulls' fortunes on his shoulders and lifting them with brilliant performances in front of millions of witnesses. Now the public phenomenon was his fall. "We agonized for him when he went through the postseason trauma," Jackson explained later that summer. "But knowing Michael so well, I put my arm around him after that first game in Orlando when he lost the ball and said, 'As many times as we've won behind you, I never expected to see this happen. Let's use it for our tool. Let's use it to build a positive. You're our guy, and don't ever forget that.'

"Michael's not the same player," Jackson added. "He's aged like everybody else has aged. But he's still Michael Jordan. He'll go back and shoot 50 percent this year, you can bet your bottom dollar on that. Will he break through all the defenses that people bring at him, the double teams and triple teams? No. But he'll probably start knowing where to pass the ball better. Michael lost perspective of where the passing would have to come from a lot of times."

Missing out on the teamwork of an 82-game season had hurt Jordan, Jackson said. "But we see Michael returning to form. . . . He saw and heard the criticism that went on in the postseason. There was a lot of the blame game going on in Chicago, a lot of people whining and gnashing teeth. Michael's going to use that for this strength."

It was obvious that Orlando's talented young team would be the main contender in the Eastern Conference, and if the Bulls hoped to win another championship they would have to rebuild their team with one purpose in mind: improving their matchups with the Magic. Specifically, the Bulls would have to find a power forward and strengthen their post play. Plus, they would have to find bigger guards to counter Orlando's trio of Anfernee Hardaway, Nick Anderson, and Brian Shaw.

With this in mind, the Bulls decided to leave veteran B. J. Armstrong, a fan favorite from the championship years, unprotected in the upcoming expansion draft. The coaching staff didn't have to look far to find a bigger guard to replace Armstrong. Already on the roster was former All-Star Ron Harper, whom Bulls vice president Jerry Krause had originally signed in 1994 to help fill the void created by Jordan's retirement. Harper's bountiful athleticism had declined with a series of knee injuries since his days as a young superstar with the Cleveland Cavaliers, but the Bulls figured he still had promise.

"When we brought Harper in initially, we felt that if he could regain some of his old skills, his old abilities after the knee injuries he'd had, he could be an ideal player for us because of his size," Tex Winter said.

The problem was, Harper had struggled most of the 1994–95 season to get the hang of the complicated triple-post offense; and just when he had started to come around, Jordan returned, taking most of his playing time. Soon the whisper circuit around the NBA had Harper pegged as finished, his legs gone, his game headed for mothballs. The circumstances had left Harper understandably despondent, struggling through the lowest point in his nine-year career. "Suicide was an option," he would say later, only half-jokingly. "Last season was something I learned from. It was frustrating, but my friend had a frustrating year, too," he said, referring to Pippen, who had spent much of the '95 season fighting with management, "and we both grew."

In the wake of the Orlando loss, Jackson realized that Harper could be part of the answer and told him so in their season-ending conference—if Harper would dedicate himself to offseason conditioning. "Phil let Ron know that we very definitely were counting on him to be a big part of the team," Winter said. "I think that helped Ron no end. Phil put it to him in no uncertain terms: 'You gotta go out and get yourself ready to play.' And Ron did that, he really prepared himself."

"Phil asked me what my role was going to be on this team," Harper recalled, "and I told him, 'When Michael returns, I'll be a player who plays defense and fills the spot. If there's a chance to score, I'll score.' I think that we felt as a team that we had something to prove. And on my own I had something to prove. I figured this was going to be a very good ball club. . . . I trained hard. I felt that last year I definitely didn't have the legs to play the style here. I had to learn that, too."

Jordan faced the same task, rebuilding his conditioning and mind-set from the months of basketball inactivity, losing what Reinsdorf called his "baseball body" for a leaner basketball body. Jordan was scheduled to spend the summer months in Hollywood making an animated Bugs Bunny film with Warner Brothers. On another team, with another player, the coaches might have been concerned about a major summer conflict taking away from the intensity of the star player's offseason work. But this was not an issue with the Bulls' coaches.

"We didn't worry about Michael," Winter said. "We figured Michael could take care of himself."

Indeed, Jordan made it clear that the situation was his source of motivation. "The game taught me a lesson in the disappointing series I had last year," Jordan would later say. "It pushed me back into the gym to learn the game all over again."

For the most part, his "gym" would be a temporary floor in the Hollywood studio he occupied while making his film. There, Jordan could work on his game yet be within reach of the film crew when he was needed to shoot a scene. "I've never seen anybody work harder than Michael Jordan," trainer Tim Grover would later say. "He fulfilled his normal summer obligations—shooting commercials, making some personal appearances—and he shot a movie. But his conditioning program always remained his primary objective."

For Jordan, the torturous offseason program was just the beginning of a year-long effort to regain the dominance he had enjoyed in the NBA as a younger man. He was nearing his thirty-third birthday, trying to prepare himself to face not only the game's talented young players but the specter of his own legendary youth. No matter what he did as an aging comeback player, he would have trouble measuring up to the standard he had set from 1986 to 1993, when he lorded over the league, leading the NBA in scoring for seven straight seasons and driving the Bulls to three straight world championships. Now, the older Michael Jordan was taking on the younger, magical version.

"I'm the kind of person who thrives on challenges," Jordan explained, "and I took pride in people saying I was the best player in the game.

"But when I left the game I fell down in the ratings. Down, I feel, below people like Shaquille O'Neal, Hakeem Olajuwon, Scottie Pippen, David Robinson, and Charles Barkley. That's why I committed myself to going through a whole training camp, playing every exhibition game and playing every regular-season game. At my age, I have to work harder. I can't afford to cut corners. So this time, I plan to go into the playoffs with a whole season of conditioning under my belt."

Heading into the 1995 playoffs, it had been Krause's concern that the Bulls lacked the meanness and nastiness in the frontcourt necessary to win another championship. After Cartwright retired, the Bulls had come to rely on a trio of centers—Will Perdue, Luc Longley, and Bill Wennington—to get the job done in the post. Perdue could block shots, Wennington had a feathery offensive touch, and Longley had the huge body necessary to struggle against giant forces like Shaquille O'Neal. None of the three Chicago centers was a complete force on his own, but collectively they formed what the press had taken to calling a "three-headed monster," a patchwork solution assembled by the coaches.

Ideally, the Bulls wanted to get a complete center to match Orlando for 1995–96—but there just weren't any around. The answer for the Bulls had been to try to develop a solid center. In this effort, Longley was their lead-ing candidate, primarily because he was young (twenty-six), and had the big body (7'2", 290 pounds) to fit the specifications. "The kid's a solid worker," Jackson said in assessing Longley's upside in June 1995. "He's got a great desire to play the game. He's very intelligent. He doesn't have fear. But he's not mean, that's one of the things that we know about him. He's not rugged mean like that. Some people think that you have to have a center that's fero-cious, that threatening type of defender."

The Bulls' coaches figured that with Jordan back full-time and commit-ted to winning a championship; with Pippen, Longley, and Toni Kukoc maturing; with Ron Harper refurbishing his game, they had just about all of the major pieces in place, except for one.

"We still needed a rebounder," Jim Cleamons said.

The Worm

Dennis Rodman had been one of the NBA's great mysteries since the Detroit Pistons first selected him in the second round of the 1986 draft. Although some people in the Pistons' organization would later claim that Rodman was fundamentally troubled, many in Detroit saw him as simply a fun-loving, immature guy who could be surprisingly sweet. One of his favorite pastimes was hanging out with teenagers in mall game rooms (growing up in Dallas, he had gotten the nickname "Worm" from his antsiness playing pinball). He was unlike many other NBA players in that he had not come up through the ranks of the great American basketball machine. He had not been on schol-arship his entire life, wearing the best shoes and equipment and staying in fancy hotels where the meal checks were always paid. Rodman had missed all of that.

Former Pistons coach Chuck Daly recalled that Rodman's first efforts in training camp were rather disappointing, but he recovered and soon found a place in the league by focusing on playing defense and rebounding. He per-formed these chores so well that most observers considered him a key factor in the Pistons' claiming back-to-back league titles in 1989 and '90. To accom-plish goals as a player, Rodman had come to rely on a natural hyperactivity that supercharged his frenetic playing style. "My friends knew I was hyper. Real hyper," he once said of his days growing up in Dallas. "They knew I wouldn't settle down, I wouldn't sleep. I'd just keep going. And now I just focus my energy in something I love to do. Now, I just play basketball, go out there and have a lot of fun and enjoy."

Daly had persuaded him to use these advantages to become a superb rebounding specialist and defender. Rodman bought into the plan and worked to make himself a marvelously versatile sub. Quick enough to stay with a big guard/small forward. Motivated enough to play power forward. Even tough enough to survive at center against much bigger bodies.

Rodman moved into the starting lineup for 1989–90 and helped the Pistons to yet another championship. It was during this period, as the Pistons shoved aside Jordan and the Bulls in the playoffs for three straight seasons, that fans in Chicago came to absolutely despise Dennis Rodman, Bill Laimbeer, and all the other Pistons Bad Boys.

Eventually, however, Detroit's guard-oriented offense declined. The Pistons were swept by Chicago in the 1991 playoffs, and although Detroit made a playoff run in 1992, Daly moved on to coach the New Jersey Nets, leaving Rodman without the fatherly coaching connection he badly wanted. Besieged by personal and off-court problems, Rodman's frustrations built, leading to clashes with Pistons coaches and management.

That October of 1993, the Pistons traded Rodman to the Spurs, thus igniting the next amazing stage in the transformation of Dennis Rodman. From all accounts, he came to San Antonio a changed man. As Rodman explained it, "I woke up one day and said to myself, 'Hey, my life has been a big cycle. One month I'm bleeding to death, one month I'm in a psycho zone.' Then all of a sudden the cycles were in balance."

This new "balance" left him searching through a series of tattoo shops, piercing pagodas, alternative bars, and hair salons to find the new Dennis, the one with the electric hair. The old Dennis, however, still played basketball like a wild man.

Jack Haley, a free agent signed as the Spurs' twelfth man, was assigned a locker next to Rodman. "I walked in," Haley recalled of that first day, "and said, 'Hey, howyadoin? I'm Jack Haley.' He wouldn't even acknowledge I was in the room or shake my hand. We sat next to each other for almost three months and never spoke a word. I would try occasionally. I'd say, 'Hey, howyadoin?' I'd get no response. Just like the rest of the team."

Haley watched in amazement that winter of 1994 as Rodman moved in and silently took control of the power forward spot in San Antonio, giving Spurs center David Robinson the kind of help that he'd never enjoyed before. Soon Rodman was regularly pulling down 20 rebounds a game, an astounding feat.

Rodman's main problem, it seemed, was that he had almost nothing to say to his teammates, particularly David Robinson. They stood in stark contrast to Rodman, with his constantly changing hair colors, his body piercings, and the cornucopia of New Age symbols etched into his well-muscled arms, shoulders, and back.

He seemed intent on living by his own rules, being late to practices and games, wearing bizarre clothing and jewelry in practices, and generally violating much of the protocol that had been established for pro basketball teams over the decades. Spurs coach John Lucas had decided the best way to keep Rodman happy and motivated was to allow him to live by a different set of rules than the rest of the Spurs, which is to say almost no rules at all.

When Rodman acted up in the 1994 playoffs, and the Spurs lost to the Utah Jazz, the policy of appeasement cost Lucas and general manager Bob Bass their jobs. Next San Antonio brought in general manager Gregg Popovich, who had a military background, and coach Bob Hill with the idea that they would provide a more structured, disciplined system.

The Spurs won plenty of games over the winter and spring of 1995, but Rodman's differences with management dogged the team like a running skirmish. The Spurs had their rules, and Rodman answered with an insurrection that cost him tens of thousands of dollars in fines.

"They were fining him $500 and they were fining him every single game," Haley would later confide. "I'm talking about every single day, $500 a day. Because Dennis made a concentrated effort to be late. It was his way of sticking it in their side."

Rodman's disruptions continued right through the 1995 playoffs, where the Spurs advanced to the Western Conference finals against Houston. But, enraged by behavior they called detrimental to the team, Spurs management suspended Rodman for the pivotal fifth game in the series. San Antonio lost that game and the next to fall 4–2 to the Rockets. Immediately afterward, Spurs management began looking around to see if someone would take their Dennis the Menace in a trade.

Rodman's contract with the Spurs held only one more season of guaranteed money. But Rodman indicated that he wanted the Spurs to give him $15 million to play another season there. He had no options for imposing that demand other than some type of work disruption, and the Spurs had had enough disruptions. He had turned thirty-four on May 13, 1995, an age when most hoops stars are looking at limited futures. It was clear that the Spurs wanted to trade him, rather than deal with another year of headaches. But they were having trouble finding takers. Rodman's ideal scenario was to get with another team for the last year of his contract, perform well, and sign a new two- or three-year deal in the neighborhood of $15 million. "I'll put $5 million in the bank, live off the interest, and party my ass off," Rodman told reporters, just the kind of talk that made NBA general managers very nervous.

"Everybody in the league was scared to death of Dennis," said Toronto Raptors coach Brendan Malone, an old Rodman friend.

Yet Rodman did have a small group of supporters, including Krause, who said he remained interested only because of Bulls scout Jim Stack. "Jim Stack came to me early in the summer and asked me to look at Rodman," Krause said. "When I put him off, he finally pleaded with me. He talked me into finding out if all the bad things we had heard were true. Without Jim's persistence, we wouldn't have looked behind all the rumors to see what the truth was."

Bulls chairman Jerry Reinsdorf wasn't surprised when Krause came to him about the possibility of getting Rodman, because the Bulls had looked at Rodman a year earlier. "I thought it was a great idea as long as he didn't play dirty," Reinsdorf said, "and Jerry and Phil could satisfy themselves that he was a good bet to not self-destruct. I didn't know Dennis. I only knew about the stories, like sitting in a parking lot with a gun in Detroit, and the problems he had with other teams. I told Jerry that if you can satisfy yourselves that it's a good risk, then I'm all for it, because we need to rebound the ball better. But I wanted him and Phil to be sure that the odds were with us, so that's why they spent a great deal of time talking to Dennis."

Friends, enemies, former coaches, former teammates—the Bulls contacted a whole group of people in their investigation of Rodman. Chuck Daly told them that Rodman would come to play and play hard.

Encouraged by what he heard, Krause invited Rodman to come to Chicago for an interview. Rodman was immediately skeptical, but agreed to come. They met at Krause's house for what turned out to be a long, frank discussion about Rodman's past. Rodman talked about his problems with Spurs management, how he felt the team had made him specific promises then failed to follow through. As they talked, Krause came to the realization that he liked Dennis Rodman. Krause was confident in his ability to judge people, and he thought Rodman was a good person. Krause also knew that Rodman had the potential to be a problem, but he believed that Jackson could take care of that.

"Anyway," Krause told *Sports Illustrated*, "Phil's no virgin. He's had his confrontations. He came from the CBA, so I guess he knows about problem children."

Satisfied, Krause sent Rodman to speak with Jackson, who spent hours talking to the forward, trying to read his attitude about the team system. It was obvious that Rodman wanted to come to the Windy City to play with Jordan. He even allowed the Bulls to talk to a psychiatrist he had been seeing.

"Phil told me I was not going to average the 15 to 16 rebounds I was used to averaging," Rodman recalled. "He told me the figure would be more like 10 or 11."

Rodman said, "No problem."

"Phil and I thought very carefully about this," Krause would explain later. "It's been under consideration for quite some time. We certainly did an awful lot of homework and were satisfied with the results we got."

Yet even after Krause's investigation turned up good news, he and Jackson hesitated before moving forward. After all, Jordan and Pippen had loathed Rodman as a Piston. "When he played in San Antonio, I used to absolutely hate Dennis Rodman," said Bulls guard Steve Kerr. Pippen, in particular, held a dislike for Rodman, who had shoved him into a basket support during the 1991 playoffs, opening a gash on Pippen's chin that required stitches. Pippen still had a scar from the incident.

"If he's ready and willing to play, it will be great for our team," Pippen said. "But if he's going to be a negative to us, I don't think we need that. We could be taking a huge step backwards."

Jackson admitted as much. "There are no assurances with anything," he said. "We're just talking about trying to take some good chances with the basketball club to put them in a championship state."

Jordan and Pippen thought about it, then told Krause to go for the deal, which sent Bulls longtime backup center Will Perdue to San Antonio for Rodman in early October, just days before training camp opened. That news elated Rodman, who badly wanted to find a basketball home. "I had no choice," he said. "I feel like I had a lot of negative energy going on in my life, and that was the best way to get rid of it."

Jackson thought of his own rebel days as a Knick and felt confident that he could coach Rodman. So the move was made, and as extra insurance for communicating with Rodman, the Bulls signed Haley to a $300,000 contract.

Haley would be placed on injured reserve and kept there all season, which allowed him to practice and travel with the team.

Rodman appeared at the press conference announcing the deal with his hair dyed Bulls red with a black Bull in the crown, and his nails done in a nifty layered Bulls motif. "I understand that they're a little leery and a little cautious of having someone like me in here," he said. "They wonder how I will respond to the team. I guess they'll find out in training camp and during the preseason. I think Michael knows he can pretty much count on me doing a good job. I hope Scottie feels the same way."

The Strangest Bull

The announcement of the trade set off the expected firestorm of media and fan interest in Chicago. But just days into training camp, Bulls insiders began to have doubts that the situation was going to work. Rodman still hadn't spoken to any of his Chicago teammates, and his silence was getting stranger with each passing day.

"It was a tough training camp because everybody was guarded," Haley offered. "Again, you're Michael Jordan. You're Scottie Pippen. Why would you have to go over to Dennis? Michael Jordan made $50 million last year. Why would he have to go over and basically kiss up to some guy to get him to talk? They came over and shook his hand and welcomed him to the team, and this and that. But other than that, it was a slow process."

"I think everybody was skeptical of what might happen," recalled assistant coach John Paxson. "But we were also optimistic as to what could happen. The optimism stemmed from Phil's personality. We felt that if there was anyone around the league who could get along with Dennis and get Dennis to respect him as a coach, it would be Phil."

Sports Illustrated came into town the first week of the preseason and wanted to pose one of the Bulls' star players with Rodman for a cover shot. Jordan, who had a running feud with *SI* since the magazine had ridiculed his attempt to play professional baseball, refused to pose. The previous spring, Rodman had appeared on the cover of the magazine in a dog collar and a bustier, one of the strangest posings in *SI* history. Apparently, this time Rodman wasn't going to wear a strange getup; still, Pippen also declined, saying privately that he didn't want to make a fool of himself. Finally, the magazine got Jackson to do the shot, which was never used.

It was just one of an avalanche of media requests for interviews set off by Rodman's becoming a Bull. In fact, several gay magazines approached the team about securing an interview because of Rodman's racy comments. Haley, however, chalked much of that interest up to Rodman's having learned to manipulate the media while dating Madonna two years earlier. He had discovered he could generate substantial news coverage by projecting a conflicted sexuality.

"He spent time with Madonna, and when he was with Madonna that increased his time in the public eye and made him more of a star," Haley explained. "So now all of the things he does are because of the shock value. He talks about, 'Oh, yeah, I hang in the gay community and I hang out with gay people in gay bars.' That's all shock value. We're best friends; we're together every single night. In the two years I've known him, we've been to one gay bar. But he talks about it all the time, because it's part of his aura and his stigma."

"Have you ever played on a team where one of your teammates lives with his male hairdresser?" one Chicago reporter asked Michael Jordan during the preseason.

Jordan said he couldn't think of any.

Yet the interest in Rodman's sexuality wasn't the reason his presence seemed a threat to team chemistry. More central to the uneasiness was the relationship between Rodman and Pippen.

"No, I have not had a conversation with Dennis," Pippen acknowledged early in the year. "I've never had a conversation with Dennis in my life, so I don't think it's anything new now."

Fortunately, things seemed to take a sudden turn for the better with the Bulls' first two exhibition games. They opened play in Peoria against the Cleveland Cavaliers, whom the Bulls defeated easily with Jordan scoring 18 points and Rodman getting 10 rebounds.

"Once he gets a little more familiar with everybody out on the floor and there's more continuity, he's going to start to shine," Jordan predicted.

Team chemistry got another boost in the second preseason game when Rodman rushed to Pippen's aid after Indiana's Reggie Miller made some threatening moves. "I'm looking forward to a lot of brawling around here," he told reporters. "We need brawling on this team."

While Rodman was a surprise early fit, the other factors would take time. Jordan wasn't so sure that his pairing with Harper in the backcourt was going to work, but Jackson advised patience. Harper's presence meant that Jordan was handling the ball more. With his offseason work he had regained his basketball conditioning. Jordan seemed like his former self on the floor. The confidence was tangible. Pippen, too, seemed more at ease with Michael back. Pippen's private life had gone through some changes, and Jackson noticed that he seemed more focused than ever.

At center, Luc Longley seemed eager to face the challenge of the coming season as a starter, and veteran Bill Wennington was comfortable in his role as a backup. For additional insurance in the post, Krause signed thirty-nine-year-old James Edwards, himself a former Piston and a friend of Rodman's, in late October, thus assuring that the Bulls would have post depth—and the oldest roster in the league. Krause had also brought in guard Randy Brown to work with Steve Kerr as backcourt reserves. Also coming off the bench were Jud Buechler, Dickey Simpkins, and first-round draft pick Jason Caffey out of the University of Alabama.

The other bubble in the mixture was Toni Kukoc's reluctance to play the sixth man, or third forward. He wanted to start instead of coming off the bench, but his role in the lineup had gone to Rodman. Jackson talked to Kukoc about the success that Celtics greats Kevin McHale and John Havlicek had enjoyed as sixth men, but it was not a concept that Kukoc embraced immediately.

"I'm very pleased with Toni," said Jackson, who had been particularly rough on the Croatian in his first two NBA seasons. "His rebounding is much better. His defensive awareness is good. He can play a variety of types of people. He's hitting key shots. He's moving the basketball. He's getting assists. He's not what I would ask for in a prototype power forward. But he has played well for us."

Changing Kukoc's mind would take patience, Jackson reasoned, but there was a whole season ahead and there would be plenty of time.

The only remaining question was Rodman. Early on, his behavior had been strange but acceptable. But how long would it last? Would he take his act too far? Could he destroy this team despite Jordan's strong will and leadership?

Rodman was obviously thrilled to be a Bull. "People have to realize that this team is going to be like a circus on the road," he said. "Without me, it would be a circus. But Michael, Scottie, and me, it's more of a circus. A lot of people want to see the Bulls again."

Indeed, Rodman's presence made the Bulls even more of a magnetic attraction, if that were possible. Yet where Jordan and Pippen had always taken a businesslike approach to winning, Rodman brought a fan-friendly, interactive, fun-filled style to the game that always seemed to set any arena on edge. What was he going to do next? was the question in everyone's mind.

Rodman admitted that even he didn't know sometimes.

"The very first preseason game of the year," Haley said, "Dennis goes in the game, Dennis throws the ball up in the stands and gets a delay-of-game foul and yells at the official, gets a technical foul. The first thing I do is I look down the bench at Phil Jackson to watch his reaction. Phil Jackson chuckles, leans over to Jimmy Cleamons, our assistant coach, and says, 'God, he reminds me of me.' Whereas last year in San Antonio, any tirade Dennis threw, it was 'Get him out of the game! Sit him down! Teach him a lesson! We can't stand for that here!' Here in Chicago, it's more, 'Get it out of your system. Let's go win a game.' "

Rodman had discovered that rather than fine him $500 for being late to practices, as the Spurs had, Jackson handled the matter with a light hand. Fines were only five bucks. "Here, the first couple of days, he walked in one or two minutes late," Haley said. "Nobody said anything. So once Dennis realized it wasn't a big deal, he was on time."

Reporters and observers began noting that Jackson, who was sporting a beard grown during the offseason, seemed to be taking a more relaxed approach to the game.

"Somewhere about the middle of training camp I realized I was having a lot of fun coaching this team," Jackson later explained, "and Dennis Rodman to me brings a lot of levity to the game. I mean, I get a kick out of watching him play. . . . He's such a remarkable athlete and has ability out there. There are some things about his individuality that remind me of myself. He's a maverick in his own way."

Most important, though, Jackson did a dipstick check on his own intensity levels. The season had opened with the NBA's regular officials on strike, which meant that the league had put together two-man replacement crews from the Continental Basketball Association. Jackson had always expended a good deal of energy each game riding the refs, but dealing with the replacements' unorthodox calls brought him to a new revelation. "I realized that it didn't matter what referees do out there, there's not much you can do walking up and down the court and yelling," he said. "I decided I was going to have to sit down and shut up and enjoy the game and coach at the timeouts and coach at the practices rather than on the floor, and practice what I preached a little bit."

The unspoken truth was that the coaches couldn't expect Rodman to behave better if they weren't doing the same. Jackson still had his moments of animation—especially when Kukoc took an ill-advised three—but he turned his demeanor down yet another notch, much to the delight of his players.

The rush of seasons had been exhausting and Jackson had found himself in 1995 heading into his fiftieth birthday with a depleted store of energy for the task of rebuilding the Bulls and coaching them back to a championship level.

For rejuvenation, he decided that he needed to step back even further from the game. That began with the process of finishing his book, *Sacred Hoops*, during which he spent time reflecting what his seasons coaching the Bulls had meant to him. Putting that in writing, interpreting his unique approach for the fans, helped him better understand it himself.

Asked about Jackson early in the year, Rodman said, "Well, he's laid-back. He's a Deadhead." Later in the season, when John Salley came to the roster, he gained an immediate appreciation for Jackson's style. "A lot of coaches on other teams get mad that Phil just sits there," he said. "It makes them look bad. But he sits there because that's his seat. He prepares us enough in practice, trust me, that he doesn't have to do all that whooping and hollering, all those sideline antics. A lot of coaches get into that yelling and whooping and hollering, carrying on and trying to demean a guy. They say, 'Well I'm trying to get them to play harder.' Well, no, some coaches are just angry, frustrated fans."

The 1995–96 season marked Jackson's seventh consecutive campaign coaching the Bulls, the second longest tenure in one job among the NBA's twenty-nine coaches. He had accomplished those things by overcoming the elements that had made casualties of many of his peers—the exhausting grind of the 82-game schedule, the daily practices, the shuffling and reshuffling of priorities, and always the pressure to win. Jackson's simple answer had been to find his sense of self elsewhere.

If that meant preaching to his players about the great white buffalo or giving them obscure books to read or having them pause amid the looniness of the NBA for a meditation session, so be it. On more than one occasion, Jackson's approach left his players shaking their heads in amusement. "He's an interesting guy," Steve Kerr said of Jackson. "He keeps things very refreshing for us all season. He keeps things fun. He never loses sight of the fact that basketball is a game. It's supposed to be fun. He doesn't let us forget about that. But at the same time, this is our job, too, and he doesn't let us forget about that either. The amount of work involved and what it takes to win, and finally the feeling of success when you do win. He's constantly reminding us of all that."

That's not to say that Jackson would hesitate to get in a player's face, Kerr added. "But when he does it you know it's not personal. That's his strength. He always maintains authority without being a dictator. And he always maintains his friendship without kissing up. He just finds that perfect balance, and because of that he always has everybody's respect. And ultimately that's the hardest part of being a coach in the NBA, I think, is having every player's respect."

Revival

It was during the preseason that veteran *Sun-Times* columnist Lacy J. Banks predicted that the Bulls would win 70 games, which brought hoots of derision. But the seed had been planted. Jordan himself reasoned it would help him make the perfect statement. He had returned in the spring of 1995 to find a Bulls roster of new faces. And that had proved to be almost as much of an adjustment as his conditioning. He seemed closer to Pippen, but his relationships with his newer teammates seemed strained. Some of them thought he was aloof, unless they happened to elicit his competitive anger. Then they felt a singe.

Steve Kerr quickly learned that in training camp that fall. "I had heard stuff about him," Kerr said, "but I hadn't experienced it firsthand. I was surprised how he just took control of the entire team's emotional level and challenged every single player in practice to improve, and never let up on anybody."

Jordan's approach was a revelation that left Kerr thinking, "Maybe this is what it takes to win a championship. This guy's been through it. He's won three of them. If this is what it takes, then it's well worth it.

"His personality raised the level of our practices each day, which in turn made us that much better," Kerr said.

Yet it also led to a fight between Kerr and Jordan one day in training camp. "It was a case of practice getting out of hand," Kerr recalled, "just a lot of trash-talking and their team was just abusing us. It was during training camp. Michael was out to prove a point and get his game back in order. So every practice was like a war. And it just spilled over one day."

It was the first and only fistfight in Kerr's life. "We were barking at each other, and it got out of hand," Kerr said. "He threw a forearm at me, so I threw one back at him, and he kind of attacked me from there.

"He was just letting us know how they were kicking our ass. I knew they were kicking our ass. He didn't have to tell me about it. Why wouldn't that piss me off? It's natural. Other guys were pissed off too. He just happened to be guarding me at the time."

"He knows he intimidates people," Jackson said of Jordan. "I had to pull him in last year when he first came back. He was comfortable playing with Will Perdue. . . . He was tough on Longley. He would throw passes that, at times, I don't think anybody could catch, then glare at him and give him that look. And I let him know that Luc wasn't Will Perdue, and it was all right if he tested him out to see what his mettle was, but I wanted him to play with him because he had a big body, he wasn't afraid, he'd throw it around, and if we were going to get by Orlando, we were going to have to have somebody to stand up to Shaquille O'Neal."

Jordan tempered the fire directed at his new teammates without banking his competitiveness. Instead, he refocused it to drive his offseason conditioning fervor. He knew that he would need the added strength during the 1995–96 season to overcome the nagging injuries that accompany age. Yet even there, he had an edge. "Between games, Jordan can bounce back from injuries that would sideline other players for weeks," Bulls trainer Chip Schaefer pointed out. "He has a remarkable body."

His capacity for recovery, his restraint with teammates, and his unique commitment would amaze the many witnesses to his 1995–96 performances, beginning with the very first tipoff. He scored 42 points on opening night in a victory over the Charlotte Hornets at the United Center, setting in motion a momentum that would carry his team to five straight wins, the best start in Bulls history.

Sensing he had latched on to a whirlwind, Rodman told reporters, "We're mean here. In San Antonio we had guys who liked to go home and be breast-fed by their wives."

Yet no sooner had Rodman started to settle in with the Bulls than a calf muscle injury sidelined him for a month.

Even with Rodman out of the lineup, Jordan continued on his tear. If the five quick wins did anything to dull Jordan's sense of purpose, the Orlando Magic were there with a reminder in the sixth game, just as the Bulls were breaking in their new black with red pinstripes road uniforms. Penny Hardaway outplayed Jordan, giving the Magic a key home victory. The Bulls responded with two quick wins back in Chicago before scorching through a West Coast road trip, winning six of seven games. The trip opened in Dallas, where Chicago needed overtime and 36 from Jordan (including 6 of the Bulls' final 14 points) to win 108–102. "As far as I'm concerned, he's still one of the best in the game," the Mavericks' Jason Kidd said of Jordan. "He still finds a way to win."

"This is a very aggressive basketball club and very confident," Jackson said afterward. "I think people are surprised who we are, or are surprised how we are playing, or they're not comfortable with our big guard rotation. It is giving us some easy offensive opportunities, so we are getting going early."

On December 2, they closed out the trip at a sizzling 6–1 with Jordan scoring 37 in a win over the Los Angeles Clippers. "I feel I'm pretty much all the way back now as a player," Jordan said, reflecting on the first month of the season. "My skills are there. So is my confidence. Now it's just a matter of me going out and playing the way I'm capable every night."

Indeed, his shooting percentage, a stellar .511 prior to his return, had dipped to just .411 during his 17-game run over the spring of 1995. Now it had jumped to .493. His scoring, too, was headed back up to a 30-point average from the nine-year low of 26.9 in 1995.

"He's right where I knew he'd be about now," Ron Harper told the writers covering the team. "And that's leading the league in scoring and pulling away from the pack. He's removing every shadow of a doubt that he's the greatest player of all time."

"I'm old," Jordan admitted. "Agewise, I think I'm old. But skillwise, I think I'm still capable of playing the type of basketball I know I can play. . . . The question [people] end up asking me the most is, how do I compare the two players, the one before baseball and the one after.

"Quite frankly, I think they are the same. It's just a matter of putting out the stats to show that they are the same. And I think by the end of the year, hopefully, you will see that it's basically the same player with two years in between.

"Right now, I'm still being compared to Michael Jordan," he said, "and according to some people, I'm even failing to live up to Michael Jordan. But I have the best chance of being him because I am him. In the meantime, I'm improving and evolving. . . . And I'm pretty sure that I'm turning some of you guys into believers."

The Bulls finished November with 12–2 record. Then December passed at 13–1. With each victory, speculation mounted as to whether Chicago could win 70 games, breaking the all-time record for wins in a season set by the 1972 Los Angeles Lakers with a 69–13 finish.

Jerry West, the Lakers' vice president for basketball operations who was a star guard on that '72 Los Angeles club, pegged the Bulls as dead ringers to win at least 70 games—unless injuries set them back.

The success also prompted reporters to ask Jordan to compare this Bulls team to other great NBA clubs. "I look at the Celtics back in '86 back when they had Bill Walton and Kevin McHale coming off the bench," Jordan said. "Those guys were tough to deal with. Those guys played together for a long time. We're starting to learn how to play together, but those guys were together for a period of time. They knew arms, legs, and fingers and everything about each other. We're just learning fingers."

It was pointed out to Jordan that most great NBA teams had a dominant low-post defender, someone to stop other teams in the paint. "We don't have that kind of animal," he admitted. "But I think Pippen compensates for that. I don't think any of those teams, other than maybe the '86 Boston Celtics, had a small forward that was as versatile on offense and defense as Scottie Pippen is."

Even without a dominant center, the Bulls seemed to have power to spare. During their big start, they had toyed with opponents through the first two or three quarters before flexing their might and finishing strong.

Observers began pointing out that with expansion, the NBA had grown to twenty-nine teams, which had thinned the talent base, making it easier for the Bulls to win. Those same observers had conveniently forgotten that the '90s talent base had been broadened by the drafting of European players and that in 1972, when the Lakers won, the American Basketball Association was in operation, meaning there were exactly twenty-eight teams fielded in pro hoops between the two leagues. Not only that, the NBA had just expanded dramatically before 1972, adding six teams in five years.

When the Bulls burned their way through January at 14–0, Jackson began talking openly of resting players just to lose a few games and slow things down. In other words, he was worried that his team would get so drunk with winning during the regular season that they wouldn't play sharp ball in the playoffs. If necessary, Jackson planned to slow them down.

"You can actually take them out of their rhythm by resting guys in a different rotation off the bench," he explained. "I have considered that."

Such talk by the coach only seemed to drive the Bulls harder to keep winning.

"What amazes me most about our team," said Jack Haley, "is that we probably have the league's greatest player ever in Michael Jordan, we have the league's greatest rebounder in Dennis Rodman, and we have what is probably this year's MVP in Scottie Pippen, and what amazes me most is the work ethic and leadership that these three guys bring to the floor night in and night out. With all of the accolades, with all of the money, with all of the championships, everything that they have, what motivates them besides winning another championship? How many months away is that? And these guys are focused now."

Particularly Rodman, who, with his constantly changing hair colors, his raving style, diving for rebounds, challenging opponents, piping off outbursts of emotion, was creating one funny circumstance after another. Each night he would cap off his performance by ripping off his jersey and presenting it to someone in the home crowd.

"I think they like me," Rodman said of the fans in the United Center. "People gotta realize this business here is very powerful. They can love you or they can hate you, but . . . Chicago fans, they hated my guts, and now all of a sudden, I'm like the biggest thing since Michael Jordan."

Not everybody, however, was completely taken with the circumstances. As the team's designated worrier, Tex Winter had concerns that Rodman was so intent on getting rebounds and winning another rebounding title that he was neglecting to play his role in the Bulls' triple-post offense. Beyond that, Winter and Jackson wondered if Rodman really had a handle on his emotions.

Still, the juggernaut pushed on, cruising through February at 11–3. And although March was interrupted by a Rodman outburst, after which he was suspended for six games for head-butting an official, the Bulls still finished the month at 12–2. The 70-win season became an increasingly real possibility, bringing with it constantly mounting pressure—which the Bulls answered with more wins.

About the only unanswered question as the Bulls headed to Milwaukee seeking win number 70 on Tuesday, April 16, was the color of Rodman's hair.

A few days into his return, he had reverted to blond, but with a swirling red streak. Then, headed into the team's historic week, he had opted for a flamingo pink. That worked for victory number 70, and 86–80 triumph over the Bucks.

After beating Milwaukee and Detroit, and losing to Indiana, they closed the regular season with a road win in Washington for a 72–10 finish. From there, Jackson refired the engines for an astounding playoff push. The Miami Heat fell in the first round in three quick games. Then came a grunting contest with the Knicks, who managed an overtime win at home before stepping aside, 4–1. Next was the rematch the Bulls had waited a whole year for—the Orlando Magic in the conference finals.

To prepare his team, Jackson spliced shots of *Pulp Fiction*, the story of two hired assassins, into the scouting tapes of Orlando. The message was clear. He wanted the Bulls playing like killers, which they did. Rodman held Horace Grant scoreless for 28 minutes of Game 1, until the Orlando forward injured his shoulder in the third quarter and was lost for the rest of the series. A slew of injuries followed, and the Magic went poof in four straight games, an immensely satisfying outcome for Jackson and his staff in that it confirmed their notions about retooling their roster.

The Fourth Championship

After battling all season to be crowned NBA champions, the Chicago Bulls climbed close enough to see their glittering prize, only to discover they'd have to sit back a while and twiddle their thumbs.

The matter of winning their fourth title developed into a waiting game over late May and early June. Their sweep of Orlando in the Eastern finals set up the problem. The Seattle Sonics had taken a 3–1 lead over the Utah Jazz in the Western finals, only to watch the Jazz fight back and tie the series. The net result for the Bulls was a nine-day layoff waiting for Seattle to claim the seventh game so that the championship round could begin. At last, the 1996 NBA Finals opened on Wednesday, June 5, but even that didn't mean the Bulls' waiting was over. What lay ahead were several unexpected delays in Seattle.

The Bulls were 10-to-1 favorites to defeat the Sonics, who had won an impressive 64 games during the regular season—which meant that the Finals carried the anticipation of an unfolding coronation. The NBA had credentialed approximately sixteen hundred journalists from around the globe to cover the event. The whole world would be watching, which had become standard procedure for just about all of Jordan's performances, particularly since the Bulls had added Rodman as a court jester. The team's resident rebounder did his part by showing up with a wildly spray-painted hairdo, a sort of graffiti in flames, with various red, green, and blue hieroglyphics and symbols scribbled on his skull.

As with every other Bulls opponent, Seattle's big concern was holding back Jordan, who was asked by reporters if he could still launch the Air raids that made him famous. "Can I still take off? I don't know," he said. "I haven't been able to try it because defenses don't guard me one-on-one anymore. But honestly, I probably can't do it. . . . I like not knowing whether I can do it because that way, I still think I can. As long as I believe I can do something, that's all that matters."

As an added measure, Seattle coach George Karl had hired recently fired Toronto coach Brendan Malone to scout the Bulls during the playoffs. Malone, during his days as a Pistons assistant, had helped devise the infamous "Jordan rules" to help defeat Chicago. The Sonics hoped that his perspective might help them find a deployment to slow down Jordan, who had averaged 32.1 points during the playoffs.

"You have to try to match their intensity," Malone advised. "Forget Xs and Os. They are going to try and cut your heart out right away, right from the first quarter."

For Game 1, the United Center crowd greeted the Sonics with a muffled, impolite boo that seemed to imply a lack of respect. In keeping with this mood, Rodman ignored Seattle forward Shawn Kemp as they brushed past each other heading toward center court for the opening tip.

The Sonics opened the series with 6'10" Detlef Schrempf playing Jordan, but when he posted up, guard Hersey Hawkins went immediately to the double team. Seldom one to force up a dumb shot, Jordan found Harper for an open three. The surprise move by the Bulls was having Longley cover the athletic Kemp, who responded by dropping in a pair of early jumpers. Longley used his size to power in 12 first-half points, with the Sonics obviously intent on forcing Jordan to pass. Pippen and Harper both found their offense, leading to Chicago opening an 11-point lead by the third quarter.

The Sonics had seemed to drag a bit, the obvious after-effects of a seven-game match with Utah in the Western Conference finals, but they found their legs and pulled to 69–67 as the fourth quarter opened. It was then that Kukoc, injured and in a slump for much of the playoffs, regained his form.

To go with his scoring, the Bulls turned on their pressure, forcing seven turnovers in the fourth quarter alone, and won big, 107–90. Jordan topped the Bulls with 28 points, but Seattle's defensive effort had meant that his teammates got off to a good championship start. Pippen scored 21, Kukoc 18, Harper 15, and Longley 14.

Rodman finished with 13 rebounds and watched as the officials ejected Seattle reserve Frank Brickowski for a dubious attempt to engage him in a scuffle, a silly little ploy played out before the network cameras.

The circumstances left Karl furious. "Dennis Rodman is laughing at basketball," the Seattle coach said before Game 2. "It's silly to give him any credibility for what he does out there."

"A lot of people don't give me enough credit for being an adult," Rodman replied. "Yesterday was a perfect example that I can be under control."

Rodman answered in Game 2 with a 20-rebound performance, including a record-tying 11 offensive rebounds that helped Chicago overcome 39 percent shooting. Rodman's total tied a Finals record set by Washington's Elvin Hayes in 1979.

Time and again, Rodman's rebounding helped the Bulls get through their all too frequent offensive lulls. Others played a factor as well. Although he struggled, Jordan willed 29 points into the baskets. And the defense forced another 20 Sonics turnovers, including a batch during a three-minute stretch of the third period when Chicago pushed the margin from 66–64 to 76–65. Once again, it was Kukoc off the bench contributing the key offense. He hit two three-pointers. Then Pippen got a breakaway jam after a steal, which was followed by a Kukoc slam on a pass from Jordan, whose anger had prompted the outburst in the first place.

"Are you scared?" he had asked Kukoc. "If you are, then sit down. If you're out here to shoot, then shoot."

Kukoc did, and the run provided enough margin. The Bulls had escaped with a 92–88 margin but had other concerns. Harper, the key to their pressure defense, had reinjured his creaky knees, requiring that fluid be drawn off one of them just before the game. That allowed him to play and contribute 12 points and key defense, but it also meant that he would miss all or most of the next three games.

Karl found himself having to acknowledge just how important Rodman was to Chicago. "He's an amazing rebounder," the Sonics' coach said. "He was probably their MVP tonight."

"The second opportunities, the little things he does," Jackson said appreciatively. "He finds a way to help the team out."

With Harper's knee hurting, the Bulls figured they were in for a fight with the next three games in Seattle's Key Arena. But the Sonics were strangely subdued for Game 3. With Kukoc starting for the injured Harper, the Bulls were vulnerable defensively. But Chicago forced the issue on offense from the opening tip. With Jordan scoring 12 points, the Bulls leaped to a 34–12 lead by the end of the first quarter. For all intents and purposes, the game was over. By halftime, Chicago had stretched the lead to 62–38, and although Seattle pulled within a dozen twice in the third, the margin was just too large to overcome. The second half was marked by Rodman's smirking antics that once again brought the Sonics' frustrations to the boiling point. Brickowski was ejected for a flagrant foul with six minutes left, and the Key Arena fans, so rowdy in earlier rounds of the playoffs, witnessed the display in numbed silence.

Jordan finished with 36, but the big surprise was 19 from Longley, who had struggled in Game 2. Asked what had turned the big center's game around, Jackson replied, "Verbal bashing by everybody on the club. I don't think anybody's ever been attacked by as many people as Luc after Friday's game. Tex gave him an earful, and Michael did, too. I tried the last few days to build his confidence back up."

Apparently it worked, because Longley's size was one of several elements of the Bulls' attack that troubled the Sonics.

"I saw Chicago with killer eyes," Karl lamented.

"These guys, once they get the grasp on a team, seem to be able to keep turning the screws down more and more," Jackson agreed, and later advanced the notion that Seattle might have been tired from taking a flight immediately after Friday night's game. "They might be learning that you don't take a Friday night flight in a situation where you have a day off and a game on Sunday afternoon," Jackson said. "You get in at 4:30 or 5:00 in the morning, and it changes up things. We've always made the statement that when you get here you better be prepared for it. It's a tough experience. The lack of sleep, the duress of travel. The energy that the games take . . . The critiquing and the overcritiquing. Sometimes a team comes apart, or joins together, in those kind of activities. Fortunately for our team, it has bonded them and helped them out, and they've become stronger because of it."

Jackson said his team reminded him of the 1973 Knicks' team, which had been built from players drafted in the '60s who grew up together. In the wake of the team's 1970 title, a host of new players were brought in. "We made some trades after we won the first championship, and Earl Monroe and Jerry Lucas came in," he recalled. "All of a sudden we had people going in different directions, with different interests. They didn't personally like each other as friends, but they liked to play ball together. This group reminds me of that group; they like each other on the court just fine. Personally, they're probably not gonna go out to dinner together. Some of them are. We tell them that's fine; that's good. Before the season started, we told them, 'As long as you keep your professional life together, the rest of the things don't matter.' I get them in the same room a lot of times. I believe in bringing them together so that they have to hear the same message, breathe the same air, so to speak.

"They're not that close, and they're not that distant. They respect each other, and that's the most important thing, especially at this level, when guys are working in this type of business, an entertainment business, where they're vying for glory and fame and commercial success. Guys understand and respect each other's game and territory. Michael and Scottie have given credence to Dennis's commercial avenue that he runs down, and they've all sort of paid homage to Michael and his icon that he carries. And Scottie's been able to take this team and do things as a leader that are very important for us. And there's plenty of room for guys who have an international appeal like Toni Kukoc and Luc Longley. Those things have all worked very well together."

With the victory, the Bulls were up 3–0, on the verge of a sweep that would give them a 15–1 run through the playoffs, the most successful post-season record in NBA history.

With Game 4 set for that Wednesday, the next two days of practice took on the air of a coronation, with the media hustling to find comparisons between the Bulls and pro basketball's other great teams from the past. ESPN analyst Jack Ramsay, who had coached the '77 Trail Blazers to an NBA title and served as general manager of Philadelphia's great 1967 team, said the Bulls just might be the greatest defensive team of all time. "The best defenders in the game are Pippen and Jordan . . . ," he said. "They're just so tough. In each playoff series, they take away one more thing from the opponent, and then you're left standing out there naked, without a stitch of clothes. It's embarrassing."

"They play as a team, and there appears to be no selfishness," Ramsay said. "There's no evidence of ego. The guys from the bench, they go in the game, and when they come out, you don't see any of them look up at the clock and look at the coach. They go over and sit down. When they come in, the guys on the floor bring them right into the game and get shots for them. They all know their roles, and they all can fill their roles."

Tex Winter was worried that the Bulls were being seduced by all the talk about the greatest team ever, and later he would kick himself for not complaining louder about it. But it wasn't just the talk that did them in. Ron Harper had been unable to practice for more than a week, and his availability for Game 4 was in doubt.

Harper had vowed he would be able to play—and sure enough, he was in the starting lineup. But his knees allowed him no more than token minutes, which left a huge gap in the Bulls' pressure.

It took the Sonics a few minutes to discover this. They missed their first four shots, but got on track shortly thereafter. The outcome was really settled by a second quarter blitz from which Chicago never recovered. In a series sorely lacking in drama, the Bulls had finally managed to produce some— by falling behind by 21 points. The Bulls pushed as Jordan furiously berated both his teammates and the officials, but without Harper the defense offered no real pressure, because there was no one to free Jordan and Pippen to do their damage.

At the next day's practice, Jackson was asked if he feared that the Sonics had gotten their confidence. No, he replied, at this level it was a matter of more than confidence.

Once again, Harper was unable to play in Game 5, which put Kukoc in the lineup. The Bulls struggled to play well, but again had no pressure in their defense. The Sonics had only two unforced turnovers at halftime. Still, the game stayed tight. The Bulls trailed 62–60 at the end of the third and pulled even tighter in the fourth.

With eight minutes to go, Pippen put home a Randy Brown miss to pull to 71–69, but the Sonics answered with an 11–0 run that the Bulls couldn't answer. Up 80–69, the Sonics crowd pushed the decibel level above 117. On the floor, a fan held up a sign that said, "Dennis's Departure Will Leave Us Sleazeless in Seattle."

Rodman showed his anger when Jackson replaced him with Brown in the fourth period. Haley tried to calm him, but Rodman knocked his hand away. Jordan and Pippen, too, had shown flashes of anger, and the media that had been ready to crown them just two days earlier began noting that the Bulls seemed fragmented and tired.

Finally, it ended, 89–78, and for the second straight game, the arena air glittered with golden confetti. The series, miraculously, was returning to Chicago. "The Joy of Six," the Seattle newspapers declared the next day in a headline.

The Bulls had shot 37 percent from the floor and only 3 for 26 from three-point land, 11.5 percent. Tex Winter looked very worried.

"It's all on them now," Seattle's Gary Payton said.

Jackson's team was rattled, but heading back home with a 3–2 series lead. Now the Sonics had to face the task of winning in the United Center. So much hinged on whether Harper could play. In the locker room before the game, he vowed he would. He had never taken so much as an anti-inflammatory, saying he didn't believe in putting drugs of any kind in his body. But he said he would play with pain. And that was all his teammates needed to know.

Game 6 was played on Father's Day, June 16, and Jordan felt the rush of emotion as he thought of James Jordan, his father, friend, and advisor. "He's always on my mind," Jordan said. His answer was to dedicate the game to his father's memory. Would it be too much to handle? Even Jordan didn't know that answer.

Once again the Bulls stayed in the locker room during the anthem, but no sooner had Jesse Campbell started singing than the United Center crowd launched into a large noise. Across the arena they were calling for the Bulls to come out and end this matter.

As introductions were set to begin, another loud prolonged applause, drowning out anything electronic, spread across the building, bringing the fans to their feet to pound out the noise. The very mention of the Sonics brought a deep and troublesome boo.

"Anhhnnnd nooww," announcer Ray Clay began the introductions, but you could hear no more after the twenty-four thousand saw that Ron Harper was in the lineup.

Taking all this in, the Sonics stood courtside, chomping their gum and setting their jaws. At tipoff, the audience sent forth another blast of noise, just in case the Bulls didn't get the message the first time. Then yet another explosion followed moments later when Pippen went to the hoop with a sweet underhand scoop to open the scoring.

With Harper back, the Bulls' pressure returned, and they picked the Sonics clean time and again. On the day, Harper would play 38 minutes, and when he paused, an assistant trainer would coat his knee with a spray anesthetic. Spurred by his presence, Pippen pushed the Bulls out of the gate in the first period with 7 points and 2 steals, giving Chicago a 16–12 lead.

The Bulls used more of the same to extend the lead in the second, as Jackson leaned back in his seat with his arms folded. Fifty feet away, Karl strolled the baseline, downcast, his hands jammed in his pockets. The Bulls saved their killer run for the third, a 19–9 spurt capped by Pippen dishing to Rodman on the break, with the eccentric forward flipping in a little reverse shot, jutting his fists skyward, bringing yet another outburst from the building, which got louder yet when Rodman made the free throw for a 62–47 lead.

Just when it seemed they would be run out of the building, the Sonics responded with a 9–0 run. To turn Seattle back, Kerr launched a long three over Perkins, and the Bulls ended the third period up 9, 67–58.

Jackson had left Jordan on the bench for a long stretch at the end of the third, so that he would be fresh for the kill in the fourth. But with Jordan facing double teams and his own rush of emotions, at least some of the momentum would come from Kukoc, who canned a three from the corner to push it to 70–58.

Later, Kukoc would knock down another trey for a 75–61 lead. Rodman, meanwhile, was on his way to grabbing 19 rebounds, including another 11 offensive rebounds to tie the record that he had just tied in Game 2. Kerr hit a jumper to drive it to 84–68 at 2:44, and the whole building was dancing. In the middle of this delirium, the standing ovations came one after another. The dagger, Pippen's final trey on a kickout from Jordan came at 57 seconds, and moments later was followed by the last possession of this very historic season, Jordan dribbling near midcourt, then relinquishing to Pippen for one last delirious air ball.

As soon as it was over, Jackson stepped out to hug Pippen and Jordan, who broke loose to grab the game ball and tumbled to the floor with Randy Brown. Pippen gave Kukoc a big squeeze, then grabbed Harper, his old buddy, to tell him, "Believe it! Dreams really do come true." Nearby, Jackson shared a quiet hug with Rodman. Then Jordan was gone, the game ball clutched behind his head, disappearing into the locker room, trying to escape the network cameras, searching for haven in the trainer's room, weeping on the floor in joy and pain over his memories on Father's Day.

"I'm sorry I was away for eighteen months," he would say later after being named Finals MVP. "I'm happy I'm back, and I'm happy to bring a championship back to Chicago."

In a nod to 1992, the last time the Bulls won a championship at home, the players jumped up on the courtside press table for a victory jig to acknowledge the fans. With them was Rodman, already shirtless. "I think we can consider ourselves the greatest team of all time," Pippen said with satisfaction.

Strangely, it was Karl who put the whole show in perspective. "This Bulls team is like the Pistons or Celtics, or some team from the '80s," he said. "This is the '90s, but they play with a learned mentality from an earlier time. This is an old-time package.

"I don't know about the Bird Era or the Magic Era. They were great teams, but this Bulls team has that same basic mentality. I like their heart and I like their philosophy."

Which had Jordan already gazing into the future. "Five is the next number," he said with a smile.

It was at the height of this greatest season that the relationship between Krause and Jackson came undone. Later, Jerry Reinsdorf would point out that the two men actually had very few differences in regard to basketball philosophy. Their disagreements were more personal in nature, the team chairman said. "It's the methods, not the philosophy," Jackson agreed. "It's how things are done.

"Jerry and I lost our cooperative nature, and it was just through the hardship of negotiations," Jackson would explain later. "I just felt that the negotiating wasn't done in a good manner. But negotiations can be difficult. Coaches and general managers, when they get caught up in it, sometimes get on the other sides of the fence from each other. That happened to us a little bit, and it's been tough to mend the bridge."

"We had a couple of negotiating things that weren't good," Jackson recalled. "And Jerry would talk to my agent and then call me up and say, 'Phil, there's no way we can do this.' "

The contract talks, sometimes emotional and acrimonious, dragged on into the playoffs, right in the midst of the NBA Finals between Chicago and Seattle. As the season wound down, the debate began about whether Jackson, Jordan, and Rodman, all at the end of their contracts, would come back for another season. Reinsdorf ultimately answered that question by agreeing to ante up a league record $59 million in salaries (not including $5 million for Jackson) for the 1996–97 season. But the negotiating was marked by turmoil.

"There was a situation in Seattle that was unfortunate," Jackson recalled. "There was all this stuff going on about coming back. I was caught in the middle of this thing. Michael was in the last year of his contract at $4.5 million or whatever he was making. We had a couple of other guys in that situation. We had a 72–10 season that year. And we were in the Finals, and there was a lot of press going on about it, and there was some bad tension about the division of the labor here."

Jackson was conducting a team practice at Key Arena in Seattle between games of the championship series when he noticed that Krause and some of his assistants had shown up. "We were practicing," the coach recalled, "and I kind of asked Jerry on the side, 'Is there a reason for you guys coming?' He said, 'We're gonna do our business here.'"

Krause and his assistants were busy conferring over the upcoming draft. The GM was so busy, Jackson recalled, that Krause spent most of the session with his back to the court, talking things over with his staff. During the Finals, each practice session was followed by a thirty-minute session of media interviews during which reporters are allowed onto the court to question players and coaches.

About 12:30 that day, the NBA public relations staff people notified Jackson that his team's media session was over. The NBA liked to closely control the scheduling of these events, because the league didn't like to leave one team waiting for the other to leave the floor, the coach pointed out.

Upon being notified the Bulls' interview time was up, Jackson used his trademark shrill, fingers-in-the-mouth whistle to get his players' attention and announce, "OK, everybody on the bus."

"The bus was right off the court," Jackson recalled. "So we wait five minutes, and Jerry doesn't show. And I drive out. The team bus leaves, and Jerry was irate at this situation. He didn't call me, but he called my trainer and everyone else. Well, one of the things is, I always call the shots on that. I'm the guy that runs the bus and the plane and that kind of stuff. It's the team. I left him behind in that situation. Now, whether he got caught with the press or what else . . ."

Jackson's implication was that Krause could have done his draft work back in Chicago, but moved his operation to Seattle to be closer to the worldwide press covering the championship series. The coach's decision to leave his boss behind rather than keep the players waiting would quickly become a factor in both their negotiations and their relationship.

"With the negotiations that were going on at the time, that was kind of an overload situation for him," Jackson said of Krause. "And at that point, when we came back to Chicago and we won, I saw Mr. Reinsdorf heap all the praise on Jerry in the final announcement.

"They started doing a spin on the fans being so great in Chicago. The reality is that Michael had come back and proven a tremendous point. He had retired and spent a year and a half away from it. Then he'd come back and had a failure of a return in 17 games. The '95 season was not successfully finished. We had lost to Orlando, which was one of the most difficult spots for Michael to be in.

"Then for our team to win the championship on a 72–10 year was just an absolute pie à la mode," Jackson said. "I don't care where the credit should have gone for whomever. But it was just an obvious slap in the face of the team. It was just like a pure snub."

Angered, Jackson said he considered leaving the Bulls. "The players all came to me," he recalled, "and said, 'Don't leave us. Don't go. Find a way to come back. Because we're all here. Scottie's here. Michael's gonna come back.'"

Jackson ultimately agreed to a one-year contract for the 1996–97 season, but his relationship with Krause had suffered heavy damage. That became apparent with the meetings the coaching staff and general manager hold with each Bulls player shortly after the end of each season. These sessions are essential, Jackson says, because the coaching staff uses them to bring "closure" to the season, discussing with each player his accomplishments and his plans for offseason conditioning and his role on the team for the upcoming campaign. For example, it was during the 1995 meetings that guard Ron Harper and the coaches discussed his pivotal role for the 1995–96 season, a role that was a key factor in the Bulls' winning their fourth title.

"We had a day off after the win," Jackson said of the 1996 end-of-year sessions, "and then we go into our team meetings where we debrief the players. We got into that thing. It was just a certain amount of rhythm. There's a half-hour for each player. You bring them in and talk. Some players only go fifteen minutes. But they have the team meeting."

The time was also used to give each player his share of playoff bonus money.

"Jerry wasn't there to start it out at 9:00," Jackson recalled. "He was in his office and couldn't get there. So all of a sudden, it was 9:30, 10:00, and we had three players backed up now. And I hate to have that happen to the players. They come in early to get it done. So we started doing players in a hurry, and started just cutting through what we normally would do with young players. I realized that he didn't care about this session. We had always gone through with the players and established what we wanted to do in the summertime. Established what they had to work on in terms of what their year was gonna be like the next season.

"In between the sessions, Jerry was like cold," Jackson said. "We couldn't get a conversation going on. I didn't try. I mean I was just kind of feeling it out. Then suddenly he had to disappear at a certain time, and he took another forty-five minutes off. We had more guys come through. I finally went to his door and said, 'Jerry, you gotta come and finish this off, or else cancel it. One way or another we cannot do this to people. You can't just not do it.' "

It was obvious that the general manager wasn't eager to work with him, and that had an effect on the quality of the sessions, Jackson said. "All of a sudden they were like meaningless."

9

THE HARD ROAD

In pro basketball, there is a simple axiom: Nothing is easy the second time around. Or the third, fourth, or fifth, for that matter. That notion has held true since the early seasons of the National Basketball Association, when the Minneapolis Lakers and Boston Celtics gutted their way to a series of championships. Yet the process of winning spoiled the fans for both teams, so much so that they struggled to sell tickets because success had become so routine. Michael Jordan's Chicago Bulls had their problems, but not that one. Heading into Phil Jackson's eighth season as head coach, the waiting list for seats at the United Center ran twenty-one thousand deep, and the ratings jumped whenever the Bulls appeared on television.

Still, there was that inevitable "spoiled" atmosphere around this team. The Bulls were so good that they were expected not just to win, but to dominate and confuse the opposition night after night with increasingly magical performances. All of which meant that in Chicago, the encore was the supreme challenge. "What the hell are we gonna do this time around?" Jackson always had to ask himself.

That was certainly the prevailing concern heading into the 1996–97 season as the Bulls attempted to follow their 1996 campaign, which the team concluded with an all-time best 72–10 regular season record and a 15–3 playoff run that netted Jackson and Bulls their fourth championship in six seasons.

No sooner had the confetti settled to the ground from that celebration than the media—and the Bulls themselves—began trumpeting the "drive for five," that overwhelming assumption that the team was going to claim its fifth championship in 1997.

Once again, the greatest obstacles seemed to be the excesses of success itself, with the players stacking up so much in new business, new contracts, and new product endorsements that they hardly had time to count the money. After all, the championship series concluded in late June 1996, and the celebration finally settled down sometime in July.

In the interim, poor Dennis Rodman had struggled to cram in the international shooting schedule for his movie *Double Team* and to start production of his MTV series "World Tour" before training camp opened in October. All the while, he managed to fit in autograph sessions, book promotional tours, and junkets to Las Vegas. He had come to Chicago in October 1995 facing bankruptcy, and a year later was the picture of financial health due to the wash of endorsement opportunities that came with being the wackiest Bull.

For Scottie Pippen, the summer included an appearance on Dream Team II, the U.S. Olympic basketball team, followed by surgery on a bad ankle. Guard Ron Harper and center Luc Longley also underwent offseason surgery and recuperation.

The first order, then, for Jackson and his coaching staff was to see just how big a toll success and all its gnarly attachments had taken on the team's togetherness.

"We were all very curious," said assistant coach Jimmy Rodgers, "as to how our team was going to respond after we won the championship and played into June and accomplished what we accomplished last season, winning over 70 games and then having a short summer. We were all curious as to how our team would reenergize and come back."

In Rodman's case, the answer was immediate and disappointing. In the media session opening the season, he told reporters just how bored he was with basketball, a jarring revelation in that the team had just agreed to pay him better than $9 million to play the upcoming season.

"I know Dennis made some statements in the opening press conference that he's not so excited about this," Jackson acknowledged later. "But in effect I tried to deffuse that with the team by saying that we're fortunate that we're all back together again."

Indeed, Jerry Krause had retained the core roster from the championship team, jettisoning only deep subs James Edwards and Jack Haley while adding forty-three-year-old Robert Parish as a reserve center.

Back were young forwards Jason Caffey and Dickey Simpkins, still charged with bringing energy off the bench; guards Randy Brown, the defensive specialist, and Steve Kerr, the three-point weapon; multifaceted Toni Kukoc, with his unique passing and ballhandling skills; Bill Wennington, the reserve center who worked so effectively as a spot-up shooter; and swingman Jud Buechler, whom the coaches called from the bench whenever they wanted to inject a little mayhem into the proceedings.

Mixing these components with starters Jordan, Pippen, Longley, Harper, and Rodman provided the Bulls' coaching staff with an enviable set of options.

"There's not another club in the league that kept its same unit together," Jackson said. "And we have this history of being together. There's so much less that we have to work at. There's so much more that we can experience as a team because we have that memory and that knowledge of how to do it out there on the court."

Amazingly, the league had been overrun with an unprecedented rush of free agency migration that saw nearly two hundred players change teams. The reshuffling of rosters created chaos on most other teams and a tremendous window for the Bulls.

"We've got the opportunity to do this again," Jackson told his players as camp began. "It's a wonderful opportunity. We had a lot of good fortune in the things that happened to us last year. A lot of little things added to our edge. From that standpoint, I just assume that 70 wins is a high plateau to aim for. We've been doing this for a long period of time, staying at the top of the league, and I think that the future is now in the NBA. Everything points to, 'Get it this year, and next year you make up your mind what you want to do.' This is the only time we'll be together as a group; or as a team, so let's do something special together."

After a brief camp at the Berto Center, the Bulls opened the exhibition season with an early October weekend swing through Las Vegas to play Seattle in a rematch of the 1996 NBA Finals.

Vegas seemed the perfect place for the Bulls to begin their campaign, because the season was something of a gamble for the organization with team chairman Jerry Reinsdorf agreeing to plunk down a league-record $57 million payroll to see if his club could complete that "drive for five."

On the court at the Thomas and Mack Center, Rodman wasted little time in making it clear just how much of a crapshoot Reinsdorf's gamble really was. He got a second technical late in the game against the Sonics and was booted, causing him to immediately rush at official Ken Maurer. Rodman snapped his head as if to butt Maurer, but teammate Randy Brown was there to pull him away.

Afterward, Jordan implied that Rodman was just showing off for his Vegas fans, which may have been the case, because Rodman cooled down immediately and trotted across the court to give his jersey to a woman in a wheelchair, all to deep applause from the sellout crowd. Jordan, though, sounded caution that Rodman's seeming indifference could be a storm gathering on the team's horizon.

Jackson agreed. "It will be a very different year," he said after the game, his face already weary. "I just don't know what to anticipate. I try not to anticipate. Just let it happen. Our whole scenario, our whole buildup of this ball club, is that we alone can destroy our opportunities."

The other big question, Jackson acknowledged, was the age of his crew. Rodman was thirty-five, Jordan would turn thirty-four during the season, and Harper and Pippen were well into their thirties. Could they withstand the grind of another championship push? What about the mental toll of meeting the challenge night after night in the 82-game schedule and mustering the competitive intensity required?

"Maybe the monotony might build, or the same-old, same-old that happens to a ball club," Jackson said. "So we've got to keep it fresh and new as often as we can so we can make it as entertaining as last year."

The press, meanwhile, wondered whether the one-year, $30 million contract Jordan had signed with the team meant that this would be his final NBA season. They also wondered whether the one-year contracts given to Rodman and Jackson would undermine the Bulls' chemistry.

"A lot of times in this modern-day game, people relax because they know they're going to be around for three or four years," Jordan said. "I think what we're showing is that we're going to play for the moment. We're gonna give our best moments, our best effort. We're not going to sit back and say, 'We've got another three or four years on our contract, maybe we can take a day, take a year off.' We're gonna come out here and play each and every game like it's our last."

He didn't say it publicly, but the negative experience of his contract negotiations still rested in Jordan's craw.

"It's put an edge on everything," Jackson would say privately of the negotiations that both he and Jordan had undergone with the team.

Reinsdorf and Jordan had enjoyed over the years what both considered a largely warm relationship. As the 1990s unfolded and it became increasingly clear that the player salaries in pro basketball were headed to previously unimaginable heights, Jordan was said to be bothered by the fact that he was signed to a contract that paid him in the range of $4 million annually while a dozen or more lesser players in the league were being paid twice that. After all, Reinsdorf and his friends had purchased the team for about $14 million, then watched it escalate quickly in value to $400 million or more. They had raked in tens of millions each season while Jordan's and Pippen's salaries remained relatively low. Reinsdorf admitted that even with an organizational payroll above $70 million (including coaches), the team was still making a nice profit.

All the same, Jordan was far too proud to ask for a renegotiation. Where other athletes had routinely pouted and fretted and demanded renegotiations, he wanted no part of that. His answer was to live up to the deal he had signed in the highest fashion.

Yet when he abruptly retired in the fall of 1993, there were the inevitable insinuations that he did so in part because of his contract. In 1994, a reporter asked if he could be lured back for a $100 million deal. "If I played for the money," he said testily, "it would be $300 million."

Actually, considering the billions his special performances had brought to the league coffers, the number wasn't entirely out of reason. With Jordan away from the game and television ratings falling, some NBA owners had approached Reinsdorf informally about the possibility of enticing the star back to the NBA with group funding from the league. Such a notion was unprecedented, but then again Jordan's impact on the game was also unprecedented. The idea of the league paying Jordan, though, was never pursued beyond informal discussions, Reinsdorf said.

In the summer of 1993, just after the Bulls had won their third straight championship and before his abrupt retirement that fall, there had been speculation in the Chicago press that Jordan's one-year playing contract could zoom to the $50 million range. That speculation all but disappeared with the murder of Jordan's father and the star's subsequent decision to leave basketball that October of 1993.

The Bulls continued to pay Jordan despite his retirement, which, according to one of Reinsdorf's associates, was a gesture of loyalty from Reinsdorf to Jordan. But more cynical observers suggested that by continuing to pay Jordan, the team also kept his salary slot open under the league's labyrinthine salary cap rules. If nothing else, the circumstances suggested the difficulty of fostering personal relationships amid the conflicts of business. Even kind gestures could be interpreted as ploys.

In one sense, Reinsdorf and Jordan were partners in the most lucrative sports entertainment venture in history. The problem was, Jordan as a player was barred from having any real equity position in the relationship. As a result, Reinsdorf was management, and Jordan was labor. The labor costs were fixed, while the profit percentages were soaring for those with a piece of the action.

Jordan, of course, was making his tens of millions off the court, using his overpowering image to hawk a range of commercial products. In a way, that position created a comfort for him. His outside income so dwarfed his player contract that he could say with a straight face that he didn't play the game for money.

Still, his relatively meager player contract created an inequity. And when he returned to the game in 1995, he returned under his old contract, which meant that the Bulls' payroll itself remained well under $30 million and that the team could continue scoring tens of millions in profit. That, of course, was in addition to the tremendous growth in equity Jordan's brilliant play had helped create for the team's owners.

So there was easily the strong sense that Jordan was "owed." And that wasn't a feeling held just by Jordan and his representatives but by virtually anyone who had anything to do with the NBA.

If the notion wasn't entirely clear, Jordan emphasized it with his play. With the close of the 1996 playoffs, Jordan's long-term contract had finally expired; then the real trouble started.

Days after the championship celebration, the star's representatives laid out his contract demands in a phone call to Reinsdorf. Jordan's agent, David Falk, wanted a one-year contract worth just over $30 million. Reinsdorf was supposedly told he had one hour to respond.

"It was cold," said one team employee.

Although he would never admit it or discuss it publicly, the team chairman was wounded. He had assumed he had a personal relationship with Jordan. After all, hadn't he extended the opportunity to Michael to begin a pro baseball career with the White Sox? Hadn't he always made the effort to publicly and privately show his respect for his star player? Reinsdorf later told close associates that he began to think Jordan had faked their friendship to take advantage of him. After the hurt came Reinsdorf's anger. But he realized he had no choice. He had to accept the terms.

Asked about the matter, Jordan said he told David Falk, his agent, "Don't go in and give a price. I've been with this team for a long time. Everyone knows what this market value may be, or could be. If he's true to his word and honest in terms of our relationship, listen to what he says before we offer what our opinions may be."

"Falk's instruction was to go in and listen, never to negotiate," Jordan explained in an interview. "Because it shouldn't have come to a negotiation. We didn't think of it as a negotiation. We felt it was an opportunity for the Bulls to give me what they felt my value had been to the organization. As I know it, no numbers were ever talked about until I was into the game. No one wanted to put the numbers out on the table. Everyone was jockeying to see who was gonna put the first number out, which we were not gonna do. We had a number in our heads, but we really felt like it was the Bulls' place to tell us what our net worth was. And to do it from an honest state, not influenced by David, not influenced by me. Just what they felt I'd meant to the organization."

Reinsdorf recalled that he could have employed Jordan for two years for $50 million and opted instead to take one for $30 million, a decision he would regret because he would later have to give Jordan a second contract for $33 million for 1998.

As for the 1996 negotiations, Jordan acknowledged that they came down to a final rushed phone call to Reinsdorf. Jordan said he was about to enter negotiations with the New York Knicks and was in fact prepared to leave the Bulls to play in New York.

"At the time they were negotiating I was in Tahoe for a celebrity golf tournament," he explained. "And we had some conversations with New York. And we were gonna meet with them right after we met with Reinsdorf, and I think that was within an hour's time. David wanted the Bulls to make their offer and discuss it before we go down and have a conversation with New York. But he knew he had a window in terms of the conversation with New York."

Even Reinsdorf had trouble arguing with the amount Jordan had asked for. In fact, the star could have pushed for far more and enjoyed the support of public opinion that he deserved every penny. But in agreeing to the deal, Reinsdorf made a comment to Jordan that would further damage their relationship: he said he would live to regret giving Jordan the $30 million.

"Michael is bitter at Jerry," explained one Bulls employee, "because when Jerry agreed to pay him the $30 million, Jerry told Michael that he would regret it. Michael stood in the training room one day the next fall and told all his teammates, 'You know what really pissed me off? Jerry said, "You know what Michael? I'm gonna live to regret this."'

"Michael said, 'What the fuck? You could say, "You deserve this. You're the greatest player ever, you're an asset to the city of Chicago and the organization. And I'm happy to pay you $30 million." You could say that, but even if you don't feel that way and you're going to regret it, why are you telling me that?' Luc was standing there and said, 'Really? Jerry told you he was going to regret it?' Michael said, 'He told me that. I couldn't believe my owner told me that.'"

"That creates tremendous bitterness," the team employee said.

"I said I 'might' live to regret it," Reinsdorf later admitted.

"Actually, he said, 'Somewhere down the road, I know I'm gonna regret this,' Jordan recalled. "It demeaned what was happening. It took away from the meaning of things. The gratitude seemed less because of that statement. I felt it was inappropriate to say that."

The team chairman had reportedly made a similar comment to another popular Bulls player a few seasons earlier. That player, a role player who had spent several seasons working under a contract that paid him relatively little, had finally earned a substantial pay raise. Reinsdorf agreed to an increased contract but upon signing the deal told the hard-working player, "I can't believe I'm paying you this kind of money."

The former player said the comment angered and insulted him and was typical of a management mentality where Reinsdorf and Krause wanted to "win" every contract negotiation with every player. That desire to get the best of the players in contract negotiations erased any good feelings between players and management, the respected former player said. And it usually resulted in an ill mood from Krause or Reinsdorf whenever they "lost," the player said.

"He's loyal, he's honest," Jackson said of Reinsdorf. "He's truthful. His word means something. But there's something about going in and trying to get the best every time. Winning the deal. When it comes to money, to win the deal.

"He has actually said those things, according to people I've been close to," Jackson said of Reinsdorf's comments, "and those things really hurt. Because most everybody really likes Jerry Reinsdorf.

"But," Jackson added with a laugh, "Jerry is Jerry. Jerry is . . . Jerry doesn't spend money freely, even with himself. He wants value for money.

Who doesn't? The salaries that have happened in the past ten years have been real difficult for owners to swallow. Large money. It's an amazing amount of money. I understand it. I'm not spending that money, but if I had to spend that money . . . Sometimes you're seeing a lot of money coming in, and then the ones going out are even bigger. You say, 'I wonder if the stuff coming in is going to match what's going out during this period of time.'

"It's a step of faith all the time for them to do it," Jackson said of Reinsdorf and Krause handing out large contracts. "But every time they've taken that step, there's been a reward for them. They've gotten more money to come in. And so it's kind of like this faith proposition. The more you seed, the more you're gonna reap."

In the final analysis, it comes down to faith in the NBA itself, Jackson said, "and faith in the people in this organization."

If there was anything about the Bulls that wasn't open to question, it was Jordan himself. There was no better proof of this than the preseason game in Las Vegas. Although it was only an exhibition, Jordan's eyes were afire and he was going full guns in an amazingly physical battle with Craig Ehlo, who had just signed on with the Sonics. They pushed and shoved and fought so hard for position that Jordan even took a quick swing at Ehlo that was missed, or ignored, by the officials.

He wanted to make it clear that he was starting off this season the way he closed things out last year. "I want to be consistent every night," Jordan explained afterward. "I want to step on the court and accept every challenge."

Cracking the Case

The Bulls whipped Boston on the road to open the regular season, then returned home to the United Center to receive their 1996 championship rings. From there, the Bulls rolled out to the best start in franchise history, eviscerating twelve straight opponents. Jordan gave the blastoff a little extra push by zipping Miami for 50 points in the third game of the season.

The motivation for this outburst could be traced to the spring before, when sportswriters and analysts began debating whether Chicago was the greatest team ever. Individually, Bulls players were reluctant to speak out on the issue. As Jordan pointed out, "Anybody else win 72 games?" Yet there was little question that Jackson made sure his Bulls saw the 1996–97 schedule as an opportunity to settle the matter once and for all.

"They're just smart," Seattle forward Shawn Kemp said of the Bulls. "They have a team where they don't make a lot of mistakes. They don't win off true athletic ability. They win off true intelligence."

Kemp said he was surprised that more teams couldn't muster the bravado to at least give the Bulls a decent challenge. "After a while, some of these teams are going to get embarrassed by the way the Bulls are sweeping through these cities."

The streak had followed the Bulls' familiar pattern of the previous season. They often toyed with a team early, then selected some point, usually in the second or third quarter, to break the opponent down with pressure defense. It was a pattern that would persist throughout the 1996–97 campaign.

"It's definitely satisfying to come out every night and feel like we dismantle people at some point in the game," said Chicago center Luc Longley. "We've done that every game so far and that's fun."

The sign was a certain look of defeat in opponents' eyes, usually after Jordan made a shot and gave them a smile or a wink, which talked louder than trash.

"I see that almost every night," Longley said. "That's one of the great things about playing on this team."

Asked about the look of defeat in the other team's eyes, Jordan replied, "Sure. You can tell."

Asked if he ever thought about pitying any of his victims, Jordan quickly said, "No. No one ever pitied me when I was [in the same situation] earlier in my career. No pity. We just want to go out and keep this going."

"It's arrogance to label people victims, I think," Longley said, adding that battling arrogance was one of the Bulls' challenges. "You got to be careful not say things that will come back and bite you. We've got to be careful to keep our i's dotted and our t's crossed. But not getting ahead of yourself is an important thing. I think we did a good job of learning that last year. We're good at it. We go to work every day and have thorough preparation for every team. We try not to be arrogant about it."

"We step on the court wanting to win every game, and I think that's a great attitude," Jordan said. "We go out there not overconfident or taking anyone for granted. We go out with the motivation that each team is trying to take something from us."

With the competition so weak-kneed, Jackson constantly reminded his players that it was important to play to their own standards. That, however, wasn't so easy when the opponent acted like a deer caught in a headlight.

"It's tough," Jordan explained, "to find perfection in your own game when the other team is going right down the alley that you want them to go down, in terms of fast shots, missed shots, rebounds, getting out on the break, playing solid defense. It's a temptation to get away from the things that make us a great team. Behind-the-back-passes, alley-oop passes, trying things that in normal situations we wouldn't try because they're not in the team concept, the team system. Phil is really trying to keep us to the basics."

"Phil is an amazing coach," Winter observed. "He has tremendous patience. I think he sees a lot of things that I can't see in these players. That's because he had the playing experience himself that he had. He doesn't get as concerned about things as I do. He can sit there and let more bad things go on in the course of a ball game than any coach I've ever been associated with or known. And it's healthy to an extent, because he wants the players to work their ways out of difficult situations. He thinks they'll have more growth and learn more that way. The players know that. Even when they make big mistakes in a game he's not critical of them. Oftentimes I am. He's not. But he lets them know in practice the next day, or in videotape review. He points out the mistakes then. Or it might be on an individual basis. He might call a player in and talk to him individually, so that he's not embarrassing them in front of the whole team. One good thing about this ball club, it's hard to embarrass them in front of the whole team because they're so open with each other. It's amazing how they ridicule each other when they make mistakes. They're supportive, very supportive, don't get me wrong, but at the same time, they're very critical of each other, and they kind of make a joke out of it. The chemistry is good because of the leadership that Jordan and Pippen provide. They kind of set the tone; they work hard in practice every single day; they're willing to step back and do what they can for their teammates oftentimes, to support their teammates. Yet they let their teammates know what they expect of them, including Dennis Rodman."

Part of the success rested on the fact that most teams continued to run isolation offenses against them. When it didn't work, those teams for some strange reason had no second option.

"That plays right into our favor, playing halfcourt offense with that isolation situation," Jordan said. "I think we have enough of a team defense to collapse. If we need to double-team, we rotate well, and we have good individual defensive players. If the other team misses, we rebound the ball and start our break."

It would have been good strategy for opponents to run the Bulls and force them to shift strategy to control the tempo. But few teams could run wisely.

With the team struggling to regain its competitive nucleus, it had been Jordan who pushed things ahead with his intensity. He was named the league's Player of the Month for November after averaging 31.9 points, 4.9 rebounds, 3.4 assists, and 1.5 steals while playing nearly 36 minutes per game. He did this while completing the renovation of his offensive game into the sport's deadliest jump-shooting weapon.

"Michael is relying a little bit more on the outside shot," observed Winter, then seventy-five, "but I think that's what he feels he can get the easiest out of the offense, that and the post-up. He's not trying to take the ball to the hole as much as he did at one time, and I think that's wise that he doesn't. He's still getting his 30-plus points a ball game, and he's getting it a little easier than he did at one time. At his age, that's a smart thing.

"In my mind it works better for the offense when he's not into the show so much, but in his mind I'm not sure that it is. In his mind, he still likes to penetrate, to take the ball into a crowd, get himself in what I call that compromised position and then make the play out of that. In my eyes, that's not necessary in the way we play the game. But he makes it successful, so I guess it becomes a plus."

On November 30, against San Antonio, Jordan scored his 25,000th career point, making him the second fastest player in league history (behind Wilt Chamberlain) to reach that milestone.

The team suffered its first loss in a road game at Utah. Rodman was badly outplayed by Karl Malone and cost the Bulls the game with a key late technical for shoving Jeff Hornacek. Afterward, Rodman said he had been bored by the proceedings.

A few nights later the Bulls nearly suffered a second loss, to the Los Angeles Clippers, when forward Laught Voy made Rodman look bad. "If we win it again, I'll come back," Dennis said afterward, wearing pink suede shoes and a blue suede jacket. "If we don't, I'm getting out. I've already made my mark in this game. I've got other things to do."

That same week the pressure on Rodman increased dramatically when Bulls center Luc Longley left Jackson and his teammates miffed after he injured his shoulder while body-surfing in California.

Longley, after all, was the giant body who anchored the Bulls' defense and played the pivotal pinch-post position in their triangle offense. Although Longley (who would be out of action until January) had been prone to bouts of erratic play, he had given the Bulls the frontcourt size that presented matchup problems for many other teams.

The Bulls returned home to face their second loss of the season, to the Miami Heat, which brought more complaints that Rodman had been outplayed—this time, by the Heat's P. J. Brown. The Heat erupted in ecstatic celebration on the United Center floor. "We'll have that memory," Jordan promised afterward.

In a loss the next night in Toronto, Jordan was clearly winded after playing more than 40 minutes against the Heat. He scored just 13 against the Raptors on 5 of 17 shooting and failed to score at all in the second half. In the fourth quarter, Jordan would post up only to kick the ball out, usually to Pippen, who finished with 28.

This time Rodman couldn't keep up with Raptors forward Popeye Jones and was ejected late in the game for disputing an offensive foul call. Afterward, in a locker room interview with The Sports Channel, Rodman spewed out a profanity-laced invective against the officials and Commissioner Stern.

The Bulls responded a day later by suspending Rodman for two games, costing him approximately $104,000 in fines (subtracted from his $9 million salary).

There had been suggestions a few weeks earlier that the team reconsidered signing Rodman pal Jack Haley, who was picked up by the La Crosse (Wisconsin) Bobcats of the CBA after the Bulls elected not to bring him back for a second season. "I don't need a baby-sitter," Rodman declared. "I don't need Jack Haley. I don't need anyone. I'm a grown man."

Jackson pointed out that Rodman had played hard in the Bulls' three losses, but "he just seemed less interested."

Rodman, however, was irritated that he could fail to win his sixth straight league rebounding title. Heading into 1997, he trailed Houston's Charles Barkley and New Jersey's Jayson Williams in the statistical rankings and was frustrated that both of those players were averaging better than 40 minutes per game while he was averaging only 33.

"Right now Dennis is struggling to find a direction to be challenged every game," Jackson said. "I keep telling him that he's going to get that rebounding title and things are going to go his way."

As he had the previous season, Rodman came back contrite and strongly focused after suspension. The Bulls, meanwhile, had continued to prosper without Rodman's full attention. They racked up a 15–1 November and sank to 11–4 in December, but finished the month by winning 10 of 11 games. The more they won, the more fans were drawn to them, making team life on the road hectic and sometimes bizarre.

"The elevators," team trainer John Ligmanowski replied when asked what part of the team's travel routine had become most difficult in the face of the crowds that greeted them in almost every city. "Just trying to get guys on the hotel elevator. All of a sudden everybody wants to get on the elevator as soon as the Bulls get there. We had some security trying to get the people off the elevator, and they would complain, 'Well, I'm staying here, too. I want to go up in the elevator, too.' You know what they want to do. They want to find out where the players are, what rooms they're in."

The on-court highlights of the first half of the season were topped by a December overtime win over the Lakers in the United Center. Los Angeles had dominated Chicago through three quarters, building a fat lead until the Bulls' pressure defense began forcing Lakers turnovers in the fourth quarter and Toni Kukoc got hot from three-point range. His 31 points allowed the Bulls to tie it at the buzzer, then break it open 129–123 in overtime, leaving the young Lakers aching and embarrassed.

Jordan had 30 and Pippen 35, making the first time in team history that three players had scored more than 30 in a single game.

The Bulls then opened 1997 by winning their first seven games, including a 110–86 thrashing of the Houston Rockets. On the 15th of January, Jordan passed Alex English (25,613) to become the eighth leading scorer in league history.

Unfortunately, that night will be better remembered for Rodman's kicking a courtside cameraman in the groin in Minneapolis, a move that brought an eleven-game suspension and more than $1 million in fines and lost income. Jordan and Pippen had never hesitated to express their displeasure with Rodman's misbehavior, but the kicking incident brought a strong reaction from teammates and fans. Observers resumed wondering why the Bulls would put up with all the shenanigans. The answer, however, lay in the videotape of 1996's playoff games, when Rodman's masterful rebounding and bucked-up frontcourt play rescued Chicago night after night.

"There was no question," Tex Winter said, "that the situation got to the point where it was, 'One more deal and you're outta here.' But at the same time it was never addressed in those terms, yet Dennis still definitely got the message.

"Jerry Krause and Phil Jackson and even Michael Jordan let him know there are certain standards that the Chicago Bulls expect of their players, and you have to meet those standards to be a part of it. Now if you can't do it, you won't be a part of it. I don't think Phil Jackson has ever run out of patience with Dennis.

"I enjoy Dennis," Winter added. "I enjoy coaching him. I'm always concerned a little bit about what might happen off the court. I talk to him about his life a little bit, but I'm not gonna correct him or tell him how to live his life. That would be a mistake. At my age, I think he sort of looks upon me as a grandfather figure. He's willing to listen, and he's very receptive, especially in the coaching aspect of it. And he's been fun to work with on the floor as far as that's concerned."

For some, the kicking incident was simply the final sign that Rodman's physical, emotional style of play had gone too far.

"I gotta have some kind of emotion out there for me," Rodman countered. "I know the other team's not gonna do it for me, so I gotta go out there and do it myself. I try to psyche guys out. Hit 'em here and hit 'em there and try to get them out of position. Try to frustrate guys. That's my game, and it works most of the time."

His coaches and teammates knew how important he was to this team. They just wanted to keep him focused enough to earn the home-court advantage for the playoffs.

"I am concerned when we go into a ball game because he is an emotional guy," Winter said of Rodman. "We don't want to take that energy away from him. One of the reasons that he's such a terrific player is that he's so energized. He gives this basketball team that same kind of energy. And if you squelch him, if you say, 'Dennis, you can't do this and you can't do that,' well then he's probably not gonna be nearly the basketball player that he is. Because of the way he is."

With the Rodman distraction, the Bulls suffered a 102–86 spanking in Houston, but then went on to win the last six games in January to close out the month with a 13–1 record. The run included Jordan's 51 points against the Knicks after New York coach Jeff Van Gundy said Jordan befriended and "conned" players on opposing teams to defuse their competitiveness. The allegation infuriated Michael, and he answered with the kind of performance that New Yorkers had come to know all too well.

February opened with another Jordan tiff, this time with Seattle coach George Karl, who had suggested what any fan could clearly see: that Jordan had resorted more often to jump shooting as opposed to attacking the basket. Jordan used this imagined slight to push Chicago to a 91–84 win over

Seattle to open the Bulls' West Coast road swing. The burst of energy propelled them to five straight wins.

Although the Lakers had lost Shaquille O'Neal to a January knee injury, they were fired up enough to hammer out a 106–90 win over the Bulls, who finished up the road trip at 5–1 just before the All-Star break.

At the All-Star festivities in Cleveland, the league celebrated its 50th anniversary by honoring the 50 greatest players in NBA history at halftime. Jordan and Pippen were among those selected, and Jackson was picked for the list of the league's 10 best coaches.

To emphasize his standing, Jordan finished the game with the first triple-double in All-Star Game history (14 points, 11 rebounds, and 11 assists). Added to Chicago's loot was Steve Kerr's win in the three-point shootout.

That success, plus the return of Longley and Rodman, helped push the Bulls on another big win streak coming out of the break. The stretch included a career-high 47 points by Scottie Pippen against Denver.

"Scottie all around might be as fine a player as there is in the NBA," Winter observed at the time. "But he's not a great shooter; he's a scorer. And there's times when he's not even a great scorer. He has very poor shooting nights at times. He seems to get out of sync, out of rhythm, on occasion, and it might even last over a period of several games. But he seems to always snap out of it—and the bigger the game, the better Scottie plays. If he feels like he has to, Scottie can take a lot of pressure off of Jordan and then suddenly he becomes a real scorer, where at other times he's satisfied not to even shoot the ball. If Jordan's having a good night and the other players are having a good night, then Pippen doesn't care about his own offense. That's one of the things that makes him a great player."

"He's had a consistent year," Jordan said of Pippen. "Last year he got off to a great start, where he was putting up some big offensive numbers. But I think you look at what he's done this year, it's been just as consistent, All-Star caliber. A lot of times he can get overlooked because of my play. But I certainly couldn't be as effective without him. We've complemented each other very well. He's certainly my MVP."

On February 22, the Bulls went to Washington and played the Bullets with President Clinton in the stands, the first time a president had attended an NBA game since the Carter administration.

"He came in the locker room and greeted everybody and knew everybody's name and made it around and was comfortable talking to the team," Jackson said of the president.

On the court against Washington, Jordan struggled for three quarters, then wowed the crowd and the president with a fourth-quarter shooting display that drove Chicago to yet another victory.

"Suddenly," Jordan said, "you find one little play, a jump shot or a certain move, you say 'OK, I'm coming back to this. . . .'"

Washington's Harvey Grant saw him hit the first two shots of the fourth quarter and turned to a teammate and said, "Oh, no, here he goes."

"It's always a matter of time with Michael," Jackson said with a smile. "He has that incredible energy level, and you know there's a point in the game where he'll just take it over and destroy a team."

It all translated into those same old feelings of invincibility, Jackson added. "We think we're doing things right, rolling along and taking care of business on the road, then going home to the United Center and playing the way we want to play, maintaining that home-court attitude that we've had. Games are a little tighter. Teams are playing us three and four times in the conference, and as they get to know us, they're stepping up their competitiveness."

After a 10–2 record in February, March brought its own sort of madness for the Bulls, beginning with Kukoc's foot injury on the 3rd and closing with a knee injury on the 27th that caused Rodman to miss the remainder of the regular season.

In between, the team still managed to roll up a 12–2 record, relying on the emergence of reserve forward Jason Caffey and the usual brilliance of Pippen and Jordan.

"I'm having a great time," Jordan said, "more so than last year even, because it's not the same pressure. Last year I had to prove myself. People didn't feel I could come back. I had a whole different motivation. This year I'm more relaxed. The team is more relaxed, yet we're being just as productive."

Even in the spring, after opponents had had the time to adjust their chemistries, they still found the Bulls to be an unsolvable puzzle. They rolled across April to what appeared to be a 70-win finish, pausing just long enough to make a White House visit with President Clinton, whom Pippen described as a "home boy" from Arkansas.

Part of the Bulls' momentum was the late-season acquisition of free-agent center Brian Williams, who gave them a solid post presence. But in the home stretch, they lost three of their last four games, including a final meeting at the United Center with the Knicks. Even so, at 69–13, they tied for the second best total in league history, matching the 1972 Lakers, and were five games ahead of the nearest competitor to claim home-court advantage throughout the playoffs.

"We want to meet every challenge," Jordan had said at the start of the campaign.

Once again, they had done it in top fashion, building hope along the way that the encore would be every bit as good as the original. For that to happen, Jackson told his players, they would have to regain their "togetherness." Their usually excellent chemistry had finally gone foul after struggling through an injury-riddled season.

Jackson addressed the problem with the film clips he spliced into the team's video scouting reports on the postseason. This time around, he chose *What About Bob?*, starring Bill Murray as a mental patient who tries to move in with his psychiatrist.

"Every time he used game clips, he'd put in pieces of the movie," Wennington said of Jackson. "Basically we saw the whole movie. He was implying that we got to come together, that we got to use baby steps to move along and start playing well. In the end, if we stick together and work together as a team, we're not gonna be crazy. We'll accomplish our goal and things will work out."

To help emphasize his points, Jackson also included clips of old Three Stooges movies.

"It's hard for me sometimes to read exactly what the message is in Phil's movies," Winter said with a grin. "On the Three Stooges it was pretty easy, because it was after a dumb play by one of our players."

"He's trying to break some of the monotony of going over play after play after play," center Brian Williams said of Jackson's approach. "The film always magnifies your mistakes. The film is not flattering. A lot of the times, the Three Stooges is appropriate, because we look like the Three Stooges out there."

"Tex Winter likes to sing a song when we get together for our morning sessions," Wennington explained. "He likes to sing, 'It's time we get together. Together. Together. It's time we get together. Together again.' That song is played once in the Three Stooges when Moe swallows a harmonica, and they're playing him on a harmonica. They're playing that song. That's part of the message. We need to stay together as a team."

That, of course, was Jackson's main idea. Over the spring the separate agendas of all the players had begun tugging at the fabric of the team.

Another factor eating at this togetherness stemmed from the questions about the future hanging over the heads of Jordan, Jackson, and Rodman, all on one-year contracts. Would they be back with the Bulls for another season? There was ceaseless speculation on this issue in the Chicago press, and the uncertainty tugged at the entire team's peace of mind. With the arrival of the playoffs, the Bulls wondered if the end of their great run was in sight.

"We've been together a long time, especially Phil and me," Tex Winter said of the circumstances. "Nine years. I think we understand each other pretty well. . . . Phil is the kind of guy who has the ability to not let things distract him. My Lord, I couldn't do it. If I were the head coach, I'd be a maniac by now. And my whole team would be out of whack. That's Phil's strength. This Rodman thing, all the things that come down along these lines, Phil kinda just handles it in a very natural, easy way. And yet he gets his message across as to how it should be handled."

"He's very good at handling distractions," Winter added. "As far as next season is concerned, he's said very little about it. It doesn't seem to bother him one bit about what is coming down. I've told him at times that maybe he might not be concerned but some of his staff members might be. On the other hand, he sets the tone. He says, 'We're just playing this thing out. Let's worry about today. Let's don't worry about tomorrow.'"

The result of all of these factors was a loss of cohesiveness.

"I think the team is a little different this year," Wennington observed in late April. "We're not as loose and relaxed as last year. We've been struggling a little bit. Things haven't been going as easy. There's a little edge on everyone. We're a little more serious. The last few weeks of the season, we weren't playing as well. We had all the injuries. They throw your rhythm off and at times make people a little testy."

Jordan, Pippen, and Harper were solid as a core. The three lifted weights together early each morning in what they called their "Breakfast Club." Rodman, of course, was an entity to himself. So was Kukoc, isolated somewhat by culture. Then there was the Arizona contingency of Buechler and Kerr, joined at times by Longley, the Australian, and Wennington, the Canadian. Then there were the new elements of Parish and Williams and Matt Steigenga, a late-season signee. Simpkins and Caffey and Brown would hang out some.

Despite the potential conflicts of their success, the Bulls got along far better than the average NBA team. But winning another championship would require more than a "better-than-average" approach. It would require a supreme chemistry.

Jackson was a master at pulling all the disparate elements of a team together. Perhaps there was no better example of this than Brian Williams. He, too, was a free agent, but salary cap restrictions and league compensation rules virtually assured that he would have to move on to another team at the end of the season. Never one to show a fondness for coaches (he had played for four different teams in his six-year career), he had taken an immediate shining to Jackson.

"I'm going where Phil goes," Williams said when asked about his future. "If he goes somewhere else to coach next year, that's where I'm signing. That's the way I feel about him. He's an excellent coach. In my time in the league, he's the most thorough, the most understanding coach I've been around."

Matt Steigenga, another late-season signee, expressed a similar appreciation for Jackson, especially his knack for using a player's mistakes for teaching instead of humiliation.

"He doesn't berate guys, doesn't get on them," Steigenga said. "But guys still know when they mess up. I had a college coach, if he wasn't yelling there was something wrong. When he stopped yelling at a player, he didn't care about that player any more. Phil's the other way. He rarely will scream or yell or belittle a player. But he really gets a guy to see his mistake and learn from it. His mental approach and mental prowess comes through. He has that grip on players, that feeling of force. You know this man is able to lead."

The Fifth Championship

The Bulls opened the 1997 playoffs by ditching the Washington Bullets in three quick games in a series highlighted by Jordan scoring 55 in Game 2. Washington came out strong and caught all of the Bulls blinking—except for Jordan, who proceeded through the evening like he was conducting a shooting drill in solitude. Jumper after jumper after bank shot after dunk after jumper. He made them from all over the floor, while the rest of his teammates seemed to stand transfixed.

With five minutes left in the game, Jordan drove and scored, pushing Chicago up by three. Moments later he got the ball back, motored into the lane, and flexed a pump fake that sent the entire defense flying like some third-world air force. As they settled back to earth, he stuck yet another jumper and followed it on the next possession with a drive that ended in a falling-down, impossible shot from the right baseline that pushed the lead to 7 and his point total for the evening to 49.

He then wrapped up a 55-point night (the eighth time in his career that Jordan had scored more than 50 in a playoff game) with two free throws that provided Chicago with a 109–104 win and a 2–0 series lead.

"He's the king of basketball," Washington assistant Clifford Ray said afterward. "He's thirty-four years old, but he still knows and understands 'Attack!' better than anybody in the game. He attacks all the time. He just kept churning away."

Luc Longley said Jordan's conditioning alone was astounding in that it allowed him to score and play intensely active defense over 44 minutes. "These are the games where he demonstrates who he really is," the center added. "Those performances you definitely marvel at. What I marvel at is how many of them you see a year. Perhaps he only had three or four 50-point games this year, but the 30- and 40-point games he has almost every night. The fact that at his age he can come out physically and do the things he does every night, that's what really makes me marvel."

"I've been watching him for—what is it? twelve, thirteen years?—and he showed me moves I've never seen before," Jerry Reinsdorf said. "Bill Russell once asked me what was the greatest thing about Michael, and I said it was his determination. Russell said, no, it was his imagination. He certainly had imagination tonight."

Reinsdorf was asked if Jordan's big night was a perfect dividend on the $30 million, one-year contract the team had given him. "He's earned it," the chairman said. "I've never had any regrets."

The Atlanta Hawks stepped up as the Bulls' next hurdle in the Eastern Conference playoffs and promptly claimed Game 2 of the series. For the first time in their incredible two-year run, the Bulls had surrendered home-court advantage in the playoffs. In fact, Atlanta became the first visiting team in two years to win a playoff game at the United Center. Chicago had won 39 games against only 2 regular-season losses on their home floor over each of the past two years. During that same period, the Bulls had been 13–0 in home playoff games.

Now, however, the Bulls were facing back-to-back weekend games in Atlanta, leaving Pippen to warn that "unless we do the things we did all season to get 69 wins, we're not going to pull another win out of this series."

The Bulls seemed far from the togetherness that Jackson was urging. Pippen, in particular, seemed perturbed with Rodman, who had struggled throughout the postseason with his return from the knee injury and with the officials, who had greeted him every playoff game with a technical or two.

"We've got to have a big effort from Dennis," Pippen said in his postgame press conference. "If he's not going to lead us in rebounding, don't lead us in technical fouls, because we don't need those."

Jackson later addressed the comments in a team meeting, reminding his players to stick together. "It's very unusual for this team," Tex Winter said of Pippen's open criticism of Rodman. "Generally they've been very supportive of each other. . . . Phil handles this by saying simply, 'We're not pointing fingers at each other. Let's go out and do our jobs.'"

The other concern for the coaches was that Jordan, who had hit just 12 of 29 from the floor in Game 2, suddenly seemed to be pressing on offense, as if he felt he had to carry the entire load. "If he's not shooting any better percentage shots than that, then he shouldn't be taking so many of them," Winter said. "Phil's told him not to force things, not to try to do too much. To move the ball. And Michael knows that. Michael's a smart player. But he's so competitive and he's got so much confidence in himself that it's hard for him to restrain. I've never been associated with a player—I don't think anybody has—who has any less inhibitions than he does."

It was pointed out that Winter was taking the diplomatic way of saying Michael had no conscience. "Well, that's one of the reasons he's a great player," Winter replied. "He has no conscience."

Yet Jordan clearly had a sense of team. With little or no complaint, he complied with Jackson's request to ease up on his aggressiveness. Although Rodman's situation saw no improvement, the Bulls rediscovered their team concept and took two games from the Hawks in Atlanta.

Then the Bulls closed out the series back in Chicago, where Rodman scored 7 quick points to stake the Bulls to a 33–27 lead and went on to finish the contest with 12 points (including a pair of three-pointers), 9 rebounds, 3 assists, and a steal. He even blocked one of Dikembe Mutombo's shots.

Rodman was ejected after a profanity-laced exchange with the Atlanta center in the fourth period, but by then he had provided the hypercharge his team needed to subdue the Hawks, 107–92, and claim the series 4–1. It was a grand way to celebrate his thirty-sixth birthday, and the crowd seemed to reconnect with his energy.

The victory sent the Bulls to their seventh appearance in the Eastern Conference finals in nine seasons, this time to face Pat Riley's surprising Miami

Heat club. There was little doubt that meeting Riley still stoked Phil Jackson's competitive fires. Since his Bulls had clashed with Riley's Knicks in the early 1990s, the two had harbored a competitive animosity for one another. An upset loss to the Riley's Heat late in the 1996 season had prompted Jackson to enter the locker room and tell his players, "Never lose to that guy."

So the 1997 Eastern Conference finals became a showdown of coaching styles: Jackson's cerebral approach versus Riley's intensity; Chicago's triangle offense up against Miami's clutching, snakebiting, overplaying defense.

The Heat had won 61 games, mainly because point guard Tim Hardaway, in his second season playing for Riley, had gotten comfortable in his surroundings and turned in an All-Star year. In Game 1, though, Rodman's rebounding and the Bulls' pressure defense propelled Chicago to a win.

"The thing that shocked me the most is just the way we got taken apart at the end," veteran Heat reserve Eddie Pinckney said after watching his team lose the first game. "The Bulls are able to pressure on all the trigger points of your offense. Next thing you know the shot clock is down and you're throwin' up a shot from 30 feet out, or you commit a charge or something. It's like a blitz defense."

Pinckney remarked that the air of confidence was tangible in the United Center, and it wasn't something that other teams liked. "I guess it's routine for teams to come in here and play hard and still lose at the end," he said. "The Bulls are entitled to that attitude."

Actually, neither team had managed to shoot the ball well in the atmosphere of frenzied defense, set in motion by Riley's brand of scrambling, holding, bumping, brushing, or anything else that worked. The final for Game 2, a 75–68 Bulls win, set an all-time NBA playoff record low for scoring. Not since the days before the 24-second shot clock was installed had teams turned in such meager totals.

Hardaway, Miami's main weapon, was just 5 for 16 from the field. And Jordan made only 4 of 15 attempts. "Both teams were frustrated with their offensive play," Jackson said.

"We played ugly against Atlanta. We played ugly against Washington. It isn't the competition. It's just us. Except for our defense. Our defense has won games," Jordan, whose 23 points included 15 free throws, told reporters afterward. "Our offense has kept people in the stands. Defense has been winning championships for us in the past."

Behind the scenes, the Bulls' coaching staff spent hours reviewing the tapes of the first two games and came up with a plan to spread their triangle offense, an adjustment they had rarely used over the years. To say the least, it caught Riley and his players flat-footed and opened the back-door lanes to the basket for an array of layups and slams in Game 3. The Bulls exploded with a 13–4 run to open the second quarter and another 11–0 spurt midway through the third.

The Miami crowd sat in misery, with only Rodman's new dye job (from his fundamental blond to another multihued look) and dark purple fingernails to keep them entertained as the Bulls smoked their way to the finish, 98–74.

"We got embarrassed out there today collectively," Miami's Alonzo Mourning admitted afterward. "They just did what they wanted to do out there, and we did nothing to counter it.

"It's tough to stop a team like that because they've perfected their offense so well. If one part of their offense breaks down, they're able to go to another option."

It was as well as the triangle offense had ever functioned against an aggressive defense, Winter said, adding quickly that the Bulls' previous championship teams, featuring John Paxson and Bill Cartwright, probably executed the offense better than the current group. Winter would eventually look back on the day as one of Jackson's finest coaching exhibitions.

The other part of the Chicago equation was their trusty defense, which included a fine low-post effort from Rodman. Chicago had forced Miami into 32 turnovers. "It's almost like an amoeba defense," Riley said. "They take away angles. They deny your trigger passes. They're long. They switch on everything. They are an exceptional defensive team. You can't rely on just scoring in your halfcourt. If you're not running and rebounding and getting second shots at every opportunity you get, then it's gonna be very difficult to score."

It seemed foolhardy at the time, but who could have known that Jordan would decide to play 45 holes of golf on his day off between games? Who would have figured His Airness to make just 2 of his first 22 shots in Game 4?

Yet no matter how deep a hole he dug for himself and his teammates Jordan found a means to bring them rushing back at the end. Finding themselves down 21 points with the clock eating away the second half, the Bulls abandoned the triangle offense that had worked so well just the day before and watched Jordan go into his attack mode.

The Heat surged right back at the beginning of the fourth, pushing their margin back to a dozen, 72–60. Jordan then scored 18 straight points for

Chicago, a display that trimmed the Miami lead to just one with only 2:19 to go. The ending, however, came down to the Heat making a final six free throws, good enough for a Miami win.

Jordan had scored 20 of Chicago's 23 points in the fourth quarter. "When he started making them, they just came, came, came, came, came," said Tim Hardaway. "He's a scorer, he's the man."

The good news in Game 4 was another outstanding effort from Rodman, who finished with 13 points and 11 rebounds, a performance he would nearly equal back in Chicago in Game 5 with another 13 rebounds and 9 points.

Jordan, too, continued on his tear from the end of Game 4. He opened Game 5 with 15 in the first quarter, good enough for a 33–19 Bulls lead and little doubt as to the outcome. The only cloud as they closed out the Heat 100–87 was a first-quarter foot injury to Pippen that kept him on the bench the last three quarters.

"They are the greatest team since the Celtics won 11 in 13 years [from 1957–69]," Riley told reporters afterward. "I don't think anybody's going to win again until Michael retires."

The Utah Jazz, winners of 64 games, emerged from the Western Conference playoffs to challenge the Bulls in the 1997 Finals.

To get his players ready for the championship round, Jackson brought yet another movie out of the dustbin, *Silverado*, a 1985 Western starring Kevin Kline, Kevin Costner, and Danny Glover as good outlaws who take on the bad sheriff in a Western town.

"It's one of those quick draw movies, quick gun movies," Tex Winter said, "and I guess the key to it is that you better react quicker than the opposition."

And certainly shoot better than they do.

That became imminently clear on Sunday, June 1, in Game 1 of the championship series, broadcast to a worldwide audience. The comforting sight for Bulls fans was Pippen grinning broadly in pregame warm-ups. He hopped around on his injured foot and seemed ready to go.

The other welcome sight for old-time Bulls fans was Utah coach Jerry Sloan, hands jammed in pockets, awaiting the introductions, scanning the Chicago crowd—a crowd better behaved and not as rabid as the one that used to cheer him on in old Chicago Stadium. For almost a decade, Sloan had been "Mr. Bull" during his playing days in the Windy City, leading the Bulls with his hard-nosed, physical style of play. He had even served as an assistant and later the team's head coach, right up until his firing in 1981.

Utah's Karl "the Mailman" Malone had just a few days earlier been named the league's regular-season Most Valuable Player. He had narrowly edged Jordan, the prime contender and four-time winner of the award. Jordan said he didn't mind the Jazz power forward getting the individual honor, so long as the Bulls claimed the team championship at the end of playoffs. Now the stars and their respective teams were meeting to settle the matter on the court, with fans in both Chicago and Utah eager to seize on the issue, chanting "MVP" when one or the other stepped to the free throw line at key moments throughout the series.

The Jazz rushed out to a solid start in Game 1 by throwing quick double teams at Jordan and working the boards hard, good enough for a quick Utah lead.

The Bulls obviously felt the tension, evidenced by their 40 percent shooting in the first half. Utah was slightly better at 44 percent, with John Stockton scoring 11 and Malone 10. Utah's Bryon Russell hit a three-pointer just before the buzzer to give the Jazz a 42–38 halftime lead.

Jeff Hornacek scored 11 points in the third period to help keep Utah in the lead, except for a brief run by Chicago that netted a one-point edge. The fourth opened with Utah clutching a two-point lead in the face of a mountain of Chicago's trademark pressure.

With just under eight minutes to go, Stockton hit a jumper, pushing the Utah lead to 70–65, which Harper promptly answered with a trey. Surging on that momentum, the Bulls managed to stay close and even took a one-point edge on a Longley jumper with three minutes left.

Malone responded with two free throws, but Harper snuck inside for an offensive rebound moments later and passed out to Pippen for a trey that put Chicago up 81–79. For most teams, that would have been enough pressure for a fold, but Stockton hit a three of his own with 55 seconds left to make it 82–81, Utah.

Then at the 35.8 mark, Hornacek fouled Jordan, who stepped to the line with the building chanting "MVP." He hit the first to tie it, then missed the second, sending the crowd back to its nervous silence. The Jazz promptly spread the floor and worked the shot clock. As it ran down, Stockton missed a trey, but Rodman fouled Malone on the rebound.

As Malone prepared to shoot his free throws, Pippen whispered in his ear, "The Mailman doesn't deliver on a Sunday." To ensure that, the crowd raised a ruckus. His first shot rolled off the rim, and the building exploded in celebration. He stepped back from the line in disgust, then stepped back up, wiped his hand on his shirt, dropped eight short dribbles, and missed again, bringing yet another outburst of delight from the crowd as the Bulls controlled the rebound with 7.5 seconds left. "I'm from Summerfield, Louisiana, and we don't have any excuses down there. So I'm not going to use any," Malone would say later. "It was agonizing, but I won't dwell on it."

Amazingly, the Jazz decided not to double-team Jordan on the last possession. Pippen inbounded the ball to Kukoc, who quickly dumped it off to Jordan, who executed a move on Bryon Russell and broke free just inside the three-point line on the left side. The entire building froze there for an instant upon the release of the shot. When it swished, twenty-one thousand fans leaped instantly in exultation. The shot gave the Bulls the win, 84–82, and the Jazz sank instantly, knowing they had just lost any hopes they had of controlling the series.

Asked afterward who deserved the MVP, Malone replied, "Obviously, it's Michael Jordan, no matter what Karl Malone says or not. Michael wanted the ball at the end and made the shot, and it's hard to argue with that."

Jordan had finished with 31 points on 13 of 27 shooting while Malone rebounded after missing 7 of his first 8 shots to score 23 on the night with 15 rebounds.

"I think anyone watching anywhere in the world knew who would take the shot," Stockton said of the game winner.

The Bulls opened Game 2 three nights later as loose as the Jazz were tight, and the scoring showed it. Jordan hit a jumper, then Pippen finished off a Harper back-door pass with a sweet little reverse, and moments later Longley broke free for an enthusiastic stuff. Like that, the Jazz were in a maze and couldn't find their way out.

Long known for their sadism, the Bulls' game management people had set up Part II of Malone's little chamber of personal horrors by declaring it Clacker Night and passing out noisemakers by the thousands to fans as they entered the building.

When Longley fouled Malone 90 seconds into the game, the clackers were waiting and rattled him into two free throw misses. Two minutes later, when Malone went to the line again with the Jazz trailing 8–1, the whole barn was rattling. This time, Malone stepped up and hit both. Given a momentary rush of confidence, Utah closed to 14–13 at the 4:41 mark of the first period.

Jordan was afire, though, and quickly squashed any momentum with a trey and a jumper. Then he fed Kerr for a pair of treys, and just like that, Chicago had stretched the lead to 25–15 with 1:30 left in the period, which had fans on their feet clapping and pounding to "Wooly Bully."

The Jazz dug in and made a run in the second period, bringing it to 31–29 with a Malone bucket. Just when it seemed Utah might find some life, the killer in Jordan emerged. He drove the Bulls to a 47–31 lead, scoring and drawing fouls like only he could. At every trip to the free throw line, the fans greeted Jordan with lusty chants of "MVP! MVP!"

How big was his hunger? That seemed to be the only question. Jordan finished the night with 38 points, 13 rebounds, and 9 assists. He would have registered a triple-double if Pippen hadn't blown a late layup, costing him the tenth assist. No matter—the Bulls coasted to a 2–0 series lead, 97–85.

"I thought we were intimidated right from the beginning of the game," Sloan said afterward. "If you allow them to destroy your will to win, it's hard to compete."

The series then shifted to Utah, where the 4,000-foot altitude in Salt Lake City had the Bulls winded for the better part of a week. The team stayed in the nearby ski resort of Park City, which had an elevation of about 8,000 feet, in hopes it would help the players adjust. But the Jazz took a 61–46 halftime lead in Game 3 and did a little coasting of their own, pulling the series to 2–1 with a 104–93 victory, during which Jazz fans showered Malone with "MVP" chants. He answered their support by scoring 37 points with 10 rebounds to lead the rout.

Game 4 on Sunday, June 8, unfolded as what was easily the Bulls' biggest disappointment of the season. The offense still sputtered, but the defense for 45 minutes was spectacular. In short, they played well enough to win, and should have. With 2:38 to go in the game, they had willed their way to a 71–66 lead and seemed set to control the series 3–1.

But Stockton immediately reversed the momentum with a 25-foot three-pointer. Jordan came right back with a 16-foot jumper, and when Hornacek missed a runner, the Bulls had a chance to close it out. Instead, Stockton timed a steal from Jordan at the top of the key and drove the length of the court. Jordan recovered, then raced downcourt and managed to block the shot, only to get whistled for a body foul—a call that might not have been made in Chicago, Jordan later pointed out.

Stockton made one of two to pull Utah within three. Pippen then missed a corner jumper, and Stockton was fouled and made both with 1:03 left to cut the lead back to 73–72. Jordan missed a jumper on the next possession, and Stockton rebounded and looped a perfect baseball pass down to Malone for a 74–73 Utah lead.

The Bulls' next possession brought Kerr a wide-open three-pointer from the right corner that missed. With 17 seconds left, Chicago fouled Malone, setting up repeat circumstances from Game 1. Would he miss again in the clutch? Pippen wanted to talk to him about that, but Hornacek stepped in to keep him away from the Mailman.

"I knew what he was doing, trying to talk to me," Malone said. "He still talked to me the whole time I was shooting."

Pippen went into rebounding position and yelled "Karl! Karl!"

His first shot knocked around the rim before falling in, smoothing the way for the second and a 76–73 lead. With no timeouts, the Bulls were left with only a rushed three-point miss by Jordan, which Utah punctuated with a breakaway slam for the 78–73 final, the second lowest scoring game in league championship history.

"I guess the Mailman delivers on Sundays out here," Pippen acknowledged afterward.

Jordan had scored 22 points, and a foreign journalist asked whether he felt mortal. "There's gonna be games where I can't live up to the fantasy or the hype of what people have built up Michael Jordan to be," he replied. "I'm accustomed to living with that."

A year later, a team employee would reveal that a Gatorade switchup had possibly cost the Bulls Game 4. A team assistant got confused and served the players Gator Lode instead of Gatorade. "That's something you drink after the game," longtime Bulls equipment manager John Ligmanowski said of the Gator Lode. "It's a high-carbohydrate drink. So they each had the equivalent to twenty baked potatoes during the game. It slowed 'em down a little bit.

"Dennis and Michael and Scottie, they all had stomachaches," Ligmanowksi added. "They were drinking Gator Lode instead of Gatorade. Dennis had to run off the floor to go to the bathroom. Scottie was laying down, and Michael asked to be taken out of the game. And he never asks that, or very rarely."

Trying to figure out what was going on, trainer Chip Schaefer discovered the mistake late in the game and was furious. But by then it was too late. The "baked potatoes" had begun to weigh heavily on the Bulls' bellies. Still, they had managed to take a five-point lead with about two and a half minutes remaining in the game when the Jazz surged past them, outscoring Chicago 13–2 to win 78–73, tying the series.

Needless to say, Gator Lode was not a problem thereafter. "We got that straightened out," Ligmanowski said.

After moving at a breakneck pace, playing every other day, the NBA Finals slowed down again, giving the Bulls an agonizing three-day wait before pivotal Game 5 on Wednesday. Asked about the time off, an obviously despondent Steve Kerr said, "I try not to think about it. It hasn't been fun."

Actually, none of the Bulls seemed too relaxed. Kukoc was shooting 34 percent for the series and averaging 7.5 points. Kerr had made only 3 of his 12 trey attempts. Harper was shooting 33 percent and averaging 5.5 points. Rodman was averaging a little over 5 rebounds in each of the first four games. Even Jordan, who had shot 51 percent in the first two games, had seen his shooting drop to 40 percent in the next two.

"They're giving us everything we can ask for," Pippen said of the Jazz. "Five, six days ago, everyone was predicting that we would sweep this team. Now everything is turned around."

Just when it seemed their predicament couldn't get worse, Jordan came down with a viral illness in the wee hours before Game 5. Never had a Bulls locker room been so quiet. About the only sound in the room was Ligmanowski whistling as he worked, trying to cut the tension. In the darkness of the training room a few feet away, Jordan lay sick. However, at least one veteran Bulls staff member wasn't fooled. "Michael's sick?" he asked. "He'll score 40."

Actually the total came to 38, including the back-breaking three down the stretch to deliver the Bulls from the dizzying altitude. Despite his well-known flair for the dramatic, this performance was no act. "I've played a lot of seasons with Michael and I've never seen him so sick," Pippen said afterward.

The Bulls had ridden their championship experience to a decisive 3–2 series lead. Jordan stood under the Utah basket jutting his fists into the air triumphantly as the game ended.

"I almost played myself into passing out," Jordan said. "I came in and I was dehydrated and it was all to win a basketball game. I gave a lot of effort and I'm just glad we won because it would have been devastating if we had lost. . . ."

He had hit 13 for 27 from the field with 7 rebounds, 5 assists, 3 steals, and a block.

"He hadn't gotten out of bed all day; standing up was literally a nauseating experience, and he had dizzy spells and so forth," Jackson said. "We were worried about his amount of minutes, but he said 'Let me play,' and he played 44 minutes. That's an amazing effort in itself."

The series returned to Chicago, and on the morning of Game 6 the players begged Jackson not to make them watch more basketball video clips. "Let's just watch the end of *Silverado*," they said.

In the film, the group of good guys had become fragmented only to come together at the end for a glorious shootout with the bad guys. Sensing the mood had built just right, Jackson agreed to run the tape through to the end.

Togetherness, of course, was the clear and perfect answer to the predicament they were in.

Jordan finished the season's business that night. A perfect Hollywood kind of ending. The Jazz valiantly took the lead early and kept it until the Bulls' pressure finally ate it away down the stretch, with Jordan driving the issue. Thirty-nine more points and two hours of defense, all capped off with the sweetest little assist to Steve Kerr, the same Steve Kerr who had been groaning in his sleep and talking to himself because he had missed a wide-open three that could have won Game 4.

"Steve's been fighting with himself because of Game 4," Jordan explained afterward. "He missed a three-pointer, and he went back to his room. He doesn't know this. His wife told me he was very frustrated. He kept his head in the pillow for hours because he let the team down, because everyone knows he's probably one of the best shooters in the game and he had the opportunity to pick us up and give us a lift and he was very disappointed."

Always looking to use everything, Jordan knew that the desire for absolution would run strong at the end of Game 6. "When Phil drew up the play at the end, which everybody in the gym, everybody on TV knew it was coming to me, I looked at Steve and said, 'This is your chance, because I know Stockton is going to come over and help. And I'm going to come to you. And he said, 'Give me the ball.'"

The response struck Jordan as something that John Paxson would have said. "Tonight Steve Kerr earned his wings from my perspective," Jordan said, "because I had faith in him and I passed him the ball and he knocked down the shot. I'm glad he redeemed himself, because if he'd have missed that shot, I don't think he could have slept all summer long. I'm very happy for Steve Kerr."

The greater glory, however, remained Jordan's—because NBA championships ultimately are a test of will, and for the 1997 title he had produced a superior display of it, in sickness and in health.

"It's been a fight," he admitted afterward. "It's all guts, deep down determination, what your motives are, what your ambitions were from the beginning. There's been a lot of soul searching. It's easy to sit back and say, 'I've given my best, I'm tired. Somebody else has got to do it.' Or whatever. I didn't take that approach. I thought positive and did whatever I could do. Every little inch of energy that I have I'm going to provide for this team."

He knew his teammates were following his lead. "If you give up, then they give up," he said. "I didn't want to give up, no matter how sick I was, or how tired I was, how low on energy I was. I felt the obligation to my team, to the city of Chicago, to go out and give that extra effort so that we could be here for the fifth championship."

Jordan would then say publicly that it would only be fair if all of the Bulls were allowed to return for one more season to defend their title. Jordan's pronouncement would offend and infuriate Reinsdorf, because it usurped his opportunity to offer that to Jackson and the players. Beneath all the glitter and excitement, the emotions within the organization were raw and ugly. Then again, the entire '97 playoff run, as beautiful as it was, had been marked by little pockets of ugliness—especially the scenes on the team bus between Jordan and Krause. Team staff members figured it was the alcohol that made Jordan do it. In the first half-hour after their playoff victories, Jordan and various teammates would pound down five or six beers and often fire up a cigar, which left the team star buzzed enough to turn loose his wicked sense of humor.

For years, Jordan had sat at the back of the bus after games, zinging teammates and anybody in range with his laserlike wit. He liked to hit the usual targets, teasing Kukoc for his showing in the 1992 Olympics, or for his defense, or for that European forgetfulness when it came to deodorant. Or there was Ligmanowski, whose weight made him an easy target for Jordan and Pippen (who would chime in when Jordan started).

Ligmanowski wanted to go back at Jordan, but it was hard to do. So the team's longtime equipment man just took aim at Pippen.

"If it gets real bad," Ligmanowksi confided, "I get on 'em about nose jokes. Like in the playoffs [against Miami] when Scottie got hit in the head and he had that big knot on his head, I told him, 'You scared the hell out of me. I thought you were growing two noses.' He got a little hot about that. They get on me about my weight and stuff sometimes. If you're gonna dish it out, you gotta be able to take it."

Jordan used the humor to police the roster, Ligmanowski said. "If he doesn't feel somebody's doing their job, or sucking it up to go play, he'll say something. He'll get a dig in and let them know how he feels."

"I don't take things too seriously," Jordan said. "I take them serious enough. I'm able to laugh at myself before I laugh at anybody else. And that's important. I can laugh at myself. But then I can be hard. . . ."

He was particularly hard on Krause during the '97 playoffs.

"That was ugly," said one observer. "As ugly as it gets."

"A lot of it was just fun," Jordan said. "It wasn't anything derogatory towards him. It was all in jest. He laughed at it, and sometimes he would respond."

"Jerry Krause! Jerry Krause!" Jordan would yell from the back of the bus. "Hey, Jerry Krause, let's go fishin'." (Krause had taken up fishing over the past few years.)

"Hey, Jerry Krause, let's go fish. It's B. Y. O. P. Bring your own pole. Don't worry. If we don't catch anything, you can just eat the bait yourself."

The back seats of the bus, where most of the players sat, exploded in laughter at these darts, while at the front of the bus, where team staff members rode, people bit their lips, some of them frowning at the discomfort of a player belittling the team's vice president and general manager. Jackson, who was never the target of Jordan's impishness, seemed to smile with his eyes.

"Those guys would get a few beers in 'em back there, and then they'd start in on him," a Bulls staff member said.

"Phil sometimes sits there and says nothing," said another Bulls employee. "You're Phil Jackson and your boss is being hammered by one of the players. At least say something. Phil does not stick up for him in any of those situations. It's just like school kids, like school kids ganging up on somebody."

"I don't know in retrospect what Phil could have done," Chip Schaefer said. "It's not like he would have turned and said, 'That's enough, Michael.'"

Krause, for the most part, endured Jordan's 1997 assaults in silence. Occasionally, when the barrage got especially heavy, Krause would turn to whoever was sitting nearby and say, "The mouth from North Carolina is at it again."

"Maybe it's a defense mechanism as far as Jerry is concerned," Tex Winter said of Krause's silence. "But it doesn't seem to bother him that much. I think he's got a pretty thick skin."

"Brad Sellers, now he was a good draft pick," Jordan would be yelling from the back.

The pace of the team bus slowed dramatically as the Bulls rode out of Salt Lake City into the mountains to their hotel thirty miles away in Park City. "Hey, Jerry Krause, this bus went faster yesterday without your fat ass on it!" Jordan yelled.

"We were reduced to like 25 miles per hour in these buses because we'd have to climb up over this big summit to get to Park City," Chip Schaefer

recalled. "You can make it from Salt Lake to Park City in a car in thirty minutes. But these buses were just terrible, and were reduced to like 25 miles per
hour and the cars were just buzzing past us. It just sort of created this situation where it went on and on."

"Krause doesn't have much to go back at Michael with. He calls him
Baldy or something silly like that," a Bulls employee observed. "When those
guys are having their beers and they're back there smoking their cigars and
they're buzzed over a victory, if Jerry said anything back to them he'd just
be feeding the fire. They would just come back with something worse. That's
the way they are."

Krause could be a tyrant around the players, but his humiliation still
wasn't a thing of joy, Chip Schaefer said. "Teasing is a cruel thing. It's cruel
when it's done on a playground with six-year-olds and ten-year-olds and fif-
teen-year-olds, and it's cruel with adults, too. Have I heard comments before
and cracked a smile? Probably. But I've also heard comments before and
wished in my heart that he would just be quiet and leave him alone."

Luc Longley admitted that while Jordan's barbs made the players laugh,
the moments could also be uncomfortable, especially if you were the butt of
Jordan's jokes. "They're a little bit tense at times. But for the most part,
they're pretty funny," Longley said.

Jordan could be wicked, the center added. "He's on a pedestal, at least as
far as he's concerned. Well, that's the wrong way to put it. But he's in a position where he can crack on people fairly securely. But people crack back at
him, and he handles that just as well. It's usually not a mean thing."

Steve Kerr said Jordan's jabs were a lot easier to take after a win, but he
also had comments after losses. "He's cracking on people all the time," Kerr
said. "Those are fun moments. Those are moments that really last in the
memory. He says some incredibly funny things. I think what makes them kind
of special is that it's just us on the bus. It's just the team. They're kind of intimate moments because they're right after an emotional game, one way or
another. The guys get going on the back of the bus, and it's very
entertaining."

"Michael is a very funny comedian," guard Ron Harper said. "He keeps
everybody loose. When it's very tense, when there are tight ball games, he
keeps you very very loose. He has an ability to say things that you don't
expect. He scores from the back of the bus a lot. He gets on Jerry Krause a
lot."

Asked if Krause takes the ribbing well, Harper laughed and said, "He don't
have a choice, does he?"

"I think Jerry has the ability to maybe recognize Michael for what he is," Tex Winter said. "He knows that Michael has the personality that likes to challenge people and belittle people and berate people. I think he just accepts that. He really doesn't have much choice, as great a basketball player as Michael is. And Jerry's the first to tell you that. Everybody recognizes how valuable Michael is to this ball club."

Asked if the conflict added to Krause's frustrations in dealing with the team, Winter replied, "I'm sure it does. I'm sure it does."

Did Jordan cross the line with Krause? "I guess maybe that there isn't even a line because he crosses it so often," Winter said adding that the situation is an obvious by-product of the mingling of "the personalities, their egos."

"Michael can be as stubborn as Jerry," pointed out another longtime team staff member. "They're both incredibly stubborn. But that's what makes people successful."

"In Jerry's case, and Michael's too, they sort of avoid each other as much as they can," Winter said. "But there are times when they've got to face off with each other and talk about things because that's part of the running of a franchise and being the superstar on a franchise.

"It's unfortunate that Michael has not had a little bit better relationship with Krause," Winter added. "I'm not gonna take sides on it, but I will say this, Jerry is the general manager. Then again, because Michael is involved in a lot of the negotiations and dealings with him, it's a give-and-take proposition. It's too bad that they can't kinda find a middle ground there. But for some reason, Michael's had sort of this resentment, and it's a shame."

The harassment only happened three or four times in Jordan's fourteen years with the team, Krause said. "Who cares? He's drunk every time. He hadn't been sober yet when he's done it. It's a young man's mistakes. He was drunk. I can live with that fine. It doesn't bother me."

Privately, Krause had come to believe that Jackson was instigating or at least condoning and encouraging the attacks. Another Bulls employee with insight into the relationship said that Krause would never believe it but Jackson had actually asked Jordan to ease up on the general manager. Jordan supposedly replied that he knew he shouldn't go so hard, "but sometimes I just can't help myself."

"I think they've visited about it," Winter agreed. "Phil has talked to Michael about trying to accept authority a little bit more as it's handed down from Jerry. I think Phil has helped a little bit in that regard. But on the other hand, sometimes I feel like he doesn't help as much as he maybe should, to be honest with you."

Winter said that he's told Jackson he needed to do more to ease the situation.

Jackson's response is that getting between the players and Krause was a question of "balance."

"Just trying to keep an even balance all the time," the coach said. "Trying to present his point of view, where it makes sense, then trying to play an even field. If I present the prejudiced side, I'm unrealistic or not truthful. . . . Jerry's felt like I've been disloyal to him in certain situations. He has guys on the team that he kinda has in his pocket who will rat on me in certain situations. That's pretty natural, and I know Jerry plays a game. He brought this up to me at one point, and I said, 'Jerry, I've only been fair. I've gotten these players to comply with so many things that I think are fairly done and we've kept them moving in the right way. But if I hadn't been honest and they couldn't read the honesty, then we wouldn't have been successful. And you know I don't have anything against you being in this job.'"

Jackson and Jordan had discussed the internal friction. "We've sat down and talked about it a couple of times, and I've asked him to really curtail it," Jackson said. "It makes it really uncomfortable for everybody else. And he says, 'Sometimes I think it's good for the team.'

"I said, 'Why?' And that was his excuse. He's taking up for Scottie. He's taking up for the team. He's airing some things for the team, and he thinks, 'If all these guys have to take this much, I'm gonna give them back a little bit.'"

Most general managers don't hover around their teams, Jordan said when asked about the issue. "That was our whole argument from day one," he said, pointing out that Jackson has tried for three years to get Krause to relent. "That shows you how much power he has," Jordan said of Jackson. "We don't want to feel like we're under a microscope the whole time while we're working. That's very important. I think that helps the team grow."

In the past, Jackson had suggested that Krause not travel with the team because he is "brusque" and "sets the players on edge with his presence." In fact, he supposedly made Krause's travel with the team an issue during his contract renewal talks in 1996. Essentially, Krause only traveled with the team during the preseason, during the team's first West Coast road trip each November, and during the playoffs. At other times, the general manager was usually off scouting college talent for each season's draft.

"Jerry felt like any exclusion or any intrusion into that territory, which is his territory, is an effort to keep him from trying to do his job," Jackson said of the issue. "I suggested a number of ways around that. Flying in the plane, then taking a private car to the games with scouts, with people who are necessary to ride on the bus at game time. Taking a private carrier back to the hotel afterwards. Flying commercially. Doing things like that to keep his distance.

"But he said, 'I don't get a feel for the team and what the team's all about.' Well, it's obvious that since 1991 Jerry really hasn't had a feel for the mood of the team. Basically, he knows how to run the show and how it goes. It's a pretty smooth operation."

"I think that Jerry feels like as general manager he should be able to make the decisions as to whether he's going to be on the bus or not," Winter said. "That is one of the sore spots as far as Phil and the players are concerned. Maybe as a coach, Phil in this case feels that the general manager shouldn't be on the bus early in the year. I think Phil has said on occasion that he doesn't think other general managers do that. And Jerry says he thinks they do.

"So what do you do?" Winter said with a laugh. "If Jerry wants to be on the bus, I think that's his prerogative. Unfortunately, if the players do respond negatively, or a player even, particularly of Michael Jordan's status, responds negatively to it, well then it's something that maybe Jerry should take into consideration and maybe say, 'Well, it's not that important to me.'"

"If anything, it was a frustration," Jordan said of his behavior. "I don't think we, as a team, should always have to walk around on our toes with the GM following us everywhere we went. So we didn't feel like we had freedom. It's like your father overlooking your shoulder all the time. So sometimes I just felt compelled to vent frustration towards Jerry, which was probably uncalled for. But I was really trying to get him away from the team, so we could be ourselves, in a sense, and do our job without having someone looking over our shoulders."

"Michael is the only player I've known who's come up with that," Krause responded. "Part of that is that there's other things involved, too. A player can have a lot more freedom if I'm not around, in the sense that you can do what you want to do and not be worried about whether I'm walking the hall. I'm coming up late or something. I'm not talking about Michael. I'm talking about anybody. But the point being that on the road I don't eat with the players, I don't play cards with 'em, I don't do any of that stuff with 'em. I never have. I do my job the way I see fit, and I resent the fact that people say I shouldn't be doing this because Michael says it. I say, 'Well, wait a minute now. It ain't been too bad, what I've done.' I resent . . . I shouldn't say resent. It's more, if I'm gonna do my job, I'm gonna do my job my way."

Jackson's point was that the players were grown men, and what's more, they had shown great leadership in winning championship after championship. They didn't need a team executive tiptoeing around their personal lives. There was the implication that Krause could use the information he gathered against the players in personnel decisions. Krause had often boasted that he traded Sedale Threatt to Seattle because the player's off-court life was too socially active.

Told of Jackson's observation, Krause pointed out that Jackson also didn't want people checking up on his behavior.

"But you know how I feel about it?" Krause said. "If a player can't handle me being there, he don't belong there. He shouldn't be on this team. But it really doesn't matter. When somebody criticizes me for that, I say, 'Wait a minute. I've got to do my job the way I know how to do it. That's the way I know how to do my job. Michael can handle it. He handles it fine. It doesn't bother his play.' "

"He likes to see the players and how they react in certain situations," Jackson said. The coach pointed out that the problem wasn't just on the bus, but in the team locker room before games.

"There have been some situations that have set the players on edge," Jackson said. "Michael is always the last one in the bathroom. It's kind of a pecking order between the taping table and the bathroom. With him going in the bathroom, and Jerry's still in there in the players' locker room in the bathroom using the toilet when Michael's getting ready for the game and he's the last one in there."

It seemed ludicrous, that the ultimate superstar of the NBA and his general manager were at odds over latrine habits. But the situation was far more complicated than that, Jackson said, although he admitted that a lot of smaller conflicts over the years had added up to a big one. "It's with those type of things, where Jerry doesn't know boundaries," the coach said. "That's really what irritates the players almost more than anything, even more than the way he has dealt with the team, the trading and not trading of players, the rumors, and everything else. Just his intrusion into the society where he doesn't belong. He just shows a lack of the idea of boundaries as to where the players stop and management begins. Those are the things you don't like to bring up, but these are the things that just alienate Jerry from the team, his behavior.

"I talked to Jerry when I took the job. I talked to Jerry in subsequent years about this really being a problem," Jackson added. "One of the things that's a great measure of an individual is how he treats people when he has nothing to benefit by it. Jerry comes up failing all the time in that territory. This is one of the things we talk about. What is important in life and what isn't. So Jerry has sort of run to the end of the rope with the guys."

There were longtime Bulls employees who had the utmost regard for Jackson and Jordan yet maintained a loyalty to Krause. They respected the general manager for the difficult stances he had taken over the years in pursuing the vision that he and Reinsdorf had for the team. The problem, said several of these employees, was that Krause seemed to harbor an unrealistic urge to "be one of the guys."

"He can't be one of the guys," said an employee who admired Krause. "It's hard to be on the bus and around these guys all the time. And then he's got to decide on their livelihoods and their contracts? I think he'd get a lot more respect if he weren't around the players all the time. He can see them during the holidays, at the Christmas party, even talk to them once in a while if he has something to say, but otherwise he should stay away. He can watch them from afar to evaluate the team. They don't even have to know he's there. If they have a problem, they should be able to go see him and respect him, instead of giving him shit on the team bus or avoiding him."

Asked about his relationship with Jackson, Krause said, "I think we've had a professional relationship that's been basically good. We've been very successful as a team. There haven't been too many other combinations that have been that successful. I respect Phil as a good basketball coach. We have our differences. We will probably have our differences the rest of our lives. But that's life, that's gonna happen."

Krause loyalists in the organization cited the bus incidents as just another sign that Jackson had grown arrogant and was trying to seize control of the team. Asked about arrogance, Jackson said, "I've tried to be really fair and tried to stay on base and on cue and not get insulted by questions that keep coming back through the media. I've done the little things that I think have kept everything on the square with the team. But that might be their view, that I'm arrogant."

As for his ambition to be general manager, Jackson said he was the person best suited to handle relationships between management and the players. "I'm the kind of person to handle both those kinds of things and find solutions for those things," he said.

But did that translate into a hunger for power? Jackson said it did not. "I've never gone behind Jerry's back to the owner," the coach said. "I've never done anything to get power."

Jackson did admit that money was a big factor in his dispute with Krause. He said that was partly because the pay for coaches has exploded, exemplified by the huge contracts and power given to coaches such as John Calipari with the New Jersey Nets. "Kind of the payoff structure for coaches has been destroyed by John Calipari getting the kind of money he's getting in New Jersey," Jackson said. "So there's precedence. Here's a guy that hadn't won at any level who is coming into the game because some team thought they were valuable at this level.

"Jerry's got a salary that hasn't done this same thing," Jackson said of Krause. "General managers' salaries didn't move up. Coaches make more than general managers. You look at it, and you say this is real tough for a guy like Jerry to negotiate. He's looking at it like, 'This guy's more valuable to the organization than I am.' I know all the personal things that must be going through his head as he's negotiating it. So it's very difficult for him to do it.

"That was my argument with Jerry Krause eight years ago," Jackson said. "I told him, 'Coaches' salaries are gonna go over a million dollars. They're gonna get paid what players are getting paid, Jerry.' He said, 'That is never gonna happen. I tell you this: It'll never happen with this organization.' And I said, 'Well, that may be true with this organization, but you know better than anybody else, this is something you should root for, because as general manager you're gonna make money on top of it, too, because of that.'

"You could see the wave coming, that this is what was going to happen," Jackson said. "Now, guys like Jerry Krause are becoming, you know, like an oddity in a way in this league. Because teams are giving total control to coaches in places like Portland and around the country. In New Jersey and Boston, you just keep seeing these teams are now making this wholehearted venture into a coach who's gonna be president and general manager. There must be seven or eight of them by now. Houston. And Miami."

The fact that Pat Riley, his rival in Miami, had that power, income, and control was particularly galling to Jackson.

The coach pointed out that Krause and Reinsdorf didn't want to give him the money he asked for in his last contract negotiations because other coaches he compared himself with were also being paid as GMs. "That actually became kind of a marketing chip against me in the last contract negotiations," Jackson said, "which I kind of laughed about because I said, 'That's not a chip. They hired these guys to be coaches, and they can employ a personnel guy for $300,000 to do the job of general manager.' That's an argument against Jerry Krause, is what that is."

The ugly contract process had started all over again when the Bulls defeated Utah for the 1997 title and Jordan stepped to the microphone to issue a plea that he, Jackson, Pippen, and Rodman be allowed to return for the 1997–98 season and a shot at a sixth championship. Krause wanted to terminate Jackson's relationship with the team after the 1997 season, but Reinsdorf wouldn't let him, the coach said.

Certainly Jackson was a big question, but no bigger than Pippen. An unrestricted free agent at the end of the 1998 season, Pippen would have to be traded, or the team would risk losing him without getting compensation for his immense talent.

Eventually all the details would be worked out to keep the team and Pippen intact, but not without another bloody round of negotiations.

Because the deals couldn't be worked out immediately, Jackson's status with the team was in limbo on Draft Day 1997. At the time, Reinsdorf and Krause were trying to decide whether to trade Pippen. Both Jackson and Jordan had said they would not return to the Bulls if Pippen was traded.

Usually Jackson and his staff made themselves available for Krause and his assistants on Draft Day, although the coaching staff had become increasingly dismayed over Krause's selections in recent seasons. When Jackson arrived at the Berto Center that day, Krause informed him his presence wasn't required.

"He just said, 'You're not needed here,'" Jackson recalled.

Soon word leaked out on sports talk radio that Jackson had been "sent home."

"Jerry has a definite sense of respect for me," the coach explained later. "It wasn't like he sent me home."

Jackson had informed Krause and Reinsdorf that if Pippen was traded, then it would also be time to change coaches because Jackson did not want to oversee the difficult process of rebuilding the team.

Jackson recalled that Krause said, "Phil, until we make a decision on this ball club, as long as we're seeing what the trade is for Scottie Pippen, whenever that's gonna be, and because of your desire not to come back if Scottie doesn't come back, there's no need for you to come in if we go in another direction, if we trade Scottie and you're not gonna be the coach. Today, you might as well let the coaching staff out."

"That was made known to me a couple of times during the draft time," Jackson said. "If they were going in another direction, if they were going to get a draft pick in a trade for Scottie Pippen, these were the guys who were gonna come in. And I wasn't going to be a part of the judging of the talent."

Krause's response was particularly jolting for Jackson, who realized that his dismissal on Draft Day might just be the last day in his long, successful relationship with the team. While it wasn't a disrespectful situation, the coach said it had the air of a brusque ending. "It was purely business," he said. "I was doing a piecemeal job. I was doing a job of handling this group of professional athletes only. That was OK with me. I understood exactly what I was asked to do. The word got out. I don't know how. I didn't try to make it public. I tried to correct it. Other people may be dismayed, annoyed, thinking that I'm not rationally handling a snubbing situation, but I'm not snubbed at all. I'm not bewildered at all. This is what my job has come down to. If I'm not on 'their team,' then I'm out. I'm basically out."

The situation resulted in the coaching staff canceling plans to hold the Bulls' annual end-of-season meetings with the players. As a result, there was no sense of closure after the 1997 campaign, Jackson said.

Draft Day passed without the trading of Pippen, and contract negotiations with Jackson became one of the team's priorities. At first, talks went surprisingly well.

"The structure that was set up for it was that Jerry is Mr. Reinsdorf's agent, Todd Musburger is my agent," Jackson said. "And so it went pretty well for a while, and then it was just explosive. It got explosive between Mr. Reinsdorf and Todd. Jerry Krause had a license from Mr. Reinsdorf to malign Todd Musburger and as a consequence was totally disrespectful and unfair."

When the negotiations stalled, Krause released detailed information stating that the team had offered Jackson the highest-paying contract for a coach who wasn't also a general manager. The tactic infuriated Jackson.

"He aggravated the situation entirely," the coach said of Krause, "and then it became a public issue in the community. They put a spin on it that made us look really negative, that I'd been offered the highest-paid pure coaching job in the NBA. It was really distorting to put out a twenty-five-page thing like that. Everybody knew it was distorted, but it was their bargaining point. It's really hard to sit still when those things are done and not come back at them."

The talks had begun while Jackson was in Montana taking care of family business. "On a Sunday afternoon while I was in Montana, Todd stepped

Jackson turned emotion loose after directing the Bulls to a fifth championship in the 1997 NBA Finals, won in Game 6 over the Utah Jazz at the United Center.

© *AllSport/Matthew Stockman*

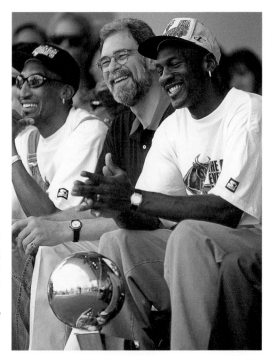

Each of the Bulls' title celebrations, including this one in 1996, were marked by an abundance of tall smiles.
© AllSport/Jonathan Daniel

Jackson with the Red Auerbach trophy after being named the NBA coach of the year in 1996.
© AP Photo/Beth A. Keiser

Dennis Rodman, Michael Jordan, Scottie Pippen, Ron Harper, and
Jackson proudly displayed the Bulls' five championship trophies during
a celebration honoring the 1997 team in Chicago's Grant Park.
© Corbis/Agence France Presse

Jackson's trademark whistle has allowed him to get his players'
attention even in the NBA's noisiest venues.
© Sports Illustrated/Manny Millan

Jackson's challenge in Los Angeles was healing the deep division between stars Shaquille O'Neal and Kobe Bryant.
© *NBA Photos/Andrew D. Bernstein*

Jackson's coaching efforts in L.A. emphasized building a strong relationship with O'Neal. Here he congratulates the center as he is taken out of Game 1 of the Western Conference quarterfinals against Sacramento after scoring 46 points, tying his career playoff high.
© *AP Photo/Kevork Djansezian*

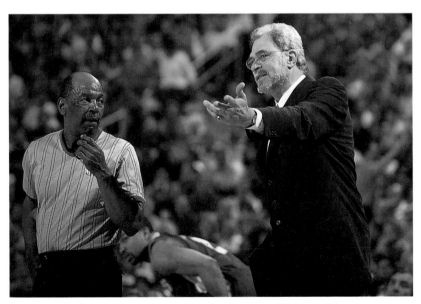

Jackson's efforts with Bryant featured healthy doses of patience and connecting with the young guard's keen mind and drive to learn.
© NBA Photos/Andrew D. Bernstein

Jackson has become a master at working NBA officials without offending them.
© Sports Illustrated/John McDonough

Jackson worked a timeout during the closing minutes of the Lakers 100–91 loss to the Indiana Pacers in Game 3 of the NBA Finals in Indianapolis, June 11, 2000.
© AP Photo/Tom Strattman

Jackson enjoyed a moment of personal triumph, waving to the crowd as the Lakers and thousands of their fans celebrate their NBA championship in downtown Los Angeles, June 21, 2000.
© AP Photo/Reed Saxon

Jackson and O'Neal embraced immediately after Game 6 of the 2000 NBA Finals in which the Lakers claimed the title with a 116–111 win over the Indiana Pacers.

© *AllSport/Ezra Shaw*

© NBA Photos/Andrew D. Bernstein

into Jerry's office," the coach said. "There was no one there but Todd and Jerry. Todd went through a half an hour, saying, 'Jerry, you know there's a lot of praise for everybody in this organization. We know that you've had a big part. The responsibility has fallen on your shoulders for five championship teams. Phil's had a big part, and Michael's had a great part. Michael's really the one.' Todd had a whole buildup about it."

Then came the part where the agent informed the general manager of Jackson's asking price. "As soon as he went to the salary we were asking for, he was [thrown] out of the office," Jackson said. "Threw him out of the office. Todd had to sit out in the hallway by the aquarium. Jerry Krause said, 'You gotta get out of the office. I'm gonna make a call. I can't believe that you're actually asking for this. I can't believe what you're thinking and what you're trying to do.' So he put him out of the office, and twenty minutes later he comes out and says, 'You'll have to leave. I'll talk to you again next week, and you'll have to come back with an offer that's better.' That was it. No counteroffer. We said, 'OK, it's gonna be negotiations. They started out, and there's gonna be negotiations.' But it came down to, 'This is our offer, and this is it. This is what our offer is.' And the next thing was purely business. It was not personal. It was over the phone, and it was totally dragging him through the mud. He tried to cross Todd.

"Jerry just spent three minutes cussing Todd out on the phone," Jackson said, "just threw all the invective and spiteful things he could say. Just cussed him out. And when he was through cussing him out, Todd said, 'Jerry, did you get it all said? Because I hope you've gotten it all said.' Todd tried to remain as calm as he could. And Jerry went through another litany of things that he said to him. The kind of things he said to him really was the final bridge for my agent. To that time, he was dealing pretty well with an uphill situation, and that just kind of put him over the edge."

It was then, Jackson said, that he realized that he was going to have to enter the fight. He told his agent, "Todd, listen. It didn't work out. I'm sorry it didn't work out. They're not gonna use you obviously. They're gonna try to disregard you. They want to negotiate with me. They want me at some level, because this is what they do. They tear it apart. They make it tough. They try to win contracts. They can't stand it. But I can deal with it. I've been able to deal with it."

"I have a good relationship with Mr. Reinsdorf," Jackson says. "In a way, I respect a lot of the things he does. That, I don't respect. That part I don't respect."

The coach was particularly angered by management's assertions that he was trying to duck dealing with Reinsdorf during the negotiations, that he was going out of his way to keep from meeting with the team chairman.

"I was traveling," Jackson said. "I was in Idaho picking up my mother, who's in a situation where she has to be in a wheelchair. She's in a walker. She's at a senior facility. So I was overnight on the road, and this kind of boiled over. And I didn't check with my agent that night. Then I came back to Montana in the late afternoon, and it's out in the media that I didn't call the owner in twenty-four hours. He wanted to hear from you. I didn't have any problem with getting ahold of him. I didn't dodge him or anything else. Unfortunately, when I talked about Mr. Reinsdorf having a good organizational sense, they didn't try to take it out on me. They tried to take it out on Todd.

"I don't think it needs to get like that," Jackson said. In the end, Reinsdorf met with Jackson in Montana and they worked out the details for the coach to return for the 1997–98 season. Reinsdorf later confided that Jackson had turned down a five-year contract offer with the team. Jackson said if such an offer was made, it was made in passing, and during 1996 negotiations.

Jackson recalled that "Mr. Reinsdorf said, 'Tell me if I'm right or wrong. From what I understand, you want to coach this team if we provide the personnel that would make it a championship team, Scottie and Michael and so forth. Because if that's the case, we'd like to offer you a five-year contract. And you'd go ahead and coach here and help us rebuild.' And I said, 'I need a break. That's really nice, but I need a break.'

"That may be what they consider a long-term offer," Jackson said. "But it wasn't clear. I said I think I've coached a couple of years too long actually for the kind of stress that this puts a person under. And for my own health, personal and mental and physical."

On July 23, the Bulls announced that Jackson had signed a one-year contract worth nearly $6 million. "I wasn't looking to do anything that would be outrageous," Jackson said. "I wanted to be fair, and I think Jerry Reinsdorf wanted to be fair. And it got to a fair point in this thing that was good."

Yet the negotiations had left Jackson's relationship with Krause in shreds. That became apparent when the general manager called a news conference to announce Jackson's signing. Krause emphasized that no matter what, even if the team went "82–0," the 1997–98 season was definitely Jackson's last with the Bulls.

"The announcement that came out of my signing was negative," Jackson said. "It was very negative. Rather than saying, 'We're gonna be able to pull this year together. We started it out by signing Phil. And now Michael and Dennis are the next two to sign, and we've begun to rebuild the championship team and allow this team to go on.' Instead of something positive like that, it started out with a negative thing: 'This is going to be the last year that Phil's going to come back and coach.'

"You could tell," Jackson said. "All you had to do was see the videotape of when I signed. It was pretty obvious that Jerry mismanaged that press release and kind of let his own feelings out."

10

THE LAST DANCE

Jerry Reinsdorf was a reserved man given to grand statements. One of his statements was the new Comiskey Park, where his White Sox played. Another was the United Center. Easily the most emotional statement of Reinsdorf's career in business and sports was the Berto Center, the Bulls' fancy practice facility in suburban Deerfield named for Sheri Berto, Reinsdorf's longtime personal assistant and friend who died in 1991 at age forty. The Bulls finished out the 1991–92 season wearing a patch on their uniforms in her honor.

The old Boston Celtics' mystique was represented by the Boston Garden, a basketball temple where the ball echoed off the chipped and aged parquet floor and sixteen championship banners hung in the rafters. Since Chicago Stadium was razed, the place that came closest to that type of expression for the Bulls was not the United Center but the Berto Center. The real fun of coaching the Bulls, said Tex Winter, was practice, "where we get to work with the greatest players in the world."

The building offered every imaginable aid or device for training and competition, from a state-of-the-art weight room to an indoor track, even a lap pool for rehabbing injuries. "It's an ideal facility for a basketball player to get a workout," said Bulls rookie Rusty LaRue, who spent many hours in 1997–98 alone in the building, working on defensive slide drills and other facets of his game. "To have the opportunity to have the weights, the medical equipment, and the pool and the sauna and all that right there as well as the court, it's really ideal. You got it all in one place. You got your track there to do your running, whatever you want to do."

Yet the most significant of these enhancements was the atmosphere itself. On the first level, the main hallway into the gym featured a giant mural photograph of fans' faces during the 1993 league championship series in old Chicago Stadium. One fan was holding up a sign that read, "We Will Defend What Is Ours." Each day as they came and went, the players could feel the expectation in those faces. It was a subtle yet powerful reminder of the tremendous loyalty the Bulls enjoyed from their supporters, a loyalty they had to earn each day on the practice floor.

A vital aspect of the building was the privacy. For much of the NBA's history, its teams had left their practice sessions open to the media, mainly because pro basketball always seemed to be a struggling business in need of any attention it could get. That situation began to change with the popularity that Magic Johnson and Larry Bird and Jordan brought to the game in the 1980s. Jordan's popularity, in fact, swelled so suddenly that it threatened to overrun his team.

A big part of Jackson's drive to create breathing space for Jordan and the team was to close off practices from the hungry Chicago media. When the team moved into the Berto Center, Jackson further enhanced the privacy by placing a large retractable screen over the windows to the press room in the building. The result of this effort was the Berto Center, a haven for all of the organization, including Krause and his assistants. Upstairs, looking over the floor, were the administrative offices of the coaches and general manager, which served as the inner sanctum for the team. There are the meeting rooms, the film rooms, the offices where the Bulls' plans and strategies for competition and personnel moves were concocted.

The media, of course, were kept at arm's length with a series of electronically locked doors, but it was a comfortable arm's length. The Berto Center press room was a cozy, well-lighted working facility, with cubicles for reporters and a bank of phones.

In this and so many other regards, the Berto Center was an extension of Reinsdorf's personality. He was intensely private, yet treasured the relationships with the people who worked for him. His car was a late-model, drab brown Cadillac, which created a contrast when parked in a loading dock at the United Center along the fancy vehicles of his highly paid athletes. His taste in dress ran to the same drab browns and muted plaids. He hardly ever inhabited a slickly tailored power suit.

"Jerry Reinsdorf is the most loyal person that I've ever met, particularly to the employees that have done well for him," said longtime Chicago radio reporter Bruce Levine. "Sheri Berto was his confidant and one of his very best friends. What more proof do you need than naming a building after her and making sure that her family is taken care of?"

Perhaps it stood to reason that a man who cherished his privacy and close relationships would have a disdain for the process of public relations. Unfortunately, that had been one of Reinsdorf's failings. A Brooklyn kid, he loved baseball and had expended much energy in the running of the White Sox, but his involvement in baseball had created one public relations disaster after another. By Reinsdorf's own admission, his early threats to move the team out of Chicago if he didn't get public cooperation in building a new Comiskey Park became the bedrock of his negative public image. In the wake of that came his role in the ugly relations between baseball's owners and its players. Added to that have been the machinations over his tinkering with the White Sox roster.

With the feud between Krause and Jackson taking on an increasingly public tenor, Reinsdorf found himself once again thrust into public view, just as he found himself trying to monitor the internal debate among his prominent employees.

That debate soon matured into hostilities within the Berto Center offices as the Bulls prepared for the 1997–98 season. In September, the Krauses had not invited the Jacksons to their daughter's wedding, but Krause had invited Iowa State coach Tim Floyd, long rumored as Jackson's replacement. Jackson had begun referring to Floyd in public as "Pinkie," an obvious attempt to irritate Krause.

"Pinkie Floyd was there," Jackson said of the wedding. "He was sitting at the table with Jerry Reinsdorf, and it was an occasion that Jerry Krause used as a business opportunity to bring Floyd to meet everyone."

The Krauses further deepened the snub by explaining it to a newspaper reporter. "Thelma [Krause's wife] spoke of it this year," Jackson said. "It was in the paper. The big deal was, 'Phil's a professional. He's an office worker. We didn't invite all of our office workers. Steve Schanwald wasn't invited.' It was that kind of thing. Jerry explained that to me the next day. But when it came out in public, that was what Thelma said. The reality is, that Jerry is all professional. He's all business. There is no personal. He's business twenty-four hours a day."

The late September wedding snub soon led to a blow-up between Jackson and Krause at the Berto Center. "He kind of was hanging around the coaches' offices acting friendly," Jackson recalled. "And he walked in the office where we were just kind of joking around as an office group. So I just stood up and walked out. He was acting like nothing had happened.

"I just walked out and went down and checked on the players," Jackson said. "When I came back upstairs, his secretary came in and said, 'Jerry wants to see you in his office.' And I said, 'Tell him he can come see me in my office.' And I went in my office. Then she called back said, 'He wants you to know that you are to meet him in his office and that he's still the boss here.' So I went in his office and told him, 'Don't come around and act friendly and everything else when you know that you're not friendly.' He said, 'Well, I didn't invite Frank (Hamblen, assistant coach), and I didn't invite (Bulls VP) Steve Schanwald.'

"I said, 'Well, you crossed a bridge right there by your definition, by your snub or whatever else. Believe me, I don't care. But when you invite the next coach that's coming in and you use that as an opportunity to introduce him to the people in the community and to the owner and stuff, and then tell me it's not business, it's personal.'

"Then he came back," Jackson said, "with how Pinkie Floyd had been his friend for five or six years. I said, 'Sure, Jerry, I know he's your friend.' I've been in that same position where Floyd is. One of his puppies. He's been watching him for a while."

Very quickly, the discussion escalated into an argument, Jackson said. "It went from there to 'Well, that's why I wanted to have the owner meet you. We wanted to make sure you understand this is your last year. I don't care if you win 82 games or not. This is your last year.' That kind of shut the door for me.

"We had an ensuing fight that lasted about ten minutes, and it was pretty loud and pretty boisterous," Jackson said. "But at the end we settled down. And he said, 'This is what the owner was gonna tell you. Instead of him telling you, I will tell you what he was gonna tell you. Make sure that the drift of your thing comes out that this is the way that it has to be. And make no doubt about it that this is our intention that this is your last year.' And I said, 'Jerry, I've known that it's been my last year since Mr. Reinsdorf came to Montana and we talked about it.' And we went through a few things that had been a hardship. And we aired a lot of things that had to be aired, and we've been much better since that time. There had been animosity and we were coming apart, so we kind of cleared the air."

Media Day

Just ahead on the schedule was Media Day, the opportunity for the press to conduct preseason interviews, which would bring a national contingent of sportswriters and broadcasters to the Berto Center. The scent of conflict was high around the Bulls, meaning that a larger than usual group of reporters showed.

Just before Media Day, Krause read some comments Jackson had made to reporters in which the coach seemed to be waffling about his status with the team. "He called me up to the office that day," Jackson recalled, "and he said, 'I want you to get this straight. This is indeed your last year. We want to get that straight to the media. We don't want any of this hedging.'"

Jackson testily prepared to comply and waited for the media to interview Krause before going onto the practice facility floor where the sessions were being conducted.

At first only two or three reporters gathered about Krause on the Berto Center floor. But then their number grew until around twenty encircled him. The GM began by discussing the effects of the NBA's new labor agreement, how unsettling it was, how it would take three years or more to understand how it would affect the economics of the league.

A reporter pointed out that the "finality of Phil rubs people the wrong way. Around town Phil leaves doors open at times in comments.

"What is the real story?" the reporter asked.

"It's both of our decisions," Krause replied. "I think you ought to ask Phil about it. But it's both of our decisions, you know. I don't see why. . . ."

He paused then and started over by referring to the public reaction to his July press conference announcing Jackson's new contract. "I think when people thought that I made the statement at the press conference, it was in the press release," Krause said. "It was right there for everybody to see. And I think when I made a statement . . . the last time I talked to you guys, some people. . . . Or one of the last times I talked to you as a group, some people thought I was saying something that wasn't in the press release. It was there."

His comments left the reporters around him with increasingly confused looks. "We had agreed to it," Krause said finally, "and that's the way it is. I don't know why it would rub somebody wrong. There's a time in life when people separate."

"People think you are saying it in such a way that you take joy in it," a reporter said.

"No, there's no truth to that at all," Krause said. "I don't take . . . I think people think . . . I've heard some people say that I'll take joy in the day when Michael leaves. I have no such thoughts in my mind. Hell, I'll probably cry when he leaves. But the point being that you have to go on. You know, this is an organization. We've been very successful. I'm really proud of what the organization has done.

A reporter pointed out that if a lot of players leave at once, a team suddenly finds itself scrambling to find the right players to replace those who left.

"A lot of them have left before," Krause replied. "We have a team that won three championships, and two years later we won a championship with ten new players. So this isn't something we haven't done before. We've done this before."

He used that example to explain that players and coaches alone don't win championships, that sound organizations do. But as he made the remark, Jackson stepped onto the floor to begin his interview session. And as they often do, reporters hurriedly departed their current interview so as not to miss anything newsworthy Jackson might say.

Within an hour after the media session had ended, a befuddled Krause found his way down to the press room looking for reporters who might have a recording of his comments. He was sure he had been misquoted, that he had said coaches and players "alone" don't win championships. Unfortunately, few media representatives remained in the press room. Eventually, Krause would get in touch with John Jackson of the *Sun-Times*, who would confirm that Krause had said that "coaches and players don't win championships, organizations do."

"I was right there when it happened," Terry Armour of the *Tribune* agreed. "He was heavily misquoted. I saw everybody run from him midway through the quote and run over to Phil. They didn't even get the end of the quote."

The group of reporters went to Jackson and told him that Krause had said that coaches and players don't win titles: "It's organizations that win championships."

"He would say that," Jackson said. "The organization is based on loyalty. Scottie sees that and has to wonder what loyalty really does mean."

The comment would come to be a theme for the players throughout the season, galvanizing their disdain for Krause and Reinsdorf. Even team employees loyal to Krause would express dismay at the GM's choice of words, at his decision to attempt to discuss the situation with the media, because Krause's comments would set in motion a nasty public relations battle that would come back to haunt the two Jerrys again and again.

Even Jackson privately expressed sympathy for Krause and how the situation had blown up in the GM's face.

Later, Krause's associates would complain privately that Jackson could have spoken up and taken the pressure off Krause. The worst part about Krause's ill-timed statements was that it left both Krause and Reinsdorf in limbo. If they defended themselves against the public anger, then it seemed they were attacking Jordan and Jackson, both very popular figures, which only made the situation worse.

As for Jackson, the coach merely followed Krause's instructions on what to tell reporters. "It would take wild horses to drag me back this time," Jackson said on Media Day. "This is the final year. It's time to start something different. In the conversation I had with Jerry Reinsdorf in negotiations, this would be the last year. We're not having any illusions, like last year. We don't want the same situation . . . if something should happen like we accidentally win a championship. I assured [Jerry Krause] I'd walk out at the end of the season, and he assisted me in that belief."

Jordan had not made himself available to the press on Media Day. But the next day, after the team's first day of practice, Jordan was ready to address Krause's comments. "I'm very consistent with what I've always said," Jordan told reporters. "That's what I mean. If Phil's not going to be here, I'm certainly not going to be here."

What if Jackson goes to another team next season? a reporter asked. Would Jordan follow?

"No," he said. "Totally. I would quit. I wouldn't say quit, I'd retire."

The assembled reporters went on to ask Jordan a host of questions, including the following:

What do you think of Krause's comment that players and coaches alone don't win championships; organizations do?

"I don't agree with him in that sense, because as a player, I feel we go out and do our job, we do what we have to do each and every day when we step on the basketball court. Sure, they [the team's management] have responsibilities to do whatever to make our jobs easier, to do what they have to do for the organization, but I mean, I didn't see any of the organization playing sick last year. In Game 5, I would have liked to see some of those organization guys step out there and play. And I didn't see that."

Were you offended that management seemed to be pushing Phil Jackson out the door?

"I think that's very obvious, because management has already said that this is Phil's last year. So, I don't know if that's Phil's step. I know Phil's not gonna go against a situation where he's not wanted. He's looked at it as if this is probably his last year. We just gotta go out and play the game of basketball this year and deal with what we have to deal with. Certainly we don't know what the future is going to hold. That's the organization's decision. That's not our decision. If Phil's not going to be here, then I'm not going to be here."

Could you use your influence with Reinsdorf to bring Phil Jackson back?

"I don't know. I've never really looked at it in that sense. I don't know what my influence is. You see how Jerry Reinsdorf operates. My influence doesn't have anything to do with his decision making. I'm not gonna sit here and knock heads with Jerry. If he has his own vision for this team and what its future holds, then we take that and we deal with it. If that means Phil's not here, that means Phil's not here."

Did the disagreement between Jackson and Krause make for a bad way to end the Bulls' great run?

"It's a bad way to end an unbelievable run. You would want it to be better down the stretch, or when the curtain is finally closing. I think that we as players can't worry about that. We have to go out there and have our own individual, our own team, goals to live up to. The management stuff is something you'll have to worry about in the future."

Although they were measured, Jordan's comments only helped cement the impression that Krause and Reinsdorf were forcing Jackson and him from the team.

Jackson then made a point of discussing Krause's comments in a meeting with his players. "We talked about it as a team actually and said, 'We have to have good mental health as well as good physical health.'" the coach said. "This is part of the mental health."

With Scottie Pippen facing foot surgery and Rodman disgruntled, Jackson was worried that the team would open the season struggling and that the discord with management would become a major distraction.

"The challenge is if the paranoia or insecurity linger with failure," Jackson said privately. "Those things can breed the kind of dark thoughts that can sway the mental health of a coach or a team. Those are the things that we have to watch for. I feel real confident about my team, about our relationships, the team's relationships. About my staff, about our dedication towards winning this year. All those things are real strong, so I can't see anything upsetting the apple cart as far as the mental or spiritual aspect of it. We're pretty unified as a team as to what we're gonna do regardless of what happens, the innuendo that are gonna go on or the slights that are gonna happen, the backhanded comments that might be made."

Krause's comments and the responses from Jackson and Jordan brought a round of media commentary nationwide lambasting the Bulls' front office. Typical of the response was a column by Gwen Knapp of the *San Francisco Examiner*, who wrote, "Krause could have let the players age gracefully into the sunset, let Jackson's natural curiosity lead him elsewhere. Instead, the general manager has sullied the whole outfit. And he hasn't even done it artfully. . . . Krause's gig is charisma free, all unembroidered pettiness.

"In Krause's fantasy basketball league," she said, "Michael Jordan is just a tool, easily replaced. And the photocopier is more valuable than Phil Jackson. Last week, Krause pointed out that the team trainer has five rings."

Later, Krause and Reinsdorf would fume privately that Jackson didn't speak up more to ease the public relations nightmare that grew out of Media Day. But the coach wasn't about to extract the GM and team chairman from the circumstances. "They created this animal," Jackson said later, "and I'm not bailing them out. I made a decision. I'm just a person they plugged into this thing, this situation. It was the right thing they plugged in, and everything's worked graciously for us behind all that. That's great, but this isn't a real estate holding, or the stock market, where you just happened to buy a lucky piece of stock. These are people you're dealing with. And that's the thing that I think they're missing."

Shaky Beginning

In reality, the Bulls' biggest concern in October had little to do with "future considerations." Rather, it was the soft tissue in Pippen's foot, injured against Miami in May in the playoffs and slow to heal. That, too, entered into the controversy when Krause faxed Pippen a letter in September threatening to take action against the star if he played in his own charity game.

It wasn't so much the content of the letter that infuriated Pippen, but the harshness of its tone and the manner in which it was delivered.

The real issue, though, was corrective surgery and the timing of the operation. Decisions were difficult in the charged atmosphere of training camp. But four days after camp opened, the surgery was performed, and the Bulls announced the star forward, so critical to the team's success, would miss a minimum of two months.

"Each year we start off with some sort of challenge and this makes it even more so," Jordan told reporters.

The week brought more news in that Rodman agreed to a one-year contract with a $4.5 million base and performance incentives that could boost it to $10 million. But then he refused to sign it, supposedly because he feared some of the incentives would be impossible to reach.

Reinsdorf had said Rodman would be welcomed back only if he gave up the bad behavior that had stained his 1996–97 performances. At first, Rodman had offered to play for free, but later changed that to a demand for $10 million with "a money-back guarantee."

"I've learned one thing: don't predict anything from Dennis," Jackson told reporters. "If you do, you just set yourself up."

Jordan pointed out that with Pippen's injury, the team needed Rodman to be on his best behavior. But a stalemate developed and dragged on through training camp and the start of the ambitious exhibition schedule.

After a preseason opener at home, the Bulls jetted to Lawrence, Kansas, to meet the Seattle Sonics in humid Allen Field House on the University of Kansas campus. After Kansas, it was back to Chicago briefly for an exhibition loss, followed by a transatlantic jump to Paris to play in the McDonald's Open in mid-October. The city was still in shock from the death of Princess Diana in an auto wreck six weeks earlier. The Bulls landed and headed immediately to practice. "*Bonjour, bonjour,*" Jordan, accompanied by his son Jeffrey, told a crowd of French teenagers after the workout.

Joining Chicago in the international exhibition tournament were Paris–St. Germain, Atenas de Cordoba of Argentina, Benetton Treviso of Italy, FC Barcelona, and Olympiakos Piraeus of Greece. The Bulls made quick work of the tournament field, but not without a cost: Jordan developed a sore toe. "It hurts him and he can't jump," Jackson told reporters. As the team headed back to Chicago, it was announced that Jordan would miss the final three exhibition games, although the injury wasn't viewed as serious.

A much bigger concern was Rodman, who still had not signed his contract by the time the team got back home. Immediately Jordan and Jackson went to work on him. "I talked to Michael a couple of days here and there," Rodman said. "He says, 'Don't leave me out here hanging to dry.' The guys gave me a lot of support. The least I can do is give something back."

With the proper prodding, the thirty-six-year-old forward signed up for another season. "The players and the people of Chicago, they gave me a lot, so I figured I might as well come back and give them one more year," he told reporters.

That Friday, October 24, Rodman accompanied the team to Chapel Hill, North Carolina, for an exhibition game at the Dean Smith Center on the UNC campus. At first, it was announced that Jordan would not play, which created a swell of fan disappointment. Then came the calls from Jordan's old friends back home. With his toe feeling better, he decided he'd better suit up after all.

Up to that point in the young season, there had been no friction, no embarrassing moments between Krause and the players. But just before game time at the Smith Center, Jordan went to use the restroom and spied Krause's feet dangling underneath the stall. From that point, Jordan, as he had explained to Jackson, couldn't help himself. Krause was just too inviting a target for a round of humorous salvos.

"He was in there," Ron Harper recalled, "and Michael said, 'I'm not going in there yet, Phil. I ain't goin' in until Jerry leaves.' It was almost time to go out on the court. It was a sad scene then. He was killing him in the can. It's a thing where Jerry will embarrass himself if Jerry gets a chance. You won't have to embarrass him. He'll find a way to embarrass himself. So we tend to let Jerry embarrass himself, and guys just laugh at him. But the guy wants to be a part of it."

"It's a ribbing situation," Jackson said. "Jerry ends up using the bathroom when the team's trying to get ready. You know, the players use a pecking order. It goes down to Dennis is taking a shower, Harp's in the bathroom, Michael's in the bathroom. And that's it. It usually goes in that kind of routine. Michael goes in the bathroom, and Jerry's in there in the bathroom. You know, it's like, 'What are you thinking about?' I don't go in the player's bathroom. This is a place where a guy wants to be alone and get his business done before a game. This is a team kind of thing. Those are the things that Jerry gets himself embroiled in that have just alienated himself from the team a number of times. So he goes back there and gets some kind of grief. I don't know what was said. I never know what's said in that situation. I just hear kind of a ruckus going on."

With one final exhibition against the Sacramento Kings the next night in Chicago, the Bulls finished their preseason schedule and turned their thoughts to the opening of the regular season the following Friday, October 31, and how they would survive without Pippen. Jordan called the upcoming season, his thirteenth in the league, "my biggest challenge ever."

He told reporters he would play 48 minutes a night if that was necessary to deliver the sixth championship. "I'm gearing myself up for a long season—

all 82 games and 15 playoff games," Jordan said. "I don't know what burnout is. I haven't burned out so far, so why worry about it?"

"We don't want to wear him out," Jackson said. "But he just wants to win, as usual. He just wants to win."

That Friday night, October 31, they opened the season in Boston, and it became immediately apparent just how much they would miss Pippen. The Bulls pushed to a big first-quarter lead against the Celtics, but without Pippen there to control the tempo of the game, Chicago couldn't hold the edge. And the young Celtics ran and pressed and ran and pressed some more, leaving the Bulls grabbing their shorts and sucking wind.

Chagrined, they headed home with a loss. The next night at the United Center, they held their ring ceremony and revealed the team's 1997 championship banner, to hang alongside banners from 1991, 1992, 1993, 1995, and 1996. The rings featured a Bulls logo made up of 46 diamonds and five sculpted NBA title trophies and inscriptions "World Champions" and "Team of the Decade."

The twenty-minute ceremony before Chicago's home game against Philadelphia brought another brace of boos for Krause. Reinsdorf was present, but wasn't introduced.

Pippen was obviously emotional when he stepped to the microphone and thanked the fans for ten years of "wonderful moments."

"I've had a wonderful career here," he said. "If I never have the opportunity to say this again: thank you."

"I said then that we'd win a championship by the time I leave," Jordan told the crowd. "Well, we're the five-time champions, going for six, and . . . we're certainly going to win the sixth."

In the short term, though, their destination was frustration.

Early setbacks leveled their record at 4–4, and observers suggested that perhaps Jordan was carrying too much of the burden. He was averaging 26 points a game but, with an inflamed right wrist and sore right index finger, his usually stellar field goal shooting had drooped to 38 percent. "When he does try to do too much it means that he feels there's a lack of aggressiveness by his teammates," Jackson told reporters. "They don't know what to do or they're floundering. So he picks up the ball and starts carrying it on his own, and right now he's not shooting well enough to do that."

What was worse, neither were his teammates. As a team, Chicago was shooting 41.5 percent and scoring 87.5 points per game. For 1997, the Bulls had averaged 103 points per game. Without Pippen, they had failed to score

100 points in any of their eight games. "Our offense has always been able to provide Michael space to score, and the other players an opportunity to hit open shots when he's double-teamed," Jackson said. "Right now, what's really frustrating is that he's finding guys off the double team and we're not making those shots."

Despite the charged atmosphere between the coach and GM during the 1997 offseason, Jackson had again attempted to persuade Krause not to travel with the team.

"Basically, in my conversation with Jerry in the preseason," Jackson said, "I had asked him not to go. I said, 'You always insist on going. I don't think this is a good year to go.' He said, 'I know you could stop this stuff if you wanted to.' I said, 'Jerry, it's what they feel like. If I stood up in this situation and tried to stop this, I would alienate this team.'"

Jackson viewed the extended trips as a time for the players and coaches to bond together, to seal their unity and commitment for another championship run. Because of that, he decided to bring the injured Pippen along. The forward wouldn't be able to play, but he would undergo limited workouts and spend extra time with his teammates. "I brought Scottie along to get him back in stride with the guys, to practice with the team," Jackson explained. "There was a chance he was going to be able to come back December 10. We didn't want him to be out too long, and this was an opportunity, his first practice chance. He wouldn't have the opportunity to practice if he stayed behind."

At the time, the Bulls were not a team brimming with confidence. They had lost all three of their road games in the young season and badly needed to reestablish their prowess in the hostile environment of another team's arena. It was a dramatic turnaround. The two previous seasons they had rung up phenomenal road records of 33–8 and 30–11. "The circumstances are different," Steve Kerr, who had a bruised knee, told reporters. "I'd be surprised if we could pull off 6–1, frankly. We're not playing well enough."

"A certain understanding of going into the enemy's territory and bonding together," is how Jordan, who was averaging just under 25 points a game while shooting just under 40 percent from the floor, summed it up. "This is a great time for it, knowing we haven't had much success on the road."

This time around, the Bulls were scheduled to open with a Thursday night game at Phoenix; then visit the Los Angeles Clippers, Sacramento Kings, and Seattle Sonics; then stop by Chicago for a two-day break at Thanksgiving before visiting Indiana, Washington, and Boston.

Without Pippen, the Bulls were averaging only 88.4 points per game, ranking them 28th among the 29 NBA teams in scoring. Worse yet, they weren't shooting the ball well and were turning the ball over 18 or 19 times a game. Without Pippen, the game also became much harder for Jordan, because other teams found it much easier to double- and triple-team him.

"You hate to keep harping on his return, but let's be honest—the guy is one of the great players ever . . . and he affects every aspect of the game," Kerr said. "Until he's back, I don't think we can consider ourselves the real Bulls."

Pippen would later admit that he wasn't exactly unhappy with the circumstances. After yet another offseason in which Krause again explored trading the star forward, the Bulls were now getting a scorching lesson in just how essential he was to their chemistry. Without him, the Bulls had no teeth.

To ease up the offensive pressure on Jordan, Jackson figured he would try starting sixth man Kukoc, which gave Chicago something of a three-guard offense. The main problem there was that doctors had just discovered Steve Kerr would miss several games with a cracked femur, meaning that the struggling bench would get dramatically weaker.

Jackson had told his assistants of his intention to make this final season one of great fun, but just weeks into the schedule it was clearly not fun. Tex Winter watched Jackson struggle with not only his own emotions but those of his players. "We have been working on the physical, mental, and spiritual sides of these players," Jackson admitted to the reporters covering the team, "to increase their appetite for the game, their hunger for playing, making basketball fun."

Winning, though, was fun, and the Bulls couldn't accomplish that against the Suns. "We lost the game in Phoenix in which Dennis had a wide-open layup down the stretch and he missed it," Jackson recalled. "We lost a game we probably should have won on the road again."

Normally, when the Bulls were dominant, the team was willing to overlook Rodman's indifference on offense. But with Pippen out, that indifference grew as yet another item in Jordan's craw.

On the plane that night from Phoenix to Los Angeles, Krause decided to approach Jordan, Pippen, Randy Brown, Scott Burrell, and Ron Harper as they were playing their usual card game at the back of the plane. The team had decided that Steve Kerr, who was injured, could go home to be with his pregnant wife. But that created a problem in that Kerr and little-used rookie Keith Booth were scheduled to make a promotional appearance with Jerry

Reinsdorf in Sacramento. The team chairman had not been around the team since the 1997 playoffs (when Reinsdorf made a point of telling reporters, "I've never had any regrets" about Jordan's big contract). With Kerr heading home, Krause now had to find another player as a replacement. So he decided to approach the group playing cards.

"I saw him going back there from the front of the plane," Jackson recalled. "I knew it was gonna be trouble. I just had that feeling, 'Gosh, he shouldn't go back there. That's really a dangerous place to go.'"

What made the circumstances worse was that Krause had a speck of cream cheese on his face from a postgame snack, creating shades of his earlier days with the team, when players concocted the "Crumbs" nickname. From several accounts of the incident, the ribbing he received was substantial. Krause spoke to the players for a few minutes but had no success in finding a replacement for Kerr. So he returned to the front of the plane.

Then, about fifteen minutes later, the GM made another run back to the group to try again. According to accounts of the incident, he still had the cream cheese on his face.

Krause's second visit to the card game reportedly drew some chiding barbs from Jordan along the lines of, "What's the matter with you, Jerry? Didn't anybody ever teach you how to eat?"

"We all know that Jerry likes to eat," Harper would say later. "He don't know that he has food on his face, though. But he likes to eat, though. MJ told him. MJ said some words to him and we laughed at him. But, you know, Jerry wants to be part of the team. He'd be very successful if he stayed away."

Jordan's answer to the losing streak was his biggest scoring outburst of the regular season, 49 points against the Clippers, the 150th time he had scored more than 40 in a game. In the game's second overtime, Jordan scored all 9 of Chicago's points, giving him a run of 13 straight points, for the 111–102 win.

"I Want to Be Traded"

After the game, *Daily Herald* writer Kent McDill noticed Pippen sitting alone in the locker room. "There was a chair next to him," McDill recalled. "So I just went over to say hi and see how things were going, when he thought he was gonna come back. And I said something about what game are you aiming for. And he said, 'Well, I'm not gonna play for the Bulls anymore.' Ron Harper was standing next to him, and Ron looked down at him and made some sort of snide remark. Scottie was laughing, and then he went on: 'I'm tired of the way I've been treated, and I don't want to play for any team that Jerry Krause is on or represents. I don't want to represent Jerry Krause.' He said a bunch of that stuff. Then he and Harper started laughing about where they were going to end up, what team they were gonna play for and this other stuff. Then Scottie finally looked at me and said, 'I want to be traded.'

"It was all too jocular for me to actually write it," McDill said. "It all seemed kind of silly. I knew that the Bulls probably wouldn't trade him even if he wanted to be traded."

McDill didn't write the story after the Friday night game in Los Angeles. But on Sunday in Sacramento he saw Pippen again. "Before the game, he was standing there before introductions," the reporter recalled. "And I just said to him, 'When are you going to have your press conference to announce that you want to be traded?' He said, 'As soon as you write the story.' So I asked a couple more questions. Then I went into the press room and started writing down the stuff that had happened Friday night as well. At halftime, I saw him again, and he said, 'Are you gonna write it?' I said, 'To be honest with you, I already did.' I told him what the story was gonna say, and he said, 'That's exactly how I feel. I want to be traded. I don't want to play with the Bulls anymore.'

"It obviously wasn't a well thought-out decision," McDill said, "because the Bulls aren't going to trade a player just because he wants to be traded. It's not like they were gonna get what they wanted for him in value, when a player announces he wants to be traded. At the time he was angry and had things he wanted to say, and I'm sure he wanted to stir the pot a little bit. Which he did."

Indeed, Pippen's comments made headlines across the country. "I ain't coming back," he had told McDill. "I want to be traded. I want to go to Phoenix or L.A." Even worse, he had insinuated he was malingering, saying, "Maybe I'm healthy" now.

"He hasn't said anything to me," Krause said when asked about the comments. "We spent a lot of money to bring everybody back and try to win a championship. I don't know anything about it."

The good news for the Bulls was that they got a second straight road victory, 103–88, that Sunday against the Kings, and their defense showed some real teeth. With an 8–5 record, the Bulls set out for Seattle, the scene of their strangest hour. On the flight up, they partied to celebrate another win.

Although the news of Pippen's comments had yet to hit the streets, he partied a bit too much, perhaps over his recent freedom of expression.

"It was a trigger to a very big event this year that was rather embarrassing," Jackson said. "Unfortunately for the players, it was an opportunity for them to unload against Jerry. It set about a mechanism between the two of us. It was embarrassing. I had to discipline the players about it, or else. And risk losing by standing in between [them and management] on what they considered an affront to their world. Or I could sit there and incur the embarrassment that followed. For the most part, I pulled them aside and talked to them personally about it. Not to do this because it's embarrassing to the whole bus basically."

When the team landed in Seattle, there were two buses waiting to carry them to their hotel, one for the players and coaches and one for the broadcasters and staff people. Krause chose to ride the team bus.

"Scottie began his tirade right after that," Jackson said. "That was the thing that sprung it all open."

Obviously intoxicated, Pippen began yelling at Krause about signing him to a new contract or trading him. The harangue went on and on and turned increasingly uglier.

"Why don't you trade me?" Pippen screamed.

"I finally turned around," Jackson said, "and grabbed a bottle of beer and held it up to Pippen and pointed to it like, 'Beers. You've had too many beers to drink.' Joe Kleine thought I was toasting him. He said, 'Were you toasting Scottie? I've never seen anything like that.' I said, 'No, I was holding up a beer and pointing at it, saying, *You've had too many. You better quiet down.* I didn't want to have to get up.

"This is beyond what normally goes," Jackson said. "I didn't like it at all. Jerry said, 'Don't worry about it. I can take it. Don't worry about it at all.' "

"These days and age, if you stare at a guy something can be said," Ron Harper said of the incident. "I think that Scottie was just letting some of his frustrations out. So he said some things."

Asked later about his conflicts with Krause, Pippen replied, "I can't say exactly where they come from. We don't have any type of relationship. There are a lot of little things that have gotten to the point where they've turned into things that are big."

"That's something that we will never understand," Jordan said later when asked about Pippen's relationship with Krause. "How that relationship formed and bridges were burned. The situation deteriorated even more when I was gone from the game and then even more when I came back."

"From my standpoint, I would love to have finished my career in Chicago," Pippen says. "It's a great tribute. And to go out on your own and not be forced out of the game."

That, in part, was his motivation for putting aside his feelings about his contract, which left his salary ranked 122nd in the league despite the fact that he had been named to the league's list of its 50 greatest players of all time.

"I had accepted the fact that I was fairly underpaid and that with the way the new collective bargaining agreement was done, it was something I was gonna have to deal with," Pippen said. "It was a process, something I was gonna have to deal with. So, you know, just go ahead and play the game."

So the anger had built in Pippen until the alcohol emboldened him to unleash it on Krause in Seattle. The incident would remain hidden from the public until after the season. As it was, Pippen might have been able to undo some of the damage the next morning when he again encountered Krause on the team bus headed to practice.

"Good morning, Scottie," Krause said.

"Go to hell, Jerry," Pippen replied.

Upon hearing that Pippen made trade demands to the media, Jackson tried to make light of it, knowing that the emotional Pippen was capable of misspeaking, particularly if reporters were gauging his sensitivity with questions. "I think he's just joking the press, personally, and throwing a barb out there," the coach told reporters that Tuesday in practice.

"We know that he's not happy with his contract," Jordan said. "He didn't have to go public but he did. I'm not shell-shocked by anything that happens. This organization is at a crossroads."

"For Scottie's situation, everything kind of broke," Jackson said. "The venom kind of broke, and he said, 'I can't play for this team anymore.' He had crossed a bridge with the organization. It was very disappointing. And it took him a while. We had to come back here and really work with Scottie. 'That doesn't mean you have to leave the team,'" Jackson told him.

"Scottie thought he had shown himself the door, because he had had too much to drink," the coach explained. "It was over the edge."

The team returned to Chicago just before Thanksgiving, and Jackson arranged for the team's therapist to spend some time with Pippen counseling him on his anger. Over the break, Pippen phoned Jackson late one night for a long discussion during which the coach realized that Pippen seemed fairly set in his position not to play for the Bulls again. The coach knew that the team couldn't be successful without Pippen, that changing his mind would take the best efforts of a variety of people, including Jordan, Harper, Jackson himself, and several teammates.

"Unfortunately, it took him a while," Jackson said. "He wasn't ready to play for another two months. And so it was a situation where he had time to cool out, to look at it and say, 'Well, my options aren't very good. I really don't have another place to go, and this is the right thing to do.' "

Part of the strategy, though, included Jackson and Jordan openly expressing their displeasure with Pippen's position. That Monday, December 1, the coach and star player both suggested that they felt betrayed by Pippen's demands. "It's all right to hold it against Scottie," Jackson told reporters. "We care about Scottie, but we're going to hold this against Scottie because he's walking out on us, there's no doubt about that. Some things are personal and some things are public. Publicly, we like Scottie, but personally there's always going to be a . . . residual effect of having gone to bat for Scottie."

Jackson and Jordan said they wouldn't have returned to the team if they had known Pippen was going to leave. "There is that kind of feeling: 'Hey, we came back to do this job together and Scottie ducked out the door,' " Jackson said.

"It would have made a big difference in terms of me and Phil and a lot of other players," Jordan said.

Jackson recalled for reporters that Jordan had come out of retirement in 1995 due in part to Pippen's great urging. "I don't think Michael forgets the fact that when Scottie was here alone in '94 and '95, that he was . . . saying, 'Come on back, come on back, Michael, and help me out with this load,' " Jackson said. "So I'm sure Michael's going to get back at Scottie, hold his feet to the fire."

A little more than a week after Pippen's explosive verbal attack against Krause, Latrell Sprewell of the Golden State Warriors ignited a media firestorm by attacking coach P. J. Carlesimo and choking him at practice, then leaving the building only to return later and throw punches at the coach. The entire incident, Sprewell said later, was aimed at forcing the team to trade him.

The Pippen incident was far too private for any of his teammates to discuss publicly. But the Sprewell news only emphasized the seriousness of the Bulls' situation.

One of Pippen's ways of dealing with the anger was to pick up the phone and call Reinsdorf for their first chat in years. "I talked to him for about twenty minutes and he was supposed to call me back but he never did," Pippen revealed later. "He just sort of talked his way around some things. I'm still waiting on that call."

December, then, became a month marked by a quiet nervousness. Would Pippen return to the team, or was the championship run about to come to a premature end? Unable to answer that question, Jackson and his players had to turn their attention to a milestone.

The game against Phoenix on December 15 marked the 500th consecutive sellout for the Bulls, the longest such streak in the league.

It was no coincidence that the next game, against the Lakers, brought Jackson's 500th regular-season victory as the Bulls' coach. He had reached the milestone sooner than any coach in league history, a fact that didn't help the public understand Krause's apparent desire to see the coach leave. "To get the guys, when they have one ring or two rings, to go out and play hard, there's the challenge," L.A. Clippers coach Bill Fitch, Jackson's old college coach, told reporters. "He ought to be able to coach here as long as he wants to coach."

His players used the occasion of his 500th victory to marvel at the circumstances of his impending dismissal. "It baffles me to understand that he's not welcome," Jordan said. "He certainly still knows how to coach the game."

In fact, the Bulls' star rated Jackson an equal to the much revered Dean Smith. "I think they're very similar in the fundamental aspects with which they coach the game," Jordan said. "With their caring about the players. Players first, management, everything else is second. I think their dedication to spreading the wealth is very evident. Their overall love for the game. I think you can see it in the way they coach. They're very poised in pressure situations. They don't let the game or the situation speed up their thought process. As a player, if you see that, then you tend to maintain a certain poise in pressure situations. So I think those are key components to winning."

Jackson used the occasion of his 500th win to do something he had said he wouldn't do—take the pressure off Krause and Reinsdorf. Their selecting him as Bulls coach in 1989 "was a miracle for me," Jackson said. "It's a great success story. A lot happened in this organization that just all clicked: the players, ownership, general manager. Motivation isn't something you teach players. They have to bring that themselves. This organization, Jerry Krause and his staff, have found players who have that kind of motivation."

Asked if he was being "squeezed out," Jackson replied, "I don't think there's any squeezing going on. This is a mutual agreement that we've made, Jerry Reinsdorf and I. We look at it as an opportunity—not as a farewell, see ya later. This is not a last gasp."

Jordan, though, refused to accept that. "It's too obvious to see the guy's success in such a short amount of time to say, 'Now, we need a change.' It's something deeper than what you see on the basketball court," he told reporters.

The star pointed out that Jackson had guided the Bulls through difficult circumstances after taking over in 1989. "We had coaches coming in and out of here," Jordan said. "We found a good one and we stuck with him and . . . he gave stability to my career. We all have so much respect for him."

That respect once again proved to be the bedrock of the Bulls' superior chemistry as they worked their way through yet another challenging season. It could be seen in the excellent year Dennis Rodman was having. "He treats you like a man," the mercurial rebounder said of Jackson. "He lets you be yourself." Rodman's December hair decoration was yellow, with a smiley face in the crown.

"Dennis has had problems with other coaches, but he knows Phil is on his side," Ron Harper observed.

Jackson, though, pointed out that one of the major differences with Rodman was the behavior clauses in his contract. "The Bulls put [behavior clauses] in the contract," Jackson said. "Rather than being a rebel, he's chosen to do the things that are appropriate. He's having a lot more fun. And he's right back at the top of the league in rebounding."

And wearing a smiley face in his hair. "I love having the most famous hair in the world," Rodman conceded to reporters. "People wonder what's going to happen next. It was Chip Schaefer's doing. Chip told me, 'Be a happy face, shock everybody.' Well, here it is."

Yet all the players knew that Jackson's respect faced a bigger challenge than Rodman's behavior. Much goodwill would be needed to lure the angry and frustrated Pippen back to the team. Fortunately, Jackson understood this and was working discreetly to pull Pippen back into the team circle. As December passed, there were clear signs that his efforts were working.

In the middle of the month, the forward appeared at the team's annual holiday party, where eight-year-old Derameo Johnson asked Pippen, "Are you going to get back on the team?"

"Yeah," Pippen replied with a shy, soft smile.

A week and a half later, he began practicing with the Bulls. "I'm just trying to get myself healthy," he said. "If I have to come back and play here, then, you know, that may be the way it has to be."

No one was more pleased than Jackson to see the return. And perhaps no one appreciated Pippen's greatness more than the coach. He often thought of

Pippen's role in the 1991 championship series and his coming of age against the Pistons in the Eastern Conference playoffs that same season.

"The real buildup was in that Detroit series when Rodman head-butted him," Jackson recalled. "He got beat up, he got thrown to the floor. He had to guard Laimbeer. He played through a physical, combative series, in which the stories were, 'They'll beat him up, and he'll pussy out in the end and he'll get a migraine headache or something will happen.' They tried to make it a negative thing about Scottie, but the truth was that Scottie was extremely tough and resilient. He has magical games, really big games."

A perfect example was the 1997 championship series, Jackson added. "If anybody looks at Michael's game against Utah last year in Game 5, and sees how Scottie Pippen played in conjunction with Michael Jordan, with Michael just playing offense and Scottie telling him, 'Look, I'll take care of the defense.' He just ran the defense and ran the floor game brilliantly. He played an absolutely terrific ball game. The combination of the two of them was devastating."

Just how badly the Bulls needed Pippen was emphasized January 8 with a smashing road loss in Miami. The Bulls took a 28–20 first-quarter lead over the Heat but scored only 44 points the rest of the way and lost, 99–72.

"There's no explanation for it," Jordan told reporters. "You just have to grin and bear it."

Jackson, of course, hated to lose to any Riley team and showed his disdain by getting ejected just before halftime for arguing with the officiating crew, which included one of the league's first two females refs, Violet Palmer. "The only thing I'll say is I'm disappointed with the league for sending a crew like that out to referee a game like this," Jackson said. "From the very first play, there was a problem."

Two nights later they journeyed to New York for their first game of the season in the Garden, where Jordan tantalized the Big Apple media by saying that he would "love" to play for the Knicks. The next night, January 11, the Bulls returned home, and Pippen appeared in uniform for the first time since the '97 championship series. The United Center crowd greeted him with joyous applause. He played 31 minutes and scored 14 points in an 87–72 win over hapless Golden State. The timing for his return was right. The Bulls had won 13 of their last 15 games and boosted their record to 25–11.

He was asked if his relations with the team's front office had been repaired. "I don't think they've been repaired at all," he said. "We haven't tried to repair them. I don't think they can be repaired. I'm just going to do my job and just allow them to do theirs."

There remained the possibility that he still might be traded before the late February 19 trading deadline, although Krause had told reporters that any deal for Pippen would have to be highly favorable to the Bulls. When asked by reporters if he was convinced Pippen wouldn't be traded, Jackson said, "I remain unconvinced about anything. It was a time in which there were hard feelings, some feelings about the loyalty issue. Some of those issues had to be worked out. The understanding that the greater glory or the greater effort had to be for the team. I felt Scottie would take the high road and I feel he has."

Back to Business

A week later, just days after Jordan had praised his good behavior, Rodman stirred the pot by missing a pregame practice after a night of carousing at a strip club in New York.

Jackson's response was to fine him, suspend him a game, and send him home from New Jersey.

"I thought it was fair and I thought Phil sending me home was the right thing," Rodman told reporters later. "When I came back from flying home by myself, I went straight to the practice facility and started to work out. I messed up and that is it. It's as simple as that. I didn't feel good physically and I stayed out a little too late."

The Bulls returned home from New Jersey and found the Utah Jazz waiting. Karl Malone scored 35 and powered the Jazz to a 101–94 win that ended Chicago's 17-game home winning streak.

Immediately afterward, the Bulls departed on their second West Coast road trip of the season, with games against Vancouver, Portland, Golden State, the Lakers, Denver, and Utah that would lead right up to the All-Star break in New York.

At 30–13, the Bulls were showing definite signs of life. "It's a bonding trip," Jordan said of the Western swing. "It's for improvement of our basketball skills, our continuity, our chemistry."

The last time he had made such a statement, the journey had turned ugly and sour, producing anything but bonding. This time, Krause would remain home, busying himself with scouting college talent. But the general manager would still find a way to reach out to the team, setting up the next round of controversy, yet another exercise in wasted effort.

It all made perfect sense in a Zen sort of way. For the third straight season, the Chicago Bulls had faced an uncertain future. They were a great team, yet the slightest disruption to their modus operandi would likely have been taken as an excuse for the team's chairman and general manager to break them apart. That meant that a major injury, internal squabbling, or just plain old everyday fear run amok could have spelled their doom. Yet that hadn't happened. One of the reasons was the Zen concept of "living in the moment," not losing concentration, not giving in to their concerns about the future.

"It doesn't affect him at all," Steve Kerr said of Jackson. "And that's to his credit. He always preaches being in the moment and living for the moment and enjoying each day for what it is. He's got a lot of little pet quotes and sayings that allude to that, and he practices that. It could be the last run for all of us, and he's gonna have fun."

Jordan agreed, saying that Jackson's dealing so smartly with the adversity of the season had been good for him "because he finally gets some notoriety as a coach. He's a wise, smart coach, not just the guy who coached Michael Jordan, Scottie Pippen, Dennis Rodman. He uses his talent to blend everybody together to have one focus. And he's doing a heck of a job of that."

By all rights, the separation anxiety alone should have been enough to splinter the Bulls into factions. But they all believed in Jordan, Pippen, and Jackson, and that bound them even tighter. Jackson loved the unity of it. Zen warriors. In the moment. Doing battle.

As the season unfolded into February, it became clear that there was plenty of battle to do, on and off the court. They opened their trip with wins in Vancouver, Portland, and Golden State, then got waxed by the quick young Lakers in Los Angeles, and one night later righted themselves against lowly Denver.

It was in Utah, on the eve of their rematch with the Jazz, that word came that Krause had decided to unburden his mind to *Tribune* columnist Fred Mitchell.

Jackson would definitely not be back, Krause emphasized. "We would like to have Michael back," he said. "But Michael is going to have to play for someone else. It isn't going to be Phil."

Krause also said that Jackson wasn't "being run out of here. Phil agreed that this would be his last year. He did not want to go through a possible rebuilding situation. Nobody is running Phil out of town. It was a well thought-out decision."

Krause also offered up an opinion on the difficulty of rebuilding with Jordan still on the roster. "Obviously, with Michael and the salary he is making now, it would be very tough to improve our team. Our cap money would be gone. It is a highly complicated thing. I would say that no NBA team has faced this type of situation before, cap-wise."

Krause should have known Jordan would take the statement as a challenge. After all, the GM had worked with the star for thirteen seasons. Krause also should have known that Reinsdorf would be angered by the statement. After all, the chairman's philosophy was to make no decision, to take no heat, until necessary. Krause had done just the opposite. He had spoken prematurely. No matter what he said, his words only cemented the impression that he was eager to pack up the current championship team, to clear the salary cap, so that he could begin rebuilding.

Krause's words created a mild media frenzy that morning at the Bulls' shootaround before the Utah game. Jordan again emphasized that if Jackson weren't retained, he would move on, too. "It still stands true," Jordan said. "That's been my thought process for the year, pretty much. I felt that management has to make a decision in terms of what they want to do with this team, the direction they choose to go in. They have to make their choice."

The Bulls lost that night in Utah, allowing the Jazz a season sweep of the two-game series and home-court advantage if the two met in the 1998 Finals. While the rest of the team returned home to rest during the All-Star break, Jordan journeyed on to New York to take part in the All-Star events. A gathering of global media awaited, more than a thousand journalists, and Jordan was ready to fire back at the two Jerrys.

"Why would you change a coach," Jordan said, "who has won five championships when he has the respect of his players and certainly the understanding of his players to where they go out and play hard each and every day. Why?"

Question: *Management contends that Phil Jackson has become arrogant. Have you seen arrogance on Phil's part?*

"I'm pretty sure that he's probably getting tired of Krause. And I've been there, a long time ago. I understand [Phil's] frustrations. Maybe they view that as arrogance. But what I see in Phil is an attitude to work with the players to achieve the best as a team. That means a lot to us."

If Phil were back, and the core of the Bulls were back, how badly would you want to play another season? Would it be something you'd really cherish?

"If they'd keep everybody intact? I'd love to do that."

Why not another coach?

"I've never had a guy come in and pacify me. I like Phil. I think Phil comes in with a certain motion, a certain thought process, a team concept, that everybody fits within that. We grew to where we respected each other, and he knew certain things to apply to me and to apply to other players. I don't want a coach to come in and say, 'Well, what do you want to do? Do you want to do this? Do you want to do that?' That doesn't motivate me. That doesn't challenge me. And now you're asking me to go into that situation unknowingly? At this stage of my career? If the system doesn't suit me, and I don't feel comfortable, or my game starts to suffer, or certain things start to change, then you leave yourself open for all kinds of speculation, which I'm not afraid of. But why would I take the risk of changing it?"

It almost sounds like a superstition.

"It's a comfort. It's a comfort. It's a respect. It's knowing what I'm getting instead of not knowing what I'm getting."

In the wake of Jordan's comments, Reinsdorf issued a statement calling for an end to premature comments about the team's future. Word spread around the Bulls' offices that Reinsdorf was angry with Krause, that the GM had lost face because of his comments.

"That's one thing that Jerry Reinsdorf does very well," Steve Kerr observed. "He stays away and doesn't get involved in all of it. He lets Jerry Krause and Phil and everybody else go about their business. Obviously, he's ended up sort of in the middle of this. But usually Krause is the front man."

Practice resumed at the Berto Center on Monday after the All-Star break, and afterward Jackson spoke with reporters, emphasizing that he was leaving. "There is no other option," the coach said. "We've made an agreement that that's what is going on and that is the direction we are going as a basketball team. It's going to be hard to say good-bye. It's going to be really tough."

Then he quibbled, leaving the door ajar that indeed he might find a way to return, which left Krause furious but muzzled.

"I'm not saying our beds are made," Jackson said, "but they are laid out and ready to go. Early in training camp I sat down with Jerry Krause and Jerry Reinsdorf and we expressly went over this again and said this is our swan song as a team."

Then he said, "Michael has a tremendous sway in this game, as we all see from the effect he had in the All-Star Game. Michael is the only one who could change it."

About Jordan's threatened retirement, Jackson said, "It makes me feel like I am standing in the way of him continuing his career. Some of it does. The other thing is that the organization is a bit to fault in it, too."

Jackson then predicted that Krause wouldn't change his mind. "That's not going to happen," Jackson said. "I think the amount of intensity we've had over the last two seasons, the directions we've changed and the divergent paths that both Jerry and I have gone on just spelled the fact that the relationship had reached its course. It's time for him to do what he wants to do in his management of this organization and it's time for me to move on wherever I have to go. Michael can throw a monkey wrench into things, but that's their decision and that's the way we have to look at it."

In his *New York Post* column during the All-Star break, NBC analyst Peter Vecsey had suggested that the Bulls were paying Jackson $500,000 in hush money not to speak out about the situation.

"I didn't get back from the All-Star Game until Monday afternoon," Jackson later recalled. "We had practice and I didn't see his column. I had questions from reporters about this, and I didn't understand it. It was totally misrepresented. There is not anything like that in my contract. Last year at some point during contract negotiations, we said at some point that if we don't come to an agreement and we have to step away what's going to happen? There was some talk about a severance. Because we actually began thinking, 'We may not reach a common ground on this and this may become difficult for the franchise.' So we talked about it in that context. But I had no intention of taking hush money, or whatever, to be quiet, or whatever it was meant as. But, you know, severance money is severance money."

In the wake of the All-Star weekend, the atmosphere around the Bulls tightened as the trading deadline neared. Would Krause dare to trade Pippen? It seemed unlikely. Not with the uproar that his comments earlier in the month had caused.

But the team did send young forward Jason Caffey to Golden State for David Vaughn, an unproven player, and two second-round draft picks. The move set off immediate speculation that Krause was intentionally weakening the team.

"This is a horrible thing to say," said one longtime team employee. "I wonder if Jerry and Jerry almost want us not to win this year, so they can have the excuse to rebuild. It's an unbelievably dangerous thing to say, especially with a tape recorder on. I'm just wondering about their emotional state. You don't want to think that, but you have to wonder."

Jordan, meanwhile, was angry, pointing out to reporters that losing Caffey, an athletic rebounder, was like losing family.

"You don't think it makes it easier to break up the team to say 'See, we told you?'" the reporter asked.

"You know, maybe we should call Oliver Stone and he could make a movie out of it," Kerr said. "He would have a field day with all of this."

Sportswriter Terry Armour of the *Tribune* figured Krause had scored one against Jackson and Jordan with the trade, a perception that also registered with many fans. "The Caffey move," Armour said, "to me is strictly—and I could be wrong here. I've been wrong before—'see if you can win with a David Vaughn.' To me, it just looks like, 'OK, let's make some minor moves that will make it hard for us to get there.' But you know, who would want to do that? Realistically, who would want to weaken their case? You can accuse somebody of that, but realistically, it doesn't make sense that somebody would want to do that."

Behind the scenes, the Bulls' assistant coaches had lobbied hard for Krause to keep Caffey, but Jackson quietly agreed with the deal. He knew that Krause had no plans to re-sign Caffey, who would be a free agent at the end of the season. Plus, Jackson was hoping that the Bulls would be able to find a player like Brian Williams, who was able to guard smaller, quick centers. Williams had been a godsend during the 1997 playoffs. Obviously, no player of Williams's quality was available in 1998, so Jackson figured that a "Dickey Simpkins–type" player, someone about 6′9″ or 6′10″, might be available to help out defensively.

"I actually wanted to bid out Caffey [for a trade]," Jackson explained. "Jason wasn't going to get a chance in this organization. He'd go through his free agency and he wouldn't be re-signed by this organization. For a kid that I liked, it was a good opportunity for him to go. But I didn't want to hurt the team. I wanted a bigger kind of a player like a Dickey Simpkins who could play centers that are small like Mourning. And Jason was a little too small to play the Shawn Kemps. He's a 6′8″ guy as opposed to a 6′10″, 265-pound guy. So that's the difference.

"I told them that what I wanted," Jackson admitted privately. "We wanted a Brian Williams–type player. I've always had that type of center. Stacey King and Scott Williams."

As it turned out, Simpkins was soon put on waivers by Golden State, allowing the Bulls to waive Vaughn after a few days and sign Simpkins.

"Dickey's that kind of guy," Jackson said. "The job is his to do. It's not a heavy-minute role. We don't see that guy coming in there and playing 30 to 40 minutes. But he can play 16 minutes a game for us and help us out if possible."

Simpkins, whom the Bulls had traded in the fall of 1997 to Golden State for Scott Burrell, was truly elated to be back in Chicago. "It's like going off to war, then coming back," he said.

Or maybe vice versa.

Behind the scenes, Krause was furious with Jackson. The general manager alleged that the coach was supposed to explain the trade to the players, but that Jackson had failed to do so, opening the door to speculation that Krause was sabotaging the team. "Phil was supposed to take care of the team, and he didn't do it," Krause said. "He was supposed to explain it to the players. But once again he left me looking like the bad guy."

With the tension, people in the organization increasingly complained to reporters that Jackson had grown arrogant. "I've heard from different circles," Terry Armour said, "that one thing that Phil may have done to rub the organization the wrong way is that he came in on a winning situation and took it to the next level.

"The belief is that, whatever reasons Doug Collins was let go for, Doug would have done it," Armour said. "Doug would have been right there to do it. Phil got arrogant. You know winning changes people, and that Phil went from being a team player as far as the organization is concerned, to saying, 'Hey, maybe I'm the guy who did this.'

"He may come across as arrogant to some people because of the way he talks," Armour added. "Some people take that as being a snob, or that he's trying to show us how smart he is. But I don't think it's that way with him. I would not consider him arrogant in his dealings with the media. He knows how to play the game, too, as far as the PR thing. You can tell when people are arrogant with the media. They embarrass you when you question them. Phil is not like that. I think, if anything, Phil might be too honest with us. Maybe it's a PR move, but Phil will answer our questions, good or bad, and he doesn't really think about repercussions."

With their "divided house" in full conflict, the Bulls entered the spring playing both for and against the organization. That seemed to work well enough. Jordan and company ran off eight straight wins, dumping Toronto, Charlotte, Atlanta, Detroit, Indiana, Toronto again, Washington, and Cleveland before finally losing again on February 25 when the young Portland Trail Blazers gave the Bulls only their third defeat of the season in the United Center. As they had done in the past, the Bulls answered defeat with another torrid burn of winning. They would roll through March at 13–1, emphasizing to opponents and fans alike at every stop that these Bulls were indeed back to their old dominant selves, or something close.

The head of steam was aided by nearly a week's rest in the schedule after wins over Sacramento and Denver. The Bulls sat at home, healed their injuries, and stoked their fires. Jordan even had time to rummage through his closets to find a vintage pair of Air Jordans to wear for what was billed as his last visit to Madison Square Garden, the game against New York on March 9 when the Bulls resumed play. Never mind that the shoes were gaudy and flimsy; they were the perfect touch to send a public message, creating further anxiety about Krause and Reinsdorf shutting down the Bulls early.

His feet covered in red, Jordan treated the adoring Garden crowd and the television audience to an old-style performance, filled with whirling, impossible drives to the baskets and reverses and dunks and whatever else popped to the surface of his creativity, all of it good for 42 precious points.

"I played up in the air a lot today," he admitted afterward. "I'm not afraid to play that way. There was a need there, and if there's a need there, I have to address it. I'm not really thinking about the moves and how excited the fans are. The oooohs and aaaahs tell you that. Some of the moves seemed to be coming from 1984."

With Jordan's outburst and Pippen's defense in full force, the Bulls drove to a 102–89 win.

Kent McDill of the *Daily Herald* said, "Krause doesn't want to be the man who chases Michael out of the game. He just wants to get rid of Phil. He wants a coach who respects him. He likes to be a kingmaker, and he feels that Phil doesn't give him the respect he deserves for putting him in a position to be considered one of the top 10 coaches in NBA history."

"To be honest," said John Jackson of the *Sun-Times*, "if I was Krause and I was in his position, I think I would want to change coaches right now too. I think it's time. I think Phil's a little burned out in this job. He has changed a lot, and he has gotten a bit arrogant. The decision to change coaches is a valid one, and I think Krause is right on about that. But the problem with it is, Jordan has aligned himself so heavily with Phil. Sometimes perception is more important than reality. And the perception is that if Krause makes a coaching change now, he and Reinsdorf are showing no loyalty to Phil, they're just kicking him in the ass."

"I don't see any reason," said Kent McDill, "why this whole thing just couldn't keep on going."

From their win in New York, the Bulls jetted back home briefly to notch a big win over the Heat before heading south for a two-game trip to Texas. First up were the Dallas Mavericks, a team stumbling through yet another misguided season.

From there, the Bulls went out and ran up a decent lead against the struggling Mavericks. Chicago was up by 18 with about five minutes to go, and the fans were leaving in droves. But then the Bulls lost focus and watched the Mavs stage a strange comeback, aided by a succession of Bulls miscues and questionable calls, to tie it in regulation and win it in overtime. It was only the Bulls' second loss since the All-Star break, but later they would look back on it as the place where they lost home-court advantage against the Jazz. In the waning seconds of overtime, a disgusted Jackson sat on the bench, clipping his fingernails.

"Sometimes you give 'em away in this game," the coach said afterward, "and we certainly gave that away. We had some help. The referees helped us give it away, but that'll happen sometimes on the road like this."

It was pointed out that Jackson seemed to be the kind of poor sport who never took losing well. "I don't think any of us do," Winter said. "Winning is nice, but losing is just awful. There's a big difference. Sometimes when you win, you're still not happy because of the way you played. But, boy, when you lose, it's just devastating. We've never lost much. It's so hard to take losing when you're not used to it. Once you get the habit of losing, it doesn't bother you quite so much."

"There's some anger and disappointment," Jackson agreed. "Most of the guys went out in Dallas and blew it off. They got rid of it that night and slept it off. We looked at the tape and put it to bed, buried it. It's past."

The Bulls assured that two nights later by playing what Winter would call their most energetic game of the season later in rainy San Antonio. Jackson surprised nearly everyone by starting Kukoc against Spurs center David Robinson. An even bigger surprise was that it worked. The Spurs pushed hard, but the Bulls shoved right back. Having learned his lesson two nights earlier, Jackson worked the officials furiously, prompting a fan to yell, "Forget it, Phil, they won't let you come back."

After outdistancing the Spurs by 10, the Bulls continued their burn through March, returning home to buzz New Jersey, then dipping down to win a big game in Indiana. They got a Friday night home win against Vancouver, then headed north into a snowstorm that left them circling for an hour over Toronto and reminded equipment manager John Ligmanowski of a few seasons back when the team jet nearly got flipped by wind shear in Detroit.

Once they landed, the Bulls found the young Raptors as problematic as the snow.

Kukoc opened the game with a rebound, and Jackson wasted no time before barking at him. At the offensive end. Kukoc held the ball on the perimeter.

"Here, here," Jackson shouted hoarsely, motioning to Pip inside.

Kukoc delivered the pass, "Now to the goal," Jackson yelled. But Kukoc had anticipated and already cut, and Pippen hit him with the return pass for a nice two-handed jam.

Things were right in the Bulls' world, at least for the moment. But that was all that Jackson wanted. On the next possession, Jordan scored and danced away from the goal with the trademark Jordan swagger, that mix of elegance and gameliness.

In the third period, the Bulls expanded the lead to a dozen, but then came the loss of focus, just as it had in Dallas. Somehow, Jordan and his teammates managed to just hold on at the end, allowing the younger Raptors to make the final mistakes. Jackson smiled. The Bulls were living on the edge, but Pippen was back, and they were winning. And best of all, they were alive in the moment. Right where Jackson hoped they would be.

The Moment

Jackson's final weeks as coach of the Chicago Bulls were marked by more turbulence. But it was nothing that Michael Jordan couldn't overcome. After all, the star lived for the playoff season, that time when every synapse in his competitive body was fused to every twitch of his muscle fiber, when his will was fully wired and hypercharged. Each spring, it seemed, Jackson and his staff would work on subtle means of reining in that immense force. Each spring, they knew the ultimate futility of their efforts. Their best hope was to preach togetherness, constantly reminding Jordan to include his teammates, to pull them along just enough so that when he needed them, they would be there to help.

Jordan knew this and complied whenever and wherever possible. He was gracious, diplomatic, and respectful. Yet that took him just so far. In the end, he was the only one who really understood his attack mentality. Only he could sense when to unleash it. And he would be the first to admit that it wasn't perfect. But it was damn near close, eerily close some nights, when he would slip into his terminator mode late in a key game with important things on the line. "He's just so damn confident," Tex Winter said one playoff night after Jordan had teetered between success and failure, what Winter referred to as the "high-wire act."

The suspense had never been greater, with the future of his team and his career on the line. In reality, the public relations campaigning of the regular season had been only fun and games, a diversion. In the end, Jordan's play would send the one single message that trumped all others.

It began in late April with the very first playoff game in the first round against the New Jersey Nets. The Bulls played sluggishly, blew a late 14-point lead, and allowed the young Nets to take them to overtime, where Jordan stole the ball from Kerry Kittles with 90 seconds to play. He sped upcourt, tongue out, and dunked and growled. New Jersey's Kendall Gill fouled him going to the basket, and he made the free throw, propelling Chicago to a 96–93 win.

The growl was a tad uncharacteristic, but these were emotional times.

"We walk away feeling lucky more than anything," said Jordan, who finished with 39 points.

"I see him being awfully close in similarity to the way he was when he left the game the first time in 1993," trainer Chip Schaefer said of Jordan. "In the early '90s, he would talk. We would have moments where we were alone while I was treating an injury of his, and he would speak of his frustrations. He would say, 'I don't think I can take this much longer.' I always thought he was just sort of venting. I was shocked when he retired the first time. But there are some things that are similar to that now. You can see the intrusions onto what he likes to do. Just a look of weariness on his face sometimes that he didn't have two years ago, or even last year. I don't know what he's going to do, I really don't. I think there's part of him that wants to stay. If it is winding down, it's almost like these guys don't want to let go, whereas months ago they spoke of wanting to end it and wanting to leave. Now, it's like you're ready to get that divorce and you think, 'One more time. Let's try it again, babe.' They're almost afraid to move on out and do something different."

On the other hand, Schaefer had a perfect read on Jackson. The coach was clearly ready to move on, despite Jordan's statements that he would quit if

Jackson didn't come back. The statements pressured both Krause and Jackson. "I can't see Phil doing it again," the trainer said.

The Bulls had been in a situation where everything worked. The spirit, camaraderie, emotion—all those elements had come together at a very special level for this team. Yet there was no question that the conflict had the potential to extinguish whatever had been achieved. That could be seen in the looks on Jordan's and Pippen's faces whenever Krause was mentioned. The situation had great potential for long-term hatred.

Even Krause and Reinsdorf showed some signs of recognizing that. But it was too late. Krause's hopes of rebuilding the team in the future had cast a deep shadow over the present.

"Sometimes it just seems that these guys get themselves in trouble by almost trying to do too much," Schaefer said of Krause and Reinsdorf. "Sometimes you just need to let it happen. They got a great coaching staff in place. They got a great roster of players. It's been made so much more complex in a lot of ways than it has to be. There's a lot of axioms about simplicity in life. It's all gotten so complicated. I don't understand how it got this way."

In Game 2 against the Nets, Chicago missed 7 of 13 free throws. Once again, they managed to hang on for a win, with 32 points from Jordan, 19 from Toni Kukoc, and 16 rebounds from Dennis Rodman. Several newspaper accounts described them as vulnerable and perhaps even distracted by the internal conflict. "I'm pretty sure that's what people have been writing," Jordan said after the second game. "Some teams probably feel that way, too. But until they actually come in and do it [beat the Bulls], it's just conversation."

He emphasized that for Game 3 in New Jersey by hitting 15 of his first 18 shots and scoring 38 points as the Bulls swept the Nets with a 116–101 victory.

It was the third straight first-round sweep for Chicago. The Bulls had run up a 24–1 record in first-round games since 1991.

The opening of the playoffs also had coincided with the first issues of *ESPN The Magazine*. As a highlight, the magazine published excerpts from Jackson's diary put together by *Sun-Times* columnist Rick Telander. At first, Jackson and Telander had been under contract to write a book based on the diary, but Jackson said he had decided to kill the book deal as the season began. The publishers prevailed upon Jackson to at least do the magazine story, and he agreed. The coach presented his diary with the understanding that he would be able to see any parts excerpted before publication. Unfortunately, there was a time squeeze, and Jackson never got the opportunity to approve what was published. It would prove to be perhaps the worst mistake of Jackson's career.

There were references to his marital difficulties with wife June (Jackson would move into a Chicago hotel for part of the 1998 season after she discovered that he had had relationships outside the marriage), snide and unkind remarks about Krause, and what seemed to be egotistical ramblings about other teams. Jackson came across as a guy campaigning to take over as coach of the Lakers or Knicks, teams that already had coaches. It was quite outrageous. Even worse, the comments provided the first real opening for Krause to attack Jackson.

The next issue of *ESPN The Magazine* bore a second installment of the Jackson diaries that proved mostly to be an apology and retraction of things said in the first installment. Even the magazine itself lampooned Jackson in a subsequent spoof comparing the Last Run of the Bulls to the final episode of the long-running TV series "Seinfeld." Each of the Bulls' primary figures was projected as a member of the cast. Jackson was designated as the strange and daffy Kramer.

Krause was understandably angry about the publishing of the diary, but kept his anger behind the scenes. "As far as me being sensitive to this issue, I don't know that I've been overly sensitive," Krause said in a private interview for this book. "I think I know where things are coming from. When you know where the gun's being aimed from, you really don't worry about the result of the bullet."

Krause also met with new *Tribune* columnist Skip Bayless and outlined his complaints against Jackson, according to one team source. Days later, Jackson sat down with Bayless in what the coach thought was a courtesy introduction. But the columnist launched into a series of inflammatory questions about Jackson's relationship with Krause. "Bayless used Krause's comments to get Phil going," said one team source.

Jackson responded to Krause's comments. "I'm not gonna let that be the final word," the coach explained at the time. Yet when Bayless's column appeared, there was little use of Krause's comments, only Jackson's angry response on issues, another situation where he appeared to be on the attack.

Bayless would then weigh in on Jackson during the playoffs as an egotist desperately seeking to take control of the team and maintain his image of being vital to the Bulls' success. "You have to wonder about Phil Jackson's motives," Bayless would write later in the season. "You have to question why he says he'll suggest to Michael Jordan that number 23 retire. Love and respect? Or revenge and insecurity? Has a vial of self-importance transformed Dr. Jackson into a wild-haired coach Hyde? Zen Master or Spin Master?

"Is Jackson trying to influence Jordan to retire prematurely in order to wreak revenge on Jerrys Reinsdorf and Krause?" the columnist asked. "Jackson despises General Manager Krause. Jackson blames Chairman Reinsdorf for sticking with Krause, who has stuck it to Jackson during contract negotiations."

The combined effect of the *ESPN* article and the Bayless columns was to leave Jackson despondent and to play a major role in his ultimate decision to leave the team. "It has not been healthy for me to be here because I have gotten a reputation now as being a backbiter, as being devious, as being ungrateful," the coach said in a private interview as the season wound down. "There have been a lot of things that I've had to suffer about my character that I've been very upset about. It's not right. I think it's a spin on the other side to portray me as that, or as worthy of being let go. I went to Mr. Reinsdorf and said I won't have my character blotted. You know this is a situation that's changing, and we can go through this without having to spoil a person's being or character or reputation. That's been my feeling, and yet it's been allowed to happen. I don't know if people seeded it.

"I may be responsible for seeding some bad things about Jerry Krause in the *ESPN* article, which I am sorry ever came out," Jackson said. "It wasn't supposed to be like that, although I did write it down and it was in my diary. The diary was in the hands of a writer. His responsibility was to let me edit it, which he didn't. It got out of my control. So there has been some rebuttal because of that. As a result, it has been a situation in which to come back would be almost unthinkable, almost an impossibility."

Tex Winter said he didn't in any form believe Jackson was the egotist portrayed by Bayless, "but I can see from the way things have come down that some people might read it that way. It's unfortunate that things came down the way they did. On the other hand, when you come out in a story, particularly one that's taken out of a diary . . . I think the mistake was that he allowed somebody to be privy to his situation and thoughts. And Phil didn't really intend that at all. That's what really hurt Phil. But those were his personal thoughts."

The assistant coach acknowledged that Jackson's diary comments had hurt and angered Krause. "I like 'em both, sure," Winter said. "I ride the fence. I'm a double agent. I find out what one side's thinking. Then I'm on the other side, find out what they're thinking. And I still don't know what either one of them is thinking."

The Final Days

In the wake of the New Jersey series, Krause granted an interview in his Berto Center office. His lung infections had given him fits all season, necessitating treatment with steroids. The steroids, in turn, had kept him awake most nights going to the bathroom. The illness, combined with the fan anger over the impending breakup of the team, made it a very difficult year. Was it the worst of all his years in Chicago? he was asked.

"On me personally? Oh yeah, this year's been the toughest," the GM said. "The first year [1985] was so damn tough because I didn't know. I knew we were gonna do some things, but I didn't know how we were gonna do 'em. The first year was pretty bad. . . . We had Quintin [Dailey] go off in a drunk tank, and had all those injuries."

Krause was asked to envision another title, more champagne, another moment with Jordan at the microphone. "That would be great with me," he said. "I got no problem with that. Six is important to me. We kept it together to win six."

Indeed, after the season he had suffered through, to not win another title would have been misery. As with the Bulls' other key figures, Krause's competitiveness was one of the elements of his success. Asked about the comment of a Bulls staff member that the friction between the coach and general manager had actually benefited the team, Krause said, "Phil and I think very differently in a lot of ways. We go at each other. It's competitive all the time. . . . I want the scouts to stand up and fight. I want the coaches to stand up and fight. I don't mind that. I gotta sit and make a decision on what people tell me and what my own instincts tell me. But I'm gonna listen to everybody and try to think every thought they express in a meeting. Somebody has to pull the trigger."

As for the current Bulls' team, Krause said, "I'm not sure that we realize what we've done. It doesn't hit you right away first of all. It hits you later in life. With me, I've been so busy doing it that I haven't had the chance to sit back and smell the roses. Jerry [Reinsdorf] always tells me, 'C'mon and sit back and smell the roses. They're blooming.' I gotta figure out a way to win next year. I think as I get older I will."

As Jordan liked to say, the playoffs never really started until you lose a game at home. If that was the case, then the playoffs started for the Bulls after the second game of the second round against the Charlotte Hornets.

The Bulls had used their trademark defense to hold the Hornets to 32 second-half points while claiming Game 1 of the series. But late in Game 2, former Bull B. J. Armstrong found the groove with his jumper and propelled the Hornets to the 78–76 upset. Charlotte forward Anthony Mason also did a nice job on Jordan defensively, using his size to take away some of Jordan's effectiveness in the post.

"It's probably been three weeks since we played a real good game," Jackson told reporters. "I thought that some of us are going through the motions and just letting everybody else take the responsibility, letting Michael take the responsibility for scoring and not carrying their own weight."

In the wake of the loss, Reinsdorf finally broke his silence with an interview with the *Chicago Tribune*'s Sam Smith. He denied that he planned to break up the team.

"If we win the championship, I would be inclined to invite everyone back," Reinsdorf told Smith. "Neither I nor Jerry Krause has ever said—anywhere—that we want to break up the team. We get accused of saying it. I read it all the time. I hear Spike Lee saying it on the Jay Leno show."

Jackson's agent Todd Musburger countered Reinsdorf's claims by telling Chicago's WMAQ radio that he wasn't convinced of the chairman's sincerity. "They are trying to put the responsibility on the players for not coming back, not the team," Musburger said. "The Bulls are having a hard time taking the responsibility for what might happen. They told us loud and clear [during the previous summer's contract talks] this would be the last year of Phil's duties as coach of the team. They have had ample time to display what they want to do."

Reinsdorf's message was that it was Jackson, not Krause, breaking up the team. Jackson himself admitted that he had been eager to leave for the past two years. "But as it gets into the playoffs, it's going to be harder and harder to say good-bye to this team," he said, adding that he had no intention of coming back. "It's being wanted back," Jackson explained. "That's the whole thing."

Jordan admitted being confused by Reinsdorf's timing. "I think all of it's been a pretty trying season," Jordan said. "We've still been able to get on the basketball court and play the game, and that's what we're going to be remembered for, not all this conversation that's going on now."

Asked if Reinsdorf was trying to put the blame for the breakup on Jackson and himself, Jordan replied, "If that's the case, it's a bad time, but it's a lot of things that have been bad timing that have happened to us thus far. But I don't know. It kind of caught us off-guard because we never really expected it. We didn't expect any more conversation about next year until this year was over and done with. So his reasoning I really don't know. But he certainly has the prerogative to make a decision like that."

"That's how out of touch things are," Chip Schaefer observed, "when you have to win a title to have the owner be 'inclined' to ask everybody back. You know how hard it is to win 62 games?"

Shrugging off Reinsdorf's comments, the Bulls rolled over the Hornets in Game 3, a contest that had the home fans heading for the exits early. At the next day's practice in the Charlotte Coliseum, Ron Harper explained the mood of the players: "On our team we got some older guys, and we know we aren't going to be around for a long period of time. We know this is our chance now to go out and to just show folks what a good basketball team we have."

Pippen had produced a line of "Last Dance" hats for sale to the public. Harper was asked when he planned to start wearing his. "My Last Dance hat ain't coming out till we get to the championship, the final round," he replied, laughing.

The Bulls' blowout win in Game 3 had left the Hornets in tatters, with Anthony Mason on the bench at the end of the game screaming profanities at coach Dave Cowens. That, in turn, set the stage for the Bulls to breeze in Game 4, 94–80, followed by a tighter win in Game 5 back in Chicago to close out the series.

Jordan finished with 33 points, while Rodman, playing on his thirty-seventh birthday, had 21 rebounds. Jordan scored 11 of his points in the fourth quarter. With less than a minute left, the crowd at the United Center began chanting "MVP, MVP." Indeed, word had already begun circulating that he had outpolled Utah's Karl Malone in balloting for the award.

As usual, Jackson had prepared his team for the playoffs by splicing pieces of a popular film around cuts from the game tapes. For the Indiana and Utah series in the 1998 playoffs, Jackson used *Devil's Advocate*, a dark film starring Al Pacino and Keanu Reeves. Pacino was literally the devil, disguised as a New York law firm executive who specialized in finding and recruiting the best talent.

Asked if it was a thinly disguised reference to Krause, Jud Buechler laughed and said, "Don't go there. Don't even go there."

"It's a little far out," Tex Winter said of Jackson's decision to select a film in which the devil was a talent-scouting executive.

It wasn't a message lost on the players.

"Who is the devil?" forward Dickey Simpkins said with a smile. "I can't answer that question. That might be trouble. I got to wait until after I sign another contract before I answer that."

The film also had ties to Jackson's circumstances. Reeves played a young Florida lawyer recruited by the devil's New York firm because he had never lost a case. In fact, Reeves was so intent on winning that he seemed willing to sacrifice his marriage in the name of competition. Jackson had made it no secret that his own marriage to wife June had suffered because of his intense commitment to the Bulls.

Jackson said the film had many applications, including several for Rodman. In the film, Reeves's wife kept changing hair colors, trying to find her identity as she sank deeper and deeper into madness.

"It has applications where needed," Jackson said, "and I try not to make a big distinction about who the applications are for. There are some things that are obviously for Dennis in *Devil's Advocate*, dealing with the darker side of life. He loves movies so much. There are just some basic statements about free will and about self-determination, that, regardless of what you believe, you are a determinator of your own life. There's other things that are about being possessed or losing control of your own life. It makes some sense to me that can be played around with."

Played around with indeed. In some scenes, certain characters' faces turn grotesquely ugly, and in another, Reeves's wife cuts her own throat while in a mental hospital. Jackson spliced these scenes into sections of game tape that showed ugly play by the Bulls.

"We had a couple of cuts of the guy's wife when she looked in the mirror and turned real ugly," Winter said. "He had that in at a time when we had a couple of real ugly plays. Finally, when we did something really bad, it showed her slitting her throat. Committed suicide. The thing of it is, this devil's advocate makes them do all these things, causes it all."

These scenes were particularly useful if Jordan seemed too intent on one-on-one play, Winter explained. "Sometimes when there was too much one-on-one, he'd maybe get the ugly scene in there, or he'd suggest we're cutting our own throat. You know."

Jordan and his teammates laughed at the ways Jackson presented these notions to them, Winter said. "It's a good way to get across points without your having to say much."

Winter saw it as Jackson's special way of speaking to Jordan, of reminding the superstar about the need to include teammates and to avoid trying to win games by himself.

"These guys, Michael and Scottie in particular, these guys have been with Phil just that long," Winter said. "They've begun to interpret a lot of things now that they didn't understand at all at first. But they've been there so long they can practically read his mind on it now."

"Phil does a lot of stuff that if you just let it pass, you don't really understand," Bill Wennington said. "But if you think about it, he's trying to get us motivated or thinking at a deeper level. Sometimes we catch on, and sometimes we don't. I think Phil's and Michael's relationship is very special. They communicate in their own way on their own level, and they do so very well. There are a lot of times when things aren't going well and we need to move the ball around, and it's in Michael's hands a lot. Phil relates that to Michael by saying, 'Hey, you know, we gotta move the ball around a little bit,' without demeaning him or saying, 'You did it wrong.'"

The other members of the Bulls sensed that Jackson could say those things to Jordan while maybe no other coach could, Wennington said.

Asked if the film could be applied to the larger issues that the Bulls faced this season, Jackson said, "A lot of it is. The thing about being strangers in a strange land. And little stuff, like there's a statement, 'Behold. I send you as a sheep before the wolves.' I've got the crowd in Indiana and Utah both and the referees' calls, and all those kinds of little distractions that go on when you're out there playing on the road. Both of those teams are involved in this movie, how you have to be self-reliant as a basketball team."

"I'm not sure what the message is supposed to be," Tex Winter said. "But there's scenes in there that are very disturbing."

The Indiana Pacers, coached by Larry Bird, stepped up as the Bulls' foes in the Eastern Conference finals, but in the first two games Chicago promptly smothered the Pacers in pressure. Scottie Pippen, in particular, so hounded and harassed Pacers point guard Mark Jackson that he had Bird pleading for the officials to bring some relief. Harper, too, played his role by shutting down Reggie Miller.

The Pacers' pain was measured by their 26 turnovers in Game 1.

"Pippen was hyped up and they let him hang on Mark to bring the ball up," Bird fussed.

In the midst of it all, Bird still had to pause and pay homage to Jordan. "No question since I've been around, he and Magic are the best I've seen," the Indiana coach told reporters. "Believe it or not, every year in this league you learn a little bit more. He might not have the skills like he did when he was young. He might not shoot as high a percentage. But you become a better player as you get older."

The league acknowledged as much by naming Jordan the MVP before Game 2 of the series, making him, at thirty-five, the oldest to claim the award. It was his fifth time to earn the honor.

"It's a cheap thirty-five," Jordan said. "I didn't play much of my second year [foot injury] and I sat out eighteen months [retirement and baseball]. I don't really have the time on the court a normal thirty-five-year-old would have if they played each and every game. To win it at this age means I made the right choice to still play the game because I can still play it at the highest level."

As for Game 3, the Bulls were up 98–91 late in the fourth when Indiana scored 4 points in less than 10 seconds to pull to 98–95. When Jordan answered with a drive, he slipped but somehow managed to keep his dribble, get back up, and cut his way through a scrum of defenders to hit a runner that bounced around and in.

Next, he nailed a 14-foot fallaway on the baseline to kill the Pacers' resurgence.

"Michael hit a lot of great, tough shots," Bird said. "Tough shots for others, routine for him."

He finished with 41 points, the thirty-fifth postseason game of his career in which he had scored 40 or more points. He shot 13 for 22 from the field and 15 for 18 from the line with 5 assists, 4 of Chicago's 15 steals, and 4 rebounds.

Rodman, on the other hand, had only 2 points and 6 rebounds in 24 minutes after being held out of the starting lineup for the second straight game. He had spent a good portion of the night in the locker room riding an exercise bike. When Jackson wanted to insert him into the game, an assistant trainer had to be dispatched to fetch him. "It was irritating having to send for him," Jackson admitted. "I will have a talk with him in the next couple days to see if we can set him straight."

For some reason, Krause chose Game 2 as the time to approach Jordan in his private room in the Bulls' locker room to discuss the star's comments critical of team management in a recent *New Yorker* article. The result was a heated exchange between the star and GM. "For some reason Jerry wanted to do this," a team employee revealed. "Jerry was representing Reinsdorf in saying they were really upset about what Michael said. Jerry tried to reason with him about the *New Yorker* article. Apparently, Michael went right back in his face, saying, 'Don't you dare try to challenge me about it, not with all the manipulating of the press you guys do.' He's not putting up with any of that shit."

Another team official heard about the incident and remarked, "Oh, gee, that's real smart, Jerry trying to go in there and smooth things over. He's the wrong person to do that."

Jordan emerged from the exchange on his way to the postgame media interview session. He looked at a team employee and said, "Fuck your two bosses."

The media, unaware of the confrontation, focused instead on Rodman's behavior during the game. "Dennis is fine, he don't have no problem with anybody," Harper told reporters. "He was late to a game. He's late to every game. Who cares? We know Dennis as a team and the guys let him do what he wants to do as long as he steps on the basketball court and plays basketball."

"I think Dennis has had to compromise his principles more than I have had to compromise mine," Jackson joked, adding, "Dennis has given up his whole life—wrestling, movies, MTV. Think of the things he's had to give up to play basketball."

Yes, Jackson told reporters, Rodman came late to games and was tardy for virtually every practice. "He doesn't like his money. We take it from him and find ways to give it back to him," the coach quipped.

On Thursday, before heading to Indiana, the Bulls' players had declined to speak with the media, which netted a $50,000 fine for the team from the NBA. In playoffs past, the players had sometimes made such refusals, and the team quietly paid the fine. But this time, Krause was incensed and lit into Jackson on the team plane in front of the players. "It's your fault," the GM yelled.

Later, on the tarmac at the Indiana airport, the two got into a screaming match as the players and support personnel watched from a waiting bus, unable to hear exactly what they were saying to each other.

Some staff members figured Krause was simply using the opportunity to vent his frustrations with Jackson. Asked about it later, Jackson said, "I did approach him in a private moment, because I thought in a private moment we could address it. I said, 'There was a better way to handle this than that.' And he didn't want to hear it. He just wanted to go ahead and proceed down the same path he had chosen, which has the tendency to make me rigid. Especially when I had come over to try and get him back on the right page.

"I realize Jerry's a . . ." Jackson said, then hesitated. "I don't want to get into ethnic slander, but from what I've known of all my encounters living with Jewish society most of my life, when the *kaddish* is said, that person becomes a nonentity. And Jerry basically said the *kaddish* [a Hebrew death prayer] over me. And the funeral was said, and I've become a nonentity to him in his life. So it had become very difficult for him to talk to me, to address me personally, and I understood that. He is not going to address me personally again. That's basically his feeling about it in some form or fashion. I've recognized that for the last couple of months. So I understood a little bit about his mentality, because he couldn't really look me in the face when he was trying to get his piece said. I understood that he was doing something he felt he had to do. He didn't want to have a personal contact with me. He still had to do this on some organizational level."

Asked if he thought Krause had also said the *kaddish* over Pippen, Jackson again hesitated, then said, "Yes. He hates Scottie. Scottie has become a nonperson in his life because Scottie called him a liar. And that's the worst thing you could do. Jerry won't admit that he lies. It's very difficult because the owner, Jerry Reinsdorf, doesn't lie. And Jerry Krause also doesn't want to be thought of as a liar. But when you're a general manager, almost by virtue of your job, you have to tell lies. It's unfortunate.

"You have to recuse yourself, is what you have to do," Jackson said. "In this job, I've tried to make it an issue not to lie, although Jerry has accused me face-to-face of lying. To which I said, 'Well, you know, Jerry, there are times I go to speak and I'm caught in situations,' particularly in front of the press, where they ask, 'Is Dennis at practice today,' or something which we're trying to avoid. I choose not to say something, or I choose to recuse myself."

Asked if he thought Krause had said the *kaddish* over Jackson, Tex Winter said, "Yes, he probably has."

With their internal conflicts flaming up before their eyes, the Bulls found a way to lose two spectacular games in Indiana over the Memorial Day weekend. Each time, Chicago had a solid lead in the fourth quarter only to see the Pacers take control in the closing minutes. In Game 3, Indiana won 107–105 to cut the series lead to 2–1. The Pacers' bench, led by forward Jalen Rose and guard Travis Best, had helped sink the Bulls. Reporters asked Jackson about his opponent's bench and he answered gamely "Wait until we get to Utah."

He created further controversy on the eve of Game 4 by telling the press that Chicago's dynasty was on its last legs. "Right now, it's an end of a basketball team that had a great run," he said.

Certainly the Pacers were trying their best to make that happen. Game 4 came down to an unusual series of events that left Jackson fuming about the officiating and countering that Bird's politicking in the media was turning the tide with the referees.

For the packed house at Market Square Arena, the officiating only boosted the drama. Miller hit a three-pointer with 0.7 seconds remaining to give the Pacers a 96–94 win that tied the series at two games apiece.

Jordan got one last shot, but his 26-footer at the buzzer hit the backboard, then rolled around the rim and out, bringing a thunderous celebration. "There were so many debatable calls late in the game, but Reggie still had to make that shot," Jackson told the gathered media. He blasted the officiating by likening it to the 1972 Olympic gold medal game when the United States lost to the Soviet Union on a bad call.

The Pacers had fought the whole game to catch the Bulls and finally took the lead, 88–87, with just over four minutes left when Derrick McKey hit a three-pointer.

The Bulls, however, led 94–91 and seemed in control until Best scored on a drive with 33 seconds to go. Then Rodman was whistled for an illegal offensive pick, sending the ball back to the Pacers. "The offensive foul by Dennis was an awful call," Jackson said. What angered the Bulls' coaches was the illegal down screens the Pacers had set all day long trying to free Miller from Harper's cloying defense. The Pacers' big men were constantly stepping out and giving Harper a forearm, which had Winter fussing. The officials, however, made no illegal pick calls until the one on Rodman in the final seconds.

Chicago was still leading 94–93 when Jordan blocked a jumper by McKey with 6.4 seconds left. Indiana retained possession, but Pippen then stole the inbounds pass after Harper tipped it. The Pacers quickly fouled Pippen, and there was an extended debate over whether Miller threw a punch at Harper.

No technical was called, leading Jackson to say the officials "backed off, acted like they were afraid," words that would bring the coach a $10,000 fine from the league.

Pippen went to the line to shoot his free throws and promptly missed both. He squeezed his head in frustration as he came off the floor for the ensuing timeout.

The Pacers' coaches called for Miller to come off yet another down screen, which he did. He ran to the top of the key and shoved Jordan backward and out of the play to get open for the winning three. The Bulls' coaches screamed yet again for an offensive foul, but the arena was already awash in pandemonium.

The Bulls returned to Chicago and responded with a 106–87 blowout victory to regain the lead in the series, 3–2.

Jordan scored 29 in the rout, which pushed his career totals to 35,000 points, including regular season and playoffs—third all-time, behind Kareem Abdul-Jabbar and Wilt Chamberlain.

Unfortunately, the Bulls had to return to Indiana for Game 6, where somehow the Pacers again managed to win with a late-game turnaround. This time the drama came when Jordan tripped on his way to the basket in the final seconds. There was no call, and the Pacers scooped up the ball and headed off with a 3–3 tie in the series.

"All teams are just kind of tired of all the things Chicago has done," Indiana's Antonio Davis said before Game 7. "They've beaten a lot of people—embarrassed a lot of people—so I'm sure there are a lot of teams out there that would like to see them lose."

The key factor, though, was Chicago's home-court advantage. They were 27–2 in playoff games in the United Center dating back to 1996. That didn't stop the Pacers from pressing the issue. Indiana took an early 13-point lead, which prompted Jackson to abandon the six-man rotation he had used for most of the series. First he inserted Rodman for Kukoc, which produced a 7–0 Chicago run.

Then Jackson turned to Steve Kerr and Jud Buechler. Kerr would finish with 11 points and Buechler with 5 key rebounds and plenty of scrambling hustle.

"We were behind, so he wanted some offense. He kind of took a chance because Best outplayed me this series," Kerr said of Jackson. "Then he went on a hunch and went with Jud, who had a great game. It says he trusts us, he trusts his bench."

"I learned something about our bench: To stick with our bench and not back away from it," Jackson acknowledged. "I think that's what I have to consider and keep considering that we can still find ways to win ball games, even though sometimes we feel a little short-handed." By halftime, the Bulls had eased back in front, 48–45. Then Kukoc took over in the third quarter as Jordan continued to struggle offensively. The Croatian would finish with 21 points, shooting 7 of 11, including 3 of 4 three-pointers.

Chicago opened the fourth with a 69–65 lead, yet even when Jordan returned with under 10 minutes to play he continued to miss shots. Finally, he began attacking the basket, driving into the Pacers' defense and drawing fouls.

"His jump shot didn't work but his free throws did," Bird said, after Jordan's show of will in the final minutes pushed the Bulls to the win. "He put his head down, went into traffic, and drew fouls."

"It's about heart," Jordan said, "and you saw a lot of heart out there on the basketball court."

His first five points of the game pushed him past Kareem Abdul-Jabbar as the leading scorer in playoff history, with nearly 5,800 points. He finished the night with 28 points, 9 rebounds, 8 assists, and 2 steals, all enough to seal Chicago's 88–83 win. "That's why he's the best player in the league and probably the greatest player ever," Bird said.

"I'm pretty sure people are going to say that some of the swagger is gone," Jordan said of his team's narrow playoff escape. "Maybe. But nobody has taken anything away from us so far."

Their next stop was the NBA Finals against the Utah Jazz, who had swept the Los Angeles Lakers in the Western Conference championship series and had been forced to wait ten days for the Bulls to advance.

"We may be a little tired, but our hearts are not tired," Jordan said when asked if his team would be ready to travel to Utah for the next round. "We haven't lost in the Finals, and that's a great confidence to have. Sure, it was a battle to get there. But we're there. Now let's just do the job."

The Sixth Championship

While there was much media speculation that the Bulls might be too weary to take on the well-rested Jazz, Chicago's confidence was high. Utah had home-court advantage in the Finals format, which called for the first two games in Salt Lake's Delta Center, the next three in Chicago, and the final two, if necessary, in Utah.

After defeating Indiana on Sunday, May 31, the Bulls jetted to Utah for Game 1, set for Wednesday the 3rd.

As expected, the Jazz seemed tight and the Bulls a bit weary in battling through a 17-all first period. Then Jackson went to his bench in the second period and quickly found disaster and a brace of turnovers. The Jazz jumped to a 7-point lead, and the Bulls' starters spent the rest of the game trying to pull close enough to steal a victory at the end. Malone put Utah up by 4 with 55.7 left. The Bulls managed to tie it on two Pippen free throws and a Longley jumper with 14 seconds to go. From there, Chicago's defense forced overtime, but in the extra period Stockton victimized Kerr on a late shot in the lane to give the Jazz a 1–0 lead in the series.

As was their trademark, Jackson and his staff made their adjustments for Game 2, which involved spreading their triangle offense and opening the floor up for easy baskets by their cutters.

In the first half, the triangle had never worked better. "Tonight it really shined bright for us," Buechler said. "It's an offense designed for everyone to touch the ball, to pass and cut. And the guys did that tonight, instead of going to Michael every time and posting up. Early on everyone got involved, and that really helped out for later in the game."

"The first half was beautiful," Winter agreed. "We followed through with our principles a lot better. Got a lot of cutting to the basket. And Michael gave up the ball. He was looking to feed cutters."

Winter's face, though, showed his frustration. "The second half we abandoned it, aborted it," he said. "We tried to go way too much one-on-one. Michael especially forced a lot of things."

If the Bulls had stuck with their scheme they might have won by a dozen, the coach figured. But Jordan had delivered a win against Indiana in Game 7 by going to the basket and drawing fouls. He attempted to do the same in Game 2 against Utah, but the officials weren't giving him the call. Instead, Jordan wound up on his back while the Jazz scooped up the ball and headed the other way for easy transition baskets. Suddenly Chicago's 7-point edge had turned into an 86–85 Utah lead with less than two minutes to go. "I don't know what it is," Winter said, shaking his head. "Michael, he's got so damn much confidence."

Jordan's late bucket and ensuing free throw propelled the Bulls to a 93–88 win, the victory they needed to wrest away home-court advantage.

The series then shifted back to Chicago, where after a practice Winter paused and admitted that where he once held out hope that the team might remain intact, he now saw that as the remotest of possibilities. "I don't think it's necessarily a shame to break it up," he said. "It's too bad that has to be, but you have to have changes. And it could be well timed."

Winter had figured the Bulls would struggle to win the title in '97, yet here they were a year later, in solid position again to rule the league. If the team returned, it would likely be too far past its prime to meet expectations in 1999, the coach reasoned.

Besides, keeping the key parties together would take some Jackson-inspired therapy. But how would Winter heal the relationship between Jackson and Krause? Only Reinsdorf could do that, the assistant coach said. As it would turn out, the team chairman tried, but it just wasn't possible.

"Well, I think time heals all wounds, but time can also wound all heels," Jackson said, toying with a riddle when posed the question in a private interview. "There are a variety of things that you can throw into the message. This is one of them that you can kind of play with.

"In retrospect, at some point, we're going to back away from this so that we're not so close and say, 'You know, this was a collection of pretty talented people. The Bulls were very successful. Even though we were enmeshed in the midst of it, we really were enjoying it.' I've always felt that way.

"Perhaps we could have enjoyed it more if we could have appreciated it," Jackson said. "I've really enjoyed it a lot, and as a consequence, I've really reveled in it the most. Tex doesn't revel in it as much as I do. But the players do. The players have this association with it, and I have an association with that, too, because I was a player."

The coach admitted that no matter how hard their feelings, he and Krause would always be bonded by their mutual success with the Bulls. In fact, their story was one destined to be told and retold.

Having acknowledged that, Jackson said there was almost no chance of his return. He said he had tried to make it clear to Reinsdorf in 1997 that it was virtually impossible for Krause and him to keep working together. The implication was that the team chairman had faced a choice, the coach or the general manager, and had clearly sided with Krause.

"Last year I felt that coming back, even though the ground had been seeded, the groundwork wasn't good," Jackson said. "I felt like my message about how a house divided against itself cannot stand wasn't really listened to by Jerry Reinsdorf. I really like Jerry, and I have a tendency to like authority figures. And Jerry has been a good one as an owner for a coach to appreciate because he stays away and stays in the background and doesn't intrude and allows things to happen. And yet he's gotta coerce both of us to work together in this atmosphere. For this group to come back, I just don't see how it's gonna happen. Right now we're in the throes of saying, 'Look at the genius of this team. Look at the collective effort between the coaching staff and the team on the floor, all the strengths of the individuals.' But the reality is that while no one wants to back away from another championship or another two championships, going through another long period of 82 games in that respect is going to be difficult. It's not a good thought."

Even so, Jackson couldn't avoid leaving the door cracked. "If it comes down to a chance of Michael playing and not playing, then my responsibility would be to him and to the continuation of his career, and I would have to consider it," he said. "I have to be a person that is loyal to the people who have been loyal to me. I feel that conviction. The only thing that would take me basically out of the mix would be my own personal well-being, my own personal physical and emotional health in dealing with this."

Clearly, Jackson had been left emotionally frayed by the season and the struggle for control of the team. Plus, he had conflict in his marriage and had spent part of the season living in a local hotel room. Now, as the season drew to a close, there was hope that he might pull the relationship with June back together. Before he could focus on that, though, there was this business of another championship.

The stress eased for everyone in Game 3 as Pippen, Harper, and Jordan took turns overpowering Utah's guards in the largest rout in NBA history. The performance established how absolutely dominant the Bulls could be as a team and Pippen could be as an individual defender.

The conclusion itself turned into the kind of dunkfest for bench players usually reserved for rec league blowouts. The game had opened with a blast of applause from the United Center crowd, followed by a brief scoring outburst from Malone. Then the Chicago defense closed out the proceedings and propelled the Bulls to a 96–54 victory. The margin was so great that a cross-country airlines flight that had radioed in for a game update for a Utah fan had to call back a second time to confirm the score. It was the worst point difference in league history, either playoff or regular season.

Jerry Sloan expressed surprise when he was handed a box score. "This is actually the score?" the Utah coach said. "I thought it was 196 [points]. It sure seemed like they scored 196."

"It was one heck of an effort, defensively, for our team," Jackson said. "We were very quick to the basketball, and we defended their offensive sets quite well. Malone did shoot the ball well, but other than that, we stopped the rest of the team."

"I'm somewhat embarrassed for NBA basketball for the guys to come out and play, at this level, with no more fight left in them than what we had," Sloan said. "[The Bulls] got all the loose balls, all the offensive rebounds, and we turned the ball over [26 times]. I've never seen a team that quick defensively."

Pippen had been assigned to guard Utah center Greg Ostertag, virtually a nonscorer, which left him free to terrorize Utah's passing lanes. "It's a luxury to have a defender like Scottie," Jackson told reporters. "He can cover more than one situation at a time. He can play a man and play a play. He can hang tight on his man and he's also able to rotate like that."

In one game, the Bulls had sent a resounding rebuke to Krause's plans to rebuild because they were too old. Tacked on was the emphasis that Pippen was too special a player to consider tossing away in any trade.

"I almost feel sorry for them," Jackson said privately in discussing how Krause's and Reinsdorf's agenda had been shattered and how they might come to be viewed by Chicago sports fans.

Just when Chicago seemed to be soaring, Rodman changed the flight pattern by missing practice to slip off to appear at a professional wrestling event in Detroit as "Rodzilla." Some accounts suggested he was paid as much as $250,000 for the appearance, while others reported that he was paid nothing. Privately, Rodman said the appearance was part of an $8 million contract.

The media took great interest in delving into the strange turn of events, which cost Rodman $10,000 in fines. When Rodman returned to practice before Game 4, Winter was ready with a lecture. "I just asked him what he thought he was doing," the coach revealed privately. "He said, 'Well, if you had a chance to give up $10,000 to make $8 million would you do it?' That's what he told me. I said, 'Don't kid me. There's no way you made $8 million.' He said, 'Oh, yes, I did.'"

Behind his frown, Winter took the matter with a smile. "You know, Rodman's no dummy," he said. "Actually, he's beaten the system. You have to give somebody credit who can do that. And I'm not so sure that maybe the system shouldn't take a lickin' every once in a while. It's a reflection a little bit on our society, though. Which is a shame, but that's part of the system, too."

The coach had talked often with Rodman about taking better care of his money but didn't think his message had gotten through, especially when it came to his gambling. "Anybody that likes him and has some compassion for him is gonna be concerned about him," Winter explained, pointing out that the reason his teammates put up with Rodman was because they liked him. "He's a very likable guy. Very generous. Generous to a fault, really. Wants attention. He's a contradiction, really. He's a very shy guy in a lot of ways. Very withdrawn. And yet he calls attention to himself on every turn. That's a contradicting personality. I think Phil's got a better read on him than the rest of us. Phil was somewhat a maverick himself. He wrote that book, *Maverick*, which he's still embarrassed about. I didn't read it. He asked me not to, so I didn't. He said, 'You don't want to read that.' Phil is more sympathetic toward Rodman than I am by a long shot."

As the plot would turn in Rodman's strange world, Game 4 of the Finals came down to his ability at the free throw line. He responded by hitting four free throws in the closing seconds to go with his 14 rebounds to seal an 86–82 Chicago win and a virtually insurmountable 3–1 lead in the series.

"The much-maligned Dennis Rodman had a wonderful game for us," admitted Jackson, who had blasted the forward's behavior just a day earlier, a ploy that Jackson knew would result in Rodman's resurgence. "As usual, he takes himself out of a hole and plays well enough to redeem himself," the coach said with a wry smile.

On a night when the Jazz responded to their Game 3 blowout with a show of fire, the Bulls managed to stay ahead by hitting 17 of 24 free throws in the fourth period. Rodman, a 55-percent shooter during the season, rolled in two for a 78–75 lead with 1:38 left. Then, with under a minute left and Chicago ahead by two, he added two more.

Game 5 clearly became a case of celebrating too early, too much of the Bulls laughing at their good fortune. The result was an 83–81 Utah win. Even Jordan admitted to getting caught up in the fallacy. "I really didn't have a tee time," he told reporters, "because I anticipated drinking so much champagne that I wouldn't be able to get up." As poorly as the Bulls played (Jordan was 9 for 26 from the floor and Pippen 2 for 16), they still had a shot to win it at the end.

Kukoc's 30 points on 11 of 13 shooting had kept them close, despite Malone's 39 points.

The Bulls got the ball back with 1.1 seconds to go, and during the ensuing timeout, Jordan sat on the bench enjoying the situation. If ever there was a moment to inhabit, as Jackson had encouraged him to do, this was it. A few moments later, Jordan missed a falling-out-of-bounds shot, but that didn't prevent his treasuring the moment. "I'm pretty sure people were hoping I would make that shot. Except people from Utah," he said. "For 1.1 seconds, everyone was holding their breath, which was kind of cute.

"No one knew what was going to happen," he said. "Me, you, no one who was watching the game. And that was the cute part about it. And I love those moments. Great players thrive on that in some respects because they have an opportunity to decide happiness and sadness. That's what you live for. That's the fun part about it."

Throughout the series, the Bulls' ability to perform reflected Jackson's work and the stress-reduction sessions with George Mumford. Repeatedly, Jordan would speak of being "in the moment," the primary focus of Mumford's mindfulness.

If the Bulls ever needed focus, it was now. They were headed back to Utah for Game 6. For Jackson and his staff, it wasn't an entirely new experience. They had lost Game 5 of the 1993 Finals to Phoenix and had to travel back to the Southwest to defeat the Suns. "Unfortunately, we have to go back to Utah, and it's a duplicate situation of 1993," Jordan said. "So when you get on the plane headed to Utah, you have to be very positive, you have to be ready to play. It's one loss, and you can't let it eat at you to the point where it becomes two losses."

The Jazz charged out early in Game 6 and Pippen came up with horrendous back spasms. The pain sent him to the locker room, where a massage therapist literally pounded on his back trying to drive the spasms out. One team employee reported Krause standing back in a corner of the room, almost transfixed, watching Pippen absorb the blows, eager to get back in the game to help Jordan. The GM didn't intrude upon the scene, but afterward, after Pippen had returned to the game and winced his way through the proceedings, giving Jordan just enough support to get to the end, some observers said that Krause seemed dramatically and genuinely changed in his opinion of Pippen.

"I just tried to gut it out," Pippen said. "I felt my presence on the floor would mean more than just sitting in the locker room. I knew I was going to come back in the second half, but I just didn't know how much I was going to be able to give."

He returned to the game to run the offense as Jordan scored a magnificent 45 points, including the final jumper in the key after which Jordan stood poised, his arm draped in a follow-through, savoring the moment, inhabiting the moment, frozen in that moment. Photos of the shot would show in the soft focus a number of Utah fans suspended there in agony with him, their hands covering eyes and ears, the ball hanging there in air, ready to swish for an 87–86 Chicago win.

"Things start to move very slowly and you start to see the court very well," said Jordan, explaining the last play. "You start reading what the defense is trying to do. And I saw that. I saw the moment."

The Jazz would get a final Stockton shot, but Ron Harper hustled to help him miss. When the ball had bounded away and the buzzer sounded, Jordan produced yet another of those moments to inhabit, this time he and Jackson together in a prolonged embrace.

The emotion would carry them away from there, first on a peaceful plane ride home, shared with Krause and Reinsdorf and free of acrimony, where an exhausted Jordan found a quiet place to curl up in deep sleep.

He would awaken, of course, from the dream to find that Jackson had ridden off on his motorcycle after turning down Reinsdorf's late offer to stay with the team. Another year trading insults and hard lines with Krause just wasn't worth it, no matter how exhilarating the finishes.

As for the rest of them, the players, their futures would be frozen in another summer of charged NBA labor deliberations. Who knew where it would end up?

All they really had, as Jackson had told them, was the moment. The sweet, sad, wonderful moment. And that was more than enough.

After the Gold Rush

The Bulls' players and coaches closed out their experience with a private, emotion-filled team dinner in the days after the championship game. They all expressed their love and regard for one another, and the tears flowed. After that, Jackson's immediate plan of escape was a trip abroad with June, the beginning of a year-long attempt to recover their relationship. "They tried," explained a Jackson friend, "but they just couldn't work it out."

There were reports that Jackson planned to have surgery to repair the troubled hip that contributed to his stiff, awkward gait. But in an interview with Rick Telander of the *Sun-Times* before he left on his trip to Turkey, Jackson said the hip was an excuse the team's management had added to the public agenda. "It hurts, but I would do a year of yoga before I would even consider surgery," he said. "I think management put the hip surgery out there, and the media seemed to pick it up."

Then Jackson told Telander that he might have stayed on. "I did feel it was time to take some time off," he said. "What would have changed things is if management had said, 'Stay on until Michael is finished, until he retires.' But they never suggested that."

Jackson said that during the spring of 1996, he and Todd Musburger had suggested a five-year coaching proposal, but Reinsdorf turned them down.

Next, Jackson had suggested a two-year agreement at about $3 million per season. Again, Reinsdorf declined.

What Reinsdorf seemed to be gambling on was that he and Krause could rebuild the team fast enough to keep the fans interested. Reinsdorf admitted that he and Krause almost broke up the team by trading Pippen in 1997. "We considered giving up a shot at the sixth title to begin rebuilding, and we would have given it up if we could have made the right deal," Reinsdorf said. "The reason we considered breaking the team up is that we wanted to minimize the period of time between winning the last championship and getting back into contention with the next team."

In other words, to minimize the time between the Jordan era and the next act on the United Center stage.

"We now have very little to trade, very little to work with in rebuilding," Reinsdorf said that July.

Then the team chairman added: "Michael couldn't care less about what happens [to the team] after he leaves." At the very least, the comment indicated something less than warmth between Reinsdorf and Jordan.

Reinsdorf's defense was that if Jackson and Jordan wanted to take control away from Krause, they never came out and said it. "There's never been a power struggle," the team chairman said. "Phil never asked for Krause to be removed. It never happened. Phil never told me he thought we were a house divided. He said it was difficult to work with Jerry Krause but not impossible. Phil never ever said that. He did express the fact that it was very strained."

Certainly Jackson and Jordan weren't going to put themselves in the position of saying outright that they wanted Krause gone, and Reinsdorf probably understood that and allowed it to work for him.

Reinsdorf said that he met with Jackson during the playoffs and told the coach that he'd been reading how management was pushing him out. This came after Jackson had informed Reinsdorf that he didn't plan to coach after 1998. "I asked him, 'Has anything changed? Do you want to coach another season?' He said, 'No.'"

After the season, Reinsdorf said he returned to Chicago and reviewed the newspaper clippings of the final weeks of the playoffs and discovered comments by Todd Musburger, Jackson's agent, suggesting that "we have never publicly or privately told Phil we wanted him back. Wednesday night after the title we had our office celebration. I sat down with Phil and told him, 'If you've changed your mind, we want you back.'"

The offer was unconditional, and it stood regardless of whether Jordan returned, Reinsdorf said. "Phil said, 'That's very generous.' I told him, 'Generosity has nothing to do with it. You've earned it.' He took a deep breath and said, 'No, I have to step back.'"

"Why people have been given the wrong impression about it I don't know, and I really don't care," Reinsdorf said.

In March, Jackson had likened the situation with the Bulls to his last days as a player with the New York Knicks.

"I was in New York," Jackson said. "We had eleven great years of a run. I was there for ten of those great years. The eleventh year things started to turn. Fortunately I got off before the landslide hit in the late '70s. But when it turned, the town turned against the Knicks, and it took them almost ten years to get it back. The people were against them because they're overcharging, they're abusing their position for power to make people cringe. They were being brusque and intrusive in the press. They said things like, 'The bottom line is the figure that really counts now, not wins and losses.' "

Of the situation with the Bulls, Jackson said, "It draws a pattern that's scary, because the people in Chicago are going to have a long memory, and they're going to remember this stuff later on down the line."

As Jackson long suspected, the Bulls hired Tim Floyd that July as the team's director of basketball operations—but the team did not name him head coach immediately. Krause emphasized in the press conference announcing Floyd's appointment that the head coaching job was Jackson's for the taking.

In September, when he and June were making their way from Montana to a new wintertime abode near Woodstock, they stopped for a few days in Chicago. Tex Winter, still hoping to patch up the fabric of the team, took Tim Floyd over to Jackson's house for a meeting. It wasn't the first time Jackson had talked with Floyd. There had also been a phone conversation, during which Jackson discovered what the rest of Chicago would soon find out— that Floyd was a nice man.

In their September meeting, Floyd made overtures about Jackson returning for another season. Jackson appreciated the visit, but wasn't about to give up the peace of mind he had found since leaving the team in June. Krause would later acknowledge the visit but said he had no knowledge of Floyd making any overtures to Jackson.

"To my knowledge, nothing like that was ever discussed," Krause said. "They discussed coaches and players around the league and stuff like that."

But as far as Floyd bringing up the issue of Jackson coaching, "First of all, that isn't Tim's place," Krause said. "That would be [Reinsdorf's] or mine."

Jordan, meanwhile, remained firm in his declaration that he would retire if Jackson was not his coach. Upon his hiring, Floyd had emphasized that he would move aside to work in an administrative capacity if Jackson decided to return as coach.

Floyd apparently had taken no offense at Jackson derisively calling him "Pink" and "Pinkie" when he sensed Bulls management was positioning Floyd to replace him.

"It doesn't bother him," Krause said. "Tim's been there. He understands. Tim's a good person and a good coach."

In a phone interview several days later, Jackson said that Jordan was probably going to retire, which was good, because Reinsdorf really didn't want him to play anyway. Through a spokesman, Reinsdorf protested that that wasn't the case. Reinsdorf said he badly wanted Jordan to play another season.

Reinsdorf said that in July he had assured Jordan that if he wanted to play, "the money [meaning his one-year contract in excess of $36 million] will be there."

That, in itself, may have been implied insult enough to drive Jordan from the game.

After all, the only clear way for Reinsdorf to be assured of Jordan's returning would have been for the team chairman to remove Krause to give Jackson and Jordan what they saw as "room to breathe."

In March, Jordan was asked if he knew about the unhappy end to the playing career of Los Angeles Lakers great Jerry West, who got into a nasty fight in 1974 with Jack Kent Cooke, then the Lakers' owner. West had wanted to play another season or two and easily could have, but he retired abruptly during training camp in 1974. "No one ever had to pay me to play basketball," West said in an interview twenty years later, the bitterness obvious in his voice. "But Mr. Cooke's manipulation made me not want to play for him. My relationship with Mr. Cooke was acrimonious because the negotiations were a game to him. I knew that. It was very frustrating."

Jordan had often made a similar comment, that he would play the game even if there was no pay.

"I never knew that," Jordan said when he heard how West's career ended, how the Lakers' great remained bitter decades later. "Will I have the same feelings?" Jordan asked. "Is that what you're asking me? I can't say that. It hasn't ended yet. Hopefully, it doesn't come to that."

Clearly, it had come to that by September.

Jackson said of Reinsdorf, almost admiringly, that the team chairman valued his loyalty to Krause over everything else, even if it meant that Jordan's untimely retirement could cost the franchise.

The financial picture for the Bulls, however, was strong. By and large, they had already maximized their revenue for the 1999 season. They'd renewed the leases on their high-priced skyboxes and had season-tickets waiting lists that ran thousands deep. Even with a 1998 payroll that approached $70 million, Reinsdorf conceded that the team still made a profit.

About the only real way for the team to improve its financial standing would be to cut costs. Jordan's contract was obviously the single largest budget item.

That move became a matter of record in January, after the lockout between the NBA owners and players finally ended. With the season set to open in early February, Jordan announced his retirement to an assembly of worldwide media gathered at the United Center on January 13. Still, he declined to make his decision any more certain than 99.99 percent.

It was important to never say never, said Jordan.

He had made the choice to retire just weeks before turning thirty-six and months after severely lacerating his finger with a cigar cutter. Even at his advanced playing age and with the long-term effect of the injury, many observers had little question that he remained the best player in the game. "It's sad for everyone to see the greatest basketball player in the world come to that conclusion," Indiana Pacers coach Larry Bird said of Jordan's choice. "There comes a time in every player's career that they have to make that decision, and he feels it's his time."

"Mentally, I'm exhausted. I don't feel I have a challenge. Physically, I feel great," Jordan said in explaining the move. "This is a perfect time for me to walk away from the game."

The game itself was not in such good shape, having spent the previous six months locked in a labor standoff. Without question, the NBA could have used his presence as it tried to regain fan loyalty. "I think the league is going to carry on, although we've had our troubles over the last six months," he said, referring to the league's struggles over a new collective bargaining agreement that caused it to miss nearly half of the 1998–99 season. "I think that is a reality check for all of us. It is a business, yet it is still fun. It is still a game. And the game will continue on."

But it would have to do so without him.

One reporter asked if Jordan might consider using his many talents to save the world. Jordan avowed that he was no savior. Indeed he had failed to save the championship team that he had desperately sought to keep together over the course of the 1997–98 season as Jackson and Krause feuded.

Yet Jordan made scant mention of the dispute at his retirement press conference, other than to point out that Bulls management would now have to live up to the standard he had set by winning six titles.

"We set high standards around here," he said with a hint of a smile.

Jordan had used his fire to drive the entire franchise, for years considered a joke in the league, to the heights of dominance. His presence had an influence that reached from the lowliest employee to the organization's board room.

"As fine a coach as Phil is, so much of it is just this unbelievable trickle-down from Michael Jordan," said Chip Schaefer, the Bulls' trainer for eight years. "As much as has been said and written about him athletically, it still hasn't been enough. People are sick of realizing it, but it's like, 'No, no. Do you really realize what this guy is? Do you really realize what this guy is? I don't think you do.'"

11

THE MIDDLE PATH

Although he had retreated to his abode in upstate New York, Phil Jackson maintained a keen interest in the Chicago Bulls throughout the 1999 season, to the point that he would phone Tex Winter to offer his evaluation of the struggles of the dramatically weakened roster.

"He calls occasionally and has left messages for me," Winter confided. "He's interested. He's followed the team. He leaves his impressions of what's happening."

Jackson's communications were typical among the group of men who used to be known as "your six-time world champion Chicago Bulls." In the months after the breakup of their very special team, the people who were the Bulls still tried to keep alive the special relationships they enjoyed as pro basketball's darlings.

Their relationships had become a matter of E-mails, voice messages, and quick courtside visits. Pippen, who was traded to the Houston Rockets, had a long-distance relationship with close friend Ron Harper, who remained a Bull. "We've just kinda been calling each other and leaving crazy messages on each other's phones," Pippen explained.

Former trainer Chip Schaefer moved to southern California, where he worked as a representative for Oakley, the eyewear company—which meant one of his new bosses was Oakley board member Michael Jordan.

Former assistant coach Jimmy Rodgers was splitting his retirement time between New England and Florida.

And Dennis Rodman was in the midst of a brief, painful tenure with the Los Angeles Lakers. Guard Steve Kerr had been signed to a fat new contract

by Krause, then traded to the San Antonio Spurs; and Jud Buechler underwent a similar process that landed him with the Detroit Pistons. Ditto for Luc
Longley, who had been sent to the Phoenix Suns.

Just like the days when he was the team's trainer, Schaefer still served as
something of a central figure, an information clearinghouse, for the group.
He had communicated with virtually every member, including Jordan himself. "There was more than a little bit of melancholy in his voice," Schaefer
said of Jordan's call to inform him of his plans to retire.

It was too soon for nostalgia, though. And the group didn't seem obsessed
with disdain for Krause, the man who engineered the demolition of the
championship roster, Schaefer said.

If there was a unifying feeling among all the expatriates, Schaefer said, it
would have to be contentment. After all, many of the players left town in
trade deals that paid them millions. With that contentment came a sense of
relief that they were no longer caught up in the acrimonious atmosphere that
engulfed the team during their last championship drive.

"Everybody was just so fried," Schaefer said of the end of the dynasty.

No one was more "fried" than Jackson himself, who had grown weary of
arguing and fighting with Krause over the future of the team. Now Krause
ran the miserable Bulls, and Jackson maintained that he had found peace
away from the stress and limelight of the NBA.

"I've been trying to do as little as possible," Jackson told the *Chicago Tribune*. "I would say right now I'm a retired NBA basketball coach. I feel great
about what I have been a part of [in Chicago], but I'm a little reluctant now
to think about going back to work."

"I made up my mind I had to retire and regenerate my batteries this year,"
Jackson said. "I'm speaking two or three times a month, talking about concepts of leadership, to companies, CEOs, church groups, though one criteria was it had to be in the Southern belt so I can keep my tan all year."

"It got so difficult to be in the middle of all that conflict last year," Steve
Kerr said. The truth be known, though, Kerr would have preferred to stay
with the Bulls. His family was comfortable in the Chicago suburbs, and he
was a favorite of the fans and the media.

But Krause believed Kerr leaked inside information about the team to the
media during the 1998 season. Even Winter tried to talk Krause into keeping Kerr and explained that the guard had not been disloyal. But Krause
would not have it. Kerr was clearly close to Jackson, and Krause was not
going to keep around one of "Phil's guys."

Kerr said Krause actually called him after his trade to San Antonio went through. "It was a nice call," Kerr said. "He thanked me for my contributions to the team."

The reason Krause was so pleasant in the phone call, Kerr quipped, "is that he was so glad to be getting rid of us."

Still, he added, it was nice to get the call. Too bad Krause hadn't made a regular practice of phoning the players every six months or so just to chat and say thanks for playing hard.

"I think it would have gone a long way for Jerry if he had called the other guys on the team as well," Kerr said.

For those who had left the team, there remained concern for the players and coaches who stayed in Chicago working among the shambles of what was. But there was also anticipation, as both former and current Bulls waited to see where Jackson landed as a coach for the 2000 season.

Jackson, after all, remained the leader of the group, and many of the members harbored hopes of working with him again in his next job. Since his move to upstate New York, Jackson had spent most of his time at home working on his relationship with wife June. When he did go on the road, it was to make motivational speeches or to raise money to boost the presidential hopes of Bill Bradley, his friend and former teammate.

Despite his success as a fund-raiser, Jackson continued to strike out with the Bulls. He approached the team about purchasing a table at a Bradley fund-raiser in Chicago but was turned down.

"He ran it by the Bulls to buy a $10,000 table," Winter said, "but I don't think they wanted to do it. From the standpoint of the organization, they felt like they'd like to stay out of the politics of it."

It would have seemed that Reinsdorf, long known as a Bradley admirer and a supporter of Democratic politics, would be an ideal candidate to contribute to Bradley's cause. "Phil hasn't hit me up," Reinsdorf said with a laugh in a brief interview.

The team chairman added that the Bulls couldn't contribute to Bradley's campaign owing to the fact that they had multiple owners, which could be a violation of federal election laws.

As for the Bulls, Winter said that Krause had spent most of his time on the road scouting and hadn't been around the coaching staff much. Considering the painful, frustrating nature of the season in those strange days after the gold rush, that was probably a good thing. Jackson maintained a particular interest in the team's efforts to continue using the triangle offense, Winter said. "Phil's impressed with the way the guys are staying with the offense, but he's also indicated the triangle is difficult for us to use because we don't have good shooters."

Winter, who had been despondent over the Bulls' poor showing in 1999, was obviously boosted by Jackson's continued interest.

"I think he's following us pretty closely and some other teams, too," Winter said, referring to the fact that Jackson was a hot commodity as an NBA coach.

As a coach, Jackson had no weaknesses, Schaefer agreed. "He can motivate players, he can discipline players, because people respect him. He has a presence about him, from his big shoulders to his contemplative nature."

At least one current Bulls staffer, however, questioned how Jackson would fare with the current team. "I'd love to see Phil come back here this year," he said. "I'd love to see how Big Chief Triangle would do now."

Other Jackson associates agreed with Winter that the coach would likely be back in the league for the 2000 season, with speculation centering again on Los Angeles, New York, Denver, New Jersey, Washington, and even Portland and Charlotte.

The speculation about Charlotte heated up in late March 1999 as rumors raced around the NBA that Michael Jordan was about to buy a share of the team and hire Jackson as the Hornets' next coach. That scenario, though, proved far-fetched. Jackson had not even responded to questions about it. Instead, his close associates said he was enjoying himself, "living in the moment," as befit his Zen philosophy, and had given absolutely no thought as to what he was going to do.

"He wouldn't want to go back into a situation where he wouldn't have a chance to win," Winter said.

"There are a couple of criteria I have," Jackson said. "If I take a coaching job, I'd like to have a chance to win. And in the Eastern Conference I see a lot of opportunity. I see the East on old or dead legs. Indiana, Miami—their [player] leaders are pretty long in the tooth. So the potential could be good in the East.

"In the West, where most of the good teams are, there are only two or three teams with a chance to win. Obviously, Utah has a great chance to win this year. L.A. has an outside chance. Portland has a chance to win in the future as a young team coming up.

"But if someone asked me to take over as an architect, a term the Bulls once used for Jerry Krause, putting a team together and a coaching staff, I may not even coach. Some of the things that happened last year were opportunities in that situation. I don't have to pound on my chest and say, 'That's my job.' "

Wherever Jackson ended up, Winter said he thought Jackson would use the triangle offense. Jackson's continued use of the offense was important to Winter, who said he viewed the triangle as his coaching legacy.

"He's embraced it, and he feels like it's as much his as it is mine," Winter said of Jackson's beliefs about the offense. "And it probably is. I like to think that through Phil the triple-post offense will live on. More through him actually than through me."

On the other hand, Jackson admitted that he might decide never to coach again.

"I am aware of the effect the game has on your health and well-being," Jackson said. "I feel really good. But I don't forget what it's like to spend relatively sleepless nights because a referee made a bad call and you lost a game or your team didn't withstand the barrage of the visiting crowd or whatever.

"I think things come to us for a purpose, so I'm willing to listen to what my opportunities are. One of the things I believed was the key to my year was to sit out and wait and make a decision this summer. That involves not jumping the gun, not trying to make up my mind before summer.

"It would be real easy to run off to the first thing that draws my attention. But I really think I need to sit back and weigh all my options and do something when the time is right. When the clock clicks back on and says, 'Let's get busy again,' I'll make that decision."

By April, young Lakers star Kobe Bryant had begun phoning Winter. The guard didn't know the elderly coach, but he wanted to ask his advice about basketball matters. "What's he doing phoning Tex?" Krause had asked when he learned of the calls.

Bryant told Winter he was in love with the triangle offense. What Bryant didn't tell the older coach was that he had long had a premonition that Winter would one day coach him. What Winter didn't tell Bryant was that Jackson was intrigued by the challenge of meshing Bryant and center Shaquille O'Neal into a team frame of mind.

"The job he'd like to have would be the Lakers," Winter said.

The Building

As coach of the Los Angeles Lakers, Kurt Rambis came to his moment of truth with stunning swiftness. One could hardly blame him for not seeing it coming. One moment his future seemed extremely bright; the next, his head coaching career was all but over.

That's just how harsh the National Basketball Association can be.

What made the experience even harder was that it was men he had known, men he had worked long and hard with, men he had enjoyed success with, men who considered themselves his friends, who terminated him, essentially deleting his options and leaving him twisting in a cold wind.

Just months earlier, Kurt Rambis, the young Lakers' assistant coach, had been the man everybody wanted to hire. There was the head coaching job of the Sacramento Kings, his for the taking. Or the Los Angeles Clippers—less desirable, given the Clippers' culture of despair, but an opportunity all the same.

Rambis, though, was given reason for pause by the Lakers. For a while it had seemed that longtime assistant Larry Drew was poised to take over if head coach Del Harris was fired. But the demand for Rambis had driven Lakers management to covet him as well. Rambis was clearly a coaching talent, and the Lakers didn't want him to get away.

The message Rambis got was that he, not Drew, would be next in line if Harris left.

So Rambis passed on the other jobs that summer and decided to wait, to see what his future held. After all, the Lakers' roster was stocked with talent. It offered the opportunity to move in and coach Shaquille O'Neal, Eddie Jones, and Kobe Bryant.

Later, when Rambis had all the time in the world on his hands, it would be easy to look back and see that the karma was all wrong from the start. But none of that was apparent at the time. When the Lakers fired Del Harris just a dozen games into the strike-shortened 1999 season, it wasn't an ideal situation. The coach who replaced him wouldn't have the opportunity to begin the season in training camp. It was there that a new coach had the time go over his system with the players, to do all the work necessary to instill his philosophy with the team.

Once an NBA season begins, there is precious little practice time for making changes. Rambis knew this would be a problem. He knew that if he accepted the job, he was faced with inheriting Harris's lax practice approach and an offense that the players often failed to execute. But Rambis assumed that after this transitional short season he would have a full training camp the next fall.

Lakers management had considered releasing Harris before the 1999 season, but then decided to give him one more try. Then the team opened with

6 wins and 6 losses, and owner Jerry Buss figured it was time to make the change.

Having earned his millions in real estate, Buss had always been a gambler. He loved poker and was known to refer to his assets, even the players on his Lakers teams, as his "stack of chips."

Rambis didn't realize it at the time, but when he took over the Lakers in February 1999, he was one of Jerry Buss's chips. Buss didn't consider the gamble on Rambis a wild one. After all, he had made the same bet in late 1981 on another young coach named Pat Riley. That season, the Lakers had opened the schedule in a turmoil that stewed as the weeks went by. Magic Johnson and his teammates didn't like the approach of Paul Westhead, even though Westhead had coached them to the 1980 league championship.

Finally, Buss decided to fire Westhead in hopes that team executive Jerry West would agree to take over the coaching chores. West, however, declined the opportunity, leaving Buss to settle for the young, unproven Riley. It took some time for Riley to learn to assert his will, but he matured quickly as a coach. By the end of the season, the Lakers were in championship form, and Buss's gamble made it appear as if he possessed some special hoops intuition.

So it seemed reasonable nearly two decades later that Buss would again decide to gamble on a young assistant with no head coaching experience. Like Riley, Rambis had been a valuable role player for Lakers teams that won titles. He had that understanding of the game. Rambis even possessed enough of an offbeat image to remind some observers of a young Phil Jackson. Rambis also had connections that ran deep in the organization. A California guy, he had been a teammate of Lakers minority owner Magic Johnson, and he was liked by West. Better yet, Rambis's wife Linda and Jerry Buss's daughter were close friends. Rambis's main flaw was that while he was lucky, he wasn't lucky enough. To start at the top of the NBA and succeed, you have to be very lucky.

The Lakers soon demonstrated there was little luck to be had in 1999.

While he was betting on Rambis, Buss decided to raise the ante, shoving more chips onto the table with the signing of oddball forward Dennis Rodman. The volatile Rodman had always proved to be a challenge for a variety of NBA coaches, but from his very first moment on the job, Rambis was faced with adding Rodman to a roster already debilitated by bad chemistry and dissension.

Rodman's basketball smarts and rebounding brought a dizzying ascent. Rambis won his first nine games as coach of the Lakers and then a bunch more. While the atmosphere around the Great Western Forum grew giddy, veteran observers harbored a sense of caution, even foreboding. And with good reason.

Not satisfied with things merely going well, Buss decided to roll the dice yet again, this time with a blockbuster trade. Buss dealt team leader Eddie Jones and backup center Elden Campbell to Charlotte for sharpshooter Glen Rice and forward J. R. Reid. The supposed upside of such a trade was the teaming of a shooter of Rice's caliber with a post weapon like O'Neal. On paper, it made an unbeatable combination. But no matter how fine the prospectus, trades always take time to work in pro basketball. It's nearly impossible to produce an instant chemistry, or to predict whether there will be a chemistry at all. Players need time to adjust to each other, to the new styles of play.

Yet if there was one commodity that Kurt Rambis didn't have in the whirl-wind spring of 1999, it was time. Even with the chaos of management's moves, he somehow kept the club moving mostly in a positive direction, despite the fact that he faced one crisis after another as March turned to April.

Later, Jerry West would make it known that he wasn't in favor of signing the troubled Rodman or of making the trade for Rice. But it was his job as team executive to try to fulfill the wishes of ownership, West explained, and Buss wanted to trade Jones because the guard's contract would be up soon and he was already expecting a substantial raise. The owner also wanted to ship Campbell because the backup center earned $7.5 million per season in a long-term contract that would only escalate.

Buss didn't like the idea of paying a backup so much, West confided.

Rambis wondered about the reasoning behind the flurry of moves, but he never really had the time to sit down with management to discuss them. They clearly had a destabilizing effect on his team; even worse, the moves only exacerbated the sour relationship between O'Neal and third-year guard Kobe Bryant.

Even with the chaos, Rambis said he didn't worry too much. He assumed at the time of the trade that he would be able to sort it out the next fall in training camp. At no time did he realize that this was it for him, that this was his one brief opportunity as an NBA head coach, that it was his neck going on the chopping block as Eddie Jones went on the trading block.

With the turmoil, Rambis found himself forced to spend way too much time talking with players' agents and parents and assistants, all of them seek-ing to be coddled and reassured over every little concern about playing time and shots and personality conflicts. Dealing with these things took immense effort in a shortened season where extra games were packed into each week to make up for the contract battles that had cost the NBA the first four months of the schedule.

As the difficulties unfolded, Rambis made an effort to talk with each of the team's three stars—O'Neal, Bryant, and Rice. What confounded him was that each one of the three offered radically different perspectives on what was needed to make the team work. He was stunned to realize that his team's three stars were not remotely on the same page. Worse yet, the three talked hardly at all with each other, meaning the team was caught up in an undeclared tug-of-war over playing styles. And as an interim coach, Rambis had little or no real power to deal with it.

As the season wore on, Rambis came to see Rice as a "one-trick pony," a marvelous shooter who was not able or willing to do the multifaceted things needed on a championship team. Rice wanted the coaching staff to devise and run plays for him that allowed him to shoot coming off screens set by teammates. This, of course, came into immediate conflict with O'Neal, who wanted to receive the ball in the post and shoot it or draw double teams and throw it out to open teammates on the perimeter.

Beyond that, Rambis was alarmed by the energy he had to expend in keeping the hard feelings between Bryant and O'Neal from flaring into open warfare.

Soon, Kurt Rambis found himself caught in a funnel, sucked away by a whirlpool of selfishness and distrust among his players. Once wry and teasing with reporters, Rambis grew increasingly testy, erupting in anger and annoyance at seemingly innocuous questions. Employees around the team began whispering, "Kurt's in way over his head."

Seeking to reverse this negative energy and salvage the season, Rambis decided to break through the barriers in hopes that he could thaw the icy relationship between his stars.

O'Neal was the leader of the team, although the big center didn't want the responsibility of dealing with his teammates. Rambis went to O'Neal and implored him to be more accepting of the twenty-year-old Bryant, who had entered the league at age seventeen fresh out of a Pennsylvania high school. Bryant was immensely talented, but his decision to bypass college had left him with no real understanding of team concepts. Under great pressure as the league's most talented center, O'Neal had quickly grown impatient with Bryant's youthfulness. Then, as the Lakers failed each year in the playoffs during their first two seasons together, O'Neal's impatience grew into an intense dislike of the standoffish Bryant.

Rambis reasoned that O'Neal should change his attitude because he was the team leader, the one player capable of pulling the group together. You can heal this rift; you can reach out to Kobe, Rambis told his center. Bryant was young and hard-working and just learning the game, the coach pointed out, and the center should make a move to reconcile with him. The coach later recalled that O'Neal's only answer was a blank, cold stare. Nothing more. That, Rambis would come to understand in retrospect, would be the moment, his one chance to heal the relationship, to bring an end to the team's deep division.

It wasn't going to happen.

Instead, the season played itself out in a sad drama, with Rodman being released in April after a drunken appearance at practice. Even with the distractions, Rambis coached the Lakers to 25 wins against 13 losses and a first-round playoff victory over the Houston Rockets. But then things fell apart against the San Antonio Spurs in the second round. For the second year in a row, the Lakers were swept from the playoffs. It was a bitter, ugly defeat, one that filled the players—especially O'Neal—with a deep anger that would linger for months. The big center left Los Angeles without bothering to attend the team's season-closing meeting and returned to his Orlando home, where he stewed in frustration.

The series loss to the Spurs was so humiliating that forward Rick Fox decided afterward he had lost all love for the game.

No one, however, was sicker at the turn of events than Jerry West, who had spent most of his fourteen-year playing career watching seasons end in frustration and shame. To Lakers fans, the sixty-year-old West was a familiar, beloved guardian of the team's fortunes. When the team moved from Minneapolis to Los Angeles in 1960, he was there to greet it, a first-round draft pick out of West Virginia University. He quickly combined with second-year forward Elgin Baylor to form the heart of a young, exciting team that made the gritty, cynical game of pro basketball a hit in glitzy southern California. West and Baylor led the Lakers to one playoff battle after another over the next dozen years, and in the process managed to capture Hollywood's hard hearts. In those early years in southern California, the celebrity crowd included Doris Day, Danny Thomas, and Pat Boone, who sat courtside in the L.A. Sports Arena and brought pro basketball its first real taste of glamour.

A taste of ultimate victory was another matter.

Six times in the 1960s, West and his Lakers faced the Boston Celtics in the NBA Finals. Six times they lost. Red Auerbach's Celtics, featuring Bill Russell, were that good. Finally Russell retired, and West and his Lakers had their opportunity.

On their seventh try for a championship, the Lakers met the New York Knicks. They lost again. They finally won in 1972, then lost an eighth time in the Finals the next year, to the Knicks team that featured Phil Jackson coming off the bench.

"I don't think people understand there's a real trauma associated with losing," West said of his championship frustrations. "I don't think they realize how miserable you can be. Particularly me. I was terrible. It got to the point with me that I wanted to quit basketball. I really did. I didn't think it was fair that you could give so much and play until there was nothing left in your body to give and you couldn't win."

The more elusive it proved to be, the more the championship came to have an almost mesmerizing hold on West. "The closer you get to the magic circle, the more enticing it becomes," he once explained. "I imagine in some ways, it's like a drug. It's seductive because it's always there, and the desire is always there to win one more game. I don't like to think I'm different, but I was obsessed with winning. And losing made it so much more difficult in the offseason."

He retired from playing in 1974 after a falling-out with then-owner Jack Kent Cooke and stayed away from the franchise for two years. Those two seasons marked the first time in their fourteen years of existence that the Los Angeles Lakers missed the playoffs. Finally courted back to the team with a settlement of his dispute with Cooke, West spent three misery-laden seasons coaching the club, discovering in the process that he was simply too high-strung, too unforgiving of lax efforts, to be around the players on a daily basis.

He found existence more tolerable in the front office, where his keen eye for talent helped him add the right players to a roster anchored by Kareem Abdul-Jabbar and Magic Johnson. The Lakers won five NBA titles in the 1980s with West shuffling the deck as an executive. But that did little to abate his ever-growing anxiety over the state of the franchise. "Jerry always seems like he's having a terrible time, or something bad is impending," Kareem Abdul-Jabbar once observed. "He's always worried."

"The bottom line is, my number-one priority in life is to see this franchise prosper," West explained. "That's my life. It goes beyond being paid. It goes to something that's been a great source of pride. I would like people to know that I do care. It's not a self-interest thing. I do care about the winning and the perpetuation of the franchise. That's the one thing I care most about. I don't care about the pelts and the tributes. I like to work in my own weird way, working toward one goal, that's a winning team here."

Through the range of difficulties over the years, West had managed to persevere as an NBA executive, a complicated job that very few did well. Most people who tried running pro basketball teams soon found themselves sunk in confusion and despair. West, though, was clearly tougher and more determined than his peers. Anyone dealing with him on trades and other NBA deals soon learned that underneath his courteous exterior he possessed a toughness hardened by his upbringing in West Virginia's hardscrabble coal fields.

He seemed to view everything as a function of his high competitive standards. There was a right way to approach every facet of the game. In Jerry West's mind, you either adhered to that standard or you failed. Most people in the NBA never seemed to even recognize or understand that standard, much less have a concern about adhering to it.

In Los Angeles, the basketball not only had to be good, it had to be entertaining and star-driven. West understood better than anyone that success was built on a star quality that could attract Hollywood's and the world's interest. The tentative nature of that formula had made itself known abruptly in November 1991 when Magic Johnson announced his retirement due to his HIV infection. "Since I came here in 1960," West said at the time, "the Lakers have always had one or two players that have been at the top of the league in talent. In perpetuating this franchise, our next move is, where do we find another one of those guys?"

With Johnson's departure and subsequent failed attempts at a comeback, West embarked on an extended period of maneuvering to pull together another championship chemistry. Identifying the players, seeing the invisible, was the first part of that very difficult task. After that, he had to manipulate the NBA's byzantine personnel structure so that the Lakers could get the rights to those special players. That had become nearly impossible with the league's salary cap and expansion over the 1980s and 1990s.

"The problem is, it's like a poker game," he explained. "Any team that has a player play ten years is probably going to be out of chips pretty soon. So you have to try like crazy within the scope of this league to keep your team young and productive. In the past, we've been able to bring in younger players and phase out older players at the end of their careers."

Despite his determination, that replenishing process stalled in the seasons after Johnson's retirement, as the franchise sorted through an array of players and coaches, trying to find a competitive mix. For five long seasons, the circumstances dragged on with West torturing himself looking for answers.

Meanwhile, the Lakers plodded through one unproductive season after another. Always a bundle of nervous energy during games, he grew into a picture of anxiety, often retreating to the Forum parking lot during games while the outcome was being settled. Or he could be seen standing near section 26, peeking past the ushers at the action, his body twisted with tension.

The circumstances pushed him to search harder around the league, looking for a sign that some supremely talented young player would emerge from the amateur ranks or that some impressive veteran from another team would find the contractual freedom to become a Laker. While the situation stretched his patience, West busied himself by acquiring the finest complementary players he could find, so that he would have the pieces in place for adding the prize talent once it became available.

Finally, early in the 1996 offseason, West saw an opportunity to attract O'Neal, a free agent with the Orlando Magic, and Bryant, a seventeen-year-old prospect entering the draft out of high school. Getting them presented a huge gamble—if he miscalculated, all of his hard work of the last five years would be wasted. It was a risk that would cost tens of millions; but after years of yearning to compete for a championship, both West and Jerry Buss were willing.

West figured he would have to come up with a $95 million offer to get his prize. But ultimately that would prove to be many millions short of what was needed. The Orlando Magic pushed their offer to retain O'Neal to $115 million, then a little more. The anxiety climbed to unbearable levels for West and his staff. To push their offer to $123 million, they released seven players, including Magic Johnson. Dumping their roster of players seemed to border on lunacy. If O'Neal stayed in Florida, the Lakers would be forced to bring in a host of low-rated talent to fill the gap.

The pressure of the situation almost drove West to a nervous breakdown, but eventually he won out, securing both O'Neal and Bryant in a flurry of deals.

Getting them in place, however, proved to be only part of the problem. The immediate expectation among fans was that with O'Neal the Lakers would challenge Michael Jordan and the Chicago Bulls for the league title. Instead, the Lakers never could overcome the veteran Utah Jazz. In 1997, O'Neal and his teammates lost 4–1 in the second round to Utah. The next season, the Lakers won 61 games and advanced to the conference championship series, only to be swept by the Jazz.

Each defeat had shredded West's emotions, but the third straight season of embarrassment, ending with the sweep by the Spurs, was clearly the worst. The team's obvious disarray had prompted calls for a coaching change. Finding someone to guide his assemblage of talent had proven to be West's greatest difficulty. Since the departure of Pat Riley in 1990, the Lakers had been through Mike Dunleavy, Randy Pfund, and Magic Johnson before West turned to Del Harris, an old friend, in 1994. A skilled Xs and Os practitioner, Harris had elevated the team's victories in each of his four full seasons, from 48 to 53 to 56 to 61. His practices, however, were not well organized, and Harris, a kind, deeply religious sort, had a tendency to drone on. West had hated firing him, but it became clear early in the 1999 season that the players had quit listening to him. Then Rambis, the hand-picked successor, had struggled during key moments of the playoffs, as rookie coaches were known to do.

West expressed irritation at these struggles, but he was fully understanding of them. From all indications he was prepared to retain Rambis, until a groundswell of support developed for a coaching change.

The name most commonly tossed about as a Rambis replacement was Jackson's. Jackson had actually sent up the first trial balloon for the job in the spring of 1998 when he had published excerpts from his diary in *ESPN the Magazine* in which he mused about coaching the Lakers and wondered whether O'Neal would be smart enough to play in Jackson's triangle offense. Like others around the NBA, West had been irritated at the time with Jackson's boldness.

West had been a good friend of Jerry Krause since the late 1970s, when Krause worked as a Lakers scout. The two men would often commiserate over the difficulties of their jobs and discuss events in and around the league. In the 1989–90 season, when West's relationship with Lakers coach Pat Riley soured, he would unburden himself to Krause. Later, when Krause began having his difficulties with Jackson, he would tell West about Jackson's manipulation, ego, and mind games.

West and Jackson had competed against each other as players. "I remember this one dubious moment Phil had with Jerry West," Walt Frazier, Jackson's old teammate, remembered with a chuckle. West's Lakers and the Knicks, with Jackson as a role player, had battled in the NBA Finals in 1972 and '73.

Sometime during those seasons—Frazier didn't remember the exact game—Jackson supposedly inflicted an injury that perhaps framed their relationship.

"The game was over," Frazier said, each sentence punctuated by another chuckle. "West was walking off the floor. Phil flared his elbow and broke the guy's nose.

"West was just walking off the floor. He was flabbergasted, like everybody else," Frazier said. "You see, West had already had numerous broken noses in his career. But he turned around and there were those elbows of Phil's."

The incident was typical Jackson, Frazier recalled. "Phil was just that way, man. He was so awkward, and those arms were so long. In our practices, nobody wanted to get near him."

Angry over the comments, Jackson would later deny that the incident ever happened. And West said he didn't remember it either, although he added that it could have happened. He said his nose had been broken so many times it was difficult to remember.

Aware of a possible conflict between Jackson and West, Winter explained that Jackson would come back into the league only if he found a team with the right level of talent. Jackson coveted the idea of coaching the Lakers, Winter revealed. To do that, however, Jackson would have to gain the blessing of West, which seemed unlikely.

On the final weekend of the 1999 season, as the Lakers were about to be swept by the Spurs, West was sitting in the nearly empty Great Western Forum when a reporter mentioned Jackson.

"Fuck Phil Jackson," West said.

Thinking that he had been misunderstood, the reporter again mentioned Jackson.

"Fuck Phil Jackson," West repeated, emphasizing the words and his disdain.

West wasn't alone in his opinion. While Jackson was wildly popular with millions of NBA fans, many coaches and team officials around the league openly loathed him. In New York, feelings against him had turned particularly strong that spring. Jackson had been cast as a potential replacement for Knicks coach Jeff Van Gundy and had quietly agreed to discuss the job with the team's front office. That decision blew up in controversy when the story broke in New York newspapers that the Knicks were talking employment with Jackson even as they had a coach under contract. Center Patrick Ewing responded to the news by declaring that he wouldn't play for the former Bulls' coach. Ewing said he'd rather be traded.

Other coaches around the league chimed in on what they saw as an underhanded move. The uproar was strong enough that it played a role in Knicks executive Ernie Grunfeld's leaving the team.

The response blindsided Jackson, according to Frazier, the Knicks' longtime broadcaster. "Coming from some of his peers. From guys in the coaching profession making derogatory comments. But it was more jealousy than anything, because he's been so successful. This is a business. Someone's going to make you an offer and you're not going to listen?"

"I think he's burned his bridges," Tex Winter said of the circumstances.

As if the Knicks' fiasco wasn't enough, in one of his rare 1999 interviews, Jackson commented that the 1999 championship would be undervalued because it was a shortened season, a statement that further angered his colleagues around the NBA. Then in early May, when he was honored by the Bulls at halftime of their final regular-season game, Jackson held a press conference beforehand and made reference to Rodman's release by the Lakers. He offered the opinion that Rodman hadn't gotten the same support in Los Angeles as he had gotten when he played for Jackson in Chicago. Although Jackson was seemingly referring to Rodman's off-court support, from agents and other professionals, West took Jackson's comments as criticism of the team's management itself. "Apparently we don't do things right," West said angrily, adding that the Lakers had done everything they could for Rodman, including paying the salaries of his two security guards.

"He might have burned the bridges," Winter said of Jackson. "It's unfortunate. With the success he's had there's bound to be some natural jealousy. It behooves him to be humble and complimentary of other people.

"I think there's a lot of resentment in the league because of the success he had here in Chicago," Winter added. "People seem to feel that Phil was lucky to coach Michael Jordan. I don't think they give Phil the credit he should receive, but at the same time Phil should have been a little more humble. There was the impression that Phil rubbed it in."

Clearly West was Mr. Basketball in Lakerland and was set to begin a new $13 million contract in 1999–2000 as team vice president. But West himself admitted that his perfectionist streak had made him a miserable coach. And there was little question that his presence as an executive added huge pressure and expectations to the people coaching and playing for the franchise.

Rambis had obviously struggled with all of the pressures and expectations.

"You also got Magic Johnson looking over everybody's shoulder," Winter said of the difficulty of coaching the Lakers. "He's another icon. That's a tough situation. I don't know if Phil would be smart to get in that situation. As long as Jerry West is there, it would be tough for Phil."

The only hope for Jackson in Los Angeles rested with Lakers owner Jerry Buss, who had acknowledged his interest in Jackson. The team was moving into the new Staples Center and had expensive skyboxes and season tickets to sell. Jackson would obviously be a marquee name in that regard. Buss, though, seemed understandably reluctant to force the issue. His efforts to get involved in Lakers management had backfired disastrously.

Meanwhile, Rambis had an uneasy feeling about his job. Even before he had been hired as the interim coach in February, there had been talk of hiring Jackson as the team's new coach.

To West, the idea of hiring Jackson seemed like another Buss gamble. But he was also aware of the need to fill those seats and skyboxes. Jackson's own public comments had served to create huge doubts in West's mind. He was the guardian of the team. He wasn't about to turn it over to a Machiavellian force. Still, Jackson clearly had star quality; something the franchise had always needed to operate in Hollywood.

West had assembled a collection of talent, but the team's play had left Lakers fans with an empty feeling. Quite simply, they had played without conviction in the 1999 playoffs, and the team had gone nearly a decade without contending for a championship.

Something had to be done to get fans excited about the 2000 season. Could the Lakers do something to bring in a player? the team's management asked. It became clear to Jerry Buss and his managers that they couldn't spend $6 million on a player and generate the kind of excitement that Jackson could. There was no player available at such a price tag whose presence would make people go out and buy tickets, or make corporations purchase skyboxes.

In fact, spending $6 million a year on Jackson would be a tremendous savings, and they would sell a lot of tickets.

Later these financial considerations would be explained to Rambis. Even the deposed coach had to admit it. In a sense, Rambis became a victim of the building and of his owner's gambling.

Discouraged, confused, and bitter, Rambis would clean out his desk at night and stay away from the franchise for weeks. But Buss would bring him back, first as a broadcaster and then as a scout. To add to his workload, Rambis would be left to conduct tours of the Staples Center for Buss's friends, tours of the very building that cost him his job.

The Seventh Championship

In the end, the decision to hire Jackson was left with Jerry West. The team vice president put away his anger and looked at the circumstances. He could rehire Rambis, who had much promise as a coach. But Rambis remained untested, and if he was retained the team could well find itself looking for a coach yet again the following the season. There had been enough change, West said. The team needed a veteran coach to deal with its internal strife.

Both O'Neal and Bryant had offered as much in encouraging West to hire the fifty-three-year-old Jackson. O'Neal had even indicated he might leave the franchise if Jackson weren't hired. West knew the center wouldn't walk away from his huge contract, but he also knew Jackson was the right choice.

In mid-June, he and the Lakers announced Jackson's hiring at a press conference, ending speculation that had dragged on more than a month. Jackson had been in Alaska, finishing up a fishing vacation with his sons, and got off a boat one day to learn from an Eskimo boy that he had been hired as the Lakers' coach.

There would be discussions and brief negotiations, but the matter was a foregone conclusion. Asked about Jackson, West told L.A. reporters, "What Phil talked about was how to get players really to trust themselves, how to get everyone to share the ball. And in the offense he plans to run, everyone has to do that, or no one's ever going to score. That to me is the most important aspect of having him here. I don't think we have to worry at the end of the season about coaches anymore. I think we have to worry about trying to improve our personnel and also trying to get to the next level."

"It was the fact that my talents and the talent of this team did match up well together," Jackson said. "I just felt that this was something that kind of meshed. I know Shaq, I've been in many situations with him. I've got a feel for him a little bit. I think he's not played to his ability in the last couple of seasons. He can be better than he is. He can be the most valuable player in this league.

"I've been very intrigued with Kobe Bryant, who I think has got Michael Jordan-esque type of ability and yet is a player that's still uneducated in basketball and in life. And he's willing to learn."

The Lakers were going to use the triangle offense, Jackson said. "When you have a system of offense, you can't be a person that just is taking the basketball trying to score. You have to move the basketball, because . . . you have to share the basketball with everybody. And when you do that, you're sharing the game, and that makes a big difference. It's like trusting each other, and when you trust each other in basketball, then it goes to the other end of the court."

Running the triangle meant that he wanted Winter as his assistant coach. Winter agonized over his decision, to remain with his old friend Krause and the rebuilding Bulls, or go to L.A. to the richly talented Lakers, where his offense would again shine in the spotlight. Krause was bitter and angry, far more than Winter had expected, when he informed the Bulls VP of his decision. "I wanted him to be upset," Winter would say later. "I didn't want him to be hurt."

Jackson also brought in former Bulls assistants Frank Hamblen and Jim Cleamons, and retained Bill Bertka from the previous Lakers' staff.

Asked if he also planned to bring in his old team, Jackson replied, "My old players? I'd like to have them all. Obviously, we had the right crew there in Chicago. But most of them are under contract and Michael's retired and Dennis has gone into some other ozone. . . ."

Although Jackson and the staff wanted the front office to obtain Pippen from the Rockets, West emphasized that he was against it. Besides, the real question on people's minds was Jordan. He immediately insisted on no plans to return to the NBA as a Los Angeles Laker. He did, however, have some kind words of advice for the young Lakers who soon would be working with Jackson. The Lakers should keep an open mind about Jackson's quirky approach to coaching, including his use of Zen Buddhist philosophy, Jordan said. "It can relieve a lot of tension in your life, and I'm pretty sure they got a lot. Actually I think they're gonna be happy with Phil. He's gonna give them a certain structure and a certain guidance that they probably need. They got the talent. It's always been there. It's just how you utilize the talent in a focused situation. And I think Phil is good at that."

There was immediate speculation that the triangle would be difficult to install in Los Angeles. In recent years, three NBA coaches attempted to install the triangle offense to help rid their teams of offensive stagnation. The three—Jim Cleamons, Quinn Buckner, Cotton Fitzsimmons—all lost their jobs after players revolted with complaints that learning the system was too difficult, too unnatural.

The previous season, Rambis had attempted to install some plays that would allow new offensive weapon Glen Rice to shoot coming off screens. O'Neal tried them for a few weeks, then informed Rambis after a players' meeting that the plays would have to cease.

"If I'm on a team where we come down and call plays every time, then it's time for me to quit," O'Neal confided later. "Then I'm not gonna be an effective big man no more. If that's the case, then they're just using me as a token to set picks. I don't want to play like that. I want to run and get crazy and look at the fans and make faces. If I've got to come down and set picks and do all that, it's time for me to quit. Then I ain't got it anymore."

How would O'Neal accept the triangle, which is a much more difficult adjustment than simply adding plays to feature a new teammate?

That question enveloped Lakers fans as training camp opened in 1999. Over the summer, Jackson, Winter, and assistants Jim Cleamons and Frank Hamblen came to Los Angeles and watched the Lakers' summer-league team struggle to run the offense.

Kobe Bryant was eager to use the triangle. But would O'Neal and the other Lakers have the patience and take the time to learn the offense? "That's the big question," said former Bull Steve Kerr. "Phil told me he thinks it takes two years, two years to learn the triangle. You tell me what NBA coach has two years to fiddle with an offense? Most of them get fired before then, and I think that's a big reason why you're seeing the same offense all over the league."

Jackson assistant Jim Cleamons had left the Bulls and taken over the Dallas Mavericks, where he attempted to install the triangle, only to find that each of his young stars recoiled at the idea of passing the ball. Each player wanted to prove that he was "the man," executing some nifty one-on-one move each time he got the ball. Their insurrection cost Cleamons his job.

Perhaps Jackson would have the status and stature to make it work in Los Angeles, Kerr said.

Whatever path the team took, one thing was clear: the young Lakers had better be ready to work—in practice. "The difference with the Bulls from every other place that I've been—every coach I've been with in the NBA has been very well organized—the difference in Chicago was the focus on fundamentals every single day," Kerr said. "We started every day with basic drills, footwork, passing, ballhandling. Every single day."

He admitted that it was hard for coaches to get modern pro players to do that, which was why the leadership of Michael Jordan and Scottie Pippen had been so valuable. "The first time I saw Michael and Scottie standing fifteen feet apart throwing two-handed chest passes back and forth for ten minutes, I realized the Bulls were really going to focus on fundamentals," Kerr said. "It's the foundation of the game, and if you don't work on 'em, you're not gonna have that foundation."

So much of Jackson's success in Los Angeles would depend on O'Neal. The coaches felt that Shaq's adjustment to the offense could be eased if he had a teammate who understood every element of the triangle and acted as a coach on the floor. The discussion came back around to Pippen, who had expressed his eagerness to rejoin Jackson in Los Angeles—so much so that he was trying to force his trade away from the Rockets. But Jerry Buss decreed that Pippen's huge contract was too expensive for L.A. to pick up.

The Portland Trail Blazers, though, were owned by billionaire Paul Allen, the cofounder of Microsoft. Eager to make the Blazers better, Allen gave Blazers GM Bob Whitsitt permission to ship six reserves to Houston for Pippen, who had just passed his thirty-fourth birthday. The vastly wealthy Allen didn't mind paying Pippen's four-year, $54 million contract, which boosted the Portland player payroll to more than double the league's $34 million salary cap.

Jackson had badly wanted Pippen, but instead the former player became his old coach's worst nightmare. Suddenly, the opposition in Portland had a player who understood Jackson's system. Worse yet, Pippen was a motivated warrior. He wanted to win a seventh league championship after winning six with Michael Jordan and the Bulls.

"When I saw Portland make its run for him, they had the reserves and the right things happen for them to get it done," Jackson would explain later. "Sometimes, it's a matter of economics. . . ."

"When it happened, I was able to say, 'We let our biggest opponent step into the gap and supply themselves with a player who could eventually end up costing us, big-time.' "

With Pippen out of the question, Jackson turned in earnest to the job of getting the Lakers up to snuff with the offense. It would be a task, but his year off had recharged his energy and he was ready. In fact, he allowed himself to be photographed bare-chested on the L.A. beaches for a *Sports Illustrated* feature, a move that strangely resonated his day as a young lion in 1973 during his Malibu acid trip. Clearly, though, he was sending the message that he was replenished.

"For me it was a very long year," Jackson said. "Obviously it was something that was definitely new. I moved out of Chicago to upstate New York. I was able to do a variety of things. I was able to take a winter vacation, which I had never done in my life. And it was spent doing some things for Bill Bradley and his campaign. It was very interesting for me just to be kind of a private citizen, so to speak. That was very good. It was very good for me, very good for my family, very good for the relationships that I've had with my family. It was very invigorating for me to feel like I can go back and come to this game with a lot more energy than I ever thought I could come back to."

When Jackson moved to Los Angeles, wife June stayed behind in New York. The couple had worked to regain their relationship following the revelation of Jackson's infidelities in Chicago. If he had elected to end his pro basketball career, they might well have succeeded in repairing the damage, several friends observed. He had been offered the job working with the Bradley campaign, and June Jackson would work on Bradley's behalf. But Jackson chose to do the thing he knew best, and accepted the Lakers' offer.

"Phil could have continued to work on Bill Bradley's presidential campaign, taught at a university, written, or stayed home in Montana and become a trout fisherman for the rest of his life," his agent, Todd Musburger, told the *L.A. Times*.

Friends said he arrived in Los Angeles and went to work with an excitement about his professional life. But his personal life left him obviously discouraged. His children delighted in visiting frequently at his beachfront home. But his choice served to chill his relationship with June. She had no desire to resume her painful experiences.

"She wants to get out of the shadow of being an NBA wife," Jackson acknowledged.

In an interview with writer Frank DeFord, Jackson would acknowledge that his life was shaped by a father who showed warmth and a mother full of drive. His relationship with his father left him craving the team relationship, he explained, and added that his mother's influence left him attracted to a woman's intellectual nature.

"Matters of the heart were not always easy with me," he explained. "I had to unlearn a lot of things about women."

The bicoastal circumstances would soon bring an end to his marriage. In the spring, the *Chicago Sun-Times* would receive a tip from someone affiliated with the Bulls that Jackson was romantically involved with Jerry Buss's daughter Jeanie, a Lakers executive who several years earlier had exposed her shapely body for a *Playboy* pictorial, even posing nude in Lakers offices at the Forum. When Rodman arrived on the scene in 1999, she had dated him briefly. It was from Rodman that she supposedly learned what a good guy Phil Jackson was. The union of the coach with the team owner's daughter did not present what Jerry West considered ideal circumstances. And critics in Chicago suggested that Jackson had finally found a way around his problems with management. Yet over his years in Chicago, Jackson had long learned to practice discretion in his private life, and he did the same in Los Angeles. His relationship with Jeanie Buss appeared to have no influence whatsoever on the team's performance.

It would, however, elevate his love life to tabloid status, yet another sign that his celebrity had grown beyond that of a mere coach. Beyond that, it gave some of his NBA critics another opportunity to sneer at the image that Jackson had projected with his *Sacred Hoops* philosophy.

Some observers snipped that Jackson had been lured back to the game by the money, but he had turned down the opportunity to earn $8 million per season with other teams to take $6 million per year with the Lakers. Jackson's close associates said he clearly missed the opportunity to teach the game, and that was what brought him back.

"This is the right place for me," Jackson said. "I believe they're a group of players who want to get there but don't know how."

Winter later observed that Jackson returned to the game under immense pressure because it was a substantial gamble in terms of his reputation. Everything he had gained as coach of the Bulls could be lost in Los Angeles, and there were critics hoping that Jackson would stumble. "I'm no savior," Jackson said, acknowledging the scrutiny.

Jackson had once explained that he based much of his decision-making on Carlos Castaneda's *The Teachings of Don Juan*: "Look at every path closely and deliberately. Try it as many times as you think necessary. Then ask yourself, and yourself alone, the question: . . . Does this path have a heart? If it does, the path is good. If it doesn't, it is of no use."

His chosen path was one he had taken before—in 1989—to take a talented, divided team and teach it the triangle. "Phil from the very beginning has been sold on this philosophy, this concept of team play that we preach," Winter would explain later. "From the very start. Sometimes even more so than me. Phil had to dig in. That he did. He had to convince Michael. That was the first thing."

Jim Cleamons recalled those first efforts to teach the triangle to Jordan and the Bulls.

"It was all new," he said. "It was new to the team. It was new to me. It was a learning process. Phil knew the team and had a good feel for them. Getting them to do the daily work was no trouble. The team had a good work ethic. But the fact is, Michael was Michael. He knew he was so talented, he figured he had to do it all, that that was the only way they were going to have success."

Teaching Jordan to share with his teammates brought waves of turmoil. Now the coaches faced a similar task of convincing O'Neal and Bryant of a new approach. But Jackson also knew so much more about what he was doing a decade later, Cleamons pointed out. "P.J. knows now what he wants out of this system, knows how to demand certain things. I think that whole teaching technique and how to build your system, he now has that down in his mind. In 1990, we didn't know what to expect.

"Now you know what you want to teach and how you want to teach it. Tex knows. We're a staff coming in together. Tex has been with him eleven or twelve years. Frank's been with him three or four. This is my eighth year. We've all had experience in teaching the triangle to teams that are resistant or less talented. All of those situations make this much more palatable."

Plus, he had prepared himself for the Lakers. Derek Fisher pointed out that Jackson hadn't been around them long before the players realized that he had spent quite a bit of time studying them.

Jackson knew exactly what he had to do to move things in the right direction. In Chicago, Tex Winter had watched in amazement as Jackson built a strong relationship with Jordan. "When you have a relationship that strong with the star player, the rest of the team just kind of falls in line," Winter explained. "Phil worked very hard at cultivating that relationship with Michael."

Now Jackson began the process by building a similar relationship with O'Neal. Winter explained that Jackson knew that O'Neal was motivated by the opportunity to score lots of points, so he fashioned a trade-off with the big center. If O'Neal would show the leadership Jackson wanted, then the triangle offense would give him the opportunity to score big numbers.

This, of course, got down to the basic conflict between O'Neal and Bryant. When Jackson was hired, Bryant had purchased *Sacred Hoops* and gone up to his hotel room in Los Angeles to greet him. O'Neal traveled to Montana to visit with Jackson. Obviously, both were eager to please their new coach, even to curry favor with him.

It was O'Neal who would take top priority in Jackson's plans. The coach began by placing responsibility squarely on the center's 7'1", 330-pound frame. "This team should be looking to win 60 games," Jackson told the L.A. media as training camp opened. "That's a realistic goal."

He paused in the middle of that thought and looked at O'Neal sitting nearby. "The ball is going in to Shaq," Jackson said. "And he's going to have a responsibility to distribute the ball. It's going to be good for the team, and good for him."

Good indeed. O'Neal would go on to average 29.7 points per game while operating out of Jackson's triangle offense, good enough to lead the league in scoring and earn O'Neal's first MVP honors. O'Neal dubbed himself "The Big Aristotle" in an MVP acceptance speech that he had been polishing for years.

For all the excitement over the big offensive numbers, Jackson reminded O'Neal and his teammates early and often that it was defense that would distinguish them. To play it, Jackson wanted O'Neal in shape and filled with desire to block shots and defend the basket.

"Maybe I could play a little defense from the bench, who knows?" Jackson joked in that first press conference from training camp. "Defense is conditioning. People get beat because they aren't in good enough condition. When you are tired, you can't have a gritty attitude. We will work on conditioning."

Still, Jackson's initial disappointment over not getting Pippen led him to forecast a 5–5 start for his team in November.

And that came before an October 13 injury forced Bryant to miss the first 15 games on the schedule. Yet even a setback such as Bryant's broken right wrist proved to be a blessing. It allowed the coaches to mold the team identity, then to add Bryant's frenetic energy to the equation in December, like some sort of super-octane fuel.

It would also allow time for the rift between Bryant and O'Neal to begin healing. On that issue, Jackson wasted little time. "I'm going to stop some of the gossiping, stop some of the rumormongering among the personnel here," he promised that first day.

At the time, Jackson and his coaches didn't realize just how deep a divide they faced. After the season, Winter would confide that he was shocked by the level of hatred O'Neal expressed for Bryant when the coaches first arrived on the scene.

"There was a lot of hatred in his heart," Winter said, adding that O'Neal didn't hesitate to vent his feelings in team meetings. "He was saying really hateful things," Winter explained. "Kobe just took it and kept going."

O'Neal's main message to anyone who would listen, including management, was that the team could not win a championship with Bryant. West had been strong in pushing aside O'Neal's desire to remove Bryant from the team, but there were signs that management had heard the message so often that they, too, entertained doubts. During the offseason, former O'Neal teammate Penny Hardaway had contacted O'Neal about joining the Lakers. The center jumped at the opportunity and phoned management. The implied message was that Bryant should be traded, but management declined that move.

During the season, as the coaches worked to heal the rift between the players, Winter explained that it had been made clear that if the coaches' efforts didn't work, then "a move would have to be made if they can't play together."

The team wasn't about to trade the massive O'Neal, which meant that Bryant would have to go.

Like West, though, the coaching staff saw Bryant as a Jordan-like player. His hands were smaller than Jordan's, but the athletic ability, the intelligence, the desire, were prodigious. What wasn't clear was whether Bryant would grow to possess the alpha male nature that made Jordan so dominant in his late twenties. Bryant was still so young, it was hard to evaluate him for that. He certainly possessed the drive and work ethic.

But Jackson put off the temptation to form a close relationship with Bryant. The coach correctly read that O'Neal's nature craved such a relationship, and Jackson turned just about all of his undivided attention to his relationship with O'Neal. The coach would later explain that the center did not have the same inquisitiveness as Jordan, and the conversations he had with O'Neal were not as expansive. Still, they spent much time talking.

Early in the season, Bryant would point out that he had yet to sit down for an in-depth conversation with Jackson. Bryant kept expecting that conversation to occur. But it never would. Jackson kept his time for O'Neal.

Some on the coaching staff pointed out that Bryant could have approached the coach about such a talk, but the young guard had such a strong sense of team issues that he seemed happy to let Jackson focus his efforts on soothing the center's harsh feelings.

For much of the healing between the center and guard, Jackson and Winter relied on their triangle. The main idea was that because the offense was so structured, it would make the relationship between O'Neal and Bryant smoother on the court. Still, the coaches found there was so much residual anger on the part of O'Neal and other veterans against Bryant that Jackson had to spend months counseling O'Neal on how to get over it.

The danger, said Winter, was that O'Neal seemed to influence the entire team against Bryant. So he and Jackson worked regularly on changing that attitude.

"The coaches voiced to us that they weren't seeing the same things we were seeing when they watched film and when they watched what was going on," Derek Fisher explained. "They didn't see the same selfishness or one-on-one play that we saw. What I tried to tell some of the other guys is that this is our fourth year now—me, Shaq, Robert [Horry], Rick [Fox], Travis [Knight]—so we still had issues that we had dealt with before this year."

And those issues were still cooking on the team agenda, Fisher said. "It was kind of similar to a relationship between a man and a woman where you get upset with all of these things from the past that come up. That's really where a lot of this stuff stemmed from. The coaches saw that a lot of this stuff would come in due time. But we were so impatient because we had dealt with it before."

For a time, it seemed that no matter what Bryant did, O'Neal and other teammates wanted to find fault with it. Winter revealed that he finally put together a videotape to prove to O'Neal that Bryant was doing just what he was supposed to do.

"I think Kobe's really leaning over backward to get the ball in to Shaq," Winter would confide as the season progressed. "If there's a problem there—and I think we'll work it out—it's that I don't think Shaq appreciates what Kobe is trying to do to help his game."

And so it became easy for the coaches to take Bryant's early injury as a blessing. The guard's absence allowed the team's entire focus to fall upon O'Neal, which worked nicely into Jackson's plans. He had named O'Neal captain and spent considerable time talking through a new approach to the game. Jackson wanted more leadership, conditioning, and defense out of O'Neal. As Winter explained, Jackson knew that O'Neal was motivated by scoring points, so he gave the center more scoring opportunities as long as he fulfilled the rest of his obligations. Jackson also regularly called O'Neal's hand if he failed to do the right thing.

His efforts with O'Neal were intended to send a message to the rest of the roster to fall in line. It soon worked.

"It's hard to not have a view of what Phil does," Rick Fox said in November. "He is our leader now. In his interaction, he's gone as hard at guys as I've seen anybody go at someone. Maybe harder than they'd ever be on themselves. And that's a challenge. He's pushing buttons to make sure guys continually come to work, come to step their games up and get better."

Jackson also showed an early liking for zinging criticism at his players in the media. "Then he'll smile about it," Fox said. "I think he's just honest."

Jackson, in fact, told *Sports Illustrated* that he doubted whether O'Neal could be a leader because his poor free throw shooting meant that he couldn't deliver at the end of games. Jackson made this comment to the magazine before he had actually discussed the issue with O'Neal himself.

"He's very open with his criticism," Fox said. "At the same time he's very open with his praise. You can live with somebody who when his mouth opens, you get the truth. Sometimes the truth hurts, and egos are bruised. But all he's doing is putting guys' egos in check. It's a fine line. He's obviously very good at what he does. We're still a group of people who will have to go through 80 or 90 games together."

O'Neal was snoozing on the Lakers' charter airplane during a late-November flight when he suddenly awakened to find Jackson leaning over just inches from his face.

"You played like shit in practice today," Jackson said and walked away.

O'Neal said it was almost creepy, because Jackson reminded him so much of his stepfather, who was just as tough on Shaq as a child. "He's my white father," O'Neal said of the coach.

"Phil is all over Shaq, all the time," Lakers reserve John Salley said. "But Shaq can take it. It works for him."

All the other Lakers saw that O'Neal was respectful of and obedient to Jackson's discipline, and they, too, fell in line. In a short time, Jackson had become the top dog in Los Angeles.

Early on, opponents made a practice of heaping fouls on Shaq. O'Neal responded with frustration and got tossed out of one game and suspended for another. Jackson forcefully reminded him that that was no way for a leader to act.

"He told me to be smarter," O'Neal said. "I always protect myself, but I shouldn't react right away when something happens. I will just wait a couple of seconds and then get them."

Opponents around the league began noticing that O'Neal was more focused, more effective with Jackson's coaching.

"He's handing out a lot of punishment, too," Phoenix coach Danny Ainge said after the Suns lost to the Lakers on November 15. "He's like the neighborhood bully. He's like a sixth-grader playing with second-graders."

O'Neal had 34 points, 18 rebounds, and 8 blocks against Phoenix.

"I'll tell you what," Lakers forward Glen Rice said. "He could do that every game."

November had brought immediate trends for O'Neal and the team. They opened the season with a big road win over Utah, only to then lose a game to Portland in which Pippen's fierceness clearly intimidated the Lakers. He seemed to know where the Lakers' offense was taking them before the Lakers knew, a development the team first saw in a preseason game.

"We used to own them," Derek Fisher said of the Blazers. "We beat them every year, regular season or playoffs. They just couldn't match up with us mentally or physically. They knew it and we knew it."

But the Lakers now saw a profound difference in their opponents to the north. Suddenly, the Blazers had a new confidence, a new awareness. They began acting like they were better than the Lakers. And they began beating them.

"They knew the plays we were going to run before we did," Fisher said. "They had this new attitude."

Pippen was having a dramatic effect on his new team. "The presence of Pippen on the court was really felt," Jackson said. "The effect that Scottie had when we played against Portland because of his ability to read the triangle, how to disrupt our offense, how to play Glen Rice, some of the things that he did are obvious."

Jackson's answer had been to sign free agent and former Bull Ron Harper, who would provide steadiness and leadership throughout the season, especially later with Bryant's return. Harper would be a steadying, calming influence whenever the young guard's competitiveness raged to the point that it pushed him out of control.

The Lakers recovered from that November setback in Portland to cruise through the month with an 11–4 record, which helped O'Neal earn Player of the Month honors.

Just before Thanksgiving, Jackson's old team, the Bulls, visited the Lakers in their shiny new home, the Staples Center—only these Bulls hardly resembled the terrorizing force that Jackson had coached.

Made up of promising rookies and castoffs, the Bulls somehow managed to stay close to the Lakers, mostly by fouling O'Neal. On one sequence after another, O'Neal was hacked, with the smacks ringing out in the dead atmosphere of the new building. Each time O'Neal made a free throw, the audience reacted wildly, only to settle back into a stupor moments later.

Many of his free throws, though, traveled a truly awful path to the basket, each of them greeted by groans from the crowd. Winter liked to call

O'Neal's free throws scud shots, which didn't endear him to the big center.

"Tell me that that wasn't a painful game to watch," Jackson said afterward. "I counted over a hundred foul shots."

"Are you trying to help Shaq with his free throws?" a reporter asked Jackson.

"I think most of L.A. is trying to help Shaq," he replied. "I have people stopping me in the middle of the street while I'm walking my dog and tell me, 'Let me tell you what I can do to help Shaq.' I told him that when I'd gotten 1,000 letters and videos and cards that I'd drop them all in his lap. But I know he's gotten that same amount."

The game also brought the opportunity for Winter to visit with Krause. The Bulls VP had finally stashed most of his anger and had brought in Don Haskins, the recently retired coach from the University of Texas–El Paso, as his basketball sidekick. Jackson and Krause, however, did not visit.

Jackson did take time to explain his progress with the collection of Chicago media present. "We're much farther along than I thought we'd be as a basketball team," Jackson said of his Lakers. "I think we've been able to do that on the strength of Shaquille's individual ability right now. We're not a very good executing team. We don't have a lot of team speed. But we have occasionally played some real good games against some very good teams and won some games on the road that maybe we shouldn't have.

"Ron Harper gives us a lot of definition on the floor," he added. "Sporadically we can play defense. I don't think we have that total effort yet. But we have a shotblocker, a force in the middle. We rebound the ball pretty well. We have some idea of how we're doing things conceptually."

Many in the Chicago media were amused by Jackson's boost in celebrity with his relocation to the West Coast, including his appearance in a national ad campaign for an on-line trading company.

"You didn't get all this attention in Chicago," a Chicago reporter pointed out. "You didn't make the cover of news magazines and all this stuff."

Jackson smiled and replied, "Number 23 was the big guy there."

Do you look at this as an opportunity to establish yourself as a coach outside Michael's shadow? another reporter asked.

"I don't look at it that way," Jackson said. "I just look at it as a team that gives me an [opportunity] to try and transcend a different age group, a different generation, with the influence that I have, and the style that I try to bring to a team. I want to see how well I can adapt to this group, this Generation X or whatever they are, these Gen X kids, and try to get our philosophy across to these young men and see if we can play our style of ball that we like to play in this element."

Two nights later, his team endured a thunderous appearance by Vince Carter and the Toronto Raptors, a defeat that left Bryant antsy to play.

His return, however, wouldn't come until December 1, when he came off the bench to score 19 in a win over Golden State.

"It was nice to have Kobe's energy," Jackson said. "He's just a wild, impulsive kid right now. He's still feeling his way."

"God, I had a headache I was so excited," Bryant told reporters. "My head was literally throbbing. The first half, I felt like I was on speed or something. I couldn't calm down. . . ."

Immediately the media began asking about the prospects of Bryant and O'Neal getting along with Bryant's energy changing the Lakers' attack.

"I don't foresee any problems," Jackson said. "If there is, we'll rein him in."

The Lakers used the young guard's presence to secure a much-needed win over the Trail Blazers the very next game. Bryant settled the issue by blocking a late Pippen shot and corralling Portland's Damon Stoudamire on defense.

All the veterans on the team had been eager to see Jackson immediately begin disciplining Bryant, Fisher recalled. But that didn't happen. "He still waited for a while before he started. He didn't just jump in. He really didn't," Fisher said. "He allowed Kobe to come in. I think Phil wanted to see firsthand how things were, how Kobe participated in the games and practice, how we felt about him, how he felt about us. Phil waited to see all that before he made any judgments about whether there needed to be adjustments. He didn't just come right in and tell Kobe he needed to curtail his game or his creativity. He really allowed things to develop, then here or there when it was pertinent, he would say something. It was never as if he was saying things to Kobe as if Kobe was the only guy on the team who needed to make adjustments, or to improve in certain areas."

The season would also bring a quick answer to the question of Jackson's own ability to get along with West. "I was worried when I first came out here," Winter admitted. A public perception existed that West and Jackson might have differing opinions on personnel issues, egged on by Jackson's penchant for offering his opinion to the media.

But Winter suspected that Jackson's presence had helped take the pressure off West, who had been faced with trying to sort out the team's gnarly chemistry problems.

"I think Phil helps get the monkey off Jerry's back a little bit," Winter said. "I think they're gonna be all right. At least I think so."

The other side of the issue was that the coaching staff took an immediate liking to West and seemed somewhat awed by his comprehensive view of the game. He saw everything, things that no one else could see. An early item of concern, the relationship with West quickly became a huge positive.

The players had also been ready to cooperate, Winter said. "The thing that impresses me is that they're all really trying to do what we want done. At this stage of the season that's really important."

That good attitude was essential as the players attempted to learn the triangle offense. "They seem to appreciate the fact that we're coaching them," Winter said. "They're trying to stay with it."

The transition to the offense was helped substantially by the Lakers' opening night win in Utah, Winter said. That was especially true for shooter Glen Rice, who had struggled adjusting to the triangle during the preseason. "He was thinking a little too much, but I wasn't worried about Glen because he's got such a great touch," the assistant coach said.

Even the early success, however, didn't change the fact that the Lakers had a long way to go to improve. "What amazes me is how poor they are fundamentally in passing the ball," Winter said.

Winter said he had been surprised by O'Neal's determination, although it was clear the Lakers' center didn't have Jordan's fire. "He's not a Michael Jordan type of leader," the assistant coach said. "He's not that vocal type of leader. But he plays hard, and everybody respects his desire to win."

The coaches were also curious to see how O'Neal would adapt to the triangle. "He's a good learner," Winter said of O'Neal. "He's picking it up pretty quickly. The only problem is, he's still thinking in terms of power. That's what he is, of course, is a power player."

The triangle, though, stressed the finesse of passing and cutting. "Sometimes he has a hard time waiting for the cutter," Winter said of O'Neal, who readily admits that patience is not one of his strong suits. "He's a little overanxious at times. As a result, he sometimes misses a lot of point-blank shots. But he's quite a player."

It was obvious that the team needed a power forward to help O'Neal with the heavy lifting in the frontcourt. Although West had clearly stated his opposition to bringing back controversial forward Dennis Rodman, Jackson continued to hint to L.A. reporters that Rodman might be an option.

Winter said he hoped the thirty-eight-year-old power forward did not join the Lakers. "He's called Phil a few times, and they've talked," Winter said. "I don't think Phil has ever actually called him. Dennis is Dennis. He's too impulsive. Phil would keep him in line better than most, but he's gonna do what he wants to do."

The Lakers would soon find that they didn't need Rodman. With the addition of Bryant, they would instead soar off to a winning streak. They would continue to show surprising poise over the coming weeks, losing a game to Sacramento before ripping off 16 straight wins that would carry them well into January. Finally they lost a January 14 game at Indiana's Conseco Fieldhouse—and just like that, the Lakers came unglued. Suddenly they found themselves in a 3–7 free fall, and all the old panic resurfaced. O'Neal's feelings against Bryant gained strength. Soon the players were again pointing fingers and blaming Bryant's desire for stardom as their problem. "We can't win with Kobe" was O'Neal's insistent message.

Winter, though, saw the problem as nothing more than bad defense and maybe a touch of self-satisfaction in O'Neal. "We're getting broken down," the seventy-eight-year-old assistant coach said. "We've been vulnerable to penetration all year long, the high screen and roll. Kobe has a real tough time with it. So does Derek Fisher. And the side screen and rolls. That's most everybody's offense this day and age, especially against us."

As for the chemistry issue, Winter said the coaches were treading softly. "Most coaches, Phil included, have always sort of had a whipping boy," Winter explained. "And I think he's very careful not to have that become Kobe, because he realizes that he's got a great young player here and he doesn't want to squelch him too much. And yet he wants to control him."

The players had admired Jackson for sitting back and letting Bryant learn from his mistakes. But it soon became apparent to the coaches that many of the Lakers were almost demanding that Bryant be disciplined.

As for O'Neal, Winter said, "My main concern is that I don't want him to be satisfied with where he is. I want him to realize what he's doing wrong, even on the free throws. . . . He's not easy to coach. He has kind of a resentment for anybody to tell him anything that he's doing wrong. He's not an easy guy to coach.

"I think Phil treads very softly on Shaq," Winter said. "I think he still is trying to read the situation as to what is the best way to motivate Shaq. I don't think he knows yet. And I certainly don't know."

Mainly, Jackson focused on encouraging O'Neal to put away his anger. The harsh feelings against Bryant could surge through the entire roster. It was an old problem, Rick Fox said. "The times that we've become frazzled and unraveled as a team it's been around situations where we embarrass ourselves."

Derek Fisher figured that the All-Star weekend had a profound effect on Bryant, as did the coaching staff's efforts to make the Lakers realize that they were silly to harbor anger from events that happened over previous seasons when Bryant was a young player finding his way along.

Bryant seemed to come out of All-Star weekend a changed man, Fisher said, as a player focused on team play. A big factor had been Jackson's quiet encouragement of Bryant not to participate in the slam dunk contest. Bryant was defending champion, and Vince Carter was drawing raves. Fisher said the Lakers knew Bryant wanted to have a go at Carter, but he set that aside so that it wouldn't bring a focus on individual accomplishments over team things. It proved to be a crucial factor in the team's growth, although O'Neal was clearly mimicking Bryant's crossover dribble during All-Star warm-ups, then tossing the ball up into the stands to emphasize the guard's turnovers. Such open hostility had to cease, Magic Johnson confided, concluding that Jackson would soon get it under control.

But another factor at All-Star weekend was Seattle's Gary Payton helping Bryant to understand screen-and-roll defense. "I don't think Gary knows how much he helped me," said Bryant, who demonstrated such dramatic defensive improvement afterward that he would wind up being named to the league's All-Defensive first team.

Ultimately, it was the winning that helped the Lakers put away the hard feelings. A late February victory over Portland sent them on another victory binge—this time 19 straight games of surging confidence. The highlight of the win streak was a win over the lowly Clippers, with O'Neal scoring 61 points on his birthday. The streak finally ended with a mid-March loss in Washington. Afterward, new Wizards executive Michael Jordan enjoyed a cigar at his former coach's expense.

"Phil has always been the master of mind games," Jordan said of his old coach's new success. "He still is."

"You know what happened in Washington?" Fox would later explain. "We had won 19 games in a row. Honestly, this was sad to say, but the game had gotten to where there was no real challenge. We were playing our best ball during that stretch. We were hitting on all cylinders. It was clicking, it was routine. Each night, we stepped out and it was rhythmic. Everything seemed to play out just as it did the game before. And so, you look at that and you realize, we started creating the challenges ourselves. We started to test the system, we started to become lax on defense. We wanted to see how big a hole we could dig ourselves before we came out. It was like we were testing how good we really were."

Immediately after losing to the Wizards, Jackson's bunch ran off another 11 wins, with the grins growing at every stop on the schedule. All the trouble, however, had not been vanquished. April brought a pair of disappointing losses to San Antonio, including one to end the season in which Spurs power forward Tim Duncan sat out with an injury.

"It wasn't the most confident way to finish a 67-win season, losing two games, including one on the road," Fox admitted. "Duncan was not in the game and we still lost. I wouldn't say your confidence wavers, but it's obvious there was a tension. You say to yourself, 'Wow, this hasn't been the way we played all year.' We were a little angry amongst ourselves, a little testy with each other. When you come from a setting where you've failed before, and the reason you've failed is because you've fallen apart, the remnants of that can always bubble up."

Some Lakers were privately angry with Jackson for playing rookies and substitutes rather than going all out in the final loss to the Spurs.

Jackson, though, continued to take the long view. The Lakers had home-court advantage for the playoffs. They had learned to play a little defense, they had learned to run the triangle offense, and they had learned to play together, to put aside their anger.

Miracles

For so many years the Lakers had been screwing up in the playoffs. Swept by Utah. Dismissed by Utah. Swept by San Antonio. It became a part of their personality.

But Jackson had helped them to a 67-win regular season. Suddenly, hopes surged that their playoff troubles were behind them.

The Lakers' coaches, though, weren't so sure. They were uneasy about how this fragile team would perform in the playoffs.

Sure enough, they struggled to put away Sacramento and Phoenix and Portland. A key win came in Game 2 of their second-round series with Phoenix. Bryant hit a last-second shot to seal the victory. Nothing had to be said; the message had been clearly sent that this team could win a title with

Bryant. As his first-round film selection, Jackson had shown his team *American History X*, a dramatic rejection of hatred that ended by quoting Abraham Lincoln's call for healing parties to choose the better angels of their nature, clearly a message to O'Neal about the futility of deep dislike.

It was the battle against the Blazers in the Western Conference finals that provided the kind of challenge that forces a team to grow up. As the series opened, Jackson figured to distract Pippen, the Blazers' leader, with a run of trademark mind games. Behind the scenes, the Lakers' coaching staff plotted a strategy designed to put even more pressure on Pippen, often criticized over the years as being mentally fragile, by making him do more and more over the course of each game. They wanted to force him into running the Blazers' show and initiating the offense.

"Ultimately," Jackson told reporters, "he's the one."

Pippen would have to do everything to lead Portland to a title. Defend. Make shots. Keep the young players from losing their cool. Keep the coaches in line.

After watching Pippen eliminate Utah in the semifinals with outstanding play, Jackson was impressed. "That's Scottie," the Lakers' coach said. "He gets into a corner, jumps out, and plays great sometimes. He can do a lot of things to create havoc at both ends of the floor for you. I'd like to think I helped him develop that ability, as a coach, but he had that resolve."

Then Jackson added his first dose of pressure. "I personally think if Scottie doesn't lead this basketball club and take this team by the horns, they're not going to get by us," he said. "He's going to have to be the one who gets them by us. Of course, I'm going to try to take that strength of his game away."

Some of the Lakers' coaching staff, especially Jackson, didn't care for the circumstances of going up against a player they held in high affection. Winter, however, acknowledged that he loved the competition of facing a player who knew their system better than perhaps anyone.

"Having had him on my side for so many years and knowing him as well as I do, it'll be interesting to see if we can get the type of matchup that still gives us an ability to corral Scottie or hold him in check . . . he's the one who has to be attended to all the time," Jackson said.

Asked if he was feeling the pressure that Jackson was trying to put on him, Pippen replied, "I know my way around the game. That's not going to affect me. I've learned from a lot of episodes I've been able to go through in my career.

"Phil feels like he's the greatest at it," Pippen said of Jackson's mind games. "He's already tried to do that, saying our team has no leader and that we're overpaid. Whatever Phil says, it's not going to be personal.

"There's nothing I can do with Phil, anyway. He's not on the court. I have to be more effective against his team and his players."

Blazers guard Steve Smith called it "trickery" by Jackson, adding: "With a young team, sometimes there is discussion about what he is saying. On our team, no one has even discussed it."

In Game 1, the Lakers survived a desperate fouling tactic by Portland coach Mike Dunleavy aimed at sending O'Neal to the line. Such efforts had long been dubbed "Hack-a-Shaq." Repeatedly squeezing, holding, and wrapping him up, the Blazers forced O'Neal to shoot 25 free throws in the fourth quarter. It did little more than delay the game to the point of irritation. The Lakers used the stopped play to set up their defense for each possession, and won handily.

After a solid all-around performance (19 points, 11 rebounds), Pippen wasn't thrilled with the O'Neal strategy. "I didn't make that call," Pippen said of the tactic. "I think everyone knows Shaq is a better shooter now. He stood up and made the foul shots. He made everyone look kind of stupid. It's a gamble to do what we did today."

The real focus of the series would fall on the Jackson–Pippen relationship. Jackson had once described Pippen as "a brooder . . . who could fall into a deep funk for days."

Jackson used Game 1 to probe Pippen's psyche. In the first half, when Pippen was working furiously on defense, the Lakers' coach called Pippen over. "I told him he can't guard everyone on the whole team," Jackson said. "He said, 'I'm gonna try.'"

Told that Jackson had revealed their conversation, Pippen frowned and said, "We'll leave it at that. I'm not even thinking about my relationship with Phil Jackson. I just want to get out of this building."

The Blazers then changed the tenor of the series by claiming Game 2 in a massive 106–77 win in Staples Center. Jackson responded by calling the Blazers "jackals" and insinuating that Pippen was leading his teammates in celebrating after the victory. Needing to make a show of their determination, the Lakers had strangely played without emotion and energy. The coaching staff left the building dumbfounded.

"We didn't expect a blowout," Jackson admitted, adding that he didn't like the way the Blazers celebrated at the Staples Center after delivering the most one-sided loss the Lakers had suffered all season.

"What we remember is the attitude Portland carried off the floor," Jackson said. "[The Blazers] were kind of jackals down there on the bench. We have to remember that when we go to Portland, that they might have been just a little bit too much so."

The Blazers contained Kobe Bryant for most of the second half in Game 3 in Portland, but Bryant produced some big plays in the game's final moments to give the Lakers a 93–91 victory and a 2–1 series lead. He blocked a last-ditch shot by Portland center Arvydas Sabonis to preserve the victory, and also had a big steal on the Blazers' previous possession.

"I had to take a chance. We've played all season long for this," said Bryant, plagued by fouls for much of the second half. "I'm not going to let a guy get a clear look just because I have five fouls."

Sabonis wailed for a foul, but replays confirmed that the block was clean.

"I feel like we did a good job of really passing the ball inside, getting penetration from the post," Pippen said. "We were getting very easy shots from the post. I mean, we only lost the game by two points, so I don't feel like we really settled for the jump shot."

"It was a surge for us," Bryant said. "Kind of a statement to Portland that we're not going to give up, that we're here to fight, that we're not going to give up no matter what the score is. I think that block was a statement to them that we're not going to give up."

With the Blazers fuming and seemingly divided, the Lakers then got another win in Game 4, with both contests marked by the Blazers' high energy to open the games and the Lakers' late surge to win.

At one point in Game 4, Jackson and Pippen engaged in a staring match. "No, there was nothing there, just looking at each other, kind of," Jackson said after Game 4. "We weren't conversing. We were just kind of checking each other out. There was nothing to be said. Scottie was playing really hard and I was just checking out what he was doing."

Harper said whatever hostilities might be arising were only temporary and only in the heat of the moment.

"Pipp loves Phil," Harper said. "He loves Phil to death. This is just a thing. They're two good friends, that's all that is. Pipp loves to play hard."

Before the game, Jackson agreed that Pippen had displayed much emotion: "Scottie's always been an enthusiastic player, maybe not to this level, but he's always played with a lot of enthusiasm, and a certain amount of love of the game comes through in his play."

Down 3–1, the Blazers returned to L.A. and found a way to win in a game that reflected Pippen's great competitive nature. Jackson had complained that Pippen threw an elbow to John Salley's head during Game 4, an act that should have brought Pippen's suspension.

Pippen responded with fire in Game 5, using the occasion to break Jordan's all-time record for playoff steals. "We know in our hearts we can outplay this team," said Pippen, who scored 22 points, grabbed 6 rebounds, had 6 steals, blocked 4 shots, and got the entire Lakers' backcourt into foul trouble. "We have throughout this series, but we haven't completed it in the games. We feel like we're going to outplay them every time out on the court."

After Game 5, Jackson told Pippen he shouldn't have been allowed to play. Jackson talked to Pippen as both were leaving the court.

"I said, 'You shouldn't even have been playing in the game and you had a great game,'" related Jackson in reference to an elbow to John Salley late in Game 4 that drew Pippen a $10,000 fine from the NBA. "He elbowed . . . clearly a cheap-shot elbow to the back of the head, and he was just fined $10,000. I told him he shouldn't be there.

"He said, 'Thanks a lot.' I don't think he meant it," related Jackson.

"Phil is not my coach," Pippen said when asked about the exchange. "I'm not listening to Phil. I'm not listening to nothing you tell me about Phil."

Pippen had scored 12 points in Game 3, and played even worse in Game 4, with 11 points on 4 for 12 shooting, with 5 turnovers and only 2 assists. "Today I didn't get in foul trouble," he said of Game 5. "It allowed me to be able to push the ball in transition and stay aggressive."

"He just took over," backup guard Bonzi Wells said of Pippen, who played well despite two dislocated fingers on his left hand. "He came out and attacked them. He stayed aggressive and played hard. That's what won the game for us."

His play helped the Blazers to again believe in themselves, and they produced a convincing win in Game 6 back in Portland. Only six other times had an NBA team come back from a 3–1 deficit to win a series, but the Blazers seemed capable of pulling it off.

Pippen's confidence had enthused his teammates. "He's our veteran player, he's our leader, and we just tried to follow suit behind him," Bonzi Wells said.

"He's been there. We just try to follow his lead. He just said we've got to play hard, we've got to be intense out there. We're the only people that are rooting for each other in this gym.

"We've got to stay together, and if we stay together, good things will happen."

"Scottie's a warrior," Blazers coach Mike Dunleavy said.

"They played desperado ball," O'Neal said.

The Lakers were strangely passive again, obviously intimidated by Pippen's mental toughness. Only Rick Fox off the bench attempted to stand up to Pippen's aggressiveness, which brought a heated exchange in the fourth period. To the fans, it perhaps seemed like a silly incident, but to the Lakers' coaches the gesture was significant. Jackson knew that someone had to stand up to Pippen's intimidation. "Being a part of those unsuccessful teams, being a part of that, you know you look back," Fox said of his decision to stand up to Pippen. "Each year at the end I looked back and said, 'What could I have done more? Did I leave something out there? Was I as emotional or into the series as I should have been?' When you sit back and you have that time, which is a whole summer, you say, 'Man, I wish I had given just a little more. I wish I had had just a little more fight. I wish I had sent just a little more of a message. I really wanted to be a champion. I really wanted to win.' That was our downfall the last few years. We never really went out in the playoffs and set a tone and sent a message that we were fighting for this game and that we were about doing whatever it took to win.

"I told myself I was just not gonna let a series go by where we went down as cowards basically," Fox explained.

"Phil's got them trying to get into my head, trying to get cheap shots on me, I know what he's doing," Pippen said.

Fox's efforts to counter Pippen's intimidation drew the ire of Dunleavy, who told reporters afterward, "They were taking fouls with a little extra mustard on them, and we didn't appreciate it."

Mainly, the Lakers lost because they were no-shows on defense, which forced them into a seventh game back in Staples Center.

"Now we have to bite, scratch, kick, and claw," Brian Shaw said.

Whenever his teammates seemed to doubt that they could win it all, Pippen would bring out one of his six championship rings from his days with the Bulls. "He's flashed me the gold a couple of times," Bonzi Wells said. "He blinded me with the diamonds. But that's Scottie. He's here to give us a taste."

All of which stoked both teams' competitive fires for Game 7 back in Los Angeles.

In the third quarter the Blazers outplayed the Lakers and took a 16-point lead, and seemed sure to end the Lakers' championship hopes. Instead, Jackson's team miraculously produced the biggest Game 7 fourth-quarter comeback in NBA history.

Portland led 75–60 with 10:28 to play, but the Lakers stopped Portland 10 consecutive times.

It was Bryant's block of Bonzi Wells's shot that led to a Shaw trey that cut the lead to 10 with 9:38 remaining.

"We all sat in that locker room after Sunday's game in disbelief," Stoudamire said. "There wasn't much anyone could say."

Afterward, the Blazers could only look on in glum, stunned silence as Los Angeles celebrated its first trip to the NBA Finals in nearly a decade.

"That was a daunting uphill battle that we had to face," Jackson said after his team had eclipsed a 15-point fourth-quarter deficit to win 89–84. "We made it back."

The Blazers had controlled the early periods by again gumming up the lane and not allowing O'Neal to do his heavy lifting. But then the Lakers did a little gumming of their own, getting stop after stop after stop in the fourth period as the Blazers settled into a mask of horror.

"You lose yourself in it," Glen Rice said of the comeback, a 25–4 run. "We were thinking, keep going, keep applying the pressure, continue to keep going down on the offensive end, and keep getting good shots, and hopefully this team will fall in the end.

"And they did."

Once the Lakers got going, the Staples crowd fed their energy, which was highlighted by Bryant's alley-oop to O'Neal for a thunderous slam and an 85–79 lead. O'Neal offered up his seal of approval afterward: "Kobe's a great player."

"When he went to the hole, we caught eye contact and he just threw it up," O'Neal said. "I just went up . . . that was an opportunity for me to get an easy bucket."

"I thought I threw the ball too high," Bryant said. "Shaq went up and got it, I was like, 'Damn!'"

O'Neal's words had much more weight than outside observers could have ever imagined. They emphasized an emerging yet still tentative bond between the two, and they rewarded one of the finest, most intensely psychological coaching efforts of Jackson's distinguished career.

Together

The Zen way is the middle path: not too high and not too low, thus avoiding both the bright and dark recesses of human nature. Jackson and his mindfulness expert George Mumford had worked at training the minds of the Lakers to avoid the rough mental edges of competition.

Kobe Bryant, in particular, had found this approach to his liking.

Not long after returning from injury in December, Bryant had made it clear to Jackson that he didn't really need the mind games and motivational ploys.

"Just coach," Bryant had said.

He liked to keep things simple, was already hypermotivated, and saw no need for Jackson's psychological approach.

Yet when it came time to introduce Mumford to the equation, Bryant welcomed the sessions because they offered specific mental training, much of it in the Zen mold, for reducing the stress of playoff competition, when the pressure hit the high side. Considering that O'Neal had set up the season as an agenda on Bryant's worthiness to serve a championship team, the pressure could have been unbearable. But the young guard seemed resolved not to let that happen.

Bryant found that he and some of his teammates enjoyed discussing the mental elements of competition with Mumford. "It was good because it gave people a chance to talk about things that might be on their mind, the hype, the pressure," Bryant explained. "I think it's good for them to talk about those things. It increased our performance a lot. It really has. I'm surprised other teams don't do that kind of stuff. Working with George helps us to get issues out of the way before they even start."

The pressure of performance, of the playoffs, can corrode a team's performance, Bryant explained. "Once it creeps into your team and your teammates, it can be destructive. Some people know how to handle it, some people don't. The pressure can get to you. You got to know how to suck it up."

Out of a sense of machismo, most NBA players don't want to acknowledge that such pressure even exists; however, Jackson and Mumford encouraged the Lakers not only to acknowledge it, but to deal with it before it had a chance to hurt their play. The mindfulness, the Zen focus on only the present moment, had been important tools for Jordan in his championship days, and that made it easier for the Lakers to accept and use.

For years, Bryant had felt the negative vibes coming from O'Neal. Jackson and his staff had worked to quell that negative element within the team, and the unfolding season brought increasing evidence of their success. Yet O'Neal's frequent complaints that the team couldn't win a championship with Bryant still rang in everybody's ears. A weaker personality would easily have crumbled under the circumstances, regardless of the coaches' efforts. But Bryant was far from weak.

"The pressure is there, the pressure is there," he acknowledged during the playoffs. "But it's how you deal with it. When you feel it, it's how you deal with it. You just give it your best. You prepare yourself as well as you can. You go out there and execute as well as you can. Then you sleep at night. That's all. Then you get up the next day and do the same thing. Keep it simple."

Likewise, Bryant found Jackson's film sessions useful. As in past seasons, the coach had worked his players through a series of feature films to prepare for the playoffs, splicing the entire feature in and around clips of the Lakers playing, using certain scenes to chide his players about their choices and actions. First for the Lakers had been *American History X*, followed by *The Green Mile*. Jackson had a way of pausing the film at the most devilish, profane moment to emphasize one thing or another, often to the great hilarity of his players. Derek Fisher pointed out that many of these video lessons seemed to point out one or another of Bryant's transgressions. Even so, Bryant said he didn't mind being singled out. "It's interesting," he said. "I like to try to figure what Phil was actually thinking when he put the clip in there. All the messages he has. It's good for you. I enjoy it. The team finds it funny. Some clips are funny. Some are made to be taken a little more seriously."

Whatever was done, it all added up to Jackson's very unique package, Bryant observed. "I think what has shaped this team, as far as his personality goes, is his sharpness as a person. He's very picky. He pays attention to detail. I think with this team that was something that we lacked in the past. We had a tendency to overlook things, just see the surface."

Jackson's approach so impressed the *L.A. Times* that the newspaper sent a reporter to question the Buddhist community about Jackson. "The Buddhist thought in following the middle path is to take life's ups and downs in a balanced and centered way," the Reverend Tom Kurai of the Sozenji Buddhist Temple in Montebello told the newspaper.

Balanced and centered, indeed. Denying ego, sublimating oneself to the team—these were themes that Jackson preached over and over again. His players didn't entirely heed the message, but they did just enough to get by during the playoffs.

In fact, it was their mindfulness, their focus on the moment, that helped the Lakers deliver that seventh-game comeback against the Blazers. And Jackson, the coach known for being so reluctant to use timeouts, used two key ones to tighten the Lakers' concentration and to shift their intentions from simply throwing the ball down to O'Neal in the post, a move that the Blazers had shut down time and again.

Through the third period, O'Neal had but two field goals for the game and would not score from the field during the disastrous third period. "What we basically told the team is that every time we forced the ball in to him, we were creating turnovers either for Shaq or for us," Jackson said. "Complete the effort, continue the action, make them have to play defense, and then look for him if he's available—and we found that and he got loose a little bit in that fourth quarter. . . . The whole team was standing in the lane around Shaq, we kick the ball around the perimeter and guys were trying to penetrate when shots were there."

Just as impressive, the leadership that Jackson had encouraged in O'Neal all season finally showed up in grand fashion. The leadership of his play had always been there, night in and night out, on the way to an MVP performance. But now it was O'Neal's dealings with his mental approach that struck his coaches and teammates. Instead of sinking into frustration in those difficult moments, he showed his teammates that he could stay focused and positive. "When you have a leader like that, everybody's watching him, to see his body language," Brian Shaw explained. "And, despite the fact that things weren't maybe going the way he wanted them to, he still kept his wits about him."

"I didn't think our players played with a lot of pressure in them," Jackson said later, with a degree of satisfaction.

The other keen development in the win over Portland had been the signs of a bonding between O'Neal and Bryant.

It was as if Bryant refused to get discouraged, and that paid off by season's end. "I think they came to respect each other," Winter said, although the coaches could never be sure what the players were merely doing as a public gesture and what they truly felt.

Asked about O'Neal, Bryant shrugged. "We just do it our separate ways," he said. "That's all we did all season long. It just depended on what we needed in certain situations. So even though we go our separate ways, it all linked up in the end."

Many observers thought that after their win over Portland, the NBA Finals against the Indiana Pacers would be anticlimactic for the Lakers. But Jackson and his staff were concerned because the Pacers were such a fine shooting team. However, they didn't look that way in Game 1. Reggie Miller made just 1 of 16 shots, and the Lakers won in a breeze, mainly by getting the ball to O'Neal and watching him work against an Indiana defense that for some reason failed to double-team. His 43 points and 19 rebounds produced a 104–87 victory in Game 1.

"This offense is designed to go away from pressure," Derek Fisher said. "We tried to attack the pressure against Portland. Indiana tried to single-cover Shaq. I'd be surprised if they don't play the next game differently."

Certainly Pacers coach Larry Bird and his assistants quickly tired of answering questions about their strategy. So the Pacers offered quicker, stronger double-teams in the second contest, and the Lakers answered by shooting out to a 33–18 lead after the first quarter. Eventually, the Pacers' double teams had some effect, and they cut the lead to two points in the third period.

To make matters worse for Los Angeles, Bryant had injured his ankle early in the contest. But the late stretches of the game became Shaw's hour to shine, just as he had down the stretch in Game 7 against the Blazers. His shooting and O'Neal's overpowering presence were enough for Jackson's group to take a 2–0 series lead, 111–104.

Hobbled and on crutches, Bryant was unable to play in Game 3, which created immediate speculation that the Lakers' coaching staff would turn to Glen Rice as a second major scoring option. Jackson, however, had watched Indiana's Jalen Rose take advantage of Rice's defensive weaknesses. He continued to award chunks of playing time to Rick Fox. Rice, Derek Fisher, Robert Horry, and other Lakers had long been troubled by the intuitive nature of Jackson's substitution patterns. Some had adjusted to the coach's whims better than others.

Rice had struggled and finally spoke out after Game 3, a game he finished with only 7 points on 3 for 9 shooting in 27 minutes. He also hadn't seen much action in the final quarters of Game 2 with Bryant injured. "I just don't think that it was a great effort of getting myself involved a little bit more," Rice told reporters. "I spent a little bit too much time on the bench."

Jackson responded, "I thought they bodied Glen well off of any screens we tried to provide for him. He caught the ball, he was crowded and pushed into driving. He got a couple of his baskets off the drive, lost the ball a couple of times off the drive. But they identified Glen very well, and I thought they prevented him from getting good looks."

"If you sit on the bench for 12 minutes and then you go in the game with a minute and something left, it's hard to get going," Rice said of the late stages of Game 3, when the Lakers struggled and Indiana finally got a win to pull within 2–1 in the series.

The issue disappeared briefly in Game 4, which will be remembered as Bryant's moment. He returned from injury and joined O'Neal in matching the Pacers bucket for bucket down the stretch. The battle went to overtime, O'Neal fouled out, and Bryant was faced with leading the Lakers by himself in a key moment. In a gesture brimming with more meaning than fans could understand, Bryant went over to the center who had questioned him so long and told him not to worry, that he would deliver. In the past in Chicago, Jackson and Winter had spread the floor in such moments and allowed Jordan to go to work. But with the Lakers, spreading the floor had never worked, Winter explained, because opposing teams would never leave O'Neal and kept the defense packed in. The spread floor might have worked if O'Neal had been willing to develop a 10- to 15-foot shot, allowing him to move away from the basket. But he had resisted that at every turn.

Now, though, he was off the floor, and Jackson ordered the Lakers to spread the formation wide to confuse the defenders. This allowed Bryant the room to work, and it was further aided by his sore ankle, which meant that he pulled up for midrange jumpers rather than trying to drive all the way to the hole.

Observers would later describe the performance as Jordanesque. In overtime, Bryant delivered the Lakers a series of key baskets and offered irrefutable evidence that O'Neal had been wrong. The victory gave them a 3–1 lead in the series.

"The system worked out well for us," Bryant said. "In the fourth quarter, the triangle offense sometimes kind of goes out the window a little bit. The system in itself allows us to spread the floor toward the end of the game and penetrate. That works because with the triangle offense everybody is a threat throughout the ball game. So the defense is scared to leave off of guys to try to stop me. They're scared to leave off of Robert [Horry] and they're scared to leave Rick [Fox] alone to try to stop me, because they know those guys will make shots.

"In Game 4 it worked really well," Bryant said. "We were able to spread the floor, and I hit a couple of jump shots for us and took us to the brink. During the season, I wanted to use the spread floor. I told him, 'Phil, man, why don't you open the court?' He said, 'We're not ready for that. We'll get to that.' I say open it up. That's when I can go to work. But I'm glad that we waited till the playoffs to use it."

Before the Lakers could be crowned, though, they suffered a terrible defeat in Game 5, which sent the contest back to Staples Center in Los Angeles for a sixth game.

That was only fitting, because the city hadn't celebrated an NBA title since Magic Johnson and Kareem Abdul-Jabbar led the Lakers to a win over the Detroit Pistons in the 1988 NBA championship series.

This time, the honor was O'Neal's. Bryant scored 26 points (on 8 for 27 shooting), grabbed 10 rebounds, and had 4 assists, two of them to O'Neal, as the Lakers charged back to take the lead late in the game.

"In the fourth quarter, we found a place where they couldn't stop us," Jackson said afterward.

With Fox and Horry hitting key shots, the Lakers moved to a 101–94 advantage, despite a stretch of O'Neal missing free throw after free throw. The Pacers, though, used free throws themselves and a Rose trey to tie it at 103 with 5:08 left.

The Lakers surged to 110–103 with 3:02 to go, but the Pacers pulled within one at 110–109 with ninety seconds remaining. This time the Lakers' coaches went to screen-and-roll action out of their offense, a surprise for the Pacers in that the Lakers rarely used it. That was enough, with O'Neal setting high screens for Bryant, to get enough late free throws from Bryant for a 116–111 victory and the franchise's first championship in a dozen seasons. The big center, so loathe to set picks and do non-scoring chores on offense in seasons past, was executing Jackson's disciplined vision of the game.

"We went back to the same thing that worked for us in Game 4, spreading the floor and penetrating, and then attacking them," Bryant said. "I was able to get to the free throw line and knock down some free throws."

"I think we needed Phil to do it," O'Neal said. "Phil and his coaching staff was a staff that was going to bring this team over the hump. We always won 50, 60 games. When we got into certain situations in the playoffs, we could never get over the hump. We had home-court advantage but we made a lot of mistakes in the playoffs. But Phil was able to keep his poise and have us watch film.

"When you look at a guy like Phil, if you're a leader, he's not worried. Why should you worry? He prepared us very well. A lot of tape. Going to the practice facility two times a day, playing, watching film. . . . Phil was a great motivator and a great people person and he did a great job with all the role players."

Could another coach have done it? the *L.A. Times* asked Jerry Buss.

"Great question," the owner replied. "I guess the answer's no. There's some great coaches, but I think this took a very special combination of talents. Pat Riley, a long time ago, was able to knit together a bunch of superstars and make them into a team. Phil has been able to do that with this team. And at least in my mind, I'd have to doubt that anybody else could have done it."

Seeing the journey's end, Jackson typically looked back to the beginning: "The first practice I had in October, I stopped the practice and I said, 'You guys can't play with the kind of energy I demand as a coach, and you have to lift that up.' They found a way to do that. But that was the key to whether we could win or not.

"I didn't think they could play with the kind of intensity defensively that it takes to be a championship team. From that standpoint, I'm very pleased they were able to bring that level up to a maximum effort this year."

Could this team win a run of championships like his Bulls?

"Wow, I don't know if I can hypothetically go to that level," Jackson said.

Jackson clearly didn't want to take on yet more pressure in that moment of celebration. But for the first time in his career, his coaching accomplishments were truly his, there for millions of NBA fans, and even his fellow coaches, to acknowledge.

Given time to think about it over the summer, Tex Winter said it was remarkable that Jackson had coached a second team to a championship. Yes, the longtime assistant had seen Jackson deal harshly with staff people over the years, and he had been just as frustrated as players by Jackson's unusual substitutions patterns at times. "They're not by themselves," Winter said. "I've been there hitting him in the ribs a lot of times, telling him he's got to get this or that guy out of the game."

The success had obviously changed Jackson in some ways, Winter said. "He's an amazing guy, but very complex, not easy to figure out. All this success can change a person quite a bit. But he's still Phil. Still very different."

Although people couldn't see it, Jackson had been under tremendous pressure when he came to the Lakers, Winter said. But over the months, the coaching staff began to see they were making a difference, and that pressure on Jackson lightened and he seemed to enjoy more of it.

As with the Bulls, Jackson's Lakers began to feel special bonds with their coach. Rick Fox, in particular, felt a strong connection. Several years earlier, he had read *Sacred Hoops* and discovered that he and the coach shared a similar background, being raised in a fundamentalist religious atmosphere, then finding a different world through basketball. Fox said he longed to talk with Jackson about the book, but he knew training camp wasn't the place.

Later, toward the middle of the season, Jackson and Fox would sit down for a deep conversation about life and basketball. "I was so astonished at how much his life kind of paralleled my life in some respects. I had always wanted to talk to him about it," Fox explained. Jackson then gave Fox another book to read, *The Poisonwood Bible*, about a missionary family.

Jackson had used his coaching acumen and his personal approach to win over his players one by one. "I've always had great coaches up until I reached the pros," Fox said as the Lakers moved in on the league title. "I had a great high school coach and a great college coach."

He had played for Dean Smith at the University of North Carolina, another man with a special approach to the game. "To me, my coaches were always guys that I looked to," Fox said. "I looked to them for more than basketball, not emulating, but trying to take what pieces they had as men and trying to see what wisdom I could impart from their lives to mine."

Jackson often used examples from his own life to talk to the players about theirs, and as the season wore on, the players realized that Jackson was going through great difficulty in his personal life, the breakup of his twenty-five-year marriage. In their own way, the players wanted to help Jackson through these difficulties the way he had helped them.

"He's been going through some things in his life," Fox said. "Things get stressful. . . . He's meant so much to us as a team, taking us to another level on and off the court. Just as he protects us as players, you kind of want to come around and protect him. He's developed a community here, he really has. He's developed a little family setting. It's what you have to have. You develop it in high school a little easier than you do in college. Sometimes in college you get it. I was fortunate to have it in both of those places.

"For a lot of years I didn't have it here," Fox said of his disappointment with other pro coaches. "As soon as he came aboard and I saw the changes that he was starting to present to our team, I said, 'Man, this is basketball again. This is what it's supposed to be about.'"

The other Lakers also came to understand what was special about their coach's approach. Brian Shaw recalled that Jackson beat his drum with a persistence on the morning of Game 6 of the Finals. "Everybody on the team seemed to perk up at the sound of it," Shaw said. Despite their differences with each other, the Lakers had found something in Jackson that they could all accept. Even Jackson's strange chanting, and the infernal tom-tom—they could embrace it all. The only hard part, they would discover, was repressing smiles in their moment of rapture.

EPILOGUE

The Lakers have long been known as an organization that generates numerous rumors. This was due in no small part to Jerry West, who over the years had included a variety of people—including officials with competing teams, reporters, and players—in his circle of confidants.

So it was no surprise that as the Lakers made their way through the 2000 playoffs, a rumor began circulating that West was planning to leave the team after four decades as a player, coach, and executive. West had seemingly contemplated retirement, or at least leaving the organization, virtually every year for a decade; but now, according to the rumor, he had finally come to the end. Since Jackson had taken over as coach, West had largely kept his distance from the team, and by spring seemed thoroughly detached from the proceedings. He had made appearances at a few playoff games, but for many others he stayed away, trusting one friend or another to keep him abreast of the score with a call to his cell phone.

Ostensibly, the reason for his absences was that the games simply made him too nervous to watch. But soon there would be indications that West had stayed away because of hard feelings over his status with the organization he had served so long. He had lost control of the team to Jackson, a development assured by the coach's success in the playoffs.

As he had every summer for years, West began agonizing over his future with the team—only this time he was closer than ever to leaving. He stayed away from the office the entire summer and offered little input on team personnel decisions.

Word of West's plans reached the press not long after the team celebrated its championship victory with a parade through downtown L.A., but no one in the organization would confirm that West planned to retire.

Then, in July, broadcaster Larry Burnett of the CBS affiliate in Los Angeles contacted Jackson at his home in Montana and received on-the-record confirmation that West's forty-year tenure with the team was indeed finished.

It would be weeks before West himself would make that declaration, after a wry aside about Jackson's sense of timing. West made his announcement in early August in a brief written statement that thanked many but made no mention of Jackson, even though the coach had just directed West's beloved Lakers to a championship.

At the time, news reports out of Los Angeles indicated that West was unhappy that Jackson, after the breakup of his marriage to wife June, had taken up with Jeanie Buss.

Not long after West's announcement, a new sort of rumor began making the rounds of the league's innermost circles. According to the story, Jackson had kicked West out of the Lakers' locker room at one point during the season as the team was making its run to the NBA title.

Although most were reluctant to discuss it publicly, an official with the Bulls said he had heard about the incident, as did former Laker Eddie Jones, who talked frequently with many of his former teammates—including Kobe Bryant and Shaquille O'Neal.

Jones said he had heard the story—and he wasn't shocked by it. "I knew it was coming," Jones said. The former Lakers' guard had recently agreed to leave the Charlotte Hornets to join coach Pat Riley with the Miami Heat. Jones, a West admirer, had even spoken with the Hall of Famer privately before West announced his retirement from the team in August.

A legendary player, West had long been considered the NBA's best personnel executive. But West had also been known for the intense competitive streak that had led him to obsess about his team, a factor that made coaching the Lakers a difficult job for anyone. Jones, an All-Star who played four years in Los Angeles before being traded to Charlotte in the middle of the 1999 season, had witnessed the situation firsthand.

"As a coach, you gotta have guys' confidence, you gotta have guys who believe in what you're saying," Jones said of the circumstances. "You don't want anybody in their ear saying this and saying that."

Los Angeles Times pro basketball writer Mark Heisler was certain no such incident had happened. If it had, West's coterie of confidants would have quickly spread the word, Heisler asserted in a radio interview and in a story for a website. Yet no sooner had he made his evaluation than Heisler heard from one of West's friends, who informed him that the rumor was indeed true. Jackson had asked West to leave the locker room, but Heisler was told that the coach asked politely.

Sources within Jackson's tight inner circle declined to confirm that such an incident took place. If Jackson did ask West to leave the locker room, said one close Jackson associate, it perhaps happened at the end of a game, when Jackson liked to speak privately with his players for a few moments without interruption.

Jackson and his associates were clearly concerned about any suggestion that Jackson hastened West's retirement. After all, West had spent most of the past decade expressing his frustration with his job and teetering on the brink of retirement each offseason, one Jackson associate pointed out.

At least one Chicago Bulls official was eager to cite the locker room situation as more evidence that Jackson was really the one to blame for the 1998 breakup of the six-time world champion Bulls' teams led by Michael Jordan.

Tex Winter, however, had never bought the scenario that Jackson was to blame for the hard feelings in Chicago. Winter offered the opinion that Jackson had spent years bending over backward to accommodate the difficult nature of Bulls VP Jerry Krause.

Certainly Krause had shown a penchant for inciting controversy and offending and alienating people long before Jackson arrived on the scene in Chicago, and after his departure as well. Milwaukee Bucks forward Tim Thomas confided to associates that while he was being recruited by the Bulls during the 2000 offseason, he found Krause and team chairman Jerry Reinsdorf to be unbelievably arrogant. The free agent Thomas, in fact, turned down many millions from the Bulls to remain with the Bucks.

Like Krause, Jackson had danced with conflict over the years—but where Krause seemed to attract it unwittingly, Jackson had always courted conflict as part of the mind games he played with opponents. Some of that certainly entered into his relationship with West.

Not long after they joined the Lakers, it became clear to Jackson and his coaches that West still enjoyed his phone conversations with Krause, and although the coaches seemed to like and appreciate West, there remained a tension in the organization. West and Jerry Buss had been against acquiring Scottie Pippen, and Jackson had questioned them publicly about it, just as he would question West over the issue of a power forward. Jackson thought he needed a good one. West thought that NBA rules changes had reduced the

need for a frontcourt banger. Winter agreed with West, but Jackson continued to question him publicly about it, teasing Lakers management by mus-
ing about bringing back Dennis Rodman, who had joined the Lakers for an
unsuccessful stint in 1999.

Jackson seemed to challenge West's judgment, which resonated of his less
public difficulties with Krause in Chicago. Long before their disagreements
became public, Jackson and his assistants reached the conclusion that Krause
was overstating his own personnel abilities.

The key example of that came in 1995, when Krause passed over Michael
Finley to take power forward Jason Caffey. The Chicago dynasty could have
been kept alive with a player like Finley, the coaches would often say later.

There was no question that Jackson longed for more control in personnel
matters. If he was going to sustain a run of championships in Los Angeles,
which is clearly what the coaching staff endeavored to do, then Jackson felt
he needed to bring in players that fit his sophisticated approach to the game.
Yet the one time he had enjoyed personnel control—during his tenure as
coach of the Albany Patroons in the CBA—Jackson had struggled with personnel chores. He had won the league championship in his second year in the
league, but after that his team's talent level declined.

With West's departure, Jackson had the personnel control that he had
seemed to want since his Chicago days. It immediately became clear what a
challenge the team's personnel issues would present. The Lakers needed a
power forward, a backup center to give O'Neal some help, and a strong
perimeter shooter. However, as training camp neared, the team had been successful in only one major offseason move—the signing of talented free agent
guard Isaiah Rider, a longtime NBA malcontent who figured to pose the kind
of psychological coaching challenge that Jackson craved.

Beyond that, however, each and every of the Lakers' personnel efforts
were thwarted by other teams. West's longtime assistant Mitch Kupchak had
become the front man in the front office. But by late August, Tex Winter
acknowledged that the team missed West.

Jackson was like Krause in that no other NBA team seemed willing to do
him any favors, Winter said. Dallas Mavericks owner Mark Cuban and coach
Don Nelson had even publicly congratulated themselves over breaking up a
trade that would have given the Lakers forward Christian Laettner.

"People think that Phil has gotten enough already," Winter mused. "They
don't want to help him."

On the other hand, West was highly regarded by all around the NBA and had offered the Lakers their best hope of dealing with other teams. Under the guidelines of his departure, West had agreed to at least accept the phone calls that Kupchak made to seek advice. Yet West had badly wanted his release from his long-term Lakers contract, which would allow him to work for another team. But Jerry Buss didn't want to give West that release.

Which meant that in the wake of his departure, West was left to stew unhappily, and the Lakers' front office seemed more than a bit disoriented. After all, West had been the heart and soul of the team for so long, the rock from which everyone else in the organization had gained a sense of stability.

Whereas owners in both Portland and Dallas had spent huge sums to beef up their lineups, the Lakers remained a frugal, mom-and-pop operation headed by Buss, who has made known his desire to cut costs in the wake of the championship.

"It will be a challenge," Winter said.

One of the big issues facing the Lakers was the status of free agent Glen Rice. The summer had brought round after round of rumored deals set up by agent David Falk to send Rice to the New York Knicks, but each of those deals fell through. Finally, his options seemingly used up, Rice appeared ready to sign a one-year contract with the Bulls in mid-September, a move that would have left the Lakers in dire straits, with little hope of getting the power forward, backup center, and perimeter shooter that Jackson's staff wanted. Indeed, Jerry Krause had already set up a press conference to announce Rice's signing in Chicago. But at the last minute, the Lakers' Kupchak helped put together a trade that sent Rice and Travis Knight to New York; the Knicks' Patrick Ewing to Seattle; and four fine Seattle players, power forward Horace Grant, backup center Greg Foster, long-range gunner Chuck Person, and 6'5" guard Emanual Davis to the Lakers. Also factoring into the deal was the Phoenix Suns, who traded Luc Longley to New York.

Foiled by Jackson's forces again, Jerry Krause cancelled his press conference, bringing to a close a long, frustrating summer for the Bulls.

Krause and Jerry Reinsdorf had dumped the players from their championship roster in hopes of signing high-priced free agents such as Grant Hill or Tracy McGrady, but the Bulls found few players willing to take their money.

Meanwhile in Los Angeles, Jackson had just the mix of holdovers and new players he needed to sustain his winning ways. He was eager to begin a new season, to help his players "strengthen the muscles of their minds," as he called his mental approach.

With his success in Los Angeles, no longer was he considered merely "Michael's coach," Winter acknowledged. Now more than ever, players seemed eager to embrace Jackson's unique approach to the game—that mysterious combination of discipline and freedom, all of it guided along by his intuition, his special understanding of the group. Above all, his players seemed eager to accept his mind games, the little flights of illusion that allowed him to keep everyone slightly off-balance, slightly unsure, mystified by the realm that only Phil Jackson understood.

INDEX